REGULATING PROFESSIONS

The Emergence of Professional Self-Regulation in Four Canadian Provinces

Regulating Professions

The Emergence of Professional Self-Regulation in Four Canadian Provinces

TRACEY L. ADAMS

UNIVERSITY OF TORONTO PRESS
Toronto Buffalo London

Toronto Buffalo London
utorontopress.com
Printed and bound by CPI Group (UK) Ltd, Croydon, CR0 4YY

ISBN 978-1-4875-0249-2

Library and Archives Canada Cataloguing in Publication

Adams, Tracey Lynn, 1966–, author
Regulating professions : the emergence of professional self-regulation in four Canadian provinces / Tracey L. Adams.

Includes bibliographical references and index.
ISBN 978-1-4875-0249-2 (cloth)

1. Professions – Law and legislation – Canada – Provinces. 2. Occupations – Licenses – Canada – Provinces. I. Title.

KE2700.A33 2018 344.7101′71 C2017-907579-9
KF2900.A33 2018

This book has been published with the help of a grant from the Federation for the Humanities and Social Sciences, through the Awards to Scholarly Publications Program, using funds provided by the Social Sciences and Humanities Research Council of Canada.

University of Toronto Press acknowledges the financial assistance to its publishing program of the Canada Council for the Arts and the Ontario Arts Council, an agency of the Government of Ontario.

Canada Council for the Arts Conseil des Arts du Canada

ONTARIO ARTS COUNCIL
CONSEIL DES ARTS DE L'ONTARIO
an Ontario government agency
un organisme du gouvernement de l'Ontario

Funded by the Government of Canada Financé par le gouvernement du Canada Canada

Contents

Acknowledgments

This book was over a decade in the making, and there were many people and organizations that helped me along the way. I'd like to take this opportunity to thank them for their support, advice, and recommendations, as well as their concrete assistance.

First, I'd like to thank the Social Sciences and Humanities Research Council of Canada for providing me with two grants to support the research on which this book is based. The first grant allowed me to trace the regulation of professions across select provinces in Canada since Confederation; the second allowed me to conduct case studies of the regulation of alternative health practices, especially osteopathy, naturopathy, and chiropody. This latter project especially forms the basis of chapter 6, although it helped to shape other chapters as well. Moreover, this book has been published with help from the Awards to Scholarly Publications program. I would like to thank this program as well for its support of this project.

Research for this book was also facilitated by the work of many research assistants. I'd like to thank (in alphabetical order) Esra Ari, Awish Aslam, Yvonne Asare Bediako, Elisabeth Bartlett, Meg Desmond, Vanessa Dolishny, Nicole Etherington, Stacey Hallman, Elizabeth Torrens, and Brendan Watts.

I would also like to acknowledge and thank the many archivists and librarians who supported my research by locating materials for me and guiding me to resources. Thanks to the librarians at Western University libraries, including subject librarians Marg Sloan and John Costello, as well as the staff at the Bitove Family Law Library, D.B. Weldon Library, Taylor Library, and the Archives and Research Collections Centre. Many thanks as well to the archivists and librarians at the Archives of Ontario, the BC Archives, the Nova Scotia Archives, Library and Archives Canada, la Bibliothèque de l'Assemblée nationale, the Legislative Library of British Columbia, and the Nova Scotia Legislative Library.

Next, I'd like to thank those individuals who helped shape my thinking and hone my ideas. Thanks to Samuel Clark who read over the entire manuscript in draft and provided very valuable feedback. Thanks also to my colleagues Kim Clark and Luz Maria Hernandez Saenz who read over portions of the manuscript, provided limitless encouragement to get the project completed, and helped to shape my thinking on these issues through our regular discussions on professions and the state. Thanks also to Keith Fleming and Chuck Levine who provided reading recommendations that shaped the final product significantly. I'd also like to thank several scholars who shaped the end product of this book – completely unbeknownst to them I am sure – by comments they made to me in chance meetings and other brief interactions: Andrew Abbott, Bruce Curtis, Elizabeth Popp Berman, Mike Saks, and Peter Twohig. Our brief conversations resonated with me and took my research and thinking in valuable directions: you have my sincere thanks.

This work is an original one but it does build on earlier research using some of the same data that was previously published in the *Canadian Review of Sociology*, the *Journal of Canadian Studies*, *Social Science History*, *Histoire sociale/Social History*, and more recently the *Journal of Historical Sociology* and the *Journal of Professions and Organization*. I'd like to thank the reviewers and editors of these journals whose critical comments helped to sharpen my thinking and therefore indirectly contributed to this present book. I'd also like to thank the two reviewers of this present manuscript who provided excellent advice for improving it and helped me to clarify my argument.

Many thanks to everyone at the University of Toronto Press, especially acquisitions editor Len Husband, associate managing editor Frances Mundy, copy editor John St. James, marketing co-ordinator Luciano Nicassio, and the many others who made this book possible.

Finally, I'd like to thank my family and friends for their support of me and this project. In particular, I'd like to thank my husband Steve and my children Meg and Rhys for their unfailing support.

REGULATING PROFESSIONS

The Emergence of Professional Self-Regulation in Four Canadian Provinces

Introduction

On 17 July 1797, ten men gathered for a meeting at Wilson's Hotel in Newark, Upper Canada (now Niagara-on-the-Lake, Ontario). The men were lawyers meeting under the auspices of the "Act for better regulating the Practice of Law," passed only a few weeks previously by the colonial government. At that meeting they fulfilled the responsibilities delineated in the act: They formed the Law Society of Upper Canada, selected benchers and a treasurer to lead it, and established regulations through which they could govern themselves, and determine entry to practice (Moore 1997; Riddell 1916). The 1797 act was path-breaking. It established law as a self-regulating profession, and granted lawyers a monopoly over certain aspects of practice in the colony. Elsewhere in the British colonies lawyers were appointed by the courts. Where they were self-regulating this was more by collegial agreement than government decree (Moore 1997). The establishment of a self-regulating law profession in Upper Canada occurred only a few years after the creation of the colony, and the redrawing of its court system. For fifty years, the Law Society of Upper Canada was the only legislated self-governing profession in the Canadian colonies; in the late 1840s self-regulation was granted to the medical and law professions in Lower Canada (Quebec). The number of self-regulating professions in Canada expanded significantly after Confederation. Today, there are scores of self-regulating professions in the country.

There appears to be something distinct about professions in Canada. Not only were self-regulating professions created by statute earlier in Canada than many other locales in the Western world, but they are still active, even as professional self-regulation is under attack in other nations. In recent decades, self-regulating professions in the United

Kingdom, United States, and Australia have faced intense scrutiny and criticism (Abel 2003; Kleiner 2006; Paton 2008; Rees 2013; Nancarrow 2015). Legislative change in the United Kingdom has transformed regulatory institutions to the point that professions like medicine and law are no longer fully self-regulating (Dixon-Woods et al. 2011; Flood 2011; Chamberlain 2013). Self-regulation is cast as an outdated practice that contributed to elitism and high prices, restricted competition, and led to excesses and abuses (Abel 2003; Chamberlain 2013). In Canada, such criticisms are present, but muted. Some scholars have called Canada one of the "last bastions for professional self-regulation" in the world (Rhode and Woolley 2012: 2274; Gorman 2014).

Is Canada merely a laggard, or do diverging trends reflect distinct traditions of professional regulation? Professions have long been a feature of Canadian society; however, heretofore, the history of self-regulating professions in Canada, across several provinces and professions, has not been told. There is a considerable body of historical research focused on single professions, especially medicine (Bernier 1989; Howell 1981; Gidney and Millar 1984), and law (Moore 1997; Miller 1991; Vachon 1962; Veilleux 1997; Watts 1984). Explorations of several professions across time (such as Dussault 1978; Gidney and Millar 1994), and province (Tipliski 2004; Twohig 2006; Fahmy-Eid 1997), are few and far between. Thus, we know little about professional development in Canada across province and period. Moreover, with a few exceptions this literature has focused on the emergence of professions generally; less has been written on professional regulation, or professions' relationships with the state. Regulation has been the focus of some government-sponsored commissions (see CNC 1970; CHA 1970; Trebilcock et al. 1979; Foulkes 1973; HPLR 1989), one comprehensive Canadian law review (Casey 1994), and a provincial policy review (O'Reilly 2000), but has yet to receive sustained academic attention.

This would appear to be a significant oversight. For many scholars, self-regulation is a core defining feature of "professions" (Chamberlain 2013; Freidson 2001; Corfield 1995). Professions have a degree of autonomy and social influence that distinguishes them from other occupations. Professions may possess some cultural authority linked with their knowledge and expertise (Starr 1982), but their social power and influence is primarily tied to their regulatory authority. Self-regulating professions have governance power. These powers are delegated to them by the state (Freidson 2001). Why does the state delegate powers to professional groups? How have professions won these powers? Few studies actually address these questions empirically; however, two types of explanations can be found in the sociological literature. On the one hand, those writing from a neo-Weberian perspective tend to see professional groups as highly influential: They request powers from the state, and if they have sufficient expertise, or advance convincing arguments, then they are granted their requests (Saks 2010, 2015). On the other hand, scholars contend that "the state" has something to gain from regulating professions: for instance, enhanced legitimacy (Spencer 1896; Evetts and Dingwall 2002), valued expertise (Halliday 1987), or an extension of the state's capacity to govern (Johnson 1993, 1995). While neo-Weberian approaches see professions as the primary driver of regulatory outcomes, alternative views ascribe a central role to state actors. Writers on each side are able to draw on historical evidence to support their claims, but the two theories have not been applied and contrasted systematically.

In light of current trends and theoretical debates about professional regulation, this book explores the emergence of self-regulating professions in four Canadian provinces between Confederation and the 1930s. This study not only attempts to fill a gap in the historical literature on self-regulating professions in Canada, it tests competing sociological explanations to determine how professions in Canada became self-regulating. When state actors regulated professions, were they simply convinced by a good argument, or did they seek to draw on professions' expertise or social position for governance reasons? Although my focus is on four Canadian provinces (British Columbia, Ontario, Nova Scotia, and Quebec), I argue that understanding the Canadian experience can shed light on professions and professional self-regulation in other parts of the world – especially in countries where patterns of professional regulation have been similar, like the United States and United Kingdom. Sociological theory has provided helpful tools to understand professional regulation, but as this study will show, these theories have limitations. This work, I hope, will help sociologists create better theories to improve our understanding of professions and their roles in society.

This chapter sets the scene for the chapters to follow. First, I define professional self-regulation. Then, I present a brief summary of the literatures on professional self-regulation, and on professions in Canada. Last, I provide an overview of the book.

Professional Self-Regulation

In this context, the term "regulation" refers to "the powers of an agency or organisation to set a framework of rules through which it holds others to account" (Davies 2004: 56). Professions, like other social entities, might be regulated in a variety of ways. The most prominent professions, however, have been granted powers of self-regulation. Professional self-regulation is a type of regulation in which the authority to govern a profession is granted to a body composed (predominantly) of professionals. The power to self-regulate is delegated to professions by the state through legislation (Freidson 2001; Rubin 1980). Among the powers granted to self-regulating professions are (1) the power to regulate (in some manner) entry to practice (or access to a restricted title), and ensure that practitioners conform to a standard of practice; (2) the power to govern practitioner behaviour in a manner that ensures professional practice is conducted ethically and responsibly (Adams 2017a; Rubin 1980).[1]

Some self-regulating professions are closed completely, while others possess a restricted title only. In closed professions, only the licensed or registered may practice. In restricted title professions, anyone may practice, but only the registered can utilize a restricted title, which is typically a marker of skill and status (historically "chartered accountant" was a prominent example). Both types of professional regulation have been common, but the extent of each varies across time and place. For instance, in the United Kingdom, very few professions have been fully closed; most possess a restricted title only (Price 2002). In contrast, in Canada, many professions have been closed.

Sociologists distinguish an "Anglo-American" model of professions and professional regulation from a Continental European model. In the United Kingdom and the United States (as well as Canada), self-regulating professions have been the norm. These professions were usually established by practitioners who banded together to raise their status and authority, and improve their market position, through lobbying states for legislation granting them privileges (Larson 1977; Collins 1990; Neal and Morgan 2000; Saks 2015). In contrast, the creation of professions in Continental Europe has been more state-directed (Collins 1990; Neal and Morgan 2000). In Germany, for instance, professional (voluntary) associations did not emerge until after licensing and education had been well established (Neal and Morgan 2000). High-status professions only have limited powers of self-regulation, and are subject to state oversight; entry to practice is regulated by the state, not the profession (Neal and Morgan 2000). Professional regulation has varied across nation (Neal and Morgan 2000; Rueschemeyer 1986).

Professional regulation has also varied across time (Saks 2015; Chamberlain 2013; Krause 1996). For example, scholars argue, the state has become much more active in professional regulation in Anglo-American contexts throughout the twentieth and into the twenty-first centuries (Krause 1996; Saks 2015; Chamberlain 2013). While historically professional regulatory bodies were often composed entirely of professionals, in the latter half of the twentieth century lay representation expanded (Stacey 1995; Adams 2017a). State actors' direct involvement on regulatory bodies (or overseeing their decisions) grew as well (Adams 2009a). Thus, today, professional regulatory bodies have a mix of members. In fact, in the United Kingdom, it is now members of the public, not professionals, who comprise the majority on regulatory boards in medicine and law (Paton 2008; Chamberlain 2013). Furthermore, in many countries, regulatory bodies' powers of self-regulation have been curtailed: by the end of the twentieth century self-regulating professions had fewer powers than their predecessors (Coburn 1999; Saks 2015; Krause 1996). Research on professional regulation has illuminated recent changes, but historical trends and patterns of professional regulation have received less consideration.

Self-Regulating Professions in Historical Context

Although some professions date back centuries, most scholars see self-regulating professions as a modern phenomenon (cf. Sciulli 2009), and a product of the emergence of industrial capitalism, the rise of the modern state, urbanization, an expanding market for services, and the expansion of higher education (Larson 2013; Macdonald 1995; Johnson 1982, 1993; Brint 1994). Legislation to regulate professions in the United Kingdom is typically dated to the nineteenth century: legislation governing medicine was passed in 1858 (Chamberlain 2013); the regulation of law was more gradual and piecemeal (Burrage 2006). In the United States, statutes governing lawyers were passed in the early to mid-eighteenth century (ibid.), while legislation regulating medical doctors dates from the late eighteenth to early nineteenth century (Shryock 1967). For the most part this legislation was rescinded in the early to mid-nineteenth century. By the 1830s and 1840s law and medicine were largely unregulated in the United States, and entry to practice was open

(Shryock 1967; Burrage 2006). Regulatory measures to govern these two professions in the United States were again enacted beginning in the 1860s (for law) and 1870s (medicine); professional regulation gradually expanded over the next several decades.

In both the United Kingdom and United States, legislation regulating professions was typically prompted by organized professional groups who appealed to state actors for the privileges of self-regulation, and restrictions on entry to practice (Larson 1977; Macdonald 1995). Those who were well organized, and who could advance a claim to expertise based on their advanced training, were more successful in achieving self-regulation (Larson 1977; Macdonald 1995). Nonetheless, professionals' social backgrounds were not irrelevant. Self-regulating professions were dominated by middle- and upper-class white men (Witz 1992; Corfield 1995). Further, professionals possessed a measure of both social respect and prestige (Corfield 1995; Brint 1994); their status facilitated their ability to win privileges from nineteenth-century states. Over time, according to Stephen Brint (1994), the bases of professionalism have switched from status and trust to expertise and training. While the old form of professionalism had a strong community orientation, newer forms direct expertise towards the market (Brint 1994: 15–20).

Sociologists contend that underlying professional self-regulation is a "regulatory bargain": states grant professions powers of self-regulation in return for the assurance that professionals will use this power in the public interest (Macdonald 1995; Gorman 2014). Some suggest that state actors cannot effectively regulate professions directly because they lack the specialized knowledge necessary to determine who is competent to practise (Sheppard 1970; CHA 1970). In contrast, others argue that state actors formed a partnership with professions, whereby the latter acted as "agents of the state" (Larkin 1995: 26). For a variety of reasons, the traditional state-profession relationship has broken down over time. British scholars have identified two principal developments. On the one hand, a series of scandals in UK professions revealed professional incompetence and misconduct, suggesting that self-regulating professions cannot be trusted to put the public's interests above their own (Dixon-Woods et al. 2011; Chamberlain 2013). On the other hand, scholars contend state agendas and political goals have changed. States are less willing to delegate authority, and have become more interventionist (Abel 2003; Chamberlain 2013; Johnson 1993). Both of these trends have combined to alter state-profession relations fundamentally, both in the United Kingdom and elsewhere.

Professions in Canada

Sociological accounts of professions and their regulation have been dominated by US and UK scholars. Nevertheless, there is a rich literature on professions in Canada. Historically, the most-studied Canadian professions have been medicine and law (see, for example, Gidney and Millar 1994, Moore 1997; Bernier 1989, Howell 1981; Watts 1984; Miller 1991; Vachon 1962; Veilleux 1997). These professions pre-dated Confederation, and were important social forces historically. Doctors and lawyers were civic leaders, active in both their local communities and in colonial governments. They not only provided services to the public, but played a central role in political and social life within the colonies (Ouellet 1980a; Moore 1997; Gidney and Millar 1994; Watts 1984). The emergence of other early professions – such as pharmacy, dentistry, land surveying – has received some attention as well (Collin 1997; Malleck 2015; Adams 2000; Thomson 1967; Ladell 1993). Much of this literature focuses on professional development generally, but the emergence of self-regulation receives attention. The picture that emerges from these studies, however, is a fragmented one, since most only document trends in one profession at a time. As Andrew Abbott (1988) has argued, professions exist within a complex ecology, or system. We cannot fully understand the events affecting one profession without considering developments in neighbouring professions. Neither can we understand the system as a whole by only looking at pieces of it.

Dussault (1978) has provided a more comprehensive picture of professions in Canada by identifying distinct "eras" of professional regulation in the province of Quebec. According to Dussault (1978), five eras or "phases" were evident between 1840 and 1970. The first phase, prior to Confederation, witnessed the emergence and expansion of professions: practitioners organized, and lobbied for legislation granting them powers of self-regulation, so that they could extend their independence and eliminate practice by the untrained. Lawyers, medical doctors, and notaries became self-regulating professions in Lower Canada (Canada East) in the late 1840s. In the second phase, which covers the period between 1865 and 1910, the number of regulated professions in Quebec expanded significantly: powers of self-regulation were extended to a variety of groups, from dentists and pharmacists, to engineers and optometrists. The third phase, between 1910 and 1940, was one of stability. Few new professions were created in this era, and most of the new professions possessed a restricted title only. For Dussault

(1978) the fourth phase occurred between 1940 and 1955, and it brought the emergence and regulation of professional and occupational groups allied to traditional and established professions, such as opticians, dental technicians, and interior decorators. The powers they received were more circumscribed than their predecessors'. The fifth phase was a period of high activity, with seventeen new professions regulated between 1955 and 1970, including dieticians, social workers, audiologists, psychologists, professional chemists, and many others (Dussault 1978). Dussault (1978) argues that the expansion of education and public administration favoured the expansion of professions during this era (see also Langlois 2011). Finally, Dussault (1978) notes that the system of professional regulation was dramatically transformed in Quebec in 1973 with the passage of the Professional Code. At this time, existing professional regulatory bodies were restructured and renamed "orders." Henceforth, professional orders would be subject to the oversight of, and accountable to, a government-appointed inter-professional council. This system maintains a measure of self-regulation, but ensures that professional bodies are subordinate to the provincial government.

Previous research has not explored whether Dussault's depiction of historical trends is applicable to other provinces; however, research has shown that there are commonalities in who is regulated and when across province (Adams 2009a, 2009b, 2010). Self-regulating professions were established earlier in Quebec than other provinces, as we will see. Nonetheless, the literature on professions in Canada has identified the mid- to late-nineteenth century as a key period of professional expansion and growth; it was in this era that self-regulating professions emerged in many Canadian provinces (Gidney and Millar 1994; Adams 2009b, 2010). Subsequently, professional regulation expanded to encompass a wide range of new groups in the health sector and beyond (Heap 1995b; Fahmy-Eid 1997; Langlois 2011; Prud'homme 2011; McPherson 1996). While the earliest professions were male-dominated, many newer professions have been dominated by women, including nursing, physiotherapy, dietetics, and others (McPherson 1996; Fahmy-Eid 1997; Prud'homme 2011; Bourgeault 2006). The emergence of "professional" technicians in the early to mid-twentieth century has also been documented (Twohig 2005, 2006).

Studies like Dussault's (1978) are helpful in providing an overview of professional development. They elucidate some of the main trends concerning professions and professional regulation over time. However, the "big" questions surrounding professional regulation remain unanswered. Why were some groups regulated, while others were not? When state actors regulated professions, did they explain their rationales? What were the social debates and concerns surrounding regulation, and how did these change over time? The literature on professions in Canada – even studies focusing on professional regulation – focus on professions' efforts to achieve self-regulation. State actors' activities and motivations remain largely invisible. Do state actors have something to gain from professional regulation?

The Present Study

This study explores professional self-regulation in four Canadian provinces through a focus on the professions regulated by provincial legislatures in British Columbia, Ontario, Nova Scotia, and Quebec, between Confederation and the 1930s. It was during this era that the predominant patterns of professional self-regulation emerged in Canada. After this period, professional regulation altered significantly, shaped by the emergence of the welfare state, Medicare, the expansion of the public sector, and other social trends. This later period is deserving of separate analysis. In this book, I not only provide a historical overview of legislation regulating (or proposing to regulate) professions in these four provinces prior to 1940, I also review the major debates and controversies surrounding that legislation. In doing so, I evaluate sociological explanations for professionalization and professional regulation. I explore both the strategies used by professionalizing groups to win self-regulation, and I examine state actors' decisions to grant it. Was regulation the outcome of professional projects? If so, what did successful professions do to achieve the privileges of self-regulation? Did state actors grant regulatory privileges to professions solely based on their lobbying, or their expertise, or is there evidence they had other agendas? And what is the role of social context? How did professional regulation vary across province and time period?

To answer these questions, I combine case studies (using both primary and secondary data) of Canadian professions with analysis of legislative and archival records, including acts of the legislature in each province, bills presented but not passed, surviving records of debates in provincial legislatures, and other assorted legislative and professional records. Since the number of professions regulated across the four provinces is so high, I have endeavoured to balance breadth and depth. Thus, I provide both general overviews of regulatory trends within and across province, and case studies of specific professions within specific provinces to reveal regulatory processes more clearly. The four provinces were chosen both for their history (all were among Canada's earliest provinces), and because they provide some variation in size, population, and historical patterns of professional regulation. Exploring regulatory trends across province can shed light on the impact of social-historical context.

Chapter 1 of this book provides a conceptual and theoretical overview. I define the main concepts at the heart of this study, and review the theoretical literature on how professions are made. I pay particular attention to different theories of state-profession relations, from neo-Weberian accounts that ascribe an important role to state actors, but do not actually theorize their activity, to Foucauldian accounts that see profession formation as central to state building, but which cast all regulatory activity as driving towards one overriding goal – governmentality. I also outline Abbott's (2005) linked ecologies approach, arguing that it may provide a fruitful frame for research, since it sees state actors as people with political and social interests of their own, which are not necessarily reducible to an overriding concern with governance, but may be contradictory, ephemeral, and political. According to Abbott (2005), regulatory outcomes may occur in those moments when state actors' interests and professional leaders' interests coincide.

Chapter 2 explores the emergence of professional self-regulation in pre-Confederation Quebec and Ontario (Lower and Upper Canada). Self-regulating professions were established by statute earlier in Canada than in many other regions, and Canada's regulatory institutions and mechanisms were constructed in this era. Drawing mostly on secondary data sources, I document the creation of self-regulating professions in medicine and law in Quebec, and discuss the extent to which they were bound up with the political and social movements of the day. I subsequently consider the emergence of a self-regulating law profession in Ontario in the late eighteenth century, and explore the short-lived effort to establish a self-regulating medical profession in the late 1830s. Although the processes that resulted in self-regulating professions in each province were distinct, emergent regulatory forms and institutions were similar. At the end of chapter 2, I contrast regulatory legislation in Ontario and Quebec with that passed in the United Kingdom and United States in the nineteenth century through a case study of the medical profession. Although all three countries share an

"Anglo-American" model of professional regulation, key differences across country are evident.

In chapter 3, I provide an overview of the emergence of self-regulating professions in the four provinces between Confederation and 1900. In the decade or so following Confederation, professional self-regulation was instituted, altered, and expanded in each of the provinces investigated here. This chapter looks at what was regulated and how. Further, it provides an overview of regulatory activity affecting professions during this era. Subsequently, the chapter explores rationales provided for professional self-regulation through a look at preambles within the legislation passed and surviving legislative debates. Variations across province in regulatory patterns are also documented. Towards the end of the chapter, I consider who won professional self-regulation during this period through a brief case study of the demographic characteristics of professional leaders in Ontario. This chapter discusses the importance of expertise and status to regulatory outcomes. While many accounts of professionalization pay little attention to state actors, this chapter documents how active they were in creating self-regulating professions in Canada historically.

Chapter 4 complements the preceding chapter by providing case studies of professional development in three self-regulating professions: medicine, dentistry, and land surveying. While chapter 3 explores professional regulation primarily through legislative records, chapter 4 brings the focus back to the professions. It explores the professional projects pursued by leaders in each of these professions, and considers whether these projects and strategies were influential in shaping state-actor decision making in these particular contexts. While much of the literature on professions sees professional regulation as the product of professions' sustained campaigns to win privileges from the state, in Canada this was only partially true. Professional organization and sustained campaigns were not always evident in this period. Rather, the case studies highlight the importance of state-profession relations, status and social capital, and especially professionals' involvement in provincial legislatures. While expertise was an element shaping regulatory outcomes, it was intertwined with many other factors such as class and gender, from which it could not be disentangled.

Chapter 5 provides an overview of professional regulation in the four provinces from 1900 up to 1940. Like chapter 3, it sketches who was regulated and how during this era, and documents the extent of regulatory activity pertaining to professions. In order to explore state actors' rationales for establishing self-regulating professions in this era, this chapter not only reviews legislative preambles, but examines regulatory debates, with a special focus on controversies surrounding the regulation of three new professional groups: nurses, optometrists, and engineers. In the early twentieth century, the debates surrounding regulation, and the nature of professional self-regulation changed significantly. Nevertheless, there is evidence that factors which were influential in the earlier period continued to matter.

Chapter 6 provides a detailed case study of the contests surrounding the regulation of "drugless practice" between the 1900s and 1930s. This case study sheds light on the strategies used by new occupational groups seeking professional status in this era, as well as the tactics employed by established professions like medicine, to undermine them. Further, it provides insight into state decision making during periods of contest and debate. When faced with competing claims respecting professional regulation, what did state actors do? This chapter focuses on Ontario and British Columbia, where the contests and inter-professional conflict were most intense, and where surviving records are richest. Regulatory debates in Nova Scotia and Quebec are touched on briefly. This chapter emphasizes the combined importance of professional projects, profession-state ties, and political concerns to regulatory outcomes. The implications of this case study for our understanding of professional self-regulation generally are discussed.

The final chapter explores the implications of the historical trends documented for our theoretical understanding of professional self-regulation. It highlights the centrality of the state to profession creation, and critiques competing theories of profession–state relations. Further, it provides new theoretical propositions that may prove fruitful in future research. While Canada's experiences of professional self-regulation are certainly distinct from those of the United States and United Kingdom, there is much that scholars in these and other countries can take away from the Canadian case that may illuminate professional development elsewhere.

Chapter One

Theorizing Professions

There is a considerable body of sociological research and theory that has sought to define professions, to explain how professions are made and how they change over time, and to shed light on the complex relationship between professions and the state. In this chapter I outline how I conceptualize "profession," and I review the theoretical melange that has influenced my understanding of professionalization, the state, and state-profession relations. I argue that no single theory is able to account for the complex nature of professional development and profession-state relations. For example, to understand professionalization or professional development over time, I find it useful to combine Weberian social closure theory, with social movement theory, and Andrew Abbott's (1988, 2005) ecological approach. In a similar vein, to understand state-profession relations, it is helpful to draw on the work of Foucauldian scholars (especially Johnson 1993, 1995), but also to consider the contributions of Spencer (1896), Durkheim (1984), and others (Abbott 2005; Streeck and Schmitter 1985; Freidson 2001). I end the chapter with a brief overview of several key themes explored in this book.

Professions

There has been extensive debate about how best to define "profession," and debate about whether "profession" is even a useful concept at all (Adams 2010, 2015; Eyal 2013; Gorman and Sandefur 2011; Saks 2010, 2012; Sciulli 2005; Torstendahl 2005). Researchers have provided "ideal types" to characterize professions (Greenwood 1957; Sciulli 2009); these were subsequently rejected by scholars advocating for historically contingent, social constructionist depictions (Freidson 1983). No single definition has gained widespread acceptance in the field. Some researchers use the term without defining it, and others have abandoned the term, preferring to speak of "expert" workers (Eyal 2013). Complicating the definition project is the fact that professions have a dual character. The term can refer to both a field of endeavour (Abbott 1988) and to a form of social organization (Freidson 2001; Johnson 1972; Sciulli 2009).

Although it is not fruitful to wade too deeply into these definitional debates, it is necessary to provide a brief overview to explain adequately the approach to professions and professional development that guides this book. In particular, it is important to touch on the debates about whether professions have a variable or invariant structure, whether and how professions differ from other occupations, and whether "profession" is simply another word for "expert."

Ideal-type models of professions attempt to outline a set of characteristics that capture the essence of professions across time and place. The most influential have been the "trait" models proposed by scholars like Wilensky (1964) and Greenwood (1957). Professions were said to be distinguished by the following traits: an esoteric knowledge base, supported by advanced training and education, the formation of professional associations, a professional culture with a service orientation, a code of ethics to guide the conduct of professional workers, professional authority, and sanction by the community (Greenwood 1957, Goode 1966; Vollmer and Mills 1965; Wilensky 1964). Trait approaches were widely criticized in the 1970s and beyond for uncritically adopting the idealized image professions attempted to project, and for ignoring power (Johnson 1972; Roth 1974; Saks 2010, 2016). However, their depiction of professions in the mid-twentieth century had considerable face validity, and guided research on professions (implicitly or explicitly) for several decades.

Subsequent definitions emphasized power. Johnson (1972: 45) saw professions as institutionalizing control over fields of endeavour; for him "a profession is not … an occupation, but a means of controlling an occupation." In a similar vein, for Freidson (1970), professions were distinguished by their "control over the determination of the substance of [their] own work" (p. xvii), and often the work of others in their field (48). Larson (1977: xvi) explains that professions seek to "constitute and control a market for their expertise." For all these scholars this ability to exercise authority over markets, work content, the labour of others in their field, and their occupation itself distinguishes professionals from other types of workers. Although it is possible to simply add power to the list of traits possessed by professions, scholars such as Johnson (1972), Larson (1977, 2013), and Freidson (1970, 1983) emphasize that professions were not invariant, but variable, and a product of specific social-historical circumstances. For instance, Johnson (1972: 38) argues that professions are "a rather peculiar historical product which can be said to have existed for a very short period and which was a product of the specific historical conditions of nineteenth-century Anglo-American culture." Larson (1977: xvi) agrees, seeing professions as a product of "modern industrial society," and she ties their emergence in Western society with "the rise of industrial capitalism, with its early crises of consolidation and, toward the end of the nineteenth and the beginning of the twentieth, with the evolution of capitalism towards its corporate form." While Burrage (2006: 593–4) agrees that professions are a product of their social-historical circumstances, he argues that this connection with industrial capitalism was greater for the United States than for other societies.

Several scholars have tied the emergence of professions to a particular set of social-historical circumstances in the West in the late nineteenth and early twentieth centuries, but Freidson (1983) goes further, arguing that "profession" is a social construction that varies across time and place. Thus, no single, invariant definition is possible.[1] He recommends that researchers treat "profession" as a "folk concept" and explore how "people in a society determine who is a professional and who is not, how they "make" or "accomplish" professions by their activities, and what the consequences are for the way in which they see themselves and perform their work" (ibid.: 20). Such a task entails, at least in part, tracing "the development and significance of the title [profession] in Anglo-American societies" (25) and "analyzing in some detail the occupations to which the title has been applied" (26). Freidson's approach is one that I and other researchers have adopted in research on professions (Adams 2000, 2010; Neal and Morgan 2000; Heap, Millar, and Smyth 2005).

Before outlining my working definition of profession, two other definitional dimensions deserve attention. The first pertains to expertise, and the second to status. These two aspects are interrelated. Today, many scholars focus on experts and expertise either because they see these terms as interchangeable with "profession," or they find the former concepts more robust and clear. Gorman and Sandefur (2011) declare that the sociology of professions has largely disappeared, to be replaced by a focus on expertise, experts in organizations, and social inequality. US scholars in particular increasingly speak of experts and expertise, rather than professions (Eyal 2013; Gorman and Sandefur 2011; Larson 2013). For Eyal (2013: 870), the sociology of professions has been limited by its focus on "organizational form: credentialing, licensing, and the formation of professional associations and lobbying outfits" that are "calculated to secure recognition" and a "legal mandate." This focus has resulted in little attention to expertise (Eyal 2013: 870) or the tasks performed by professionals (Abbott 1988). Andrew Abbott's (1988) work has been tremendously influential, particularly his claim that it is the relationship between the professional or expert and his or her work that is crucial. Battles between professions for control of a jurisdiction – battles over who does what – are the determining force shaping professional development. Abbott's (1988) approach combines a focus on professional work, with attention to power and authority. Recent literature on expertise, however, discounts this focus on professional power, instead turning attention to the institutional arrangements that facilitate task completion. Eyal (2013: 898–9) argues that a sociology of expertise can replace the sociology of professions because it is "more comprehensive," exploring all those who can advance a claim to expertise. The sociology of expertise asks "not only who controls a task and how jurisdictional boundaries are assembled but also what arrangements, devices, concepts and other actors are necessary if an expert statement or performance is to be formulated, reproduced and disseminated" (Eyal 2013: 899). With these words, Eyal (2013) joins Gorman and Sandefur (2011) in signalling the death of the sociology of professions, advocating a research turn towards expertise, experts, and their work.

Such claims are premature, and do not sufficiently acknowledge the multifaceted nature of professions elucidated by several scholars (Collins 1990; Johnson 1972, 1982, 1995; Freidson 2001; Saks 2012; Scott 2008). These scholars argue that professions are not simply groups of experts (Saks 2012). For Randall Collins (1990: 18–19) it is not technical knowledge or expertise per se that distinguishes a profession but the social organization of knowledge and the link between knowledge and status. Burrage's (2006: 18) sweeping study of the emergence of the contemporary legal profession in the United States, United Kingdom, and France also highlights this linkage, suggesting that it is status, or more specifically the "desire for recognition," that drives professional activity. To enhance their status, professions organize and self-regulate. Recall the arguments made by Johnson (1972) and others (Freidson

2001; Scott 2008) that professions are not simply fields of work, but they are also, historically, a component of social organization and social regulation. In Freidson's (2001: 2) terms, professionalism has its own organizational logic, and it exists in structural form as "a set of interconnected institutions providing the economic support and social organization that sustains the occupational control of work." In a similar vein, Scott (2008: 223) argues that "professions function as institutional agents – as definers, interpreters and appliers of institutional elements," and moreover are "the most influential, contemporary crafters of institutional elements." All professionals may be experts, but not all experts are professionals. While a sociology of expertise may be valuable in illuminating the institutional arrangements surrounding the performance of expertise, it implicitly neglects the ways in which professional workers differ from other workers who advance claims to expertise. Professional workers are distinguished from others by their status, institutional authority, cultural authority, organization, and regulation (see also Scott 2008; Adams 2010). Although their work is shaped by the organizational logics governing large bureaucracies in capitalist economies, which so strongly shape the work of all expert workers (and others), they are also influenced by the organizational logic governing professionalism (Freidson 2001).

While the lines drawn between professionals and other experts have become increasingly blurred in sociological discourse, historically the terms were distinct. In fact, Eyal (2013: 869) himself explains that the term "expertise" was not commonly used before the mid-1960s, although the emergence of the term "expert" in popular discourse dates from the late nineteenth and early twentieth centuries. Thus, a focus on experts and expertise is of limited use when studying the emergence of professions in the mid-to-late nineteenth century. Indeed Stephen Brint (1994) shows that the link between professionalism and expertise only became dominant in the United States between the 1920s and 1940s. Nineteenth-century notions of professionalism were rather tied more closely to character and gentlemanly behaviour, although knowledge, education, and competence were also important aspects (Gidney and Millar 1994; Brint 1994). Thus, when exploring professions historically, one cannot abandon the sociology of professions for the sociology of expertise; doing so in modern studies of professions also risks losing sight of key organizational and regulatory dimensions.

Building on Burrage's (2006: 18–21) work, it is important to recognize the extent to which the desire for recognition – of oneself and one's work – shapes professionalism and professional activity. Professions are occupational status groups: workers who typically have more social status, and a different legal status, than other workers (Adams 2010). According to Weber (1978), such status groups emerge when "in the context of some association [they] effectively claim a special evaluation of their status" and seek "monopolistic appropriation of powers" (61–1). Professional workers often enjoy some measure of social status or esteem, and many also enjoy a special legal status, conferred upon them by legislation granting them practice privileges. Professionals enjoy a degree of cultural authority that not only encourages customers and clients to seek out their expertise, but can also shape societal discourse, influence social policy, and shape social practices on a broader level (Starr 1982; Scott 2008). Professional projects are aimed at achieving or maintaining status. Experts may be recognized as having important job-specific knowledge, but this does not necessarily carry the social weight that certain types of professionals historically possessed.

A good definition of professions will facilitate research into their changing nature (as per Freidson), while acknowledging the centrality of power, status, and structured social relations to the organization of professions in the Anglo-American world since the mid-nineteenth century. My working definition has been shaped by my research into professional regulation in Canada. As I outline in my 2010 article "Profession: A Useful Concept for Sociological Analysis," a look at professional regulation in Canada over time reveals that certain types of occupations – almost always labelled professions in legislation and discussions about it – were regulated differently than other occupations. My own research, then, sees professions as "organized occupational groups with a (somewhat) accepted claim to legal and/or social status" (Adams 2010: 54). My focus has been on regulated professional groups. Historically, professions have been distinguishable from occupations (and other "experts") by the nature of their regulation. Self-regulating professions were granted more autonomy and authority, more regulatory privileges and responsibilities, and more work-related rights and protections than other workers (Adams 2010: 65). In this manner, the privileges and authority of doctors and lawyers differ substantially from those traditionally held by private investigators, beekeepers, and electricians (Adams 2010; Manitoba Law Reform Commission 1994). Regulatory legislation is important, structuring professionals' relationships with the state, other professional and non-professional workers, and the public, as well as their relationship to their work (Adams 2010).

Thus, organizationally, professions are distinguishable from occupations, at least historically, not so much for their services, their expertise (per se), or even their claim (or lack thereof) to a monopoly in their field of endeavour; rather they are distinguished through their status, organization, and their legal right to regulate themselves, and in certain circumstances to govern their field of endeavour.

Here I differ from some scholars who emphasize the establishment and enforcement of monopolies as the defining characteristic of profession (Freidson 2001: 198; Brockman 1998). Following Larson (1977), I instead emphasize powers of self-regulation and attempts to shape or control the market for professional services through regulation and other social closure strategies (see also Witz 1992). While many professions seek to obtain a market monopoly, very few have actually managed to do so.[2] Since obtaining a full monopoly in a market is so rare, it is not fruitful to make "monopoly" a defining characteristic of a profession.

Professionalization

Professionalization is the set of processes that combine to constitute a profession and control a labour market (Berman 2006: 188), and specifically those processes that combine to raise an occupation's professional status, or maintain its status. The ideal outcome of professionalization is status as a self-regulating profession, but this goal is out of reach for some professionalizing occupations. In this work, I use "professionalization" somewhat interchangeably with "professional development" to capture professional change over time. The term "professionalization" has been criticized and rejected by many scholars. Earlier formulations that attempted to denote a series of stages an occupation had to move through to obtain professional status (Caplow 1966; Wilensky 1964) were justly criticized for being ahistorical, and unable to capture variations in process or outcome (Abbott 1991). Some, like Witz (1992), prefer to use the term "professional projects" to highlight the endeavours of organized occupational groups to increase their status, whether they are successful or not. While I agree with Witz that "professional projects" is a useful concept, it cannot adequately capture all the processes that shape professional development. As Witz (1992: 57–9) herself suggests, many social actors and social groups shape the formation of professions – occupational leaders, and other occupational practitioners, various state actors, members of the public and practitioners' clientele, workers practising in the same or adjacent jurisdictions, and business and other social interest groups. I use the term professionalization to capture the historically variable confluence of factors, processes, and activities that shape the emergence of professions and professional development. The term professional projects is used only to refer to aspiring (or established) professionals' strategies to advance their occupation and increase their status.

To capture the complexity of professionalization, I find it useful to combine four different theoretical strands: Weberian social closure theory, social movement theory (especially resource mobilization and political process models), theories of professions and the state, and Abbott's (1988, 2005) ecological approach. Professionalization in Anglo-American contexts is typically a product of collective mobility projects, wherein occupational groups organize, and their leaders mobilize an array of resources – notably skills and knowledge, education and training, economic and social capital, and ideological resources –to win over audiences – specifically, the state, public, and employers – and convince them of their claims to a privileged market position (Larson 1977; Abbott 1988; Shortt 1983; Howell 1981; Witz 1992; Berman 2006). Aspiring professional groups pursue social closure to acquire and mobilize resources to cut off access to opportunities, such as education, training, entry to practice, and practice rewards, to advance or protect their own claims to status (Murphy 1988; Saks 2010; Witz 1992). Although many groups pursue these professional projects, only some are successful. Those who have "fewer resources of power" (Johnson 1972: 43), and who are unable to convince their target audiences of their claims, are less likely to achieve professional status. Also, professional projects can be undermined by the efforts or projects of other workers – especially professionals in the same or related jurisdictions – who counter-mobilize against them (Abbott 1988). Even with resources, however, a professionalizing group will not succeed in achieving regulatory recognition unless state actors decide to grant it. At times, neo-Weberian models cast state actors as passive audiences for professional leaders' claims. Theories of profession–state relations and ecological theory are useful in filling this gap, allowing us to recognize the agency and agendas of state actors, and their influence on professional development. In the sections that follow, I elaborate on each of these theoretical elements.

Neo-Weberian Social Closure

Building on the work of Weber and Parkin, researchers have looked at professionalization in terms of social closure, exploring how occupational groups have pursued professional status by closing off access to opportunities, knowledge, education, and practice by drawing on a variety of status criteria (Murphy 1988; Parkin 1979; Saks 2010, 2015; Weber 1978; Witz 1992). Through social closure these groups "seek to regulate market conditions in their favour, in the face of competition" (Saks 2015: 9). With the assistance of the state, professional practice is limited to those who possess prescribed levels of education and credentials. A variety of status criteria have been drawn on historically. For example, studies have shown how, in the nineteenth century, access to professional education, training, and licences to practise in fields like medicine was restricted to white men from middle- and upper-class backgrounds (Starr 1982; Howell 1981; Witz 1992); formal restrictions were put into place to limit the participation of women, minorities, and working-class white men. Occupational groups enacted social closure not only around education and training, but also around social characteristics such as gender or citizenship. Social closure can take the form of exclusionary strategies in which members of a dominant group close off access to resources and opportunities to subordinate groups. It can also take the form of usurpationary strategies in which subordinate members attempt to mobilize power against dominant groups – to fight their exclusion and subordination, to gain access to professional employment, and/or stake their own claims to professional status (Parkin 1979; Witz 1992).

Social closure is a central element in processes of professionalization, but as a concept its explanatory power is limited. First, there is ambiguity surrounding how social closure is enacted. In Weber's formulation, occupational status groups (like professions) are communities of privileged people who attempt to monopolize their cultural and material opportunities to exclude others (and thereby protect their position) (Weber 1978: 48–52). Thus, the theory captures processes through which status groups draw on their status to get more status, or a different type of status – for instance, transform social status into legal status and privileges, conferred by the state. How exactly do they do this? Research tells us they organize, and attempt to erect institutional barriers that limit entry to practice: professional practice examinations, expensive and competitive education programs, practical training with established practitioners (Saks 2010; Witz 1992). But what of those aspiring professions without much status originally? How do they enact social closure or professionalize? Accounts of professionalization typically start with an occupation with limited status and influence whose practitioners organize to increase their status and form a profession (Adams 2000; Starr 1982; Larson 1977). How do social groups come to acquire status and opportunities that they seek to "hoard" (to use Tilly's 1998 term) for themselves? To answer this question, and add depth and detail to social closure models, I turn to social movement theory – especially resource mobilization models.

A second limitation in neo-Weberian social closure theory is its lack of explicit attention to the state. As Chamberlain (2013: 46) argues, neo-Weberian approaches tend to overemphasize professional autonomy, and minimize other actors involved in the professionalization process, especially the state. While neo-Weberian scholars argue that social closure is enacted with the assistance of the state, which establishes legal boundaries privileging them in the market (Saks 2015; Burrage 2006; Witz 1992), state activity is not actually theorized. The theory does not address why state actors legislate for professionals, and enact social closure. In some accounts the state appears only peripherally in the narrative, merely offering "an administrative rubber stamp, with perhaps a minimum of policy review" (Gilb 1966: 223). Others acknowledge that "the attitude of the state … is crucial" to the success of a professional project (Witz 1992: 57). More recent neo-Weberian accounts demonstrate how active and interventionist the state can be in professional regulation (Saks 2015; Kuhlmann and Saks 2008), but they tend to see the active and interventionist state as a recent development (Saks 2015). Thus, neo-Weberian accounts of professionalization in the nineteenth century typically cast state actors as reactive; they simply respond to the claims put before them. This limitation can be addressed by drawing on theories of the state and state-profession relations.

In the paragraphs that follow, I discuss what each of these additional theories brings to the study of professions, beginning with social movement theory.

Social Movement Theory

Social movements have been defined as the means through which collectivities express their "grievances and concerns about the rights, welfare, and well-being of themselves, and others" through collective action (Snow, Soule and Kriesi 2008: 3). They are "attempts by excluded groups to mobilize sufficient political leverage to advance collective interests" (McAdam 1999). Social movements are catalysts for social change (Della Porta and Diani 1999). The focus of social movement activity is varied, but it often involves protest and opposition to the actions and policies of dominant groups, and/or identity claims (ibid.; McAdam 1999). In this light, social movement theory might at first seem to be of little use to the study of professionalization, as professions are often high-status groups, attempting to expand their power, not oppose those in positions of power. Indeed, social movement scholar Charles Tilly (2004: 5) argued that professional groups, like medical doctors, are better understood as "organized interest groups" who have "achieved special political rights to speak and act collectively," but rarely have they done so through "social movement means." Nonetheless, many scholars see professionalization as a collective mobility project (Larson 1977; Macdonald 1995; Parry and Parry 1976). To understand this project better it is helpful to draw on certain insights in social movement theory.

Aspiring professions are not social movements per se, but social movement theory can shed light on their strategies and tactics. The social movement theories that appear most adaptable to the study of professions are the *resource mobilization* and *political process* models (especially Tilly 1978, McCarthy and Zald 1977; McAdam 1999). Resource mobilization models explore the campaigns and strategies social movement organizations pursue to voice their concerns and achieve their goals. Basically, the approach turns our focus to the structural power and resources – economic, organizational, political, network, and ideological/cultural resources – that are drawn on (or mobilized) by actors involved in a social movement, as well as the political and social context in which this mobilization takes place (McCarthy and Zald 1977; Tilly 1978; McAdam 1999). At the risk of oversimplifying, social movement actors who organize and mobilize many resources to their cause may be more successful in achieving their goals. Social movements are more likely to form when social change disrupts existing societal power relations and expands political opportunities, providing a context favourable to collective action (McAdam 1999: 41).[3]

Adapting these models to the study of professionalization enables us to identify the mechanisms through which practitioners of an occupation enact social closure and win professional status. As such, they combine nicely with neo-Weberian social closure theory to illuminate processes of professionalization. Professional groups organize, attempt to draw on a variety of economic, political, social, ideological, and cultural resources – including their knowledge and skill – to advance their claims. Those who mobilize more resources, and advance more convincing claims, have a better chance of achieving their goals. To succeed, however, the political and social context must be favourable: "The timing and ultimate fate of movements [are] powerfully shaped by the variable opportunities afforded challengers by the shifting institutional structure and ideological disposition of those in power" (McAdam and Snow 2010: 55). Politically, state actors must be open to the claims advanced by professionals, if they are going to legislate in their favour.

To shed light on state actors' activity, it is helpful to consider theories of the state and state-profession relations.

The State and State-Profession Relations

Abrams (1988) has encouraged historical sociologists to view the state not as a unified entity, but as a social construction and ideological project. As Curtis (1997: 9) elaborates, the state as a "unitary, internally coherent entity, possessing will and intention, separate from but capable of intervening in society" does not exist. Rather there is a cluster of political institutions, staffed by particular groups of people, or "state actors." Abrams and Curtis encourage sociologists to dig behind the ideological image of the state to uncover the practices and actions of people who work within state institutions, and to identify those groups that "draw on the capacities of the state system in the interests of organizing the political subjection of others" (Curtis 1997: 10). These latter activities may be called "state projects." In these projects, groups mobilize a variety of state resources to purse their objectives, which may, in fact, conflict with the objectives and goals of other groups and institutions that make up the state system. To understand these projects, especially those pursued in the nineteenth century, several scholars have turned to Michel Foucault (1991) and his work on governmentality (Curtis 1997, 2001; Johnson 1993, 1995).

For Foucault, government is "a form of activity aiming to shape, guide, or affect the conduct of some person or persons" (Gordon 1991: 2). In this sense, governance can occur at any level. At a personal level, individuals can govern their own or others' behaviour. At a societal level state actors endeavour to govern a population. There are also additional levels and locales in which governance of a group or population may occur (Foucault 1991: 91). For Foucault, population meant not simply "a numerous human group, but living beings penetrated, compelled and ruled by processes, by biological laws" (Foucault in Curtis 2001: 40). In societies where power is decentralized, governance through discipline is more predominant (Foucault 1991); it is to these types of societies that "governmentality" applies. Here, individuals, their lives, and social institutions become political targets. In Curtis's (2001) words, "Individuals become the objects of projects that seek to change their conduct by effecting their bodily forces, by tying them to physical space or social categories, by colonizing their wills, and by developing selectively and encouraging pointedly their capacities for reflection and self-discipline" (41). To govern a population, however, actors need to define and acquire knowledge about that population. Key to this process have been statistical projects, like censuses (Foucault 1991; Curtis 2001; Clark 1998). Through such projects state actors attempt to take "exceptionally complex, illegible, and local social practices" and create social categories whereby they can be "recorded and monitored" (Scott 1998: 3). Efforts to define, investigate, categorize, and govern population are central components in state formation (Curtis 1997, 2001; Scott 1998).

Professions and professionals have played an important role in these governance and state-building practices, according to Terry Johnson (1982, 1993, 1995). Governing the population builds on expertise and knowledge, and therefore experts "became crucial in the development and maintenance of this governing capacity," and further, "the institutionalization of expertise in the form of the independent professions was integral to the emergence of the modern state" (Johnson 1993: 142; Evetts and Dingwall 2002: 163). As Foucault (1991) outlines, expertise plays a key role in governmentality and regulation. Experts are in a position not only to acquire knowledge about the population, but also to regulate behaviour. They record, document, evaluate, and assess behaviour, and make normalizing judgments (Evetts and Dingwall 2002: 163–4; Foucault 1979). For example, medical doctors are central actors in a healthcare system that collects information about individuals within a population: these records are used to construct rates of health, disease, morbidity, mortality, fertility, and so on. At the same time, medical doctors help to regulate or "govern" social behaviour, by shaping conduct – for instance, monitoring the sick, encouraging people to engage in healthy behaviours, limiting the movements of the ill to minimize the spread of disease, and so on. From a Foucauldian perspective, professions are governance institutions that not only govern populations themselves (for instance, professional practitioners and their patients), but are also instruments of governmentality at the level of the state. For Johnson, professions are part of the state system, broadly defined (Johnson 1982, 1993); however, he also argues that professionals and professional bodies are autonomous from "the state" (Johnson 1993: 150). Johnson's views have been criticized by Freidson (2001: 134), who cautions researchers against collapsing professions into the state, arguing that while states and professions "interpenetrate, if we do not treat the state as if it were an entity separate from professions in particular and civil society in general, we are awash in a fog-bound sea of ambiguity" (see also Saks 2015: 7).

It is important to recognize that professional development and state development are linked: processes of professionalization and state building occurred in conjunction historically (Goebel 1994; Johnson 1982). Professionals have contributed to governance by state actors, and in turn have earned legitimacy and power through their relationship with state actors, and their own governance activity (Evetts and Dingwall 2002: 164; Johnson 1993). Recent changes in professional regulation, and state-profession relations, have been spurred by changing government objectives (Johnson 1993: 149; Chamberlain 2013). In the United Kingdom, changing state goals, and state-profession relations, have modified how professional expertise is used, and concomitantly have reduced professional autonomy, altered professional regulation, and limited professional jurisdictions and powers (Evetts 2002; Kuhlmann and Saks 2008; Chamberlain 2013; Larkin 1995).

Although many scholars exploring state-profession relations have been influenced by Foucault, other scholars, taking substantially different theoretical perspectives, have also concluded that the fate of states and professions have been closely intertwined in industrial capitalist societies. Evetts and Dingwall (2002) have highlighted the contributions of Herbert Spencer (1896), who similarly saw professions as integral to state formation in the modern era. For Spencer, professions help to provide legitimacy to a state system no longer as reliant on military force to sustain its political authority. Professions not only serve a legitimating role, however, but they also exercise some independent regulatory authority. In this manner, "collectively, the professions constitute a key part of the regulating system of industrial society" in which "significant elements of social control are decentralized and loosely coupled, leaving space in which change can occur" (Evetts and Dingwall 2002: 164, 170).

Durkheim (1984, 1992) also believed professions could fulfil important regulatory functions. For Durkheim (1984), professional associations and other similar organizations could occupy "a distinct role between the state and civil society" (Streeck and Schmitter 1985: 16). Such associations established ethical guidelines for their members, and regulated their behaviour, in the conduct of their business and life, in a manner that a distant state was incapable of achieving (Durkheim 1992: 30–9). These professional associations were (or should be) governed by state legislation. For Durkheim (1992: 96), professions were intermediaries between the state and individuals, preventing the state from oppressing the people, while ensuring the state was "sufficiently free" from the latter's direct influence.

These ideas have been elaborated by Streeck and Schmitter (1985), who see professional associations and similar groups as one of four institutional bases of social order (along with community, the market, and the state). For them, as for Durkheim, professions and related associations are private interest groups, but their institutional design (and regulation by the state) ensures they can act in the public interest (ibid.: 16). State actors delegate authority to "private interest governments" like self-regulating professions and enable them to act autonomously with the threat that if they do not wield their power responsibly, the state will intervene directly. For these scholars, professions are one social institution that facilitates state governance, and contributes to social order.

Although they draw on very different theoretical assumptions, Foucauldian scholars and others influenced by Spencer and Durkheim claim that professions were historically a key element in state formation, and that professions have historically supported state activity, and have contributed to the maintenance of social order. State actors may regulate and draw on the labour of professional workers to serve their own governance goals or state projects. These arguments are in sharp contradistinction to much of the sociological literature on professionalization, which casts state actors as merely the audiences for claims advanced by professionals, who sometimes grant privileges when a particularly compelling case for regulation is made. In contrast, for these state-focused scholars, state actors are active in creating and regulating professions because the latter serve political, social, or governance goals.

These approaches are valuable because they cast state actors as agents, and explore how profession creation may help state actors meet their goals. Further, the concept of "state projects" is useful, and it may be fruitful to explore the interplay between these "state projects" and the "professional projects" identified by neo-Weberians. Nonetheless, Foucauldian and Spencerian approaches are not without their limitations. As touched on earlier, it is problematic to collapse professions into the state, although we must acknowledge that professions and the state interpenetrate (Freidson 2001; Saks 2015). Further, the theories may apply only to some regulated professions. For example, Johnson (1982) demonstrates the interconnections between states and professions through a case study of the legal profession. Law would appear to be a profession that is highly interconnected with the state, but is this true for other regulated professions, for instance, optometry and chiropractic? Probably not. Foucauldian approaches do not generally acknowledge variations in state-profession relations across profession. Lastly, the approaches ascribe a narrow range of interests to state actors, or minimize their decision-making capacity, at least respecting professions. State actors are said to embrace professions to achieve governance goals (Johnson 1993, 1995), or enhance legitimacy (Spencer 1896; Evetts and Dingwall 2002).[4] State activity, here, then seems aimed at achieving one overarching goal: social order or governance. For some Foucauldian scholars, however, state actors' interests may be irrelevant. Governmentality is an outcome of state actors' activity, but not necessarily one pursued intentionally (Johnson 1993). The end result is that these approaches have a somewhat narrow view of state actors' decision making and their activity. State actors are not seen as individuals who possess a range of interests, or whose decision making can have a variety of outcomes.

Abbott's Ecological Theory and Linked Ecologies

Andrew Abbott (1988, 2005) has advanced an ecological theory of professions (and states). He contends there is a system of professions, in which professional groups fight for jurisdiction and dominance in their field of practice. Professional development is shaped by these battles over jurisdiction, and the outcomes of these battles. Potential outcomes include the dominance of one profession over another, a compromise where professions share a jurisdiction, or even one profession's eradication of a competitor (Abbott 1988). Jurisdictional disputes involve professional groups advancing claims to expertise to key audiences, including the state, the public, and employers. Thus, although professions exist in an ecology, they interact with institutions in other ecologies, and in fact, for professionals to achieve their goals (which for Abbott pertain to jurisdictional claims), their claims must resonate with actors in ecologies that are linked with their own, such as the state and university ecologies.

In Abbott's (2005) work on linked ecologies, he explores linkages between the professions' ecology and the state ecology. For Abbott, ecologies are "complex interactional structures" composed of actors, locations, and the linkages or relations between actors and locations, which may vary from one ecology to the next (2005: 247–8). For him, "the concept of linked ecologies recognizes that events within any particular ecology … are hostage in some sense to events in adjacent ecologies" (254). To illustrate how the ecologies of professions and states have historically linked together, Abbott uses the example of medical regulation in the United States and United Kingdom. He argues that "to succeed in one ecology, a particular competitive strategy must … provide results to allies in an adjacent one" (255). In this instance, medical licensing (or deregulation) emerges when it works in both ecologies: when both professionals and state actors have something to gain from it. The gains for state actors are not necessarily broad and general (governance and social order), but can be short-term and political. Supporting or opposing licensing might contribute to a political party's or set of actors' broader or short-term political agenda. If licensing serves no one in the political arena, then professionals' legislative goals are unlikely to be realized. Similarly, regulatory instability may arise if the gains to be made by different groups are contradictory or shifting. Abbott's approach is valuable in ascribing multiple and varying goals to institutional actors. It draws researchers' attention to alliances between actors within linked ecologies, and those moments when professionals' goals and state actors' political goals intersect. Further, it highlights the centrality of politics to professional regulation (see also Burrage 2006).

Adapting Abbott's (2005) approach, one might postulate that professional regulation is shaped not only by professional projects (involving social closure and resource mobilization), but by state actors' projects and goals.[5] Professional regulation may arise when it not only benefits members of an aspiring professional group, but some state actors as well (Abbott 2005: 255). Since the state and professions are just two ecologies within a complex social reality, we would also assume that other ecologies may be linked, and could also influence professional regulation at certain points in time. Nonetheless, we would expect that the state and professions ecologies would be two of the main ones shaping professional regulation.[6]

When using Abbott's model, one must be careful to take social-historical change into account. In the earliest period of profession formation, the profession's ecology is in formation as well. In fact, one could argue that the system of professions was not fully established until the twentieth century. In a similar vein, the size, shape, and nature of the state ecology changes dramatically over time, and was still being defined during the earliest eras of professional regulation in Canada. The shifting boundaries, changing actors, and new institutional structures make it difficult to determine the precise shape and nature of professional and state ecologies, especially in the years around Canadian Confederation. Nonetheless, Abbott's model is still helpful, even in this earliest period, because it encourages us to explore the goals, interests, and beliefs of state actors, and the extent to which – and moments when – these coincide with, or at least do not run counter to, the goals, interests, and beliefs of professional actors.

Making Sense of Professional Regulation in Canada

In the chapters that follow, I build on the concepts and theories outlined above to make sense of the regulation of professions, and state-profession relations across four Canadian provinces, from Confederation to the mid-twentieth century. I build upon, and compare and contrast, three models of professionalization: the neo-Weberian social closure model (augmented by social-movement approaches that provide insight into how social closure can be achieved through resource mobilization), Foucauldian and other state-centred approaches, and Abbott's ecological approach. I argue that professionalization and professional regulation is an outcome shaped by a combination of forces and processes, which include social closure, professional projects, and resource mobilization, as well as state actors' projects and interests, and the interplay between professional projects and state actors' projects. Also important are a host of other factors including social context, public concerns, and the lobbying of various public and private interest groups, especially other professional workers. In the pages that follow, I pay particular attention to state actors' decision making and activities. Professional groups may organize resources and engage in sustained campaigns to win professional regulation, but when do state actors grant them these privileges and what rationales do they provide for doing so? Throughout I treat state actors as agents, keeping in mind that even saying "yes" or "no" – or ignoring a request outright and doing nothing at all – is a form of action.[7] To understand professional regulation and profession creation, I argue, we need to consider both professionals' and state actors' activities.

Previous research on professional regulation has focused disproportionately on the regulation of prominent professions, especially law and medicine, or, occasionally, explored the rise of several professional groups in a specific time period (Gidney and Millar 1994). To understand professional regulation and profession–state relations in all their complexity, I explore all regulated professions in the provinces of British Columbia, Ontario, Quebec, and Nova Scotia over a seventy-year span of time. This approach has advantages as well as disadvantages. The approach is helpful in providing an overview of regulatory trends, identifying general concerns informing and shaping professional regulation, and revealing variations across time, locale, and profession. Such an approach, however, can obscure small details that are often important in shaping regulatory outcomes for specific professions. Further, the approach limits my ability to test my theoretical model completely. Professionalization and regulatory outcomes may be shaped by professional projects and state projects, but it is regulatory decisions at the legislative level that occupy much of my attention. To capture regulatory trends across profession, time, and locale, I focus more on legislative debates and outcomes, and rely more heavily on government records, than I examine professional projects and draw on professional records. The large number of professions considered here (approximately fifteen per province) makes a serious study of professional projects across time and place too unwieldy. Fortunately, the existing literature on professions (in Canada and abroad) has the opposite bias – focusing on professions to the neglect of state processes. I am able to draw on previous research on these professional projects to understand professions' contribution to regulation. Moreover, in the chapters that follow, I present several case studies where I take a closer look at the various parties and actors shaping professional projects and regulatory outcomes.

Because the scope of the project is so broad, I have tried not only to provide an overview of key historical trends, but also to narrow the focus by considering the implications of my findings for two current sociological debates and questions. The first concerns the role of the state in professional development. When they regulated professions historically, did provincial state actors merely respond to requests advanced by organized professional groups (as depicted in many neo-Weberian accounts), or did they actively seek to achieve their own governance goals or political goals as state-centric approaches and Abbott respectively contend?

A second area of focus is "expertise." As the above review of the theoretical and sociological literature reveals, "expertise" has emerged as a central concept in debates on both professions and state-profession relations. Professionals are experts, but does the concept of "expert" capture what it means to be a professional? Further, Foucauldian studies of state-profession relations suggest that it is in the role of expert that professions contribute to state projects. Halliday (1987) argues that professions provide expertise in service to the state. Others, however, like Spencer (1896) and Streeck and Schmitter (1985), place more emphasis on professionals' institutional roles, rather than their "expertise" per se. This study explores how significant "expertise" was historically to professions and professional regulation, and how meanings attached to "expertise" have changed over time.

In addition to these two primary themes, there are two other goals worth mentioning. First, I have tried to be attuned to variations in regulation across time and place. Sociological and historical research on professions has typically seen regulation as a key element in professionalization; however, the exact nature of that regulation, and how it varies across time and place has seldom been analysed in any detail (exceptions include Krause 1996; Burrage 2006; Saks 2015). A distinction has been drawn between professions in Anglo-American contexts, which tend to be "self-regulating," and professions in European contexts, which are more aptly described as "state-regulated" (Collins 1990; Krause 1996; Neal and Morgan 2000; Rueschemeyer 1986). However, as I will show in the next chapter, patterns of self-regulation in the United States, United Kingdom, and Canada have differed in meaningful ways. Canada has regulated professions slightly differently from other, similar countries. Further, each province in Canada has its own regulatory traditions. These distinct traditions not only lead to different trajectories in professional development, but they may be indicative of differences in state-profession relations that are theoretically important. Although this book briefly touches on international regulatory differences, it focuses more on regional differences in regulation across province, profession, and time. To understand these latter processes, I draw on the work of DiMaggio and Powell (1983) and others writing on organizational fields and institutional isomorphism (Suddaby and Viale 2011; Scott 2008).

Second, although my focus is on professional regulation at a broad, provincial level, I have tried not to lose sight of the actors driving professional processes. I sometimes use general terms like "the state" and "professions," but I focus on the actors within these institutions and organizations that generate social change by pursuing their own interests. The class, gender, and race of these individuals, their status and resources, and their efforts to expand their status power, or defend their livelihoods and political interests against the perceived infringements of others, drive their social activity. Where possible, I take pains to identify the key actors in these various projects and consider how their backgrounds shaped their activity.

A Note on Methodology and Sources

To explore professional regulation in five Canadian provinces from Confederation to the 1930s, I draw on a variety of historical sources. Since the focus is on regulatory patterns and state-profession relations, I rely heavily on provincial legislative records including acts passed, bills proposed but not passed, surviving records of legislative debates, and where possible professional records. To understand the path of professional legislation through legislative assemblies, and explore some debates, I use the *Journals of the Legislative Assembly* in each of the four provinces. Newspapers were also a valuable source of information. Prior to the mid-twentieth century in many provinces, transcripts of legislative debates were not published, and newspapers provide the only detailed records. Historical newspapers contain information on professional activities and public opinion as well. Moreover, provincial government commission reports often capture contemporary debates about professional regulation. I also draw on archival sources; for instance, state actor correspondence and memos on professional regulation. Records housed in the provincial archives and legislative libraries, and to a lesser extent Library and Archives Canada, have been helpful in some contexts. To explore professional developments I rely heavily on published histories of professions in Canada, along with some professional records. Where possible I have also considered demographic information, using genealogical and census records to obtain information on the backgrounds and occupational histories of professional leaders and state actors who actively shaped professional projects and regulatory outcomes.

It must be acknowledged that these records are incomplete. There is no surviving record of legislative debate on many bills proposing to regulate professions; many key legislative votes and important discussions occurred behind closed doors and were not recorded. Even when records of debates surrounding legislation exist, state actors rarely explained their decisions, or conveniently outlined the set of principles guiding their actions. Despite these data gaps, a review of all these records provides an unprecedented look into the history of professional regulation in Canada, and illuminates the factors shaping professional development, and how these changed, over time.

Chapter Two

The Emergence of Self-Regulating Professions in Pre-Confederation Canada

The majority of self-regulating professions in Canada were established after Confederation, but the very first self-regulating professions date back to the country's colonial days. In this era, patterns of professional self-regulation, which would become dominant in later decades, were first established. This chapter explores the emergence of professional self-regulation in Lower and Upper Canada (Quebec and Ontario). I begin with a look at the emergence of self-regulating professions in law and medicine in Lower Canada, through a consideration of both professionals' activities and political events from the late eighteenth century to 1850. Subsequently, I discuss the establishment of a self-regulating legal profession in the late eighteenth century in Upper Canada, and legislation to create a self-regulating medical profession in 1839, which was ultimately disallowed by Queen Victoria in December 1840. Last, I contrast the regulation of medicine in Upper and Lower Canada from that which emerged in the United Kingdom in 1858, and in many US states beginning in the 1870s. I argue that, while Canada was strongly influenced by both the United States and the United Kingdom, the pattern of self-regulation that emerged in pre-Confederation Canada differed from that which subsequently developed in the other two nations.

Sociologists have identified an Anglo-American model of professional regulation, in which groups of practitioners organize, lobby the state for privileges, and win the right to restrict entry to practice (Larson 1977; Collins 1990). While this model has been helpful in distinguishing professional regulation in the United States, England, and other nations like Canada, from that common in Continental Europe, it has the disadvantage of homogenizing social-historical trends and patterns of regulation within groupings. Social-historical circumstances and events shape professional development and may lead to particularities in regulation that are obscured by sweeping generalizations (Bernier 1989; Macdonald 1995). Larson (1977), for example, links the rise of professions with the emergence of industrial capitalism. This argument may work for the United States, where professional regulation dates from the late nineteenth century (Burrage 2006), but in Canada, where self-regulating professions arrived comparatively early (late eighteenth to mid-nineteenth century), and industrial capitalism comparatively late – the 1860s and 1870s (Rinehart 2006; Pentland 1959) – such arguments are not as easily sustained. Historically, the structure of professional regulation in Canada, the United States, and the United Kingdom has differed in significant ways that have seldom been explored.

Lower Canada (Quebec)

Early in the seventeenth century, France established a colony in what is now modern-day Quebec. Although not a terribly large settlement (especially compared to those established by England in the American colonies), New France was land- and resource-rich. The colony was governed under French law and custom, with some accommodations for local conditions. Leaders attempted to reproduce France's "Three Estates" within the French colony, and a dominant place was established for the Catholic Church and a landed elite with seigneurial rights,[1] while the majority of colonists of more modest means laboured as farmers, and in a variety of other capacities, including as fur trappers, tradesmen, and merchants (Ouellet 1980a). In the mid-eighteenth century, Britain and France were at war (the Seven Years' War), a conflict fought in part in the colonies. Britain defeated the French militia at Quebec and Montreal in 1759 and 1760, respectively, and New France fell under British rule. The Treaty of Paris, signed in 1763, formalized the transfer of the colony of New France to Britain. The colonists were promised freedom of religion in the treaty, but in other aspects their fate was unclear (Vachon 1962).

After some difficulty and uncertainty during the first few years of British rule, Britain passed the Quebec Act in 1775 which re-established French civil law in the colony, but also continued the implementation of English common law. Quebec would be a British colony, loyal to the British Crown, but would combine English traditions and forms of government with French custom (Vachon 1962; Garneau 2009). These decisions would fundamentally shape Quebec (and Canadian) history for centuries to come.[2] The next few decades saw the size of the population in the colony more than double (Vachon 1962: 83; Ouellet 1980a: 8). The former French colonists (*les Canadiens*) had a very high birth rate, and their population continued to grow, while the American Revolution brought thousands of English Loyalists into the British colonies of Quebec and Nova Scotia. Many of the Loyalists chose to settle west of the main French settlements, in what is now Ontario. These Loyalists wanted nothing to do with French civil law and French customs. Rejecting the seigneurial system, they sought "not only English law, but grants of land in English freehold tenure" (Ouellet 1980a: 10). Fearing ethnic conflict, Britain decided to divide the colony into two provinces: Lower Canada would continue as before, characterized by French civil law and English common law, while Upper Canada would be established as entirely English (Ouellet 1980a).

The rise of professions in both Upper and Lower Canada dates predominantly from this period of British rule. The laws of New France forbade lawyers, so there were none practising in the colony before the 1760s.[3] In 1764 the British governor of the colony (James Murray) established an English court and judicial system, and the following year gave commissions to four Canadiens to act as lawyers ("procureurs et avocats") in the courts established (Veilleux 1997: 24).[4] The first organized profession in the region was the notariat (Vachon 1962: 3), whose presence in Quebec dates back to the 1620s. Around 1663, two categories of notaries were established: "royal" notaries, who were appointed by the (French) king or his representative in the colony, and "seigneurial notaries," who were nominated by seigneurs to work in their regions (ibid.: 17). Ordinances from King Louis XV attempted to regulate aspects of their work in 1733 (30–4). Until the English era, however, notaries were a fairly small and precarious group. Variably trained (if trained at all), these men were distinguished from their fellow colonists by their ability to read and write,[5] perhaps their dignity and morals (which were verified before a commission was granted), and their officially sanctioned roles; however, they had difficulty sustaining a living unless they combined their notarial work with other occupations (for instance, land surveyor, architect, bailiff, and clerk, but also innkeeper, shoemaker, and merchant) (39–43). The British government's decision to maintain French civil law in Quebec confirmed a place for notaries in the colony, and the two legal professions (lawyers and notaries) continued to split their duties according to French custom. Notaries would be public officers who write official documents and contracts (e.g., marriage contracts, wills, land grants), and provide legal advice, while lawyers represent or advocate for people, in court or outside, on legal matters (civil suits, criminal cases, contract negotiations), and also provide legal advice.

In the late eighteenth century, there was also a small number of medical doctors in the colony, but they were mainly associated with the military. Local and untrained healers abounded (Ouellet 1980a: 71). Under British rule, the number of medical doctors also increased. Most of these doctors were foreign-trained (and often foreign-born), coming from Britain, France, Germany, and the United States (Bernier 1989; Tunis 1981). Like their lawyer and notariat counterparts, all were men.

The first laws to regulate all three of these professional groups in the colony were passed between 1785 and 1788. The ordinance of 1785 affected lawyers and notaries. Historians explain that this act was shaped by lawyers' (and notaries') complaints that commissions to practise in these two fields were being granted on the basis of patronage, not qualification (Veilleux 1997; Vachon 1962; Garneau 2007). In the years since the British took over, the colony's governors had issued many commissions to individuals seeking to practise as lawyers or notaries. These commissions were granted not infrequently to individuals who had no training in the law (Vachon 1962; Veilleux 1997); often, lawyers and notaries complained, well-connected individuals who had met with failure in other fields decided at an advanced age to secure their livelihoods by requesting a commission (Garneau 2009; Vachon 1962; Martineau 1967). Governors were willing to grant commissions to such individuals, even as they turned away others (less well-connected) who had some training (Vachon 1962: 65). Governors were also willing to hand out multiple commissions to the same person; it was not uncommon, for instance, for men to practise as both notaries and lawyers in the colony (Garneau 2007; Veilleux 1997). The situation came to a head in 1784, when a notary of advanced age and little training sought a commission as a lawyer. Quebec lawyers endeavoured to block the appointment, claiming that commissions should only be granted to those who had worked continuously for several years under a supervising lawyer to learn the profession, and those who could provide proof of their good conduct and ability (Veilleux 1997: 30–3).

The lawyers were not successful in blocking the appointment, but in response the following year, the governor passed an ordinance establishing entry-to-practice requirements for lawyers and notaries (Veilleux 1997). Candidates required five years of clerkship under contract to a trained notary or lawyer, and examination by two practitioners before judges of the Court of Common Pleas, before they were eligible to practise in their fields (Garneau 2009; Martineau 1967; Veilleux 1997). The 1785 ordinance also provided some guidelines for the practice of law and work as a notary, and forbade individuals from combining professions (Vachon 1962; Martineau 1967). Henceforth, law, notarial work, and land surveying would be separate occupations. Individuals who had been practising more than one profession in 1785 were granted twelve months to make their choice. Notaries and lawyers objected to the latter clause, which was not a development they had sought. Many individuals had practised both branches of the law and felt that their ability to sustain a living would be undermined if they had to give up one for the other (Vachon 1962: 73; Martineau 1967). Nonetheless, in establishing entry requirements, the ordinance "assured a certain identity, if not coherence for the profession(s)" (Garneau 2009: 132; Veilleux 1997).[6]

The 1788 ordinance pertained to the practice of medicine (and pharmacy), and limited practice in the province to those who had obtained permission, and a certificate, from the governor (Canada 1788). In Montreal and Quebec, those attending childbirth also required permission. The preamble to the act explains that incompetent and ignorant practitioners had caused many difficulties for people in the province (ibid.). According to historians, the act was a response to the advice of British military surgeons, who believed strict regulation was required to improve healthcare in the colony (Collin 1997), and who sought to control the influx of American doctors into the province (Bernier 1981). To practise, individuals would have to pass an exam before a board in either Montreal or Quebec. Examiners were predominantly British, military, and urban medical doctors, and in their minds British education and degrees were superior to all others (Collin 1997; Tunis 1981). Those who could afford to go to Europe for their medical training were rewarded in this system, but the average French Canadian (and English Canadian) medical student was at a disadvantage (Collin 1997; Tunis 1981).

Although the 1780s legislation raised entry requirements for professions in Lower Canada, it did not repress professional growth. The first four decades of the nineteenth century witnessed a rapid increase in the number of professionals. From a mere four lawyers in 1765, by the opening decade of the nineteenth century, the province had thirty-four. In the same era there were also fifty-seven medical doctors, and eighty-nine notaries. By the following decade, the number of professionals in these three fields had increased by 59 per cent: drawing on the Quebec almanac, Ouellet (1980a: 364) finds 145 notaries, 64 lawyers, and 77 medical doctors in 1811–20. Between 1820 and 1838, the numbers increased 110 per cent from the 1820 mark. The growth was particularly notable among les Canadiens. Over 90 per cent of notaries were French Canadian (not surprisingly given the French origins of this occupation, and its basis in French civil law). Over the period roughly 60 per cent of lawyers were also French Canadian: the percentage of Canadiens practising law in urban centres increased substantially between 1786 and 1805 (Garneau 2007, 2009). Medicine was the only English-dominated profession; approximately one third of practitioners were French Canadian. Nonetheless, the percentage of practitioners who were francophone increased over the period from 27 per cent in 1801–10 to 38 per cent in 1821–38 (Ouellet 1980a). As noted, medicine's entry requirements privileged those who earned European degrees or diplomas (Tunis 1981), not the more locally trained. Nonetheless French Canadian medical doctors increased their numbers in both urban and especially rural areas during this period (ibid.).

Professional growth was tied to the expansion of the population, commerce, and business in Lower Canada, as well as opportunities to obtain a classical education (Ouellet 1980a; Garneau 2007). Professions were not only occupations for the sons of the elite, but were open to those of more modest means (e.g., the sons of tradespeople and artisans) who could afford to send their sons to school for a classical education (Garneau 2007, 2009).[7] Such training opened up opportunities in all branches of the professions (including the clergy, not otherwise discussed here). Young men educated in the Quebec seminary or similar institutions could subsequently obtain a clerkship with an established lawyer or notary, train and study for five years, and enter practice (Garneau 2007), or seek out medical education, both through apprenticeship and through formal education in the United States, the United Kingdom, and by the mid-1820s in Lower Canada (Tunis 1981). As the number of practitioners increased, their efforts to join together, establish schools and societies, and obtain professional rights and privileges also increased. In Quebec, these professional projects were intertwined with political projects.

According to historians, French Canadian professionals, along with many of their English Canadian counterparts, became frustrated with their perceived lack of opportunities and voice in the affairs of the province, especially from the 1820s on. Many were upwardly mobile, but with appointments to various offices and civil roles being granted on the basis of patronage – and hence disbursed largely to the English urban elite – several avenues were closed to them (Vachon 1962). In Ouellet's (1980a: 63) words, it appeared "as though French Canadians were being systematically blocked from the higher echelons of the civil service at a time when they had become most eager to accede to them." In the early nineteenth century, pathways into the professions still went through the governor, who issued licences to those who met the criteria laid out in the 1780s ordinances. These rules were advantageous for professions because they required training for entry-to-practice, but their benefit was limited. For example, the ordinance respecting lawyers and notaries required five years of clerkship attached to an established practitioner, but said nothing about the content of clerks' training. Some individuals likely received very good training at the hands of experienced professionals, but others did not. After all, students could be apprenticed to practitioners who themselves were appointed on the basis of patronage, not ability or training. Lawyers and notaries wanted more opportunity to determine training, education, and entry to practice; they were frustrated that entry was in the hands of the governor. Medical doctors had similar frustrations with the lack of clear standards for entry to practise medicine (Tunis 1981). With no rules in place, medical board members began setting their own standards: for instance, in 1821 the Montreal board denied a candidate seeking a licence because he only had apprenticeship training; they requested that he "seek further education at an American university, an action outside the powers conferred on the Board by the Act" (ibid.: 87). Such arbitrary decisions fostered anger and resentment. Professionals across all three professions began to organize and advocate for improved regulation and the right to determine their own fate.

Parallel frustrations were experienced on a political level, where professionals in the legislative assembly felt their efforts were being blocked by the elite. When the British colony was separated into the two provinces of Lower and Upper Canada, parallel political institutions were established. Each province had an elected legislative assembly, and an appointed upper house, the legislative council (Ouellet 1980a; Vachon 1962). Each also had a lieutenant governor and an executive council at the head (Ouellet 1980a). Above them all was a governor appointed by Great Britain, who had ultimate authority over both provinces in the colony. Under this system, those at the top of the state hierarchy were all appointed either by authorities in Great Britain, or by the governors. The leaders were friends and associates of the governors and they formed "une oligarchie puissante et très loyaliste" (Vachon 1962: 82). The British elite and their friends dominated not only the top state positions, but also most of the paid government offices and posts as well. According to Ouellet (1980a), authorities in Great Britain sought to balance out the democratic legislative assembly with a strong executive controlled by English appointees and the French landed elite.

Members of professions increased their representation in the legislative assembly from 18 per cent in 1792 to 35 per cent by 1810 (Ouellet 1980a: 80). Between 1815 and 1824, they held 38 per cent of the seats (ibid.: 187). Most professionals in the legislature were in the Canadian party formed in 1806, in opposition to the English elite (80). The majority were French Canadian – most of the notaries, and eleven of fourteen lawyers in the assembly after 1792 (Garneau 2009: 139). Les Canadiens found that legislation they advanced was frequently overturned by the appointed upper house. (In turn, they blocked legislation advanced by anglophone merchants.) Thus, on a political level, as well as on a professional level, French Canadians of ability saw their aspirations and endeavours undermined by an English minority that held the key power positions. In response they organized to bring about effective change.

The legislative assembly became a focal point for both professional and political struggles, with a group of French Canadian professionals (and several English professional and business allies) leading the charge. For professional leaders, what was needed was legislative change that would grant professionals the collective ability to determine entry to practice, and govern their own professions. Some merely sought more of a voice in shaping entry to practice. Others went further, requesting the right to self-regulate. These goals were shared by French and English Canadian professionals alike; shared interests and similarities in training appear to have reduced the impact of ethnic tension within professions.[8] In the 1820s and 1830s, professionals formed societies, began to establish schools and journals, and prepared bills to be introduced in the legislative assembly to revise their regulation (Bernier 1989; Vachon 1962; Veilleux 1997). For example, bills pertaining to the regulation of notaries were presented by notary members of the legislature in 1824, 1831, 1834, and 1835. On several occasions the bills were passed by the elected assembly, but they disappeared or were rejected when sent before the legislative council (Vachon 1962). Lawyers introduced bills on their profession's behalf in 1821, 1823,

1824, and 1831 (Veilleux 1997). These too failed to proceed. From professionals' point of view, their ability to determine their own futures was thwarted by the conservative element leading the province, who feared that any such independent body would threaten their authority to govern (ibid.: 53).

Medical doctors alone found some limited success in their legislative requests. In 1818 non-military medical practitioners in Quebec petitioned the legislative assembly, "protesting the military composition of the medical boards, and their own lack of participation in the administration of the profession" (Tunis 1981: 72). They were unsuccessful. Five years later, controversy erupted in Montreal when a member of the Montreal board wrote to the governor to request that the current board be dismissed, and that a new board made up of professors at the Montreal medical school affiliated with the Montreal General Hospital be installed (Tunis 1981). The governor agreed. All members of the new board were British-educated (those educated elsewhere were excluded from appointments at the hospital and school). French Canadian and some English Canadian practitioners vociferously opposed this decision, and they petitioned the legislature in 1823. In subsequent years, there were repeated attempts to reform the medical act in the legislature. Some degree of success was achieved in 1831 with the passage of a new medical act which allowed medical doctors to elect medical board members (with governor approval) (Bernier 1981; Tunis 1981).[9] The act also clarified entry-to-practice by limiting entry to those twenty-one years of age or older who had undertaken five years of training (apprenticeship and formal education at a recognized medical school), and passed an exam (Bernier 1981). Those with a university diploma (obtained in "her majesty's dominions") could acquire a licence without examination. In some periods, American diplomas were accepted in lieu of examination, but in others they were not. This act was only in effect until 1837, when the political impasse between the assembly and the council contributed to its expiration (Tunis 1981: 73).

Faced with repeated roadblocks to their professional and political endeavours, the Canadiens in the assembly radicalized. Seeing themselves as not simply professionals seeking more independence, but articulate representatives of the entire French Canadian population, they began to voice their discontent against the discriminatory policies and practices of the English government and elite, who they felt were marginalizing the French people economically and politically (Ouellet 1980a: 60). Professionals of British origin were somewhat divided. Some enjoyed considerable prestige, important posts, and an elite clientele (ibid.: 63). They were invested in the current system, and wanted to maintain it. Nonetheless, there was not room for all English-speaking professionals at the top, and many English professionals (especially, in medicine, those not trained abroad) joined their francophone counterparts in both their professional and political projects. Professionals, as educated men of ability, believed that they were well situated to be public and social leaders. Further, they believed that through improving their situation, they could bring about positive change for all Canadiens. Thus, when fighting for their interests, they did so in the name of the people of Lower Canada, and they successfully earned the latter's support (Ouellet 1980a).

The solution for these French Canadian professionals – active along with others in the Canadian party, and later the Patriot party – was an expansion of elected authority. Professionals should be allowed to govern themselves, and elect members from their ranks to take on leadership roles. They should not have their fate decided by the English elite. On a political level, they sought reform to the upper appointed legislative (and executive) councils. The people should be governed by those they elected (Ouellet 1980a). Thus, the fight for representative government and the fight for professional self-regulation were intertwined. Each was a fight against English domination, for an extension of democracy, and for the acquisition of rights that should already be theirs.

For all that professionals advocated for political and professional reform, they tended to be somewhat conservative in their views, rather than radical (Ouellet 1980a; Curtis 2012). Throughout the 1820s and into the 1830s they expressed loyalty to Britain and British institutions: "They saw no contradiction between their [French Canadian] nationalism and membership in the British Empire" (Ouellet 1980a: 74). They rejected American republicanism, and saw capitalism as a system encouraging the rule of a dominant few Englishmen (ibid.). Their focus was on eliminating the forces stacked against them, by bringing about social and political change to expand their voice and their opportunities. In Ouellet's words, the French-Canadian professionals were "a class aspiring to power for itself, but on behalf of the 'nation'" (ibid.: 84). Their cohesion and commitment made them an important political force.

Demographic and economic trends in this era – specifically population expansion and a prolonged economic and agricultural crisis – exacerbated the political situation. The English oligarchy was blamed for the province's woes (Ouellet 1980a). Although in the assembly the "English" party had faced off against the "Canadian" party for decades, the two parties were not ethnically homogeneous (i.e., there were French Canadians in [and voting for] the English party, and prominent anglophones in the Canadian party), but both the parties and the vote polarized in the tumultuous 1830s (Ouellet 1980a; Tunis 1981). There was an upsurge of support for les Canadiens (since 1826, *les patriotes*), who enjoyed the vote of the French Canadian population, while the English maintained the support of the small English population, but lost more general support.[10] Feeling threatened, the English minority clung to power more vociferously and continued to block the Patriots' political efforts. The Patriots tried to appeal to Britain for support against the tyranny of their English government leaders, and for government reform, but were denied.

It was in this context that the more radical among the Patriots and their supporters began to foment rebellion. Believing that legal and political methods had failed them, the only option for some was armed conflict. The leadership, based in Montreal especially (the Quebec base was more moderate), sought to mobilize the support of people in the towns and countryside, to follow their American neighbours' lead, and overthrow the British government (Ouellet 1980a). They managed to garner a considerable amount of support, and even won a few battles, but ultimately the rebellions of 1837 and 1838 failed. The leaders were predominantly professionals and merchants: 186 professionals (just less than a third of the estimated number of professionals in the province) and 388 merchants participated in the rebellions (Ouellet 1980a: 340); the professionals held positions of leadership and influence (Vachon 1962: 85). They were skilled thinkers and good orators, but not well equipped to plan and execute a military endeavour. Further, they did not have sufficient resources (weapons) to carry out their aims. When faced with the British military, they faltered. Some professionals led their charges into battle, while others quickly abandoned their posts, or refused to engage.

In response to the 1837–8 rebellions (and a small rebellion in Upper Canada in 1837), the British government sent an investigator, Lord Durham, to identify the problems and propose a solution. In 1840, Britain followed his recommendations and united the two provinces into one colony, divided into two parts (Monet 2006): Canada West (Upper Canada) and Canada East (Lower Canada). The colony would have one government and a shared legislative assembly with representation from both of the former provinces. Representation in the assembly would be equal in the two regions, even though Canada East had the larger population (Monet 2006). Through the union, it was believed, the colony could be anglicized; several anti-French measures were implemented at the same time, which angered French Canadian leaders and provoked opposition (Ouellet 1980b; Curtis 2012). Nonetheless, the drive for French Canadian independence had diminished (Ouellet 1980b). By mitigating their political influence, the new colonial structure may have encouraged French Canadian professionals to focus on professional advance. Professionals who had been divided politically during the rebellions (many reform-minded professionals refused to join their radical colleagues), once again began to work towards common professional goals.

Lawyers in Canada East formed new associations to share information, knowledge, and build professional ties. Both the notaries and lawyers in Canada East began to regulate themselves. In 1840 in Quebec City the "Barreau du Quebec" was formed. This association established requirements for entry to study and to practise law, created an examining board, and fixed dates for exams (Veilleux 1997: 62–3). Lawyers practising in the community agreed to these standards, which were implemented without legislative sanction. An association of notaries in the Quebec district was founded that same year, and similarly established regulations governing practice and discipline (Veilleux 1997; Vachon 1962). Medical doctors also organized associations and schools in Quebec and Montreal. Like their colleagues in other professions, they sought to raise the standard of education, shape entry to practice, and have a voice in the regulation of practice (Bernier 1981).

Notaries continued to strive for legislation allowing them more self-governance. They presented bills in the new colonial legislative assembly between 1842 and 1846; in 1847 they presented a bill amended to take into account concerns raised in 1846, and succeeded in obtaining an act (Canada 1847b). The act established a Board of Notaries in each of three districts: Quebec, Trois-Rivières and Montreal (Canada 1847b). These regulatory boards were elected by notaries located in each region every three years. The boards were empowered to regulate entry to study, entry to practice, their own functioning, and they had the power to discipline and suspend notaries who were not conducting their practices ethically (Canada 1847b; Veilleux 1997). They were also empowered to construct a fee schedule.[11]

To enter practice, a candidate had to have served a "regular clerkship" under articles for five years with a notary, or have served a clerkship of four years, if he possessed a classical education – consisting of "Belles Lettres, Rhetoric, and Philosophy, (comprising Logic, Ethics, Mathematics and Physics)" – at one of the seminaries or colleges in the province (Canada 1847b: s. xiv). He also had to provide proof of good conduct, and undergo an examination. The boards were allowed to summon witnesses to testify about "the life, morals and qualifications of the applicant" (s. xiv). Those who were approved would be recommended to the governor for a licence, and would be registered with both the board of notaries in their district and the protonotary office of the Court of Queen's Bench. The ideal entrant, then, was male, ethical and moral, classically educated, and possessed a practical training in his work.

Although the act was requested by notaries, its preamble argued that "it is of the utmost importance to the peace and welfare of families that the Notarial Profession should be exercised by well-educated and duly qualified persons." Further, the preamble declared that "abuses" had "crept into the exercise of those [notaries'] functions, for which it is expedient to provide a remedy with regard to admission to the Profession, and the general organization of the Profession in Lower Canada." Thus, the act was declared to be in the best interests of the public and the province, as well as in notaries' interests (Canada 1847b).

Notaries were pleased with the act, which allowed them to govern entry to practice and practice conduct. Nonetheless, problems soon became apparent (Vachon 1962). The principal problem was the regional nature of the regulatory structure. In the following decades, new regional boards were established, and professional unity was increasingly undermined. Different boards began to operate differently, some (especially those in the countryside) refusing to uphold the same examination and entry standards as those in other regions (Vachon 1962). Despite these problems, the regulatory act was not revised to establish a single board to unite the profession across the province until after Confederation.

Medical doctors also organized further in this era. The seeds were sown in the 1830s. The 1831 medical act authorizing elected medical boards provided a reason for practitioners to get together, to choose candidates and exchange information (Bernier 1981: 319). The newly elected members of the boards had much in common: they were urban, active in civic affairs, predominantly francophone practitioners with an interest in professional advancement. Practitioners vocalized their shared interests in professional advance – increased autonomy and decision-making power, improved education, higher status and rewards (Bernier 1981). These seeds took root and grew in the 1840s, as various medical societies were created or revived. These medical societies sought legislative change during this era: various bills related to medicine (schooling, anatomy, and bills to harmonize entry to practice across Canada) were introduced in the legislature. Organizational and professional activities increased in 1845 and 1846. A meeting took place in Montreal in 1845 to which organizations across Canada East and Canada West were invited. Canada West practitioners declined to attend, reportedly because they wanted to pursue their own legislative project (Bernier 1989: 55). The Canada East organizations were well represented, and they continued to work together, meeting in 1846 as well to develop a bill to establish a self-regulating medical profession and improve medical education. Their bill was presented in the legislature in 1847 by an English Canadian medical doctor, Wolfred Nelson, who had been a former member of the Patriot party and an active leader in the rebellions.[12] Within the assembly, the bill was sent to a special committee (three-fifths of its members were medical doctors), and received favourably. It was amended by the legislative council (to facilitate the entry of those with British or Canadian medical degrees), but passed with amendments in fairly short order (Bernier 1989).

The legislation established a self-regulating medical profession (Canada 1847a). All practitioners would be combined into a body corporate entitled the College of Physicians and Surgeons of Lower Canada. This college would have an elected board of governors (with regional representation), and was granted the right to regulate itself, entry to study, and entry to practice. The college's board would be known as the Provincial Medical Board, and would also function as an examining board with the authority to review credentials and approve students for entry to study, and examine candidates (and review qualifications) for entry to practice. It was illegal to practise medicine ("physic, surgery, and midwifery") without a licence; those who did so were subject to a fine of five pounds per day. Although the act gave the board the right to regulate entry, it also prescribed criteria for entry to study – "a good moral character, and a competent knowledge of Latin, History, Geography," and after 1850 knowledge of both English and French (Canada 1847a). Entry to practice required a mixture of apprenticeship (four years), a specified period attending a school of medicine, and attendance at a hospital. Anyone who had a medical degree or diploma from "any University or College in her Majesty's Dominions" could obtain a licence without an examination.[13] The preamble to the act provided the following rationale for it: "It is highly desirable that the Medical Profession of Lower Canada ... be placed on a more respectable and efficient footing, and that better means should be provided for the conviction and punishment of persons practising the same without a license."

Why did this bill succeed, when medical professionals' previous efforts to achieve self-regulation did not? Bernier (1981) points to a more favourable social-historical context. Several members of the legislative assembly were medical doctors (and members of medical societies and boards), as were a few members of the legislative council. While medical doctors were politically active in previous eras, the power struggle between the assembly and the legislative council resulted in the rejection of professional initiatives. In the new context of the integrated colony, there was more political stability and less ethnic conflict (Ouellet 1980b). Further, during the period there was a trend towards political decentralization (Bernier 1981; Ouellet 1980b). Bernier (1981) argues that in this context of decentralization, it is not surprising that the legislature was willing to delegate medical matters to local (medical) institutions.

Perhaps encouraged by these developments, lawyers too sought their own act. Lawyers achieved self-regulation in 1849, in a context of great judicial reform (Veilleux 1997). They assessed the advantages and disadvantages of the notaries' and medical doctors' acts, when preparing their own (Veilleux 1997).[14] The lawyers' act established a single "Barreau du Bas-Canada," which like the medical doctors' regulatory college included every practitioner in Canada East (Canada 1849a). An elected general council would govern the entire profession, and was granted the power to regulate entry to study and to practice, manage property and pass by-laws to regulate its work, and maintain the "discipline and honour of the profession" (Canada 1849a). The council was also charged with resolving general disputes and representing "the members of the Bar, whenever the interests or rights of the profession shall require it" (s. vii). At the same time, as with the notaries' act, three regional districts were established (Montreal, Quebec, and Trois-Rivières). Each district would have its own elected council charged with overseeing admission to study, entry to practice, and discipline in their regions. The act required local councils to determine the ability and morals of candidates seeking admission to study. Students were required to have demonstrated ability in English or French and knowledge of Latin, and to possess a liberal education. After five years of clerkship with a practising lawyer (or four years if they had attended a college or seminary; or three if they had formal college training in law), candidates for entry would be examined by the district council about their legal attainments, qualifications, training, and morals. If these were found satisfactory, the district council would issue a certificate allowing them to practise (s. xxiv). The bar (and the councils) was allowed to charge member fees, and was authorized to manage those funds (Canada 1849a).

To summarize this lengthy discussion, by 1850 Lower Canada had three self-regulating professions. The fight for self-regulating professions in the province was part of a broader struggle among French Canadian professionals and businessmen (with some of their English counterparts) for a greater voice in their own affairs. This struggle, in the name of democracy, was led by a group of men seeking more social authority and autonomy through organization and legislative change. Their efforts were increasingly viewed as a potential threat to the authority of the British colonial elite. In response, the elite became more rigid, and rejected the legislative initiatives of the reformers. The situation escalated to the point that some of the most radical professionals turned to rebellion. After the rebellions, professional organization increased, as did professionals' efforts to obtain self-regulation. In the calmer political environment of the 1840s, with a unified central parliament, combined with an increasing openness to political decentralization, they were ultimately successful. State actors no longer considered self-regulating professions a threat. It is worth noting as well that the establishment of self-regulating professions occurred around the same time (1848) as responsible government arrived in the colonies (Massicotte 1989; Wiseman 2007). Change in the regulation of professions, thus, was concomitant with state reform. The fact that self-regulating professions were already in existence in Upper Canada may have further encouraged a positive reception to these legislative requests.

Upper Canada (Ontario)

In Lower Canada, the British elite sought to enforce British policies, practices, and institutions, despite a predominantly French population with their own traditions and French civil law. Their counterparts in Upper Canada faced no such constraints. Geographically placed in between the French-English hybrid of Lower Canada to the east, and the revolutionary Americans to the south, officials in the new province endeavoured to ensure that Upper Canada was staunchly British from the beginning (Moore 1997; Gidney and Millar 1994). According to the province's first lieutenant governor, John Graves Simcoe, it was important "that British customs, manners, and principles in the most trivial as well as serious matters should be promoted and inculcated to obtain their due ascendancy, to assimilate the colony with the parent state, and to bear insensibly all their habitual influence in the support of that British Constitution which has been so wisely extended to that country" (Simcoe cited in Moore 1997: 20).[15] However, this was a difficult task. When the new province came into existence in 1791, its laws were the French-English hybrid of Quebec.

The English system of law – and the legal professions of barrister and solicitor (attorney) that supported it – were centuries-old institutions that had evolved through a complex set of historical circumstances and social events.[16] How could they be recreated in, and adapted to, the colony? A Lincoln's Inn barrister, by the name of William Osgoode, was sent to the colonies as chief justice and legal adviser to work with the first lieutenant governor, John Graves Simcoe, with the goal of establishing a legal system and judicature for Upper Canada. His Judicature Act, passed by the legislature in 1794, brought an English court system to the province. However, there were virtually no lawyers to work within the system. Legal historians report that there were probably only two trained lawyers in the province in 1794 (Riddell 1916). One was John White, an unsuccessful English barrister (called to the bar in 1785) who had travelled to Upper Canada with William Osgoode to assume the position of attorney general (Firth 1979). Another was British-born Walter Roe, a member of the Royal Navy who settled in Canada after the American Revolution, and who had studied law in Montreal. He received his commission to practise there in 1789 (Farrell 1983). To implement an effective judicial system, the government passed an act authorizing the lieutenant governor to appoint additional men as lawyers (up to sixteen over two years). Appointees were to be male British subjects who on the basis of their "probity, education, and condition of life" were deemed "best qualified to act as Advocates and Attornies [*sic*]" (34 Geo III c. 4 [UC], cited in Riddell 1916: 8). The lieutenant governor appointed men who were "already in the royal service and leaders of local communities," some of whom had served as "lay advocates in the old courts" (Moore 1997: 25). One of these was Robert Isaac Dey Gray, an American-born Loyalist who received his education (and some training in law) in Quebec, and who had been appointed a district court judge in 1796 (Burns 1983).

The first self-regulating legal profession in Canada was established shortly thereafter in 1797. In other British colonies, including Nova Scotia, entry into the profession was determined by court judges. However, such a system could be potentially problematic when those judges (as in Upper Canada in the eighteenth century) were appointed laymen, with no formal training in the law (see, for example, Phillips 2009). Perhaps to avoid potential problems, and with the goal of establishing the authority of lawyers in the province, the Upper Canada government granted the right to control entry to practice to lawyers, not judges. Unfortunately, there is a dearth of surviving records to explain exactly how (or why) this came to pass. Records of the legislation's path through the assembly and council are lost, burned during the War of 1812–14. Further, there is no evidence of a group of lawyers advocating for the legislation; there were very few lawyers in the province. The preamble for the act indicates that its promoters had the following goals: "the establishment of order amongst" lawyers, and "securing to the Province and the profession a learned and honorable body, to assist their fellow subjects as occasion may require, and to support and maintain the Constitution of the said Province" (in Riddell 1916: 10). Thus, this would appear to have been a government bill, which was seen to be in both the profession's and the public's interests.

Some historians have credited Attorney General John White for being the major author of the legislation (Riddell 1916). As an English-trained barrister, steeped in the history of the Inns of the Court, he may have wanted to establish a self-regulating profession in Upper Canada, in accordance with English practice. Controversially, the act would also create a distinction between barristers and solicitors, again following British tradition, but not common practice in North America (Riddell 1916). At the first meeting of the Law Society of Upper Canada in Newark (Niagara-on-the-Lake) in 1797, White was the only lawyer in attendance who supported this division, which was eliminated less than two weeks after his death (Firth 1979). Thus, it seems likely that White had a hand in the legislation. Yet, Law Society historian Christopher Moore (1997) argues that a more likely author of the bill was Robert Gray, who in 1797 was both a member of the legislative assembly and solicitor general in the province. Gray was more active than White in the society in the succeeding years, and seems to have taken a personal interest in keeping it active. Moreover, in a report to the colonial executive in 1797, Gray explained that the act was intended not only to further the law as a learned and honourable profession, but also to provide some protection to lawyers trained and commissioned in the colonies, in the face of immigration by lawyers who were more regularly trained elsewhere (Moore 1997). The act allowed English-trained lawyers to practise in Ontario, but they were subject to the discipline of the Law Society, just like everyone else. Thus, Moore argues (1997: 30–2), irregularly and untrained colonial lawyers like Gray had a great deal more to gain from such legislation than did the status-conscious English barrister White. The limited historical evidence, then, suggests that both White and Grey influenced the act: the legislation was a government-initiated measure, shaped by lawyers who were also state actors. The act appears to represent another attempt to implement and adapt British institutions in Upper Canada.

The 1797 "Act for better regulating the Practice of the Law" established the Law Society of Upper Canada, which would be composed of all lawyers in the colony. The society would be governed by a group of "benchers" appointed by society members from the senior ranks of lawyers in the province, and was authorized to pass by-laws to govern itself, and govern entry to practice. Only members of the society could practise at the bar in the province's courts. The act established some criteria for entry to practice. The Law Society was empowered to establish additional criteria and clarify entry standards. As noted, the act also distinguished between barristers and attorneys. Under the act, and the regulations passed by the society, students-at-law (studying to be barristers) had to be listed on the books as actively training for five years (similar to the previous 1785 law regulating entry to practise law in the entire colony). Attorneys were expected to be on the Law Society books for three years (Riddell 1916). Proof of training and character had to be provided by candidates' supervising lawyers. While the Law Society could pass by-laws, these laws had to be approved by the Judges of the Court of King's Bench (Riddell 1916).

What is immediately striking is that while this law established a self-regulating legal profession similar to that in existence in Great Britain, it also deviated from English practices significantly. While the British distinction between solicitor (attorney) and barrister was made (somewhat tentatively at this point), both would be regulated under the same society, unlike in the United Kingdom. This did change between 1822 and 1857, when attorneys were not regulated by the Law Society (Moore 1997: 109). However, for much of this period, virtually all lawyers practised as both barristers and solicitors (Riddell 1916). The nature of the act itself, and the regulations passed under it, did not directly copy British law. The fact is that the creators of this institution – the writers of the act and the first lawyers in the province (other than John White) – did not have intimate knowledge of the operation of the Inns of the Court in England. Indeed, in 1833 a Law Society committee explained that in defining "procedural standards of the society, it had worked 'almost entirely from first principles, having no satisfactory information as to the course adopted by the Inns of the Court in the Mother Country'" (Moore 1997: 34). Thus, for early Upper Canadian lawyers, the English Inns of the Court were more "a sketchy ideal rather than a practical model for Ontario's Law Society" (35). In attempting to establish British institutions in Upper Canada, professional and government leaders could not help but alter them, both intentionally (to fit the different institutional and social context) and unintentionally.

While decades later the British colonial leadership in Lower Canada saw demands for self-regulation as a threat to the state, in Upper Canada a strong independent legal profession seems to have been seen as a support for the state, or at least for British institutions and values. Indeed, several historians have argued that provincial administrators saw professions (like law) as a mechanism for establishing a social elite, or a colonial pseudo-aristocracy (Gidney and Millar 1994: 17; Garneau 2007: 132). Further, Moore (1997) explains that an independent legal profession provided career opportunities for the sons of Upper Canada's elite, who had few other prominent positions open to them because the very top positions were reserved for British appointees (see also Gidney and Millar 1994).

A shortage of lawyers in the province prompted legislation in 1803 that empowered the lieutenant governor to create another batch of lawyers out of distinguished laymen. However, after 1815, there was increased immigration from England and Ireland that brought more lawyers to the province. It was this influx of lawyers that seems to have motivated the 1822 legislation that incorporated the Law Society and allowed it greater control over the entry of British lawyers (previously under the control of provincial judges) (Gidney and Millar 1994). Some criticized the new legislation, seeing in it a move by lawyers to restrict entry to practice. However, lawyer-politicians declared the changes were necessary in part to protect the Canadian-trained and their families: "Parents were educating their sons at great expense for the profession of the Law, and it would be great injustice to the parents of these children to admit gentlemen coming from other countries" (Baldwin cited in Gidney and Millar 1994: 19). Further, Attorney General Robinson explained there were dangers in admitting strangers into the profession without knowing them, or having proof of their character (ibid.: 20). Here, we can see that the regulation of law in the province was not simply about granting privileges to a group of experts, or even ensuring an adequate supply of expertise for the colony, but was also intended to provide opportunities for young Canadian men (with the sufficient competence and character), and ensure that people in positions of social trust were actually trustworthy and loyal. The 1822 act extended the Law Society's powers of self-regulation through incorporation, and by granting the society authority over the entrance of the foreign-trained.

In the colony's early years, there was also discussion of regulating entry into the medical profession. Indeed, there were several acts passed, beginning in the 1790s, but these were shortly thereafter repealed, and were largely ineffectual (MacNab 1970). It was not until 1827 that medicine was regulated on a permanent basis (MacNab 1970; Baehre 1995). At this time, an appointed board, the Medical Board of Upper Canada, was granted the power to examine candidates who wished to practise in the province. Candidates who passed were recommended to the lieutenant governor, who after assessing "the loyalty, integrity and good morals" of the applicant would issue a licence to practise (Gidney and Millar 1994: 22). All practising doctors in the province needed a licence, except for military physicians and surgeons, but those who held a previous licence or a diploma could receive a licence without an examination (MacNab 1970). There are few early records to document how this medical act (and its predecessors) came about. Certainly, it seems likely that medical doctors sought out such legislation, but there are also records of discussions in the legislative assembly about medical regulation dating back to 1792 (ibid.). Medicine was not formally organized at this time, but some practitioners were well connected and may have used their influence to sway state actors to regulate the field. At the same time, it seems likely that the lay public and colonial leadership were also concerned that standards be established in the province, and (as with law) that the profession be guided by "respectable gentlemen of assuredly loyal politics" (Gidney and Millar 1994: 415 n. 85).

A variety of men participated on the Medical Board of Upper Canada at its various sittings (Baehre 1995). Among the most influential members in the earliest years was Dr Christopher Widmer, a distinguished military surgeon and a member of London's Royal College of Surgeons who fought in the War of 1812; Widmer sat on the board from 1819 until his death in 1858 and held a leadership role throughout most of this period (Canniff 1894; Baehre 1995). Other early board members included judge J.W. Macauley and doctor/magistrate Grant Powell. Baehre (1995: 107) explains that the early "presence of judicial representatives on the Board" reflected its dual role as a medical and legal institution. In determining suitability for entry to practice the board concerned itself not only with candidates' knowledge and capacity to practise, but also with their morals. Both medical leaders and the colonial elite wanted "to ensure that colonial medical graduates acquired and then exhibited the correct moral and intellectual attributes of British gentlemen, including a strong sense of loyalty, in addition to receiving proper training in his profession" (ibid.: 106). Although the number of licences granted increased substantially during this time period, the medical board was not hesitant to fail men who came before them. Between 1830 and 1837, only 61 per cent of those examined by the board (100/164) passed, and it took several candidates multiple tries to do so (ibid.: 108).

Resistance and resentment against the medical board and the state of medical regulation in Upper Canada was voiced in the 1830s by Scottish- and Irish-trained medical doctors who had immigrated to the province.[17] Under the 1827 act, graduates from the well-respected medical programs in Scotland and Ireland had to submit to an examination by the medical board, while graduates from England's Oxford or Cambridge Universities did not. Given the reputation of their programs, the Scottish- and Irish-trained doctors felt this to be unfair and beneath their dignity.[18] In their complaints they implicitly challenged the authority of colonial medical men to assess (accurately) their knowledge (Baehre 1995). In 1832 a group of Scottish doctors recommended that a self-regulating medical profession be established along similar lines to the profession of law. The medical board resented this challenge to their authority and expressed the opinion that legislative change was not needed (ibid.). In the face of such criticisms, board leader Widmer argued that educated men should not protest any request to demonstrate their knowledge and competence (ibid.). Further, he argued that examinations were intended not only to test knowledge, but to ascertain "loyalty, integrity, and good morals" as well; without such a review, how was the suitability of immigrant men to practise in the province to be assessed? Complaints were also received by Irish graduates who felt they were being denied hospital privileges, as well as membership on the board (ibid.). Thus, some medical doctors in Upper Canada were feeling marginalized in the 1830s. Many different groups called on the legislature to revise the medical act (MacNab 1970: 7).

By the late 1830s, even the medical elite was starting to feel excluded from major decisions. Board leader Christopher Widmer had a good working relationship with provincial lieutenant governor John Colborne, but the latter was replaced by Francis Bond Head late in 1835; Widmer and Head did not get along (Baehre 1995). Their main conflicts surrounded plans to create King's College in Toronto, a provincial, Anglican university to be established with government support. Although a medical department was planned for the university, Widmer and the medical board were excluded from the planning process. Medical leaders were not pleased with the plans revealed to them: a medical curriculum that was not secular, but at least partially moral and religious, and the placement of individuals outside the profession in key roles (Baehre 1995).

While in the early 1830s the medical board opposed the reform advocated by educated medical newcomers in the province, by the mid-1830s the situation had changed. Fed up with the small oligarchy that ruled the province, many in positions of importance were reform-minded, although few actually went so far as to participate in the 1837 rebellion (Romano 1995). Several medical doctors did get implicated in the rebellion, but likely no more than twenty were involved (Baehre 1995). Many more remained loyal. Those active in the rebellions escaped to the United States or were imprisoned (Romano 1995). Following the arrival of a new lieutenant governor in 1838, the medical board was reconstituted, this time including several reform-minded medical men. Shortly thereafter, the Medical Board took the lead in demanding new legislation that would establish a self-regulating medical profession (MacNab 1970; Baehre 1995).

In their petition to the legislative assembly, the representatives of the medical board and their supporters – including many Scottish- and Irish-trained practitioners (Kett 1967) – explained that the current regulatory system was not working. The province had become overrun by improperly trained and unlicensed practitioners from the United States, and this was endangering the health of the people in the province (Canniff 1894: 109–10). This situation was deemed "detrimental to the peace and tranquility of the country, and degrading and humiliating to the honourable and useful profession of medicine" (ibid.). The members of the legislative assembly appear to have been convinced by these arguments, perhaps swayed by a pervasive anti-American sentiment and concern for social order, which were both high immediately after the rebellion. Kett (1967: 348) explains that in the 1830s there were "widespread and not unjustified fears that lax enforcement of licensing laws would invite a descent on Canada of battalions of American quacks armed with republicanism as well as charlatanism." The act, then, not only pursued professional goals, but aligned with political goals as well (Kett 1967: 348). In this era, the political leadership sought to reinforce social order and British institutions (in part by excluding American sentiments and agitation) (Gidney and Millar 1994). The 1830s marked both the beginning of a decline in American medical regulation and training and the rise of medical sectarianism (Shryock 1967), as homeopathic, botanic, and eclectic medical practice gained adherents.[19] All these trends likely increased fears of an impending invasion by American charlatans (Kett 1967).[20] The fact that some prominent politicians were also physicians likely aided the legislative initiative (Romano 1995).

The "Act to Incorporate certain persons under the style and title of the College of Physicians and Surgeons of Upper Canada" (Upper Canada 1839), incorporated all licensed practitioners in the province under "one Body Corporate and Politic in deed and in Law" (s. ii). A medical board (with broader membership than the previous one) was established with its members deemed "fellows" of the college, who could elect from college membership other fellows. This structure mirrored that of the London Royal College of Surgeons (Parry and Parry 1976: 106). The fellows were made governors of the college with the power to pass regulations governing college members. Only the licensed were entitled to practise in the province, with the exception of medical men in "Her Majesty's Naval or Military Service" (s. xi). Anyone with a degree, diploma, or licence from somewhere in Her Majesty's dominions was entitled to a licence to practise. The act itself actually said next to nothing about entry to practise or education; the governors were granted the right to fix regulations and by-laws in these areas themselves (Upper Canada 1839). The focus of the act was rather on defining an "in group" – scores of individuals were listed by name, most of them with British degrees, diplomas, or licences (others were their Canadian-trained students) – and an outgroup (not explicitly identified, but presumably the

American-trained and untrained). Further, the act empowered a broader number of individuals (predominantly trained in Ireland or Scotland, or affiliated with the Royal College of Surgeons, London) to participate in the governance of the medical profession. Last, it established penalties for those practising illegally.

In 1839 and 1840, the medical profession established the college and began operations, examining candidates for entry, and formulating regulations. In 1840, however, they received news from England that the legislation was going to be disallowed. The disallowance was justified on three grounds. First, the act was deemed to violate the rights of members of the Royal College of Surgeons (RCS) of London to practise anywhere in the dominions. Second, the legislation granted powers that were extensive – "greater than any ever granted to any existing body or college" – but which were poorly defined (Canniff 1894: 152). Third, the provisions of the act appeared to establish a monopoly, and infringe on the privileges of the RCS "and several other bodies in this country" (ibid.). A committee was appointed by the College of Physicians and Surgeons of Upper Canada to consider and respond to these concerns, and they wrote a lengthy reply, rejecting each one (reported in full in Canniff 1894: 151–60).

To counter the first objection, they explained that the rights of RCS members to practise in the colonies had been upheld: the legislation allowed those affiliated with Britain's royal colleges to obtain a licence to practise in the province. However, committee members elaborated that they did not believe that members of the RCS should, in every instance, be allowed to practise *all* branches of medicine without examination in Canada (Canniff 1894: 152). Just because someone was trained as a surgeon did not mean he was a competent physician:

> Your committee does not bring this forward as applying to British surgeons generally, but simply to show that however well informed they commonly are, the few exceptions that occur render it imperative on the College, to whom this important duty is assigned, to take care the ignorant individuals shall not receive the same license as those who are fully competent." (in Canniff 1894: 152)

This change was likely the RCS's main bone of contention. Members of the RCS had previously been automatically entitled to practise all branches of medicine in the colonies, but the new college – dominated by colonials who practised all branches, and the Irish and Scottish graduates who were trained in all branches – suggested that they be required to submit to examinations in the branches of medicine in which they lacked a credential.[21]

In their reply, members of the college also countered the second complaint, arguing that since there was no institution precisely like theirs elsewhere, it may be true that they possessed powers not possessed by other bodies, but these powers were similar to those possessed by the medical board, and were neither unreasonable nor ill-defined (in Canniff 1894: 153–4). Last, they indicated that they did not understand the final, ambiguous complaint that their college infringed on the privileges of other bodies. No such privileges (or bodies other than the RCS) had been identified. In its lengthy reply, the college went on to elaborate and justify their body, drawing on a variety of evidence, to request that the decision be overturned, and offering to discuss these issues further. This request was turned down, and in early 1841 they had to disband the college, and get rid of its property and assets (Canniff 1894). With the disallowance of the act, the previous act and regulatory structure came back into effect.

A brief moment of unity, and an influx of reform-minded Scottish- and Irish-trained practitioners in the province, had led to the emergence of self-regulation in medicine.[22] In the immediate post-rebellion environment, the political context was favourable. It is worth noting that the drive for change came primarily from the medical board – a group of professionals serving on a state-appointed body – not from a separate association of medical doctors (emphasized in neo-Weberian accounts). In creating the regulatory college, these professional actors sought to recreate a British institution (by establishing a self-governing "college" of practitioners). At the same time, as with the establishment of the Law Society, the end product was distinct. Not only was the college granted extensive rights and privileges, but it included both branches of medicine. Another distinction was the college fellows' assertion that membership in a high-status English college should not inherently grant one the right to practise all branches of medicine. Status was important, but it did not necessarily trump competence or character – both of which were emphasized in colonial entry requirements.

It would be three more decades before medicine in the province was permanently established as a self-regulating profession. Medicine in the 1840s became increasingly divided (Romano 1995; Kett 1967). Different medical schools were established, and conflict and rivalry arose among practitioners affiliated with each (Romano 1995). Rural-urban divisions also intensified: rural practitioners were not supportive of legislative schemes they believed would privilege urban doctors and medical schools. Complicating matters further, irregular practice (homeopathy, eclecticism) spread in the province, and irregular doctors mobilized against the efforts of regular doctors to legislate in a manner detrimental to them (Romano 1995). Some historians suggest that anti-elitist sentiments that undermined medical regulation in American states in the 1830s and 1840s had some support in Upper Canada in the 1840s and 1850s, and may have also contributed towards the lack of support for regulatory change (Kett 1967). Between 1840 and 1860 there were six different bills introduced to re-establish the college, but none of these was successful, at least partly as a result of dissension among medical men in the province (MacNab 1970).

By 1850, there was only one self-regulating profession in Upper Canada (then Canada West), and that had been established over a half-century before. A self-regulating law profession had been established by state actors (who were also professionals), with both professional and political goals in mind. The emergence of a self-regulating medical profession in the late 1830s was the result of a professional initiative (and the government's political interests), but when this act was disallowed, there was not enough professional unity (and perhaps political will) to re-establish a self-regulating medical profession in the province. While the development of self-regulating professions in Lower Canada owes much to professional organizing, lobbying, and a political reform movement, self-regulation in Upper Canada, in both law and (to a lesser extent) medicine was associated with efforts by state actors to extend British institutions in the colony, secure positions of authority for loyal and competent English Canadian men, and minimize the impact of Americans and their republican ideals in theregion. Nonetheless, the form and structure of self-regulation in each province were not dissimilar: both incorporated bodies of practitioners charged with regulating entry to practice, and entry to study. The Lower Canadian professions tended to be more democratic, since regulatory boards were elected. Similarities were likely encouraged by similar social conditions experienced in the colonies (e.g., few universities, shortages of practitioners in rural areas, and the desire to establish social order across a broad territory with few institutional antecedents). Professionalization in both locales was also shaped by a desire to adopt and adapt British institutions to fit practice and social concerns prevalent in the colonies. Moreover, professional developments in each province appear to have been influenced by developments in the other. The end result appears to have been the beginnings of a pattern of self-regulation for professions in Canada that was distinct from that which was developing elsewhere.

Self-Regulation in the Canadas, United States, and Great Britain Compared

When establishing self-regulating professions, political and professional leaders in Upper and Lower Canada were constantly looking to Great Britain and the United States. Great Britain served as an example towards which early professional and political leaders aspired, even as they altered British institutions, both intentionally and unintentionally. The connection with the United States was more complicated. At times, the United States provided the counter-example for colonial (and even professional) leaders in the late eighteenth and early nineteenth centuries: for some, republicanism led to revolution, and the decline of professional regulation, fostering social disorder (see Kett 1967). However, many settlers in the Canadian colonies had lived in the American colonies, and some lived in the United States of America after the American Revolution. A minority of professionals had received some of their training and education there. When they moved to Canada, they also brought their positive experiences, their training, and their opinions with them, and these shaped professional practice and professional projects. In the mid-nineteenth century, the Canada-US border was a porous one, and many people crossed back and forth to live and to visit. Thus, to understand the development and regulation of professions in Canada, one needs to acknowledge these dual influences. Canadian professional leaders were always measuring themselves by, and frequently influenced by, their counterparts in the United States and United Kingdom.

At the same time, the structure and formation of professions in Canada came to differ from professions in the other two nations. Although all three nations established many self-regulating professions in the nineteenth and twentieth centuries, what that self-regulation entailed was not identical. A comparison of early legislation regulating the medical profession in Upper and Lower Canada, with the 1858 UK Medical Act, and legislation passed in several US states in the 1870s and 1880s, is illustrative.[23] Table 2.1 compares the two early Canadian medical acts, the 1869 Ontario Medical Act (discussed in more detail in chapter 4), and the 1858 UK Medical Act, with medical acts passed in five American states in the 1870s and 1880s, the beginning of the revival in medical regulation in the USA (Shryock 1967: 55). The American states represented were chosen to encompass a variety of registration practices. In the nineteenth century, the Illinois medical act was considered by the medical profession to be one of the most effective and advantageous (Dunglison and Marcy 1883; Shryock 1967; Sandvick 2009). This act was duplicated, in whole or in part, by other states. New Mexico's legislation was also extensively copied in other states: partly because it brought the different medical sects together under one board (Baker 1984). In contrast, New York's legislation was viewed as disappointing, since it "degraded the regular practitioner to the level of anyone … however unworthy he may be in the ranks of the medical profession" (Dunglison and Marcy 1883: 391). Alabama had "one of the most powerful state medical societies in the country" that sought to control entry to practice itself (Hamowy 1979: 77). Virginia's legislation seems fairly typical of the period. The table compares the acts along several lines, with attention to the regulatory structure (what bodies were created and what their powers were), criteria for entry to practice, and whether it was illegal to practise without a licence. Looking closely at the table, several differences and variations across locales become evident.

Variations are most evident when one considers the regulatory bodies created through the legislation. The Canadian acts alone establish incorporated bodies, comprised of all practitioners, which have the power to elect officers to a governing board. These boards also have more power and privileges than most of their counterparts. That is, they not only maintain a register, review qualifications, and examine candidates for practice, but they have the power to establish entry requirements, and regulate themselves and the practice of medicine to a broader extent. The other acts do not create colleges or societies; they create councils or boards only. Membership on these boards is typically appointed.

The Illinois and Alabama acts appear to come closest to the Canadian acts. The Alabama act recognizes a pre-existing society, and allows it to regulate entry to practice (State of Alabama 1877). The Medical Association of the State of Alabama (MASA) had requested broader powers to regulate practice itself (MASA 1877); however, their powers were diluted by the state legislature, which inserted clauses granting exemptions to irregular medical practitioners, and removed clauses granting MASA the right to review practitioner conduct and hold hearings. The

Table 2.1 Nineteenth-century self-regulation in medicine: Canada, the UK, and US compared

Legislation	Lower Canada	Upper Canada	Ontario
Date of Act Analysed	1847	1839	1869
College or Society of Practitioners created or recognized?	College of Physicians and Surgeons of Lower Canada	College of Physicians and Surgeons of Upper Canada	College of Physicians and Surgeons of Ontario (CPSO)
Is a Regulatory Board established?	College has Board of Governors, also called "The Provincial Medical Board"	Governors of the College	A "Medical Council" was established to govern the College and its members (originally including Homeopathic and Eclectic representation).
Is the board elected or appointed? By whom is it appointed?	Elected by members of the College	The Governors are named, but leadership positions and future governors will be elected.	Members from specified Medical schools were appointed and the remaining members (the majority) were elected by the members (most to represent practitioners in specified regions).
What is the Regulatory body and/or board empowered to do?	College is a body politic and corporate with all powers that entails. This includes the power to regulate the study of medicine, surgery, midwifery, and pharmacy; examine candidate credentials, administer oaths to candidates undergoing scrutiny, determine the qualifications of students and those seeking a licence, assess credentials and qualities for entry to practice, and establish fees for College members, and students entering the study of medicine	College is a body politic and corporate with all the powers that entails. They may also make statutes and rules for the government of the College, and its members, election of officers, entry to practice, review and assess candidate credentials, examine candidates for entry to practice, collect fees and fines from members and others affected by the act. The College can also pass regulations affecting Apothecaries.	The College was empowered to appoint a registrar, and maintain and publish a register of qualified practitioners, review qualifications, examine candidates. The Council was empowered to regulate the register, the Board of Examiners, regulate admission to study or matriculation (subjects specified in the act), and establish a medical school curriculum.
Is a Licence to Practice and/or a register established?	Yes. College issues certificate, on which basis the governor will issue a licence. A register is also established.	Yes, licences issued by lieutenant governor after approval by College. No mention of register, but list of College members will be kept.	Yes, a register is established.
Can the unlicensed practice (legally)?	No	No (only military)	No (only those registered under this or previous acts, or those with commissions in the military)
What are the education or training requirements for a licence	Medical degree or diploma obtained in her majesty's dominions; or four years of apprenticeship combined with schooling in specified subjects (for a specified length of time) in a school or college in her Majesty's dominions.	The act does not specify education or training requirements. The College may establish them. All holders of diplomas or licences from university or college in her majesty's dominions is eligible for licensure, as are military physicians and surgeons.	Those previously licensed are entitled to register. Also, candidates with medical training (diploma) who have passed Council exams.
Is an exam required?	Yes, but those with medical degree from her Majesty's dominions are exempted.	The act does not specify (but exams were conducted under the act)	Yes
Are requirements for the study of medicine established?	Yes, knowledge of Latin, history, geography, mathematics, and philosophy; Knowledge of French and English	No	Yes, including English language (grammar & composition), arithmetic, algebra, geometry, Latin, and one of Greek, French, German, or natural philosophy.
Are there other requirements for a licence?	yes, good moral character, 21 years of age	None specified. College may establish (emphasis traditionally on loyalty and character)	No

United Kingdom	Illinois	Virginia	Alabama	New Mexico	New York
1858	1877	1884 / 1888	1877	1882	1874
Existing bodies named and acknowledged; will have representation on Council.	No	No	Medical Association of the State of Alabama (MASA), and chartered medical schools	No	Not explicitly
General Council of Medical Education and Registration of the United Kingdom.	State Board of Health	Board of Medical Examiners	MASA board and med faculties recognized as Boards of Medical Examiners	Board of Examiners (composed of allopathic, homeopathic, and eclectic doctors)	No
Several members appointed by Queen and Privy Council, others chosen by various colleges, schools, and organizations.	7 individuals appointed by the Governor, with the advice of the Senate	Medical men are appointed by the governor.	MASA elects or appoints (and presumably the medical schools)	Medical men are appointed by the governor.	N/A
Appoint council registrar and other officers. Maintain register, and establish rules for regulating the registers. Collect information from medical bodies and colleges about qualifications required. Report to privy council when qualifications required seem inadequate.	With respect to medicine: review qualifications, examine candidates, take testimony.	Examine candidates seeking to practice medicine or surgery, collect fees for examinations.	MASA may regulate qualifications for entry to practice, rules governing Boards of Examiners, and may regulate practice and practitioner conduct. They may hold trials and revoke certificates of those found guilty of immoral, ungentlemanly or unprofessional conduct.	Board of Examiners is charged with reviewing medical diplomas, conducting examinations on those without diplomas, and reviewing evidence of candidate / practitioner conduct.	Existing medical societies are asked to spread the news that medical practitioners in the state should obtain a certificate from a medical society.
A register is established	County clerks will maintain a register of qualified MDs	A certificate is awarded, and a register is maintained in the county clerk's office	The Boards issue diplomas or certificates. These are recorded by Probate judge into a Register of Licensed Practitioners.	Yes. A certificate is awarded, and a register is maintained in the county clerk's office	County clerks will maintain a register of those with diplomas or certificates from medical schools or societies.
Yes, but the licensed obtain certain privileges.	No (exemption for those in armed forces)	No	No. But the act exempts homeopaths and other irregular practitioners, so in effect, yes.	No	No
These are determined by pre-existing colleges and bodies (many of which are governed by their own acts)	Diploma in Medicine, or successful completion of Board exam.	None specified.	MASA may determine	Candidates will hold a diploma from a medical school, or pass examinations in anatomy, physiology, chemistry, pathology, surgery, obstetrics, and the practice of medicine.	None are specified. Medical schools and societies in the state may determine their own.
Not under this act.	Yes (for those who do not have legitimate diploma)	Yes	Yes	Yes (for those who do not hold a diploma)	If school or society demands (not specified in act)
No	No	No	No	No	Not until 1889 Medical Act
No	None specified in act. In practice character taken into account.	None specified.	No, but those convicted of immoral, ungentlemanly or unprofessional conduct will have certificates revoke, so good morals are implicitly required.	Ethical conduct is reviewed, and certificates may be denied or revoked for those violating standards of professional conduct.	None specified (societies may determine).

content of the Illinois legislation appears different (State of Illinois 1877). The state established an appointed board of health to regulate not only health, but also entry to medical practice. The legislation does not specify that board members will be medical doctors. In reality, though, the board of health was a medical board, and the medical doctors on this board used the power the state legislature gave them, not only to regulate entry to practice, but practice itself, and some aspects of the healthcare field more broadly (Sandvick 2009). When critics and the courts protested that the board had overstepped its legal mandate, the state legislature revised the legislation to extend the board's powers (ibid.).

In contrast, the powers of medical boards in some other states were fairly limited – Virginia's appointed medical board was charged simply with examining candidates (State of Virginia 1884). New York did not even have a state medical board in this period. This state's legislation simply took steps towards establishing a register of practitioners, and urged medical doctors to get some kind of qualification from some established body (State of New York 1874).

The UK Medical Act established a General Medical Council (GMC), made up of representatives from the various established medical colleges and schools, and others appointed by the government.[24] The GMC was charged with establishing and regulating a register, as well as providing some general oversight over the various bodies. The council had little regulatory authority. Of course, in the United Kingdom entry to practice was regulated by separate societies and colleges governed by their own charters and legislation (which appear to have been the inspiration for Canada's). Further, it is worth noting that under the UK Medical Act, the practice of medicine was not closed to the unlicensed, although registered practitioners enjoyed certain privileges.

Turning to entry requirements, we can see that the Lower Canada medical act goes further than all the others in not only specifying criteria for entry to practice, but also entry to study. In Upper Canada, criteria were not specified in the act (beyond affirming the right of those trained in British universities or colleges to obtain a licence); rather, the regulatory body was given the right to establish regulations to govern both entry to study and entry to practice. This is a significant delegation of authority to one body, as the (London) Royal College of Surgeons emphasized in its protest against the act. The 1869 Ontario Medical Act prescribes requirements for entry-to-study, but empowers the Medical Council of the college to shape the medical school curriculum. The UK act does not specify criteria for entry-to-practice, since these were determined by various medical schools and societies (and the acts governing them). The entry requirements in the five US states reviewed in table 2.1 are variable, but most states required either a diploma or an exam (with some requiring both, and New York neither). Some of the acts, such as New Mexico's, explicitly mentioned additional qualifications, like ethical conduct and gentlemanly behaviour (State of New Mexico 1882). Ethical conduct was not mentioned in Illinois's act, but historical evidence shows that it was taken into account (Sandvick 2009).

To summarize, medicine's powers of self-regulation in Canada, as seen through the lens of these nineteenth-century medical acts, appear more extensive and comprehensive. Canadian medical doctors' legislation granted them more control over entry to practice, and entry to study. Further, the acts established corporate bodies, in which all practitioners had membership, and (at least in Lower Canada in this era) all were on equal footing, and could vote for their representatives who would govern their profession. The UK and US acts established different regulatory structures, and delegated different regulatory powers.

How do we account for these differences in professional regulation? And more to the point, what factors contributed to a Canadian regulatory pattern that both resembled and differed from that which emerged in the United States and United Kingdom? Some tentative answers can be found in the existing literature on the emergence of professions in the United Kingdom, United States, and Canada.

Comparing Canada and the United Kingdom, it is clear that Canada sought to establish "colleges" that were similar to the College of Physicians and College of Surgeons in London. In early-nineteenth-century England, there were three main medical orders: the physicians, the surgeons, and the apothecaries, each with their own regulatory mechanisms (Parry and Parry 1976: 104). The Royal College of Physicians received its charter from King Henry VIII in 1518 (RCP 2015; Shryock 1967). The Royal College of Surgeons was a newer body, having received its charter in 1800; its predecessor the Surgeon's Company was chartered in 1745 (Shryock 1967). These colleges (along with the Apothecaries' Society established in 1815) had similar regulatory powers to their Canadian counterparts: they controlled study, entry to practice, and to some extent practice itself, in their branch of medicine, in their region of practice. There were also many other organizations, associations, and schools representing a variety of medical practitioners in the early nineteenth century. In the early part of the nineteenth century, medicine was a complex institutional field with over twenty different organizations representing different groups (Berman 2006; Parry and Parry 1976; Reader 1966). When the movement for medical reform and a variety of professional projects emerged in the early nineteenth century, there were already centuries-old traditions in place.

The 1858 Medical Act was limited in its reach, but it represented an attempt to reform medicine, while balancing the interests and goals of so many different groups, some of them quite powerful (Berman 2006; Parry and Parry 1976). With 14,000 to 18,500 medical practitioners nationwide (Berman 2006: 163), represented by two score organizations (Parry and Parry 1976), it was impossible to duplicate the structure implemented in Lower and Upper Canada: that is, establish one regulatory body that encompassed all practitioners, and grant to that body the authority to govern aspects of professional education and practice. Instead, the UK compromise was to establish one register that built upon pre-existing associations and colleges, each with their own rules and regulations surrounding entry to practice and discipline, and with their status distinctions largely intact.

As limited as the 1858 Medical Act appears, it was the result of decades of struggle, conflict, and negotiation (Berman 2006; Reader 1966; Parry and Parry 1976). Neither the reformers, nor the traditional colleges and societies were willing to compromise substantially (Berman 2006). There were too many institutions with their own traditions, legacies, and status hierarchies, to implement something new. Thus, the result was the beginnings of a regulatory system that tried to accommodate everyone by threatening no one. This would be a system that built upon existing practices and status hierarchies, even as it altered them. Nevertheless, the act brought about some degree of unification in medicine, ensured that all registered practitioners were recognized (equally) before the law, and established a form of professional (self-)regulation bolstered by the "prestige and authority of the State" (Reader 1966: 67; Parry and Parry 1976: 126).

In Canada, practitioners numbered in the hundreds (at best) rather than the thousands. Professional groups and other interested parties were few and far between, and only in some instances, well organized. Thus, there was opportunity for state and professional actors to step in and create something new. The result was self-regulating professions that were similar in name and form to traditional British professions, but were adapted to the needs of the colony.[25] In Lower Canada, the balance struck was to establish professions partially modelled after British custom, but adapted to the concerns for democracy and self-determination prevalent in the province between the 1820s and the 1840s. In Upper Canada, the aim was to establish British institutions and maintain loyalty, while creating a class of educated gentlemen equipped to take on positions of leadership and authority in the colony. Professionals would provide support for state policies and plans, even as they operated separately from it. When Medicine became more internally divided in Upper Canada around mid-century, medical leaders once again turned to the UK as a model, and sought a medical act in 1865 that mirrored the 1858 Medical Act closely, establishing a General Council of Medical Education and Registration for Upper Canada (but with council membership being partially elected) (MacNab 1970). This act proved unsatisfactory, and three years later, the medical profession sought legislative change, which ultimately re-established a "college" model once again (see table 2.1).[26]

American legislation did not create bodies similar to Canada's (or the UK's) regulatory colleges in the late nineteenth century. Some medical acts recognized existing societies, and allowed them to regulate entry to practice (which both Alabama and New York did in different ways), but their powers remained very limited. The examining boards established in many states were largely charged with overseeing entry to practice; they had limited powers (some had more power than others, as the case of Illinois shows) to regulate medical practice. They typically did not even hold the register of licensed practitioners, which was lodged in county clerks' offices. Although US policymakers and health professionals faced many of the same concerns as their Canadian counterparts (health epidemics, comprehensive medical practices [i.e., blending physic and surgery], a variety of health providers with variable training), their institutional and political responses were quite different. The decline of medical regulation in the 1830s is usually attributed to an American culture characterized by anti-intellectualism, an abhorrence of monopolies, and commitment to individualism (Shryock 1967: 31; Macdonald 1995: 80–1). Professions' claims to status conflicted with the American democratic ideal (Starr 1982: 37), and professionals were not able to limit access to markers of status, such as the title "doctor" or a medical diploma (Starr 1982: 43). Educational institutions became entrenched and shaped medical education, without heavy professional association oversight (see also Burrage 2006). By the 1870s and 1880s, there was a renewed interest in medical licensing among practitioners – regular and irregular alike (Starr 1982: 102; Saks 2015). Lacking unity, and seeking a change in their status (and protection from the competition of the untrained), they accepted legislation that granted licences to those with a credential, with a variety of credentials recognized as acceptable. Several states established separate boards for the different medical sects (like California), while some others established a single board with representation from the various medical sects (New Mexico) (Baker 1984: 182).[27]

Nevertheless, the medical profession was not always the driving force behind the legislation. Goebel (1994: 313) argues that the impetus for Illinois's medical act was not the medical profession, but state actors who appear to have been concerned about public health. He argues that "the goal of securing the welfare of its citizens provided a strong incentive for the state to assume responsibilities in medical affairs" (ibid.). In this instance at least, medical regulation was tied with the regulation of health and healthcare. The piecemeal and gradual implementation of medical licensing across the American states suggests that state actors in other regions may have had different priorities, or that they could not identify any immediate political gains to themselves from medical licensing (see Abbott 2005). Thus, regional culture and priorities shaped state actor and professional group decision making, contributing to variations in regulatory outcomes. Medical schools were also influential in shaping professional regulation and professional development (Starr 1982; Brint 1994).

Cultural differences appear to have shaped not only the form of regulation, but the content of it as well. Canadian legislation tended to give weight to both competence (training and education) and character (morality, loyalty, ethical conduct of practice). The balance of character and competence is evident in the emphasis in Lower Canada, and to some extent Upper Canada (especially by the 1840s: MacNab 1970), on qualifications for entry to study: a classical or liberal education was required, not simply because it provided suitable background knowledge for professional training, but because it created gentlemen (Gidney and Millar 1994). While ethical conduct was certainly a concern for nineteenth-century professionals in the United States, it appears to have been less a concern for policymakers. As noted, legislation typically established a general standard of competency (a medical diploma or examination); it did not privilege specific diplomas over others, as Canadian legislation usually did. Attention to gentlemanly conduct was relevant in the 1870s, invoked by professional leaders on boards and in professional associations; it did not, however, figure prominently in legislation.

Further, when American state actors established professional regulation, they did not typically delegate power to professional groups, but established appointed state boards to examine candidates for entry to practice. Rather than bringing different types of practitioners together under one corporate body, they allowed them to associate (or not) in different voluntary associations as they saw fit. In contrast, Canadian state actors created incorporated professional bodies, and delegated power to them.[28] These differing patterns may reflect different traditions in the two countries: Scholars have argued that Canada has more of a collective or group orientation, in contrast to the USA's individualist orientation (Wiseman 2007: 74–6). Variations were likely also related to trends in higher education in Canada and the United States. While there were few Canadian universities in the mid-nineteenth century, when professions were first regulated, universities and professional schools (which in the United States were more commonly separate from universities) were more prevalent and influential. These differences resulted in distinct roles for professions: Canadian professions were more involved in determining entry to practice than their US counterparts. Further, differences in state-profession relations are evident across the two nations. For Canadians in the mid-nineteenth century, professional regulation was as much about governance as it was about establishing standards for practice. Regulatory bodies in Canada were established to function at arm's length from other state institutions, but to uphold the values and principles that underpinned the state.

Discussion

This chapter has provided an overview of the social-historical circumstances and events surrounding the creation of self-regulating professions in law and medicine in Upper and Lower Canada in the opening half of the nineteenth century. It has also explored how the content and nature of that regulation was influenced by, and yet distinct from, patterns of professional regulation established in the United Kingdom and United States. Professions were regulated in the Canadian colonies from early on, but medicine and law became self-regulating in Lower Canada in the late 1840s. Here self-regulation was the product of organization and resource mobilization on the part of professional practitioners (in accordance with Neo-Weberian theory), but it also owed much to changes in colonial governance in the period. In Upper Canada, the law profession has been self-regulating since 1797. Self-regulation in this context was not the result of a professional project, but rather was implemented by state actors (who were also practitioners) to serve social and political goals. In both provinces, self-regulating professions adopted a form and structure that differed in several ways from that characterizing the colonies' two main referents: the United Kingdom and the United States.

Differences with professional regulation in the United States are perhaps to be expected, given the strong current of anti-Americanism among the colonial elite during much of this period. Differences with the United Kingdom are more ironic. In several instances, professional and political actors sought to re-create British institutions in Canada, but in the process, ended up with something distinct. At least five forces and factors appear to have been at work here. First, familiarity with British institutions was, at times, limited. Thus, despite Upper Canadians' intentions to re-create the British Inns of the Court, lack of familiarity with that institution resulted in a law society that resembled it only superficially. Second, the realities of practising in the colonies – its institutional context, the small population scattered across a broad area, a limited money economy, and so forth – were different, and hence British institutions could not be imported, but had to be modified to fit the realities of practice (for instance, eliminating distinctions between barristers and solicitors, and physicians and surgeons; the existence of notaries tied with French civil law in Quebec). Third, some differences were intentional, aimed to eliminate some of the internal status hierarchies inherent in British professions: this is particularly the case in Lower Canada, where professional projects were tied with democratization and ethnic empowerment movements. Fourth, the mere act of intentionally creating institutions that had developed more organically in the United Kingdom produced different institutions. Macdonald (1995) links the development of the legal and medical professions in England to decentralization – a commitment to "lesser governments" through granting local and special-interest groups the right to control their own affairs (see, for example, p. 76). In attempting to implement this structure in Upper Canada, political leaders were more hands-on – at times creating these self-regulating professions themselves. Fifth, the involvement of professionals in state roles was significant. Professional projects were not always pursued outside state institutions, but professionals used their political positions, and political mechanisms, to achieve their goals.

Before ending this chapter, it is useful to reflect briefly on the key implications of the history described here for the two central themes highlighted in chapter 1. These include processes of profession formation – especially the role of state actors in professionalization – and the centrality of "expertise" to the making of professions.

In chapter 1, I argued that professional regulation is the result of the interplay between professional projects, and state or political actors' projects. The history of the emergence of self-regulation in Upper and Lower Canada shows that while professional actors shaped regulatory outcomes, state actors were also very much involved. Most notably, the establishment of a self-regulating legal profession in Upper Canada owed very little to a professional project. Even in Lower Canada, where professional projects are quite evident, regulatory outcomes were strongly shaped by state actors – especially those who were also professionals. Overlapping membership in state and professional bodies appears significant. Moreover, it seems evident, as Abbott (2005) contends, that regulatory initiatives occurred when the interests of professionals and state actors coincided, such as in the 1840s in Lower Canada, when a political commitment to decentralization accommodated professionals' drive for self-regulation.

Chapter 1 also discussed the significance of expertise to the formation of professions. From the historical overview provided here, one can see that while requirements for entry to study and entry to practice were central concerns for early Canadian professionals, there was little discussion of expertise per se. In fact, early professional leaders spent as much time defining education requirements for entry to study (a classical or liberal education), as they did education for professional practice. As Gidney and Millar (1994: 12) explain, in the nineteenth century, "profession" was an indication of social ranking more than a symbol of expertise. Professions married expertise to gentlemanly status and conduct; they linked competence to character. When professionals in Lower Canada fought for self-regulation, more opportunities, and a greater voice in public affairs, they were not solely concerned with expertise, or raising standards for entry to practice, but with their social authority and place in society. When medical doctors (and state actors) in Upper Canada sought to prevent American doctors from practising in the province, they were as much concerned with the latter's ideologies and comportment as with their medical knowledge. Entry to practice in both law and medicine at this time required references and assessments of individuals' character (Gidney and Millar 1994). Thus, in this era, we can see that expertise and competence were central components to professionalization and professional regulation, but they were embedded in a complex web of other social concerns and characteristics.[29]

The following chapter continues to explore these themes, through an examination of the emergence of professions – and various forms of professional regulation – across four Canadian provinces, in the post-Confederation period.

Chapter Three

Self-Regulating Professions Post-Confederation

In 1867, the separate colonies of Canada (East and West), Nova Scotia, and New Brunswick joined together to form the new independent nation of Canada. Confederation was the result of three years of negotiations, largely driven by Canada East and West. Many in the latter regions were not happy with the united colony established in the early 1840s. Confederation promised to divide them again into provinces, so that each could continue with their distinct traditions and customs (Creighton 2012; Evans 1992; Waite 1963). At the time, Great Britain had become disillusioned with the colonies and was encouraging national independence (Miller 1991). Confederation also promised to provide the colonies with a distinct national identity, and hopefully protect inhabitants against possible American annexation, which some feared following the American Civil War (Waite 1963; Senior 2006). In Nova Scotia, many people were against Confederation, but the Nova Scotia premier, Charles Tupper, supported it (Miller 1991). New Brunswick was also ambivalent about joining Canada, but Fenian raids originating in the United States in 1866 helped to swing opinion towards Confederation (Senior 2006). These four original Canadian provinces were joined within a few years by Manitoba (1870), The Northwest Territories (1870), and British Columbia (1871), stretching Canada from the Atlantic to the Pacific oceans.

The British North America Act (1867) established the terms of the new country, dividing governance between a bicameral federal level and the provincial level, in which Nova Scotia's and New Brunswick's colonial governments could continue largely as they had previously (Canada 1867).[1] Each province also had a lieutenant governor (representing the British Crown, and appointed by the governor general of Canada), as well as a provincial leadership including a premier, and an executive council with an attorney general, a provincial secretary, a treasurer, a commissioner of Crown lands, and a commissioner of agriculture and public works (Canada 1867, s. 58). In each province there would be an elected legislative assembly, and most (Nova Scotia, Quebec, and New Brunswick) had an appointed legislative council as well. According to Elisabeth Wallace (1950), the division of powers between the federal and provincial levels aimed to confer authority over important areas to the Canadian government, and to assign to the provinces the "unimportant and inexpensive functions of government, among which education, hospitals, charities, municipal institutions were then reasonably numbered" (Wallace 1950: 384). To the fathers of Confederation, health and welfare were considered merely "local and private concerns" and "primarily personal and of no concern to the state." (ibid.). Others have maintained that the goal was to move to the federal level areas common across provinces, but leave to the provinces matters that "might be defined as cultural" (such as social welfare) (Granatstein et al. 1990: 6), to retain "the rights and privileges they had before Confederation" (Evans 1992: 142). Regardless of the motivation behind the division, the end result was the same: the regulation of professions – and their fields, including provincial law, health, land, and infrastructure – would remain within provincial jurisdiction, and existing legislation at the provincial level could continue to apply post-Confederation.

Nevertheless, in the decades following Confederation, professional regulation changed substantially. At Confederation there were a total of five self-regulating professional bodies across the four provinces studied here: Quebec, Ontario, Nova Scotia, and British Columbia. Three of these were in Quebec (lawyers, notaries, medical doctors), and two were in Ontario (law and medicine). Medicine and law were regulated in Nova Scotia and British Columbia, but they were not self-regulating. By 1900 there were twenty-five self-regulating professional bodies across the four provinces. Although there were significant variations in how this regulation was structured, and what powers were conferred upon professional bodies, a dominant pattern of regulation had emerged: one that resembled the regulatory college structure established earlier in the century in Lower Canada, and in Upper Canada's profession of law.

In this chapter, I provide an overview of the emergence of self-regulating professions in these four Canadian provinces from Confederation to 1900.[2] I begin by outlining which professions were regulated, and when and how they were regulated. I consider how patterns of professional regulation varied across time, province, and profession. Next, I provide an overview of the origins of regulatory legislation to ascertain who provided the impetus for professional self-regulation in this era. Subsequently, I explore rationales provided by state actors for professional regulation. When they established self-regulating professions did state actors explain their reasoning? And if so, what did they say? I complete the overview of professional self-regulation in this era with a small case study of the characteristics of professional leaders in Ontario to explore the significance of social background to professionalization. In chapter 4, this general overview is augmented by three case studies (of medicine, dentistry, and land surveying) to explore in detail the forces shaping the emergence of self-regulating professions between the late 1860s and 1900. Together, chapters 3 and 4 will illustrate, in breadth and depth, how state and professional actors combined to create self-regulating professions, and will document the changing nature of state-profession relations.

Overview of Regulation across Four Canadian Provinces

Law and medicine were regulated in each of the colonies at Confederation. In Ontario and Quebec, professional regulation had changed little since the mid-nineteenth century. The principal changes concerned medicine. In Quebec, Montreal homeopaths had been recognized through legislation in 1865. In Ontario, separate provincial medical boards to regulate entry into homeopathy and eclectic medicine were established in 1859 and 1861 respectively, and an 1865 act established a General Council of Medical Education and Registration for Upper Canada (as noted in chapter 2). With these changes, the medical profession in Ontario enjoyed some measure of self-regulation in 1867. Land surveying was also regulated – but not self-regulating – in Ontario and Quebec. In Nova Scotia, medicine and law had been regulated since the early nineteenth century. The 1828 medical act prevented anyone from practising medicine (for fee or reward), unless they held a diploma or had been licensed by the governor (Nova Scotia 1828). The 1811 act to regulate the practice of "attornies, solicitors and proctors" restricted practice to those who had apprenticed and been examined by judges (respecting their "fitness, capacity and qualifications"). Up to 1860, solicitors (attorneys) could become barristers after one year of practice, upon admission by the judges of the Supreme Court (Nova

Scotia 1811); after this time the two branches of the profession were fused (Miller 1991). Professional regulation in the colony of British Columbia was limited. An 1863 proclamation granted the Supreme Court of the colony authority over lawyers' conduct and entry to practice (Watts 1984). In medicine, an 1867 ordinance empowered the governor to appoint a registrar and establish a medical register to record the names of those who held diplomas or licences to practise medicine or surgery from some body based in the United Kingdom or other countries (see British Columbia 1877). Anyone falsely claiming to be a registered medical doctor was subject to a fine.

Professional regulation changed fairly dramatically in the years immediately following Confederation. In Ontario, self-regulating professions were established in dentistry and pharmacy, and medical regulation was altered, between 1868 and 1871. Legislation respecting the self-regulating legal profession was revised in 1868, 1869, and 1872. In Quebec, legislation revising the regulation of advocates, medical doctors, and notaries was passed in 1869 and 1870. Further, dentistry (1869) and pharmacy (1870, 1875) were established as self-regulating professions. In Nova Scotia, the law profession became self-regulating in 1872 (Nova Scotia 1872b), and a provincial medical board was established that same year to regulate entry to practise medicine. Self-regulation was slower to develop in British Columbia, but a self-regulating law profession was established in that province in 1874. Thus, the number of self-regulating professions across the four provinces increased rapidly from five in 1867 to twelve in 1874.

Table 3.1 shows the self-regulating professions established in these four Canadian provinces up to 1900. As this table shows, Ontario and Quebec established more self-regulating professions in this era; Nova Scotia and British Columbia had fewer, and BC established them later. Ontario created by statute a few self-regulating professions in the years immediately following Confederation, and then refused to establish any others for over a decade. In fact, of the four professions recognized by statute between 1882 and 1891, three had very limited powers. The pattern in Quebec is similar: after the post-Confederation flurry, four new professions were established, but three had limited powers and privileges. Nova Scotia established three self-regulating professions in law, medicine, and pharmacy in the 1870s. The province came close to regulating dentistry in 1870, but in the end, did not confer the privilege of self-regulation on the dental profession until 1891. Self-regulating professions in British Columbia were established in 1886 (medicine, dentistry) and 1891 (pharmacy, land surveying).

Table 3.1 Self-regulating professions in 1900, by date self-regulation achieved

Profession	Ontario	Quebec	Nova Scotia	BC
Lawyers	1797	1849	1872	1874
Medical doctors	(1839, 1865)	1847*	1872	1886
Notaries public	1869	1847		
Dentists	1868	1869	1891	1886
Pharmacists	1871	1870	1876	1891
Land surveyors	1892	1882		1891
Architects	1890	1890		
Chartered accountants	1883	1880**		
Civil engineers		1898		
Stenographic / shorthand reporters	1891			

* Quebec (1865) also regulated homeopathy separately from regular medicine in Montreal.
** The 1880 legislation applied only to chartered accountants in Montreal.

This look at the establishment of self-regulating bodies in these Canadian provinces is informative, but it hides the full extent of legislative activity affecting professions during this era. Table 3.2 and figure 3.1 provide a clearer picture. During this 33-year period, there were 182 acts passed concerning the regulation of professions across the four provinces. Some of these acts made substantial changes, establishing regulatory bodies and outlining their powers. Most were minor in nature, making small changes to clarify or alter some aspect of existing regulatory legislation. There were an additional 164 bills introduced in the provincial legislatures that did not pass. Most of these unsuccessful bills represented attempts by occupations to obtain or expand their professional privileges. A few were bills introduced by legislators to reduce the powers claimed by professionals, and to open up professional practice.[3] Overall, there were 346 bills pertaining to professions introduced and discussed in the four provincial legislatures during this 33-year period. Hence in an average year, there were 10.5 bills considered across the four provinces; 2.6 bills per province per year. Professional regulation was oft-debated and discussed in provincial legislatures. It was also controversial: 47 per cent of bills introduced failed to pass. The most contention occurred in Ontario, where more

Figure 3.1 Total bills, 1867–1900

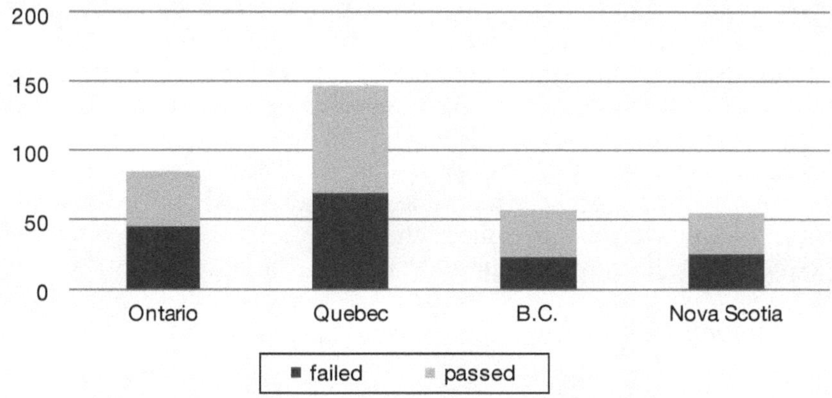

Table 3.2 Bills introduced pertaining to professional regulation, 1868–1900

Bills	Ontario	Quebec	BC	Nova Scotia	Total
Failed	45	70	24	25	164
Passed	41	77	34	30	182
Total	86	147	58	55	346

bills failed than passed between 1868 and 1900, in part as the result of controversies over medical regulation in the 1870s and 1890s. As many as 60 per cent of bills proposed in BC passed between 1868 and 1900, compared to 55 per cent in Nova Scotia and 53 per cent in Quebec.

In most provinces (except Ontario), the largest number of bills concerned the regulation of the legal profession. For instance, there were 26 bills introduced to regulate law in Nova Scotia: 16 of them passed. Of the 27 bills to regulate law debated in British Columbia, 16 became statutes. In Quebec, 31 bills to regulate lawyers, and 50 bills to regulate notaries, were considered.[4] Only 17 acts respecting lawyers, and 28 acts respecting notaries passed. The regulation of medicine was controversial and frequently debated in both Ontario and Quebec. In Ontario 22 medical bills were presented, and only four of them became law. In Quebec, 26 medical bills were introduced, and 14 of them passed. Some of the other failed bills concerned groups (unsuccessfully) seeking regulatory status. For instance, civil engineering was the subject of seven bills across three provinces during this era, but regulatory legislation only passed in Quebec in 1891. In a similar vein, there were ten bills to regulate architecture considered in three provinces during this era, but only four passed (three in Quebec, and one in Ontario).

Thus, professional regulation appears to have been a major concern within all four provinces during the period between 1867 and 1900. Legislators in each province spent time almost every single session debating and discussing the regulation of professions. The number of failed bills suggests considerable ambivalence about professional regulation, although it also reflects the contentious nature of provincial politics at this time (Massicotte 1989; Robin 1978; Wiseman 2007).

Regulatory Patterns across Profession and Province

In the decades following Confederation, professional regulation varied across province, but signs of convergence were nonetheless evident. While there were variations in who was regulated, each province regulated law, medicine, dentistry, and pharmacy by the end of the nineteenth century. Patterns also emerged in the structure of professional regulation. By 1900, there were three modes of professional self-regulation. The first resembled the regulation of lawyers and medical doctors in Quebec in the mid-nineteenth century: legislation established an incorporated body (usually called a college or society), that included all licensed practitioners, and an elected council or board that governed entry to practice and often practice itself. Entry was closed: only those who were licensed could legally practise. The second mode resembled the regulation of medicine in earlier decades in Ontario and many US states (described in chapter 2): legislation established a regulatory or examining board that was either appointed by the lieutenant governor or (partially) elected by practitioners. The board was charged with overseeing entry to practice (usually by examining candidates and reviewing credentials); it might also be empowered to remove or suspend licences for professional misconduct. Under this mode of regulation, practice was typically closed as well; only the licensed could practise. The third mode of regulation granted fewer powers, typically establishing a restricted title. Under this mode, an incorporated body might be created (or an association recognized), and its members were granted the right to use a protected title (e.g., "chartered accountant"). The body usually had an elected council that could govern association members, hold examinations, or otherwise ascertain who was deserving of the

Table 3.3 Regulatory structure by profession and province, 1900

Profession	Closed, incorporated body	Regulatory board only	Restricted title
Law	ON, QC, NS, BC		
Medicine	ON, QC, BC	NS	
Notaries		QC	
Dentistry	ON, QC, NS	BC	
Pharmacy	ON, QC, NS, BC		
Land surveying	ON, QC,	BC	
Architects			ON, QC
Chartered accountants			ON, QC*
Civil engineers	QC		
Stenographic reporters			ON

* Montreal only

title. Practice was not closed. Anyone could practise, but only association members could claim the restricted title.

Over time, across provinces, there was a decrease in the number of professions regulated by a board only, and an increase in the other two modes. Ontario and Quebec established several closed professions with an incorporated regulatory body (labelled a college, society, or institute) early on (Quebec 1840s, Ontario 1868–71), but few after. The professions they established in the late nineteenth century were predominantly restricted-title professions. In British Columbia and Nova Scotia, it was common for professions to begin with a regulatory board only (in dentistry, medicine, and in BC land surveying), and for a regulatory college to be established subsequently. Some of these transitions occurred before 1900, and some shortly thereafter. A snapshot of self-regulating professions in the four provinces in 1900, by type of regulation, is provided in table 3.3.

As this table shows, by 1900 the majority of self-regulating professions in these four provinces were closed and governed by an incorporated body of which all practitioners were members: 65 per cent or 17 of the 26 professions fall into this category. There were also clear differences across province. Ontario had no self-regulating professions governed only by a regulatory board. Quebec had one. British Columbia had two: dentistry, which obtained a regulatory college in 1908, and land surveying, whose incorporated body dates from 1905. Nova Scotia did not establish a college of physicians and surgeons until a century later. Ontario established three restricted title professions in the late nineteenth century (in architecture, accounting, and stenographic reporting). Quebec established architecture as a restricted title profession in 1890, and legislated a restricted title for Montreal chartered accountants in 1880.[5] As the table shows, there are clear commonalities across the provinces, with four to five professions being granted more powers of self-regulation (incorporated body or board) and a few being granted a restricted title.

Across these provinces, most professions were closed with an incorporated body. As noted in chapter 2, this distinguished Canadian professions from those emerging in the United Kingdom and United States. In the United Kingdom the dominant pattern of regulation that emerged was the "qualifying association" (Millerson 1964). Qualifying associations "examine and qualify individuals, wishing to practise," and typically establish different grades of membership based on "examination levels, age, [and] position of occupational responsibility" (Millerson 1964: 37–8). Although these associations were usually incorporated, they did not typically have the authority to govern entry to practice (in its entirety) or practice itself. Further, practice of these professions was not usually closed. Rather, practitioners in most simply enjoyed a restricted title. Qualifying associations like the College of Physicians examined physicians, and conferred a credential, but did not govern entry to practise medicine. As we have seen, a separate body, the Medical Council, oversaw registration, but it had limited authority. In the United States, the regulatory model in healthcare was a regulatory board, not a college (Gevitz 1988a; Shryock 1967). Professional regulation in Canada was differentiated not only by its basic structure, but also in the powers sometimes granted to professional bodies.

Regulatory Powers

The powers conferred upon professional regulatory bodies varied widely across profession, time, and province. Some professions were granted fairly sweeping powers (especially the earliest self-regulating professions), while others were granted very few. At the bare minimum, bodies were granted the right to oversee entry to practice (or access to a restricted title), but the vast majority enjoyed considerably more powers than this.

Regulatory boards tended to be granted a narrower range of responsibilities than incorporated bodies. For instance, the powers conferred by the BC legislature on the dental profession in 1886 were limited. This act simply established a board of examiners appointed by the provincial lieutenant governor. The board was charged with keeping a register of those licensed to practise and was empowered to "make such rules, regulations and by-laws, not inconsistent with the provisions of this Act, as may be necessary for the proper and better guidance of said Board" (British Columbia 1886a, s. 9). These regulations could be annulled by the lieutenant governor. Some regulatory boards enjoyed broader powers. For example, the 1872 Nova Scotia medical act empowered the provincial medical board to do the following: (1) regulate the study of medicine, surgery, and midwifery; (2) appoint people to conduct matriculation examinations; (3) examine all degrees, diplomas, licences, and credentials presented for entry to practice; (4) maintain a register of the licensed; (5) make by-laws concerning the register; (6) appoint medical examiners to conduct final examinations for entry to practice; (7) appoint officers of the board (president, secretary, registrar, and others); and (8) pass additional by-laws for carrying out its duties (with the governor's approval) (Nova Scotia 1872a).

The powers granted to self-regulating professions with an incorporated body tended to be more extensive. The 1868 Ontario Dental Act, for example, established a regulatory college with an elected board of twelve. The board was empowered to pass by-laws not only for the operation of the board and regulatory college, but also for entry to practice, and practice itself. That is, they could "make such rules, regulations, and by-laws as may be necessary for the proper and better guidance, government and regulation of said Board and College, *and said profession of Dentistry*" (Ontario 1868, s. 13; italics added). These regulations could also be annulled by the lieutenant governor of Ontario. Ontario dentists' power extended to the establishment of a dental school, the holding of exams, and the ability to assess the integrity and character of applicants and cancel licences of those who are deemed "guilty of acts, detrimental to the interests of the profession" (s. 15). In this manner, incorporated bodies were often granted the ability not only to regulate entry to practice, but also to regulate professions and professionals – from matriculation and study, through entry-to-practice examinations, and into practice itself.

Restricted-title professions were typically charged with regulating their own associations, and with making rules governing entry to the restricted title conferred upon them. Some restricted title acts specified what education was required for entry. Others did not, allowing the professional bodies themselves to establish rules. Table 3.4 provides an overview of the content of legislation establishing self-regulating professions.

As this table shows, 22 out of the 26 professions self-regulating in 1900 had incorporated bodies in which all practitioners, or in the case of restricted-title professions all who possessed a restricted title, were members. The acts regulating all 26 established some kind of regulatory board, and 23 of these boards were at least partially elected. Twenty were completely elected by registered professionals, and three (all in Nova Scotia) had a mix of government-appointed and profession-elected members. Seventeen of these regulated professional boards (65 per cent) were granted the right to govern entry to study in some manner, for instance, through establishing matriculation or intermediate exams, matriculation criteria, or training programs. Entry-to-study or matriculation standards increased steadily throughout the period. Some provinces and professions specified specific courses. These often included English literature and composition, Latin, history, geography, math, and for health professions some science (see also Miller 1991; Howell 1981). Specific professions had their own requirements; for example, the BC land surveyors' matriculation exam required a test of penmanship and orthography (British Columbia 1891). Other legislation did not specify courses, but granted professions the power to establish criteria, or set a general standard such as university matriculation. Most professions restricted access to literate, well-rounded students – those who possessed a broad and general education before they began studies in their professional fields. None of the restricted-title professions enjoyed the privilege of setting standards for entry to study.

Seventeen of the incorporated-body and regulatory-board professions were granted at least some authority over professional discipline; at minimum they had the ability to suspend or cancel the licence of a practitioner who was guilty of misconduct. Some legislation merely allowed a board to cancel the licence of practitioners proven guilty of a crime in a court of law. Others empowered boards to conduct hearings and seek out evidence of professional misconduct or unprofessional behaviour. Penalties for illegal practice were established in all but one of the closed professions (there was no penalty clause in Quebec notaries'

Table 3.4 Regulated professions, 1900: Privileges and modes of regulation

	Incorporated body created (or recognized). All practitioners belong.	Board of examiners or regulatory board created.	Board is elected and not appointed by the state.	Board governs entry to practice.	Board governs entry to study.	Board disciplines practitioners (right to suspend, exclude).	Penalties for illegal practice (practice is closed).	Penalties for illegal use of title.	Entry to practice determined by competence and character.
Self-regulating professions									
Lawyers	QC, BC, NS, ON	QC, BC, NS, ON	QC, BC, NS, ON	QC, BC, NS, ON	QC, BC, NS, ON	QC, BC, NS, ON	QC, BC, NS, ON	QC, BC, NS, ON	QC, BC, NS, ON
Medical doctors	QC, BC, ON	QC, NS, BC, ON	QC, NS,* BC, ON	QC, NS, BC, ON	QC, NS, ON	QC, NS, BC, ON	QC, NS, BC, ON	QC, NS, BC, ON	
Notaries public		QC	QC	QC	QC	QC			QC
Land surveyors	QC, ON	QC, BC, ON	QC, ON	QC, BC, ON	QC, BC, ON	QC, BC, ON	QC, BC, ON	BC, ON	BC, ON
Dentists	QC, NS, ON	QC, BC, NS, ON	QC, NS,* ON	QC, BC, NS, ON	QC, NS, ON	QC, BC, NS, ON	QC, BC, NS, ON	QC, BC, NS, ON	QC, BC, ON
Pharmacists	QC, BC, NS, ON	QC, BC, NS, ON	QC, NS,* ON	QC, BC, NS, ON	QC, ON		QC, BC, NS, ON	QC, NS, ON	QC, BC
Civil engineers	QC	QC	QC	QC	QC		QC	QC	QC

Table 3.4 Regulated professions, 1900: Privileges and modes of regulation (*cont.*)

	Incorporated body created (or recognized). All practitioners belong.	Board of examiners or regulatory board created.	Board is elected and not appointed by the state.	Board governs entry to practice.	Board governs entry to study.	Board disciplines practitioners (right to suspend, exclude).	Penalties for illegal practice (practice is closed).	Penalties for illegal use of title.	Entry to practice determined by competence and character.
Restricted title professions									
Chartered accountants	QC, ON **	QC, ON	QC, ON	QC, ON Entry to title		QC			ON
Architecture	QC, ON **	QC, ON	QC, ON	QC ON Entry to title only				QC, ON	
Stenographic reporters	ON **	ON	ON	ON Entry to title					ON
	** All association members belong to body corporate.		* Mixed, roughly half appointed by state, rest elected.						

legislation until later). Penalties for the illegal use of a title were established in twenty professions (three restricted-title professions had no penalty clause in this era).

Legislation also established entry-to-practice requirements, usually in some detail. Sometimes, they established only general criteria and allowed the profession to create their own by-laws. At other times, legislation detailed education and examination requirements. Fifteen of the twenty-six self-regulating professions (58 per cent) had character clauses that restricted practice to those who not only possessed the proper training, but could provide proof of their integrity and good morals. Character clauses were uncommon in medicine and most common in law: legislation regulating lawyers in each of the four provinces had a character clause, as did that regulating Quebec notaries. They were also common in dentistry (in three out of four provinces), and to a lesser extent pharmacy and land surveying. Character clauses became even more popular in subsequent years.

Overall, in these four provinces a substantial number of self-regulating professions were established in the thirty years immediately following Confederation. Most of these professions were closed and governed by an incorporated body granting the right to regulate not only entry to practice, but also entry to study, their own operation, and practice itself. A few enjoyed only a restricted title. Where did these professions come from? What factors and processes shaped their ability to win self-regulation? And what rationales did legislators provide when they regulated these professions? These issues will be explored in greater depth in the next section.

Explaining the Emergence of Self-Regulating Professions

In Canada, the creation of self-regulating professions involves an act of delegation: legislators delegate some of the state's regulatory authority (to regulate certain areas and aspects of social life) to a group of professionals. Why would they do this? Johnson (1982, 1993) argues that the formation of professions is a crucial element in state building and governance (see also Halliday 1987; Goebel 1994). Such arguments seem plausible in the Canadian context, where so many self-regulating professions were created immediately after Confederation. During this era, Canadians were debating and discussing what exactly the proper function of government was (Wallace 1950: 383). Professions may have historically contributed to governance, supporting small and nascent provincial governments, whose main legislative activity took place during the two to three months of the year that provincial legislatures met. Professions could ensure year-round governance in areas of social life that state actors did not have the capacity or interest in governing closely themselves. In contrast, social closure theory and collective mobility models would suggest that the surge in professional regulation at this time reflects an increase in requests for regulation. The rise of industrial capitalism (which historians date in Canada to precisely this era), growing occupational specialization, the expansion of education, and the rise of associations to represent various interests and endeavours, may have combined to increase demands for regulation (Dussault 1978; Howell 1981; Larson 1977). Through professional regulation, educated and trained practitioners sought to defend their livelihoods in the face of competition from the untrained (Adams 2000; Bernier 1989), and to extend their social influence (Howell 1981).

To assess which theories capture historical events most accurately, it is valuable to explore where the various acts establishing self-regulating professions originated, and what justifications or arguments were provided in support of the regulatory legislation.

Whose Interests?

If state actors believed they had something to gain from professional regulation, then one might expect them to the primary force behind it. Social closure theory would suggest that professions were the driving force behind the legislation. It would appear a comparatively easy test of the theories, then, to identify the source of the bills presented and debated in parliament. Unfortunately, this is a difficult task. The best records of the 346 bills presented in the four provincial legislatures between 1868 and 1900 are found in the *Journals of the Legislative Assembly* (and in bicameral systems, the *Journals of the Legislative Council*), which record the name and number of the bills, and track their progress through the legislature. Unfortunately, these records do not always record the source of a bill. There are few surviving records of legislative debates (outside Nova Scotia) in this era to provide more information. When we do have records of debates (from newspapers or official sources), sometimes the source of a bill is mentioned; other times it is not.

From the *Journals* and the published acts themselves, one can usually tell whether an act was private or public. Private bills were created on behalf of an individual, group, or organization (to incorporate, solve a will or land dispute, or grant them some specific request) (Massicotte 2009). Private bills were usually passed when they were believed to provide some assistance to the individual or group, or enable them to meet their goals, without infringing on the rights of, or doing harm to, someone else (Adams 2005); as Massicotte (2009) shows for Quebec, private bills had a high success rate. Looking at the original acts establishing self-regulating professions in all four provinces, about 40 per cent originated as private bills in this era. Here occupational leaders petitioned the legislature for an act to incorporate them and grant them special privileges. Often they, and their supporters, wrote the act themselves. The act was introduced in parliament by their local representative or another member of the legislative assembly (MLA) willing to take on their cause. If occupational practitioners and professional association members supported the bill, and there was little to no evidence of opposition, the bill would pass. In contrast, about 60 per cent of the acts establishing self-regulating professions originated as public bills: they typically were introduced by a member of the governing party, and were debated in terms of the public interest. Thus, it appears that a slight majority of legislation establishing self-regulating professions was public and hence came from state actors.

A look at the historical records, however, shows that whether a bill was public or private is not a perfect measure of whether a bill was a professional or state actor initiative. It is not uncommon for legislators presenting and discussing government bills to indicate that they originated with the profession. Even some public bills, then, could be profession-driven.

Legislators – especially in British Columbia – debated on numerous occasions whether bills to regulate professions were best classified as public or private. The discussion surrounding an 1881 bill to regulate the legal profession in British Columbia is particularly revealing, of both this debate and the contentious nature of BC politics at the time. In February of 1881, the attorney general and Premier George Walkem introduced "An Act relating to the Legal Professions" (British Columbia 1881: 18). When a week later the order for the second reading of the bill arose, MLA John Ash objected to the bill on the grounds that it was being presented as a public bill, but in reality it was a private bill, serving the interests of the profession. Because public notice had to be given weeks prior to the introduction of a private bill, the bill could not then proceed (British Columbia 1881; *Victoria Daily Colonist* 1881a). Mr. Walkem countered that the "the bill was for the protection of the public generally" (*Victoria Daily Colonist* 1881a: 3). The Speaker of the House reserved judgment, but the following week ruled in favour of Ash's objection. Although all bills affecting the legal profession in both England and British Columbia had been treated as public bills, because this bill touched on the incorporation of the Law Society it was deemed a private bill (British Columbia 1881: 25).

The speaker's decision killed the bill during this session; through his point of order, Ash successfully defeated the measure. The newspapers quoted Ash expressing "surprise that lawyers should have made such a blunder as to seek incorporation when they are already incorporated" (*Victoria Daily Colonist* 1881b: 3). His opposition is striking since Ash was often a political ally of Walkem, and he was a medical doctor. Legislators often displayed considerable antipathy to the law profession in this era. Indeed, the *Colonist* newspaper quoted another MLA who joked that he was glad the bill was ruled out of order, since it aimed to protect the lawyers, when what was needed was a bill to protect the public from lawyers (*Victoria Daily Colonist* 1881b: 3). Only five years later the same objection was made to the 1886 medical bill, this time by Robert Beaven. On this occasion the speaker ruled that the medical bill was a public one since it was "being introduced in the interests of the general public and … the powers that have been given to incorporate were incidental to legislation on the subject" (*Victoria Daily Colonist* 1886b: 1). BC politics in this era were contentious, and legislators demonstrated considerable ambivalence towards professional regulation, and the regulation of law in particular. Challenging whether a bill to regulate a profession was truly "public" was a political tactic used to undermine professional legislation in this era, but in most instances, the speakers ruled that professional legislation was "public" in nature.

Even when a bill was "private," state actors might be quite involved with its creation and path through the house. Private bills were sometimes produced by professional organizations; however, at other times, professions requested legislation from government leaders, who had government employees write the legislation. Presumably in these moments, state actors were in a position to shape the content of the bill, and if government leaders introduced it, it is reasonable to assume they supported it. Further, there are records suggesting that at least two private bills introduced in Ontario were in part spurred by a state actor. For example, on the surface, the act to regulate architecture appears to be a typical private bill. Architects organized, petitioned the legislature for a private bill, and one was introduced on their behalf. Their bill, however, was not introduced by a house backbencher, but by Minister of Education (and future premier) George Ross (Ontario 1890b). Simmins's (1989: 28) history of the Ontario Association of Architects sheds light on this anomaly. Architects credit Ross for being the driving force behind the formation of their association. He met with a group of Toronto architects to discuss a post-secondary educational matter in 1888, and at that meeting recommended that they form a province-wide association and seek legislation to establish criteria for entry to practice. In this manner, Ross provided not only the opportunity, but also the impetus, for architects' professional project. George Ross also provided support for the stenographic reporters' legislation. A group of court, legislative, government, and some newspaper reporters (recorders) organized in 1890 and decided to seek incorporation. After a conversation with an encouraging Ross, they chose to pursue professional legislation instead. Ross introduced the bill to regulate chartered stenographic reporters as a government measure and shepherded it through the house (Chartered Stenographic Reporters Association 1892).[6]

Overall, it is difficult to determine whether the state or profession was behind the majority of legislation establishing self-regulating professions in the four provinces. What is clear is that both professional leaders and state actors were very involved. While professionals did lobby for legislative privileges during this period, it was not unusual for state actors to take a leading role. Even when a bill was produced and presented by professionals, the legislation was significantly altered by legislators. Evidently, state actors were not passive in the process of establishing professional self-regulation – simply approving or denying requests presented to them – but were active participants in writing, revising, and challenging professional legislation.

Legislators' Reasoning and Rationales

Why then did state actors establish self-regulating professions between 1868 and 1900? It may be impossible to know for certain. Unfortunately, legislators did not bother to record their reasoning for future historians. Evidence of their rationales, however, can be found in the legislation they passed, and surviving records of their legislative debates – which, while generally scarce and incomplete, are nonetheless informative. These rationales sometimes refer to general principles, such as the public interest, protection of professional practitioners, service quality, or consumer choice. Quite often, however, legislators simply focused on the merits of the specific bill before them. With respect to the late nineteenth century, Wallace (1950: 391) explains that Canadians tended to conceive "of the state as simply the citizens in their organized capacity, and not as an entity with rights and duties of its own, much less a soul." State actors were there to represent and legislate for the people. Thus, when presented with a bill – especially a private bill – they attempted to discern whether it appeared fair, and considered who it would help, and who it might hurt (Adams 2005). If the bill appeared to do no harm, and no one (or few people) objected to it, then it typically passed.

Preambles are one source of information about the principles that underlie an act of provincial parliament. Many pieces of legislation do not have preambles explaining their purpose or background, but some do, especially those that originated as private bills. These preambles usually justify legislation regulating professions on the grounds that it serves the public interest by either raising the quality of services provided or enabling the public to identify who is competent to practise. Some preambles also argue that the legislation will provide protection or privileges to professional practitioners. The preambles to the dentistry act passed in all four provinces are virtually identical: "It is expedient for the *protection of the public,* that there should by enactment be established a certain *standard of qualification* required for each practitioner of the said profession, and that certain *privileges and protection* should be afforded to such practitioners" (Ontario 1868; British Columbia 1886a; Quebec 1869a, emphasis added).

Other preambles contain the same themes: public protection, establishing (or raising) practice standards, and providing some benefit to trained practitioners. Each of these aspects is evident in the preamble to Ontario's (1890a) 'Act respecting the Profession of Architecture':

> It is deemed expedient for the better protection of the public interests in the erection of public and private buildings in the Province of Ontario, and in order to enable persons requiring professional aid in architecture to distinguish between qualified and unqualified architects, and to ensure a standard of efficiency in the persons practising the profession of architecture ... and for the furtherance and advancement of the art of architecture."

As a private bill, this act also aimed to allow the architects' association to reach intellectual goals. A similar clause is found in the preamble to Ontario's (1883) 'Act to Incorporate the Institute of Accountants of Ontario': this act was said to allow the Institute of Accountants to reach their aims as "an intellectual and educational movement to raise the standard of accountancy."

Early medical acts in British Columbia (1867), Ontario (1865), and Nova Scotia (1972) provide a shorter rationale: "It is expedient that persons requiring medical aid should be enabled to distinguish qualified from unqualified practitioners." The 1869 Ontario act was passed simply "to make more effectual provision for regulating the qualifications of practitioners of medicine, surgery, and midwifery, and to incorporate the medical profession of Ontario." Nova Scotia's 1876 pharmacy act was justified as contributing to "the safety of the public" by ensuring that "all persons engaged in the sale or dispensing of drugs and medicines within this Province should be acquainted with their properties and uses, and possess a competent practical knowledge of pharmacy" (Nova Scotia 1876).

Thus, legislation preambles suggest that professional legislation passed in the late nineteenth century was intended to protect the public by requiring that practitioners possess training and knowledge, and enabling consumers to distinguish the trained from the untrained. Legislation also provided benefits to practitioners: either granting them some protection from the untrained (as in the dentistry act), or enabling them to advance their discipline (as in architecture and accounting). While these preambles provide insight into the rationales underlying professional legislation, they present only a partial picture. Regulating professions was often quite controversial. We can learn more about professional regulation by taking a look at the recorded debates surrounding both successful and unsuccessful bills.

When legislative debates touched on general regulatory principles, they too discussed the public interest, but also considered access to services and consumer choice, professional protections, and sometimes expertise. Perhaps one of the main points of contention in provincial legislatures was whether a bill could serve both the public's interests and the professions' interests, or whether the latter should be a consideration at all. Legislators promoting Ontario's 1869 medical act claimed the bill was "in the interest of the public and medical profession" because its goal was to "raise the standard of education" (Mr Cameron, *Globe* 1869a: 4). Another commentator editorialized that the act should be judged on the likelihood it would benefit the public, but that question could only be answered by considering if the bill would "tend to elevate the profession" (*Globe* 1869b: 4). For some, then, professional interests could serve the public interests. According to this view, entry standards and tests of competence benefited both the profession and the public. Many legislators questioned these claims, arguing that legislation creating self-regulating professions served the profession, and not the public. Such legislation threatened to create monopolies, and provide protections to people who did not need them. The mood in the provincial legislatures varied across province and time period, with the view that self-regulating professions were in the public's interest predominating in some moments, while the opposite view prevailed in others.

When BC's 1886 medical act was being considered, the mood of the house favoured doctors' regulation as supporting the public interest: "The public were not always in a position to judge the qualifications of a physician and if they discovered incompetency in such persons it was generally at the expense of experience when the mischief had been done. The bill was not to create a monopoly in the medical profession but was to protect the public" (*Victoria Daily Colonist* 1886a: 1). Legislators supported "any bill that prevents all but qualified doctors and surgeons from practising in the province," claiming that "many men, women, and children now in their graves would have been alive at the present moment had it not been for the work of imposters and quacks" (ibid.).

Nevertheless, there were always legislators who viewed professions as self-interested groups who pursued their own interests at the expense of the public. Timothy Pardee, in opposing the 1869 Ontario medical act, declared "it was contrary to the spirit of the age, that a close corporation such as this should exist" (*Globe* 1869a: 4).[7] In debate over the 1891 BC pharmacy bill, several legislators claimed the act was solely to benefit pharmacists and not the public, and that it sought to create "an immense trade union." The bill's supporters countered that the act contributed to "the safety of human life" (*Victoria Daily Colonist* 1891: 2).

In British Columbia, the legal profession was a particular target of attacks, with opponents claiming that regulatory legislation was "passed entirely for the benefit of the profession," not the public (*Victoria Daily Colonist* 1881a: 3). Critics claimed the law profession was overprivileged, enjoying "legislation of a restrictive character and hedged about with privileges that no other profession asked for or would get if they did ask" (*Victoria Daily Colonist* 1888: 4). One lively debate occurred over an 1886 bill that concerned the entrance of lawyers trained outside of British Columbia. The contentious issue was whether those lawyers trained outside the province should be required to fulfil a residency requirement, so that they could spend time learning the laws of the province, and so that practitioners in BC would have time to assess their character (*Victoria Daily Colonist* 1886c: 1). Supporters claimed that the restrictions would provide some protection to young BC men of good character who were pursuing the study of law (by limiting their competition from foreign-trained lawyers).[8] In this sense, they declared, the bill served the public interest. Critics attacked the lawyers for seeking protections, arguing they were more than capable of protecting themselves. In the end, the bill was defeated.

Many legislators were willing to grant professions privileges, but believed professional power and privileges should be delimited. Some wanted to eliminate professions altogether, although they were in the minority in most eras. For instance, BC legislator (and businessman) Robert Beaven argued for the removal of restrictions on the practice of law in 1893: "Merit would come to the top every time. He was surprised at lawyers hedging themselves around with so many safeguards to prevent competition, and would like to see all close corporation legislation abolished" (*Victoria Daily Colonist* 1893: 6).

Others believed strongly in "the necessity for laws of this kind for the protection of the public against imposition by incapable or unworthy persons presuming to carry on the practice of a barrister or solicitor without having been duly admitted to membership in the profession" (T. Davie in *Victoria Daily Colonist* 1894: 6). These differences of opinion led to some lively discussions in the legislature, especially since four of the twenty-five legislators were in fact lawyers. The other legislators were predominantly farmers or merchants and businessmen; they were often not in favour of such restrictions. These controversies were particularly evident in the 1880s, during which only three of thirteen bills introduced respecting the law profession were actually passed.

Regulation may have been more controversial in British Columbia in this era due to the low number of lawyers in the legislature. In both Ontario and Nova Scotia about 20 per cent of MLAs were lawyers; usually some MDs sat in the legislatures as well. Boily (1967) and Massicotte (2009) have shown that the Quebec legislature was dominated by lawyers, notaries, and medical doctors in this era. There were fewer professionals of any kind sitting in the BC legislature at this time. The participation of professionals in provincial legislatures at times shaped regulatory outcomes.

In addition to professional privileges and protections, legislators also demonstrated a concern with access to professional services. In each province, there were many regions that were sparsely settled. Some legislators expressed the view that professional regulation might be fine for the cities and larger towns, but not for the countryside: perhaps any practitioner, even if untrained, was better than no practitioner at all (*Victoria Daily Colonist* 1879a: 3). This concern prompted BC legislators to pass an Inferior Courts Practitioners Act in 1873, which allowed non-lawyers to appear on behalf of clients in local courts (police court, county court). The small supply of lawyers also encouraged the expansion of notaries in the province to perform some tasks otherwise under lawyers' scope of practice (Brockman 1999). In the 1886 debate on the BC medical act, Mr Galbraith expressed concern respecting "the difficulty of obtaining medical assistance in remote districts," and Mr Robson hoped that the bill would not "prevent the medical treatment of Indians and Chinese by their own countrymen" (Victoria Times Colonist 1886b: 1). Originally the BC pharmacy act "operated only in larger towns and cities in the province" (Malleck 2015: 203). In these instances and others, legislators voiced reluctance to establish entry standards that were unduly restrictive, and limited practice in such a way that public access to needed services would be curtailed.

Concerns over access and choice were common in Nova Scotia as well. In the late nineteenth century, Halifax was six times as large as the next largest town (Yarmouth); 15 per cent of the Nova Scotian population lived in Halifax city or Halifax county (Canada 1882). The rest of the population was spread across rural areas and small towns. Legislators frequently voiced concern about the impact of professional regulation on people in the countryside. Professional regulation might be suitable for Halifax with its plethora of practitioners, but what of those areas where professionals were in short supply? Legislators rejected legislation if they believed that it would eliminate valuable, if informally trained, practitioners in more rural areas. Legislators also voiced the fear that regulation would raise fees, to the extent that the common people would not be able to afford professional services (Nova Scotia 1870, 1871). Some acts (especially in the twentieth century) exempted rural areas from their provisions.

These core-periphery distinctions were also evident in Quebec, and to a lesser extent Ontario. Quebec passed several acts that only had force within specific urban centres (usually Montreal) (see, for example, Quebec 1880). In Ontario, legislators expressed concern in 1871 that the bill to regulate pharmacy "would do an injustice when applied to rural districts" (*Globe* 1871: 2). However, concern over the rural-urban divide arises less often in surviving legislative records from Ontario, than in Nova Scotia or British Columbia, perhaps because the province had numerous urban areas spread across the south, central, and eastern regions of the province.

Concerns over practitioner supply dovetailed with support for consumer choice. During the debate on the Inferior Courts Practitioners Act, one legislator asked his colleagues, "Why should a man be prevented from employing *any* legal adviser?" (*Victoria Daily Colonist* 1873: 3). Legislators believed that when possible, consumers should be allowed options. This was particularly evident in medicine. For instance, the 1869 Ontario medical act recognized and regulated three branches of medicine: orthodox, homeopathic and eclectic (Ontario 1869a). Both homeopathic and regular doctors were regulated in Quebec.

Some legislative debates about professional regulation focused on competence and training. Recall that the preambles sometimes justified regulation on the grounds that it would distinguish the qualified from the unqualified. If legislators were not convinced that trained practitioners knew more than untrained practitioners, then they were not in favour of professional regulation. Such debates are clearest in Nova Scotia. For example, part of the debate on the (failed) 1870 bill to regulate dentistry focused on whether dentistry was "almost entirely mechanical" and like other trades, or whether it required some medical and scientific training (Nova Scotia 1870: 146–7). Medical doctors (including the MD MLA who introduced the bill) argued the latter, but many others were not convinced. Legislators traded anecdotes about people who (on one side of the debate) were reputed to be excellent practitioners despite having no training, and those (on the other side) who were subjected to great pain and hardship because they visited a dentist who was not properly trained. Similar concerns were raised in debates about an 1898 bill to remove some privileges from the pharmacy profession. One legislator (Mr Finlayson) argued that "it did not follow because a man had a certain knowledge of Latin, botany and chemistry sufficient to enable him to pass the examination prescribed by the society that he was in a better position to dispense drugs than another man who had practiced for fifteen years but had not passed the examination" (Nova Scotia 1898: 128). Here, too, legislators questioned whether formal education was actually necessary for practice.

Overall, then, we can see that legislative debates on professional regulation centred around concerns for public safety, access to services, education and expertise, and sometimes controversially, protections to professions. It must be acknowledged, however, that legislative debates did not always focus on general values and principles, but also often the particulars of the case before them, and legislators' own particular concerns. For example, debate on the 1883 pharmacy act involved not only a discussion of the principles behind the proposed legislation, but some legislators' temperance concerns, controversy over one country pharmacist's sale of alcohol, and the damage that could be wrought by intemperance (Nova Scotia 1883: 250).

Although records of legislative debates reveal legislators' key concerns about, and rationales for (and against), professional regulation, they rarely speak directly about self-regulation. Earlier in the chapter, I argued that legislators in these four provinces favoured the establishment of self-regulating professions that were closed, and were characterized by an incorporated legislative body that had been granted fairly extensive regulatory privileges. Although this regulatory model resembled modes of professional regulation then emerging in the United States and United Kingdom, it also differed from them. There are few surviving records that explain Canadian legislators' choices. Certainly, legislators were aware of other models, as they periodically refer to them in their debates. One plausible rationale for self-regulation appears in the 1886 debate over the BC medical act, which would establish a self-regulating medical profession. The attorney general spoke strongly in favour of self-regulation based on the ability and character of medical doctors in the province:

> He asked the members [of the assembly] if they did not think those of the medical profession here were competent to decide upon the qualifications of those presenting themselves for examination. Those here constituted a numerous, influential and competent class; they were humanitarians in the best sense of the word, always required to go when called upon, and who always did so go, and it was not right to impute any selfish ground or motive on their part in the introduction of this bill, whose object was not to keep out of the province qualified physicians and surgeons, but to protect the public against incompetent persons and quacks. (*Victoria Daily Colonist* 1886b: 1)

The attorney general's speech, according to the newspaper, was accompanied by calls of "hear, hear" suggesting that many in the legislature agreed with him. In Ontario in the mid-1890s attacks on medical self-regulation similarly focused on the character of medical leaders, arguing that the state should not "devolve" its regulatory "responsibility upon an irresponsible body of men" (Haycock, quoted in Naylor 1986: 12). Further, when Nova Scotia was debating extending lawyers' powers of self-regulation in 1885, MLA Otto Weeks argued that since legislators were about to delegate legislative power to the Law Society, they "ought to have some guarantee that this power would be exercised in such a way as the legislature would approve" (Nova Scotia 1885: 300). The solution he proposed was to place the attorney general on the council (ibid.).[9] Legislators, then, believed that the professionals they delegated power to should be trustworthy. It appears that they considered the competence and character of professionals when making regulatory decisions.

Debate over an 1879 BC medical act provides additional insight about the appeal of self-regulation for government leaders. The original draft of the bill called for the government (the lieutenant governor) to appoint members of the medical board, but Premier Walkem objected: "The Government would much rather be relieved of this responsibility" (*Victoria Daily Colonist* 1879a: 3). The compromise proposed was that the government appoint the first board, but that subsequent boards be elected by the profession. Hence, the potential burden on state actors and institutions was also a consideration for legislators. Overall, it would appear that when practitioners were deemed competent and honest, and state-directed regulation was viewed as a burden on limited state resources, then self-regulation was an attractive regulatory solution.

Further, once some self-regulating professions had been established, a precedent had been set. During the debate over the pharmacy act in Ontario in 1871, MLA Dr William McGill argued that "what was asked for [by pharmacists] was what had been granted to other professions, and there was no reason why the provision should not be applied to druggists" (*Globe* 1871: 4). McGill also explained that the bill was similar to that passed in the United Kingdom and some American states, and was less "stringent" than that which existed in Quebec. A few years later, an amendment to Quebec's pharmacy act was passed that brought it more in line with Ontario's (Bernier 1989: 101). In this way, legislation passed for one profession (in one province) influenced legislation discussed for others. The similarity of legislative preambles noted in a previous section provides additional evidence of this trend. Nonetheless, legislators still needed to be convinced that the practitioners in question were deserving. In the Ontario 1871 debate, MLA

George Perry disagreed with Dr McGill, arguing, "There was a great difference between the granting of such a Bill to doctors and to druggists" (*Globe* 1871: 4). In his eyes, the latter were not necessarily deserving of self-regulation.

When it was granted, self-regulation was viewed as an act of delegation of state authority, and hence a privilege that could be rescinded. On numerous occasions legislators threatened to do just that. One instance involved the BC pharmacy profession, which was granted self-regulation in 1891; however, in 1895, when pharmacists sought amendments to their legislation, they faced some angry legislators, one of whom introduced a bill to repeal their regulatory act and strip them of their powers. Legislators complained of the "arbitrary manner in which the pharmaceutical association have exercised the power conferred by the act of incorporation" (*Victoria Daily Colonist* 1895a: 6). In the end, the act passed with amendments, and the controversial repeal act was withdrawn.[10]

In Ontario in the 1890s, there were also attempts to remove the privilege of self-governance from the medical profession. The Patrons of Industry, an agrarian political party opposed to professional and economic protections, proposed a bill to remove the powers of the regulatory college, and bring about state regulation of medicine in 1895 (Naylor 1986). Although this bill, and others to curtail the medical profession's authority, were defeated in the legislature, in the face of such pressure and considerable popular support, the Ontario government did introduce legislation to lower matriculation requirements and eliminate regional fee schedules in medicine (Naylor 1986).

Legislative efforts to reduce the medical profession's control over entry to practice also occurred in Nova Scotia (1888). MLA Otto Weeks introduced a bill to amend the Nova Scotia medical act, which would have facilitated the practice of the unlicensed. He explained that the goal of his legislation was to allow the non-physician inventor (for instance, of a cure for cancer), to be able to bring his invention to the public. In presenting the bill in 1888, Mr Weeks attacked the medical act then in force in Nova Scotia, describing it as "far and away more stringent than that to be found upon the statute book of any other country" (Nova Scotia 1888: 79). He held up English law as the ideal: medical practice was not closed in that country, but the medical register allowed the public to distinguish between the qualified and the unqualified.

In response, the medical doctor MLAs in the house, and their supporters, defended the Canadian practice of establishing closed, self-regulating professions: "We have gone further than they have in England, perhaps because we are more enlightened. We have seen them and have gone one better. We have done and are doing more for the people in protecting them from being injured, by unqualified practitioners … than they do in England"[11] (Dr Munroe, in Nova Scotia 1888: 81–2).

Although several legislators agreed with Mr Weeks and criticized the medical profession, many others spoke in favour of the profession and against the bill. I recount this exchange, because it reveals both legislator ambivalence about professional privileges, and the fact that those who supported professional regulation – and these included professionals who held seats in the legislature, in addition to many others – were confident that their system of professional self-regulation was superior. Even though it did not completely eliminate incompetence in the professions, it still improved the quality of services provided (Mr Fraser, in Nova Scotia 1888: 96). Opening up practice to the unqualified would only do harm.

Bringing these different ideas together suggests that for legislators in these four provinces, self-regulation was justified as being in the public's best interest, in certain instances, as long as concerns over access and consumer choice were addressed. The characteristics of professionals requesting such powers (their responsibility, integrity, and training) appear to have been relevant considerations for legislators. Further, it seems plausible that provincial governments did not believe that they had the capacity to be heavily involved in professional regulation, and hence were willing to delegate this responsibility to professionals, as long as they used their powers wisely.

Professional Characteristics

In the previous section, I argued that legislators were concerned with the characteristics of the professionals to whom they delegated regulatory authority. Legislators appear to have been more likely to grant self-regulation when professionals demonstrated both competence and character. Regulating professions was controversial in this era, as the legislative debates and number of failed bills reveals. Legislators were not reluctant to reject requests from groups seeking privileges. Professionals frequently lamented their lack of influence over governments (Howell 1981). Even after privileges were granted, legislators revised legislation governing the operation of self-regulating professions, and occasionally threatened to remove those powers. Who then succeeded in becoming self-regulating professionals? What were their characteristics?

As previous research has shown, professionals were almost exclusively men in this era (Adams 2000; Brockman 1995; Kinnear 1995). Where formal restrictions against women's practice were not in place, existing restrictions were interpreted in a manner that excluded women (Brockman 1995). At the moment of regulation, all professional leaders were male, and all authorized practitioners (with the exception of pharmacy and stenographic reporting) were as well. The first women to enter medicine in Ontario (in the 1880s) and British Columbia (1890s) did so well after their professions had achieved self-regulation (Hacker 1974; Davies 1994). The first women to enter law and dentistry in Ontario did so in the 1890s. There were only a few women practising pharmacy in the late nineteenth century. The privilege of self-regulation was, then, only granted to men.

Professional practitioners were overwhelmingly white. Asian men were formally and informally excluded from BC professions (Brockman 1995). African Americans faced difficulty entering law: in 1900 there was one black lawyer in Ontario, and one in Nova Scotia (Adams 2006; Fingard 2003). Other professions were predominantly, and in many cases exclusively, practised by white men. Professionals were also overwhelmingly of British descent. Some professions had formal citizenship requirements in this era restricting practice to British subjects (Adams 2016b). Other professions accepted none but those trained in Britain or Canada, thereby tacitly restricting the practice of non-citizens. Architects and stenographic reporters in Ontario did not have citizenship requirements to practice, but participation on regulatory boards was restricted to British subjects who were twenty-one years or older (Adams 2016b). Here, the criteria for participating in professional governance were the same for participating in provincial governance. Only those who were male, British, and over the age of twenty-one could serve in the legislature.

Research has also suggested that class was important to professional projects. Professionalization has been seen as a collective mobility project pursued by members of the rising middle class (Millard 1988), seeking to extend their social authority: "Professions became a vehicle through which members of the newly emerging middle class could improve their status, security, and social influence" (Adams 2000: 16). To advance, leading professionals sought to disassociate themselves from those who were lower in status: they excluded women, minorities, and the poor, and recruited the sons of the prominent and educated. Miller (1991: 63) argues that Nova Scotian lawyers in the late nineteenth century endeavoured "to keep the profession in the hands of the elite." Similarly, in the Maritimes medical leaders spoke in favour of recruiting "the sons of the wealthy" to ensure that medical doctors were "a more liberally educated and independent set of men" (Howell 1981: 14). In Ontario, Naylor (1986) argues, the opposition of the Patrons of Industry to medical self-regulation was in part predicated on the fact that the profession's entry standards were so high that a career in medicine was all but closed to the sons of farmers and ordinary folk. By the latter decades of the nineteenth century, professions were seen as respectable careers that would grant men the ability to maintain a middle-class life-style, and also take on local and community leadership roles (Holman 2000). I have suggested that state actors were more willing to regulate in favour of respectable men of influence who were seen to make valuable contributions at the community level. At the same time, professionals' involvement in local leadership positions, provided them with skills and contacts that assisted them in their professional projects.

Then, as now, class background was intertwined with education. Middle-class status (and professional status) was closely tied to advanced education, and the nature of professional work, which required knowledge and intelligence, rather than physical strength (Holman 2000). Education was not only a source of knowledge, but also of refinement and respectability (Holman 2000: 164–5; Gidney 2005). Although social mobility was possible, advanced education was largely limited to the wealthy and the middle class. Professional training was lengthy and expensive, thereby limiting admission into professions "to those with financial resources and social standing" (Miller 1991: 64; Gidney 2005). The relationship between class and education is important for understanding the implications of regulatory requirements. When professional regulation distinguished the trained from the untrained, it also distinguished the educated from the less educated, and, therefore, separated the well-to-do from the poor. Legislation required not only practical training for entry to practice, but a liberal education (Gidney and Millar 1994; Miller 1991; Howell 1981). To enter professions, individuals needed knowledge of English literature, Latin, sometimes Greek, and a variety of other subjects, as we have seen. The ideal professional practitioner in this era combined gentlemanly education with practical skills: he was "learned but pragmatic" (Miller 1991: 63; also Pue 1995).

To determine if other characteristics were influential in winning self-regulation, I conducted a case study of occupational leaders seeking regulation in nineteenth-century Ontario. It was common for professional legislation and draft bills to name the individuals who would comprise the first regulatory board, and those who petitioned for the act. Using these names, I reviewed census records to determine leaders' basic characteristics (age, ethnicity, religion, declared occupation, and so on) when legislation granting them self-regulation was first passed. My purpose was to determine the characteristics of those who were successful, and to ascertain whether those who received more regulatory powers differed from those who received less. I also, when possible, searched these individuals in Dun and Bradstreet's historical records to determine credit ratings, and obtain an assessment of their wealth (Dun and Bradstreet Reference Book 1867–81). The latter records were incomplete: pharmacists were most likely to be listed, as were many dentists, and some medical doctors, but only a few others were named. I also drew on professional histories, and biographical information (from sources such as the *Dictionary of Canadian Biography*) to identify additional characteristics that may have shaped regulatory outcomes.

Table 3.5 provides a summary of the main demographic characteristics of professionals and aspiring professionals across profession.

Almost all professional board members were male.[12] The average age of board members at the moment of regulation was in the mid-forties, with architect leaders being older, and dentists and stenographic reporters being younger. A significant number of leaders were foreign-born. Percentages are particularly high in pharmacy, where almost all professional leaders were born in the United Kingdom. Only a few were born in Ontario or the United States. The majority of accountants were also born in England or Scotland (see also Richardson 1989). Just over half of dentists were American-born, while a substantial majority of stenographic reporters and land surveyors were Canadian-born. The vast majority of professional leaders claimed English, Scottish, or Irish origins in the census, with English being the most common for most professions. Almost all professional leaders were Protestant, with Presbyterian and Anglican being the two most common religions claimed. Leaders in the different professions tended to cluster in certain regions, with the majority being based in Toronto, and several from central and eastern Ontario.

This analysis suggests that professional leaders were a homogeneous bunch. They were unlikely to claim ethnic minority or religious

Table 3.5 Demographic characteristics of professional leaders by profession in Ontario

	Year reg.	Avg. age board at regulation	Percentage foreign-born	Modal ethnic origins	Modal religion	Region
Medicine	1869	43.6	46	English/ Scotch	Presbyterian	Cities, Toronto
Dentistry	1868	39.4	45	English	Presbyt./ Anglican	Eastern Ontario
Pharmacy	1871	45	92	English	Methodist	Urban, central, east
Accountancy	1883	44	76	English	Anglican	Toronto
Land surveying	1892	46.4	36	Irish/Scotch	Anglican	Central/ eastern Ont.
Stenographic reporters	1891	37	27	English	Anglican	Toronto
Architecture	1890	50.5	55	English	Presbyt./ Anglican	Toronto

minority status, and they tended to cluster in larger urban centres, especially Toronto. The few differences across professions (age, place of birth, and region of practice) do not appear to be influential in shaping professional outcomes; however, it may be the case that leaders' proximity to the legislature in Toronto assisted their efforts.

Data on wealth and credit ratings are incomplete, but the available data suggest that pharmacists were the wealthiest group of professional leaders. Nevertheless, their professional privileges were more narrow and circumscribed than their counterparts in medicine and dentistry. Dentists, in particular, were considerably less wealthy and influential, but still received more legislative authority. During the late nineteenth century, funeral directors and embalmers also sought professional legislation, unsuccessfully.[13] Leaders in this profession tended to be prosperous as well. Within professions, there was a tendency for the most financially secure to be the most professionally active. However, in absolute terms, wealth does not seem to be a key factor in shaping professional legislative outcomes.

This initial look at professional leader characteristics is not particularly informative. More insight is provided by a review of professional histories. These reveal the importance of social connections and political ties. Many of the professional leaders held important posts, and were well connected to prominent people, and especially legislators. The importance of connections is most dramatically demonstrated in the case of accounting. The Ontario Institute for Chartered Accountants was formed in 1879, modelled after its counterpart in the United Kingdom, and in 1881–2 sought regulatory status without success (Creighton 1984). Legislators seemed unwilling "to give special consideration to a group of downtown Toronto businessmen" (ibid.: 11). To win over the legislature, the institute recruited influential, savvy, and politically connected Samual Bickerton Harman as president (Creighton 1984, 1990; Richardson 1989). Harman was an accountant and lawyer who had been very active in Toronto municipal politics, serving two one-year terms as mayor. His impact, according to historians was immediate:

> In the space of a year he revamped the council to make it politically important, enlarged and to some extent inflated the membership, stage-managed a public meeting of Toronto's business élite that demanded incorporation, lobbied Toronto's MPPs and the appropriate cabinet ministers, and retained the best legal talent. The result was incorporation in February 1883. (Creighton 1990)[14]

The new Council of the Institute "included everybody with connections whom the institute could muster" (Creighton 1984: 12). For instance, John James Mason was a former Hamilton alderman and mayor who was active in the Masons and the militia, and who worked for some prominent companies and other institutions (Creighton 1994). Other accounting leaders had experience in local politics and public office, and held prominent accounting positions. For accountants, having a politically savvy, well-connected leadership appears to have been important to their obtaining legislation.

There is reason to think that political and social connections were important for other professions as well. As noted earlier, it was architects' meeting with minister of education George Ross that spurred their professional project, and Ross himself shepherded their bill through the house. Ross also influenced the Chartered Stenographic Reporters' legislative drive. Many land surveyors were government employees. Professional leaders were among the most prominent in their field, having been granted federal and provincial commissions to conduct important surveys on unchartered territories, or for state projects (for instance, to chart a path for railways). Otto Klotz, the first president of the Association of Dominion Land Surveyors was characterized as a lifelong organizer, and involved in a wide range of associations and societies, including the Royal Society of Canada (Jarrell 2005). Given the nature of their work, which was often commissioned by the national, provincial, and municipal governments, land surveyor leaders were well connected.

While dentists were less connected politically, they did use the connections they had to their advantage.[15] Their petition for legislation in 1868 was accompanied by a petition signed by not only the majority of trained dentists in the province, but also medical leaders, and a few other prominent individuals including the mayor of Toronto (Gullett 1971). Dentists' clients were almost exclusively middle-class and well-to-do individuals. These connections may have also helped to sway legislators towards their cause (Gidney and Millar 1994). Medical doctors were in an even better position than dentists. Regular and homeopathic medical leaders often enjoyed an elite clientele. Further, some medical doctors sat in the legislature, where they could potentially shape legislative outcomes from within.[16]

As we have seen, pharmacist leaders were prominent drug merchants and manufacturers. Some of these men were also socially and politically active. It is not clear whether they had strong political ties that were influential, but it is possible that the lack of such ties was the reason why they had difficulty obtaining legislation, and why their regulatory powers were more limited than others'. Pharmacists tried unsuccessfully to obtain regulatory legislation in 1868 and 1869 before succeeding in 1870–1. Further, they tried to amend their legislation three times in the 1870s, but were turned away each time. They finally succeeded in amending their act in 1884.

It is also important to note that most Ontario professions were organized at the time of their regulation. Professional leaders in these organizations endeavoured to unite practitioners in pursuit of a professional project, and met with legislators to discuss regulation.[17] Most of these organizations were not particularly large, and some (such as dentists', architects', and reporters' associations) only met a few times before presenting a bill to the provincial legislature. Establishing a bill was often the primary motivation for organizing in the first place. For these early professionals, then, there was often not a sustained professional project prior to regulation. Some simply formed an association, produced a bill, petitioned the legislature once or twice, and then got their regulatory act. In this sense, while organization was an important element in the professionalization process, the success or failure of a project in Ontario in this era appears to owe less to a sustained campaign to mobilize resources, than to the short-term effort by professional leaders to draw on their social and political connections and demonstrate their character and competence to legislators. This will be discussed in more detail, and interprovincial variations explored, in chapter 4.

In sum, a look at leaders in early self-regulating Ontario professions shows considerable homogeneity. Leaders tended to be male, middle-aged, of British origins, and Protestant, and possessed varying degrees of wealth. More crucial to winning self-regulation were social connections. Leaders in self-regulating professions were politically and socially well connected, or at the very least were able to successfully draw on the connections they had to win legislation, often shortly after they organized or decided to seek regulation. In this era, professional leaders resembled many of the legislators from whom they sought benefits. For example, in Ontario after Confederation, 92 per cent of legislators claimed English, Irish, or Scottish origins; 47 per cent were foreign-born, most in the United Kingdom. The vast majority were Protestant. Further, roughly 26 per cent were in "professional" occupations (most of the rest were merchants and farmers). Legislators granted professional privileges to individuals who resembled them along several dimensions.

Nevertheless, as we have seen earlier in this chapter, Ontario's pattern of professional regulation was somewhat distinct from that of many other provinces: it regulated more professional groups than Nova Scotia and British Columbia, and regulated a few groups that were not regulated elsewhere in this era. Precisely who early professionals were and what they did to achieve self-regulation is deserving of a closer look. The case studies in chapter 4 will do this.

Discussion

This chapter has provided an overview of professional self-regulation in four Canadian provinces from Confederation to 1900. During these decades, the number of self-regulating professions increased substantially. Each of the four provinces examined here established (or reaffirmed) self-regulating professions in law, medicine, pharmacy, and dentistry, and several other self-regulating professions were established in some provinces including land surveying and architecture. Professional regulation was an area of considerable state activity, discussed in virtually every sitting of provincial legislatures. Patterns of professional regulation varied across provinces. Nova Scotia regulated only four professions, while Ontario and Quebec regulated eight each. British Columbia regulated five in 1900. Ontario and Quebec established several closed, incorporated regulatory colleges early on, but then seemed reluctant to extend such authority to other groups. They created several restricted title professions instead. In contrast, British Columbia was slow to establish self-regulating professions, and when it did so, it first created a regulatory board, not a college. This changed in the late nineteenth and early twentieth centuries, when it too adopted the closed, regulatory college model of regulation. British Columbia was the newest of the three provinces, and legislators may have thought that the number of practitioners (and their "quality") was insufficient for a regulatory college. Overall, though, a common pattern began to emerge.

The impetus for professional regulation often came from professionals, but state actors at times encouraged these initiatives, and certainly played an active role in shaping the legislation before them. Legislators were often ambivalent about professional regulation. When they passed legislation to regulate professions, they typically declared the legislation to be serving the public interest and sometimes professionals' interests by raising the quality of services available, and allowing members of the public to distinguish the trained from the untrained. They sought to raise standards, while still ensuring that services were available outside city centres, and sometimes while protecting some degree of consumer choice. As we have seen, they were likely to delegate authority to professionals who in terms of their background resembled themselves: Protestant men of British descent who appeared respectable, and were socially and politically active and connected. When establishing self-regulating professions, legislators considered the characteristics and competence of professional leaders. The disciplinary provisions in regulatory legislation would presumably allow these upstanding leaders to keep rank-and-file practitioners in line. Self-regulation was a privilege and not all were deserving. Legislators appear to have been aware that their regulatory legislation differed from that in the United States and United Kingdom, but on occasion some expressed a belief that the emergent Canadian pattern of regulation was superior.

This chapter has provided only an overview of professional self-regulation in these four Canadian provinces, setting aside the discussion of exactly how professions were made in this era, which will receive more detailed treatment in chapter 4. Nonetheless, this overview finds considerable support for the theories presented in chapter 1. As social-closure and resource-mobilization models would predict, legislation to regulate professions often came from the professions. Nevertheless, legislators were not passive recipients, but frequently introduced, actively debated, rejected, and amended legislation regulating professions. Certainly, as collective-mobility approaches suggest, there appear to have been moments when provincial legislatures were more favourable to professional requests than others. One of these moments was immediately after Confederation, when provincial legislatures were still defining their roles. The fact that professional regulation was substantially redrawn immediately following Confederation provides support for those who link professional regulation with state building (Johnson 1982; Goebel 1994). Although legislators rarely speak of professional regulation explicitly in governance terms, they saw it as a delegation of the state's governance authority, and only granted self-regulation to those they deemed capable of handling the responsibility. State leaders appear to have had little interest in regulating these fields (health and law) directly.

As in the previous chapter, there is some evidence that expertise was important to professional regulation, but it tended to be tied to a host of other characteristics, including gender, class, status, ethnicity, and character. Competence was closely linked with education, but in this era, education was tied with socio-economic status. Thus, when legislators and professional leaders implemented education requirements for entry to practice, they were also limiting the ability of those outside the middle and upper classes to enter practice – a fact of which contemporaries seemed well aware.

In this era, when class distinctions were so crucial to professions, it is perhaps not surprising that "the public interest" was sometimes tied with professionals' interests. As long as professionals were broad-minded, educated gentlemen, they were trusted (by some legislators at least) to act in the public's interest. This said, there were legislators in some periods who depicted professionals as self-interested men whose actions might have negative implications for the public (higher fees, lower access to services). These beliefs, though, sometimes spurred professional regulation. Upstanding leaders were asked to control the behaviour of rank-and-file members to ensure they acted in a manner that benefited rather than harmed the public.

Chapter Four

Case Studies in Self-Regulation: Medicine, Dentistry, and Land Surveying

In the three decades following Confederation, professional regulation in Canada changed dramatically. Chapter 3 provided an overview of what was regulated and how, and touched on the rationales and debates surrounding the establishment of self-regulating professions up to 1900. This overview, however, shed little light on how professions came to be regulated during this era. The actions of professional leaders and state actors which ultimately determined regulatory outcomes remain unclear, as do the provincial social contexts shaping professional development. To enrich and enliven the picture of professional self-regulation in the four provinces, this chapter will present case studies of three professions that acquired self-regulation during this era. These case studies provide the opportunity to draw on theoretical concepts and models introduced in chapter 1 to illuminate regulatory processes, and explore similarities and variations across province. It is only through such case studies that one can parse out the roles of professional leaders, state actors, social events, and local conditions in shaping the emergence of self-regulating professions.

The first case study focuses on the medical profession. Medicine has probably been the most studied of all professions in North America (with the possible exception of law), and it was the profession that most subsequent professions sought to emulate. The medical profession was also influential in shaping the regulation of other professions in the healthcare field in both this era and subsequent ones. The attraction of medicine as a case study is enhanced by the plethora of records on the profession and its regulation: while the regulation of some professions warranted virtually no mention in newspapers or other contemporary accounts, the same cannot be said for medicine. Further, there are several published histories of medicine in Canada, which provide additional evidence and insight. For all these reasons, medicine makes an ideal case study. Here I pick up the story of medical regulation in Ontario and Quebec introduced in chapter 2, and expand it to include Nova Scotia and British Columbia.

The second case study considers dentistry, which of all the professions to achieve self-regulation in this era is perhaps the most intriguing. While professions in medicine and law (and even pharmacy and land surveying) had English and French antecedents dating back to medieval times, dentistry as a distinct occupation is largely a product of the modern era in the West. Law, medicine, pharmacy, and land surveying were all regulated in some fashion in most colonies prior to Confederation, but the same cannot be said for dentistry. Dentistry, then, may be the first truly modern profession, and it was one that acquired self-regulation in Canada and the United States before it was regulated elsewhere in the world. Further, it is also a profession that was regulated differently across Canada. As we have seen, fairly sweeping powers were granted to dentists in Ontario and also in Quebec within a few years of Confederation, but the profession had difficulty winning regulation in Nova Scotia, and did not achieve its own regulatory college in British Columbia until the twentieth century. For all these reasons, dentistry as a case study promises to illuminate processes of, and variations in, professional regulation in Canada.

The final case study presented here concerns land surveying. Research on the sociology of professions rarely – if ever – touches on land surveying. Yet, land surveyors were regulated in some fashion in the Canadian colonies dating back to the eighteenth century, and by the end of the nineteenth century, they were self-regulating professionals in Ontario and Quebec, and regulated in British Columbia. Although there is a dearth of scholarly sources on land surveying, and the profession was not high profile enough that legislative debates were recorded in detail in the newspapers of the day, it is important to take a brief look at this profession. Sometimes the clearest insights into a phenomenon come from the anomalies and outliers, and such appears to be the case with the regulation of land surveying in Canada.

Towards the end of the chapter, I tease out the similarities and differences across the case studies and discuss their implications for our theoretical understanding of professional development and regulation.

Medicine

In 1867, medicine was regulated in Quebec, Ontario, Nova Scotia, and British Columbia; however, it was only in Quebec that a regulatory college had been established. Ontario was governed by a medical council, and medical leaders there wished for regulatory change. In Nova Scotia and British Columbia entry to practise medicine was restricted, but the profession was not self-regulating. Over the next several decades, medicine's powers of self-regulation were extended in each of the four provinces. This process was not an entirely smooth one, as the last chapter demonstrated. As medical doctors sought bills to expand their authority, they faced legislators who were at times ambivalent about their requests, if not outright hostile. Further, medical doctors faced a great deal of competition from other formal and informal care providers in the late nineteenth century (Bouchard 1996; Connor 1991). These challenges shaped medicine's professionalization.

Historians argue there were a variety of healthcare providers available to ailing Canadians in the late nineteenth century (Bernier 1989; Bouchard 1996; Romano 1995; Connor 1991). Botanical, eclectic, and homeopathic practitioners had made inroads into Ontario, Nova Scotia, and Quebec (Connor 1991; Howell 1992; Bernier 1989). Like regular medical doctors (allopaths), homeopaths, and eclectic doctors were usually formally trained, although their philosophies of practice differed. In Ontario at Confederation, all three groups were regulated medical doctors. In Quebec, the Montreal Homeopathic Association had been given the right to establish a dispensary, a hospital, a school, and a board of examiners to license trained homeopaths (Canada 1865b; Bernier 1989). Nova Scotia also recognized alternative healers (Howell 1992). In addition to the formally trained and regulated, there were a variety of other healers with less training, if any at all. Medical doctors from the United States, with variable levels of training, found their way across the border and set up practice (Bernier 1989; Bouchard 1996; Romano 1995; Connor 1991). Moreover, midwives were common throughout the countryside and attended many births. In Quebec, under the law of 1847, medical doctors could examine midwives in the towns of Quebec, Montreal, and Trois-Rivières, but this provision had little effect on the practice of midwives in rural areas throughout the province (Bernier 1989). In Ontario and Quebec, by the late nineteenth century many medical doctors saw midwives as ignorant and dangerous practitioners, whose practice cut into their own. By the turn of the twentieth century, regular medicine had largely succeeded in marginalizing (and even in places eradicating) midwives' practice (Bernier 1989; Biggs 1983).

Folk medicine – whether provided by family members, neighbours, or travelling practitioners – was also popular, especially throughout the countryside (Bouchard 1996). In Quebec, the church by tradition provided care to the sick in local parishes (ibid.). Purveyors of patent medicines who travelled from town to town also drew the patronage of many. Bouchard's (1996: 535) observation for the Saguenay region in Quebec in the nineteenth century, seems to hold for many other regions as well: "L'intervention du médecin était associée à des circonstances très graves." For many, seeing a medical doctor was a last resort. When people were sick they would first turn to home remedies, and more informal care providers (ibid.). Some regions did not have access to a licensed medical doctor (Bernier 1989: 95–6).

This state of affairs spurred regular medical doctors initially to seek and then to revise regulatory legislation. Through legislation they sought to undermine their competitors, who they felt were doing more harm than good. Medical leaders also fought for legislative change in this period to extend their social influence. It was in the late nineteenth century that provincial governments became more involved in public health initiatives. In earlier campaigns against infectious diseases, medical doctors were involved, but their roles varied. State actors pursued initiatives with little consultation, and medical doctors often felt shut out of the decision-making process (Howell 1981). In a similar vein, early hospitals relied on a skeleton medical staff, instead relying on nurses and other workers (Bernier 1989). Throughout the nineteenth century, hospitals expanded, as did medical doctors' place within them. In this era, medical doctors attempted to enlarge their social, public, and political roles (Howell 1992; Bernier 1989). They lobbied state actors for a position of leadership in the emerging healthcare system, and in public health initiatives. By the turn of the twentieth century, they had succeeded in securing many official positions on municipal and provincial health boards, in hospitals, and in the collection of vital statistics for state agencies (Bernier 1989, Gidney and Millar 1994; Ferguson 1930; Howell 1992). They obtained a virtual monopoly on these official positions, excluding and/or marginalizing their competitors in the healthcare field. This, however, was a long and difficult process, and in 1867 their future success was by no means assured.

In Quebec at Confederation, medical doctors were self-regulating, and held a legal status that may have been the envy of medical leaders in other provinces. However, the 1847 act regulating medicine was not fully enforceable. Medical doctors faced competition from unlicensed (both trained and untrained) care providers, and they were internally divided. Bernier (1983) argues that the regulatory college was not terribly effective prior to regulatory change in the 1870s. It was difficult to police illegal practice, especially in the countryside. Even formally trained practitioners might not bother to register with the College of Physicians and Surgeons of Lower Canada (ibid.). Further, the college had little disciplinary control over its members. Faced with this situation, some reform-minded medical men pushed for regulatory change. Historians credit a group of young, francophone medical doctors within the Société médicale de Montréal for driving the process, which resulted in a new medical act in 1876 (Bernier 1983, 1989). Although there was dissatisfaction with the state of medicine and medical regulation at the time, the catalyst for legislative reform in the mid-1870s appears to have been the establishment of the Canadian Medical Association in 1867 (Bernier 1989; MacDermot 1935). Quebec medical doctors were quite active in this association, which in its early years pursued regulatory legislation at the federal level with the goal of establishing nation-wide standards for entry to practise medicine. To some within the Société médical, it seemed prudent to consolidate the College of Physicians and Surgeons' powers in the province, so that regulatory control did not pass into others' hands at the federal level (Bernier 1989: 90; MacDermot 1967).

Minor amending acts affecting medical regulation were passed in 1869, 1872, and 1875: these were short and dealt with minor housekeeping issues only. In 1876, however, the college petitioned the legislature for an entirely new act, which redefined its powers. Another bill was introduced during the same session by the provincial secretary (seemingly without consulting the profession; *Globe* 1876: 4). The two separate bills were eventually combined, and referred to a special committee, consisting of ten MD MLAs, three lawyers (including the two movers of the two bills), and one MLA trained in both medicine and law (Quebec 1876a). There appears to have been some resistance to the legislation from several medical doctors in Quebec City who petitioned against the act. In the end, however, the legislation passed with little controversy in the House of Assembly.[1] The legislation itself renamed the regulatory college the College of Physicians and Surgeons of Quebec, and altered board membership (Quebec 1876b). The size of the board increased to forty members, and included regionally elected and medical school representatives. The board's powers of self-regulation were expanded, especially around entry to practice and the operation of the college. Entry requirements were revised, and a matriculation exam formalized. Fines for practising without the college's authorization were raised. Further, the first discipline provisions were implemented: practitioners who were convicted of a felony would be forced to forfeit their registration. The board's powers concerning the regulation of midwives were also extended (ibid.).

These changes had the combined effect of consolidating and strengthening the power of the College of Physicians and Surgeons of Quebec, at least over entry to practice, and the practice of trained practitioners in the province (Bernier 1989).[2] Subsequent legislation in 1879 extended this power by tweaking entry requirements, and revising rules concerning the entry of those trained outside the province (Quebec 1879). Those trained in non-British institutions had to pass the provincial matriculation exam, attend a Quebec medical school for six months, and then write the professional entry examinations (ibid.). The regulatory college's powers were extended further in 1898 (Quebec 1898). At this time the college was granted the right to establish a discipline committee, which had the power to conduct investigations, hold hearings, take evidence, and render decisions respecting the suspension or removal of the licences of those proven to be conducting practice in an unprofessional manner. Nevertheless, the profession was not without its challengers in the late nineteenth century. For instance, in 1881 and 1882 there were attempts by an MLA, M. Gagnon, a notary and editor, to pass legislation to regulate (lower) medical fees.[3]

By 1900, the Quebec medical profession had a regulatory college with fairly extensive governance powers, and control over entry to practice and professional conduct. Further, medical doctors' relationships with state actors had expanded; they were more often consulted on public health issues and held important institutional roles. They had used their newfound powers to identify and prosecute illegal practitioners, especially in the 1880s (Bernier 1989), and these actions may have reduced illegal practice in the province. Despite this strengthened position, medical plurality persisted: homeopaths still practised, and people (especially those in the countryside) continued to patronize other practitioners in times of illness. The public was more convinced of medical doctors' expertise than it used to be, but MDs did not enjoy universal respect. The profession's power was by no means absolute.

While the regulatory status of medicine in Quebec was stable and established at Confederation, in Ontario, medical regulation was in a state of flux. Medical doctors had attempted to revise medical regulation throughout the 1850s, with no progress. The profession was too internally divided to come to an agreement on any regulatory solution (Gidney and Millar 1984). A bill proposed by one faction would be immediately rejected by another. One of the main divisions was between the medical elite in Toronto and country doctors spread throughout the province. When the former proposed legislation creating an appointed board and establishing registration fees to fund professional buildings and libraries in Toronto, the latter protested that they wanted more of a say in medical regulation (and hence supported an elected board), and they did not want to support professional perks that only Torontonians would use (Gidney and Millar 1984: 72). Another principal division was between various school men. Feuds between rival proprietary medical schools derailed legislative initiatives: when bills appeared to favour one school over others, there were protests. Some practitioners wished to see the influence of the "school men" undermined altogether (Gidney and Millar 1984; Romano 1995). The expansion of homeopathy, eclectic medicine, and other alternative practices in the province further prevented legislative change in this era. If regular medical doctors proposed legislation which threatened the existence of alternative practices (which they were eager to eliminate), then alternative health providers rallied and petitioned against them (Romano 1995). The legislature was not willing to legislate for any one group at the expense of others, and so in the early 1860s the profession continued to be regulated in the same manner it had been since the late 1820s (despite the brief experience with self-regulation in 1839–41).

At Confederation, there were three acts regulating the medical profession in Ontario. Homeopaths in 1859 and eclectic doctors in 1861 won legislation establishing elected medical boards, which were charged with regulating entry to practice in their respective medical specialities (Canada 1859, 1861). The regular medical board still formally regulated entry to practise medicine, but by the 1860s had less control over the process. The medical act exempted anyone with a diploma from a medical school in the British Empire from writing the exam for entry to practice. With the spread of medical schools in the mid-nineteenth century, most doctors in the province were Canadian-trained, and hence received a licence upon graduation (Gidney and Millar 1984: 66; Romano 1995). Frustrated with the state of the medical profession in Ontario – especially rising numbers of practitioners, the challenge of alternative therapies, dissatisfaction with the state of the medical schools, and a sense that their status was not what it should be – members of the regular profession united long enough to support an 1865 act establishing a "General Council of Medical Education and Registration for Upper Canada" (Gidney and Millar 1984, 1994). Regular medical doctors were not formally organized on a provincial level at this time, but professional leaders cooperated to pursue legislative change (Gidney and Millar 1994). The 1865 act resembled the 1858 UK Medical Act, to the extent that it neither closed medical practice nor did it do anything to undermine alternative therapies and the status of the various medical schools (Canada 1865a). As in the United Kingdom, this was a compromise that achieved little, and therefore offended no one. Its main innovations were twofold. First, most of the medical council would be elected, not appointed, so authority would no longer remain in the hands of the Toronto medical elite; council representatives would be drawn from ridings across the province. Seats on the council were also reserved for appointees from the medical schools in the province. Second, the act gave to the council the power to set matriculation standards and shape the curriculum of the medical schools (MacNab 1970; Gidney and Millar 1984).

Disagreements within the new council erupted almost immediately over matriculation. In the context of concerns that the status of medicine was slipping (or at least was not what it should be), and that medical school proprietors were more concerned with profit than education, the elected council representatives "declared war on the schools," and endeavoured to establish high matriculation standards (Gidney and Millar 1984: 80–1). Controversy arose over the implementation of Greek as a compulsory requirement for entry to study (Gidney and Millar 1984; Romano 1995). Medical school representatives protested, but the supporters of the high standard outnumbered them. In the end, they reached a compromise to delay its implementation.[4] Lacking control over entry to practice, medical council members endeavoured to ensure that only well-educated gentlemen could obtain entry to study.

Although the new medical act had its advantages, the elected council members were dismayed that they had so little control over the medical schools (whose public bickering and public misconduct embarrassed the profession) and entry to practice (Gidney and Millar 1984). Thus, in 1868, the medical council struck a subcommittee to develop a new bill. When Member of Provincial Parliament (MPP) and medical council member Dr William McGill introduced the new medical act in the legislature in November 1868, he explained that the measure was intended to correct an oversight in the previous act, by making clear rules for council elections. He claimed the medical council had decided to use this opportunity to make some "slight amendments," of which the only notable one was the establishment of a board of examiners to govern entry to practice (McGill in MacNab 1970: 12). The proposed act would also strengthen the council's power over entry to study. During its path through the legislature, however, the bill was transformed in ways the profession had not anticipated.

In the legislature, some concerns were raised at the second reading of the bill – specifically over its relevance for homeopathic and eclectic doctors – but it passed this phase and was directed to a special committee, which included several medical doctor MPPs, for further consideration (Ontario 1869b). The special committee altered the bill (Gidney and Millar 1984). The original bill continued the General Medical Council established in 1865; the committee, however, made provisions for the creation of the College of Physicians and Surgeons of Ontario (CPSO), with an elected council at its head. There are no records of legislative committee meetings from this era, so the source of this change is not clear. Some medical leaders desired a regulatory college (Gidney and Millar 1984), and hence the change could have been prompted by an MD MPP. However, the Ontario legislature had established a regulatory college for the dental profession earlier that year; establishing parallel regulatory structures for both health professions (similar to the structure then in place in Quebec, and resembling that in the United Kingdom) likely seemed reasonable and appropriate. The special committee reported the bill, with amendments, and it was sent to the committee of the whole house.

It was here that events took a dramatic turn. Legislators argued that the act should not only apply to regular medical doctors; its provisions should be extended to include homeopaths and eclectic doctors. Legislators and many members of the general public supported medical pluralism (Gidney and Millar 1984, 1994; Connor 1991). Homeopathy especially appealed to members of the middle class and the well-to-do (Connor 1998; Gidney and Millar 1994). Thus, legislators revised the bill, expanding the medical council to include representation from homeopaths and eclectics. Each group would have some separate exams, and the ability to appoint examiners (Ontario 1869a; Gidney and Millar 1984; MacNab 1970). The separate homeopath and eclectic boards would be abolished: there would be only one regulatory board for all three branches of medicine (for more details on the 1869 Ontario Medical Act, see table 2.1). Many medical leaders were outraged.[5] To those keenly concerned with status distinctions, being grouped with lesser-trained practitioners whom they regarded as "charlatans" and "quacks" was an offence. Others were more sanguine, and reasoned, over the following months, that a united board might enable the regular profession to undermine these alternative therapies more subtly and effectively (Gidney and Millar 1984, 1994).[6] Indeed, within a few years, eclectic medicine was fully integrated into regular medicine: eclectic doctors were educated as regular doctors, and chose not to register as eclectics (Connor 1991). Homeopathy, though, remained strong for several decades.

In the years immediately following the passing of the 1869 medical act, some difficulties arose. Tensions between regular and homeopathic doctors persisted, to the point that homeopaths sought to leave the confines of the medical act in 1874. Legislators were unreceptive to homeopaths' request. They had embraced "therapeutic diversity within a unified profession," and "were unwilling to abandon that principle" (Gidney and Millar 1994: 97). Instead, they revised the medical act to provide some protection for homeopaths: the composition of the board of examiners was altered, and provisions for a homeopathic college were made (Ontario 1874). With this legislative change, the medical profession entered a period of stability, and there were few major alterations (or attempts to alter the medical act) until the late 1880s and early 1890s.[7]

The next major revision of the Ontario medical act occurred in 1887 (Ontario 1887). This act altered council representation by limiting school representatives to several named institutions. Moreover, it established disciplinary mechanisms for the profession. Under earlier acts, the medical council could erase from the register practitioners guilty of a felony, but the new legislation allowed the council to penalize people deemed guilty of "infamous or disgraceful conduct" in the practice of their profession (Ontario 1887, s. 3). Similarly to the 1898 Quebec act, the Ontario Medical Council was empowered to establish a discipline committee that could conduct investigations, hold hearings, take evidence and testimony from witnesses under oath, cross-examine witnesses, and recommend to the council whether a practitioner should be erased from (or restored to) the medical register (ibid., ss. 4 and 5).

Their decisions could be appealed to "any Judge of the High Court of Justice for Ontario" within six months (ibid., s. 6). This legislation expanded the medical profession's powers of self-governance, and provided the council with the ability to regulate practitioner behaviour more effectively.

As noted in chapter 3, the Ontario medical profession experienced some significant challenges to its authority and high standards from two sources in the early 1890s. The first challenge was internal. The Medical Defence Association was formed by a group of predominantly rural practitioners, who felt that the medical council was dominated by homeopaths and school representatives who were making decisions that were not in the best interests of rank-and-file practitioners. They also resented council policies, specifically the annual registration fees – which the council wanted to increase to cover expenses such as the establishment of "expensive headquarters" in Toronto (Naylor 1986: 10). This group sponsored a bill introduced in the legislature in 1892 that would eliminate medical school representation on the council, increase the number of territorial representatives, and eliminate the annual registration fee (ibid.: 10; MacNab 1970: 26). MD MPPs and their supporters opposed the bill, and they succeeded in having it referred to a special committee to which they all were named. They killed the bill in committee. The Medical Defence Association tried again in 1893, and this bill was referred to a large committee, which included Premier Oliver Mowat. This committee struck a compromise, which resulted in an increase in the number of territorial representatives on the medical council (Naylor 1986: 11).

The challenge by the Patrons of Industry to the medical profession was a more substantial one. The Patrons of Industry political party garnered the support of many in rural Ontario in the 1890s with their anti-monopoly stance. Having obtained several seats in the provincial parliament in 1895, party members introduced a bill that would remove the power of self-regulation from the medical profession. The Patrons claimed that professional entry standards were too high, making medical education out of reach for the common people, and reserving the occupation for the elite. They sought to open up medicine, while maintaining some form of regulation. The bill they proposed would have removed the powers of the medical council and established an independent council, which would examine candidates, but would be more publicly accountable (Naylor 1986: 13). The bill would have also removed the profession's power to discipline practitioners. To the Patrons such powers "should not be given to any such body of men" (Haycock, ibid.). This bill was defeated (overwhelmingly) by a vote when the order for its second reading occurred (Ontario 1895). The Patrons continued to agitate for reform, however. In 1896 they introduced a bill that would limit registration fees (MacNab 1970).

Ontario medicine successfully survived this challenge, and in 1900 was a profession with considerable powers of self-regulation, which had successfully fended off opposition, in part due to the presence of MDs' in the legislature. Provincial organization followed, rather than preceded, self-regulation, and by 1880 the Ontario Medical Association advocated for medical doctors and endeavoured to enhance MDs' public image and to shape state policy (Ferguson 1930). Like their counterparts in Quebec, respect from the public and belief in their expertise was slow to develop, but Ontario medical doctors began to take on more public and institutional roles as the government introduced public health initiatives and hospitals expanded.

At Confederation, Nova Scotian medical doctors were regulated, but not self-regulating. Like their Ontario counterparts in 1865, their medical act dated from the late 1820s. It restricted practice to those who could present a diploma, or who had undergone an examination, by examiners appointed by the governor. In 1856 the Nova Scotia legislature established a register, located in the provincial secretary's office (Howell 1992).[8] Five years after Confederation, members of the Nova Scotia Medical Society, formed in 1854, approached government leaders seeking a change in their regulatory status. The bill "to regulate the qualifications of practitioners in medicine and surgery" was presented in the provincial legislature in the spring of 1872 by the attorney general, Hiram Blanchard (Nova Scotia 1872a). Although both the Quebec and the Ontario Colleges of Physicians and Surgeons were established by this time, the bill proposed a form of regulation similar to that emerging in the United States in the 1870s.[9] It established a provincial medical board, which would be tasked with regulating entry to practice, examining candidates, and reviewing credentials. However, this bill went further than many in the United States, and had some provisions similar to its provincial counterparts: the board would be elected, and it had the power to regulate not only entry to practice, but entry to study as well, establishing a matriculation exam. Further, while a medical diploma was required for entry to practice, it was not in itself sufficient. Candidates would also have to pass an exam.

The bill engendered little controversy within or outside the legislature. There was some discussion in the Committee of the Whole about requiring exams for those with diplomas. Attorney General Blanchard defended this clause on the grounds that those with skill would not object to demonstrating it before their peers and, further, that requiring an exam was the practice in England (Nova Scotia 1872c: 169). While some objected to the bill's restrictions, Blanchard argued, "Some stringent remedy was necessary to prevent the growing evil of quackery," which harmed the public (ibid.). The provincial secretary was one of several legislators opposed to the bill, but he withdrew his opposition after making several amendments – the principal one affected the make-up of the board. Just under half would be elected by medical doctors; the rest would be appointed by the lieutenant governor (ibid.: 170). The bill, as amended, passed. The legislative council agreed with the bill in principle, but recommended a few small amendments, which were approved by the assembly, and the bill became law in April 1872.

While medical legislation in Ontario was the subject of internal conflict, and intense debate, it appears to have provoked little controversy in Nova Scotia. In the past, the legislature had expressed a "lack of faith in [regular medicine's] therapeutic effectiveness" (Howell 1992: 8). However, in 1872, legislators did not outright oppose the act, but rather voiced concerns about certain measures. The new medical act of 1872 aided the regular medical profession in its battle against unlicensed practice, but it could do little to combat more informal forms of practice, and patent medicines. As in Quebec, alternative treatment methods were plentiful and popular. It was not until the early twentieth century that the medical profession was able to establish itself on firmer ground in Nova Scotia (Howell 1981, 1992).

In the decade following the passing of the 1872 medical act, the Nova Scotia medical profession was busy implementing its provisions. Small administrative changes to medical legislation were made in 1877, 1880, and 1881. The medical board requested a minor extension of their power to regulate entry to practice in 1883, in order to "secure the public from fraudulent registration of practitioners" (Nova Scotia 1883: 239); however, legislators were not open to the proposed changes, arguing that the board had enough power, and they seemed to be trying to prevent "persons of ability from getting an opportunity of practising in this Province" for their own gain (ibid.: 324). The controversial elements seem to have been the college's matriculation requirements and preliminary exam, which excluded some US-trained doctors whose pre-medical education was deemed lacking (ibid.: 324). The board appears to have reversed its position on this issue shortly thereafter, and admitted several (American-trained) MDs to practice in the province without their having completed the matriculation exam. Legislation required that the board mark such men with an asterisk in the medical register (Nova Scotia 1886: 382–5). When the board returned to the legislature for an act to remove the asterisk in 1886, a debate on the value of the matriculation exam was reignited (ibid.). Nonetheless, the bill passed.

It was in 1888 that the medical profession in Nova Scotia faced its greatest challenge. As recounted in chapter 3, MLA (and lawyer) Otto Weeks introduced a bill that would open up medical practice to ensure that medical breakthroughs reached the public quickly (Nova Scotia 1888: 80). For Weeks and his supporters, the medical profession in the province had been granted excessive powers out of line with those conferred in the United States and United Kingdom, to the detriment of the people. He elaborated: "Does it not seem rather a stringent regulation, if a man shall, by investigation, hit upon some discovery to relieve the sufferings of humanity, that, because he does not happen to be registered under the act we have passed in this province, the benefit of that discovery shall be entirely lost to humanity?" (ibid.).

The bill spurred a lengthy debate in the legislature about the value and legitimacy of medical regulation, and there were a number of legislators who sided with Weeks in opposing the privileges possessed by the profession. The MD MLAs spoke at length against the measure, but many others did as well. The discussion provoked an impassioned defence for professional self-regulation, and the principle that professional practice should be limited to the trained to protect the public. In this era, over a third of legislators were members of regulated professions (doctors and lawyers), and hence it is not surprising that so many would reject a challenge to medical regulation. Nonetheless, Weeks and some of his supporters were lawyers. After a lengthy debate, the bill was finally defeated by a vote of 25 to 11. Most professionals in the house voted against the bill, but so did a majority of the merchants and all but one of the farmers in the assembly. Despite this challenge to professional regulation in 1888, the majority of Nova Scotia legislators supported medical self-regulation. By 1900 the regulatory status of medical doctors in the province was secure.

The history of medical regulation in British Columbia provides an interesting counter case to the other provinces. In 1867, medical regulation was brand new in the province, and very rudimentary. The medical profession was not formally organized, there were few practitioners, and at the point when British Columbia joined Canada (and for several decades after) there were very few MD MLAs serving in the legislature. Given this state of affairs, it is not surprising that regulatory change was slow to occur.

In 1879, a revision to medical regulation was proposed by the lone MD MLA, Dr John Ash. In doing so, he claimed, he had no "personal interest" in the measure, but thought it beneficial to place "the profession of medicine on a proper footing in the province" (*Victoria Daily Colonist* 1879b: 3). The 1867 ordinance had proven ineffective. Debate in 1879 revealed that many trained medical doctors had not bothered to register under the act, while it was believed that several untrained men had done so (ibid.). The bill would establish a medical council to regulate entry to practice, but in many other respects was similar to the 1867 measure in restricting practice to those with a medical diploma who had registered. In general, there was a fair amount of support for the bill, but legislators did voice concern that the measure would restrict access to practitioners in outlying areas (ibid.). Further, the bill apparently privileged those with diplomas from British universities, and there was a feeling that the American-trained should be allowed to practise as well. In the end, the bill did not pass, in part because it was introduced very late in the session, and legislators refused to be rushed in their deliberations. MLA Mr Williams, for instance, was reluctant to "hurry" the bill through, without consulting the medical profession. He preferred that medical men themselves initiate the process (ibid.).

Although a bill affecting medicine was introduced in 1885, it was discharged before its second reading. It was not until 1886 that a medical council with regulatory powers would be established in British Columbia (British Columbia 1886b). The 1886 bill was accompanied by petitions from medical doctors, but it was presented to the assembly by Attorney General A.E.B. Davie as a public bill. The medical profession was not organized on a provincial level at the time, although the Vancouver Medical Association formed that year (Rose 1972). Political opponents objected that the bill was actually private not public, but in this instance, the Speaker of the House ruled the bill was indeed in the public interest, and hence discussion of the bill could continue. Debate focused not on the principles behind the bill, but rather on particular clauses, such as the proposed education requirements, and the bill's potential impact in rural areas (*Victoria Daily Colonist* 1886b: 1). One issue that raised debate was a proposal by MLA Simeon Duck, a carriage-maker, to exempt "practitioners of the Hygio-Therapeutic school" who possessed diplomas from the provisions of the act (*Victoria Daily Colonist* 1886d: 3). According to the newspaper, this proposal "met with a most vigorous opposition" (ibid.). There was general agreement that *all* medical doctors, regardless of their therapeutic school, should be regulated under the act. In this way, BC legislators, like their Ontario counterparts, supported medical pluralism.

This point was reaffirmed in 1887, during the consideration of a bill to amend the medical act, when legislators struck out a clause which would have excluded magnetic healers, solely on the basis of their therapeutic preferences. Further, in 1889 a bill to exclude homeopaths from the provisions of the medical act was proposed (*Victoria Daily Colonist* 1889a: 4). Medical supporters defended the council's treatment of homeopaths and other alternative practitioners, explaining that in some instances, homeopaths might be excused from some of the regular practitioners' exams. When they were examined it was "by a practitioner of the same school [branch of medicine] as the candidate" (*Victoria Daily Colonist* 1889b: 4). There was some debate over accommodation for homeopaths in the legislature (British Columbia 1889), and in the end the admission requirements for homeopaths were amended such that only a diploma was necessary. Many legislators were not happy with this turn of events, and the act was further amended in 1890 to require homeopaths to complete exams before the council in specified subjects (British Columbia 1890). Legislators upheld the power of the medical council to determine entry to practice, but supported medical pluralism.

In the 1890s, BC medical legislation was revised along two lines. First, there was debate and discussion about entry requirements, especially the entry of the foreign-trained into practice in British Columbia. Second, as in many of the other provinces, discipline provisions for BC medical doctors were extended in 1898. Medical doctors were empowered to establish a discipline committee, and their ability to police practitioner conduct was extended. All these developments occurred prior to the establishment of the British Columbia Medical Association, formed in 1900 (Rose 1972).

Although the precise context and events shaping the regulation of medicine in these four provinces differ, several theoretically important similarities are evident. First, regulatory legislation was sought by medical doctors to marginalize their competitors; hence, social closure was a key process at play. Nonetheless, members of the legislature were not passive responders to professional demands, but actively debated, discussed, and amended legislation placed before them. Many acts were introduced and supported by government leaders because they were deemed to serve the public interest. At least in certain moments, legislators generally supported the principle of self-regulation, and primarily debated the particulars. Regulatory outcomes were the product of the interplay of both professional interests and legislators' beliefs about what was fair and reasonable. Second, the presence of medical doctors in legislatures was undoubtedly of import in helping medical leaders achieve their goals. MD MLAs in each province – even in British Columbia, where they were in short supply – introduced legislation, supported legislation in medicine's favour, and undermined legislation not in the profession's interests. Further, they helped behind the scenes: having insiders familiar with the operation and mood of the legislative assembly no doubt shaped legislative requests, increasing the odds of a favourable reception. Many lawyers in the legislatures also supported medical regulation, though some did not. Third, while medical organization was valuable in shaping regulatory initiatives (in Nova Scotia and Quebec especially), it does not appear to have been essential to winning self-regulation in every instance. The presence of a professional leadership that was politically connected and respectable was more important. Fourth, each province had its own regulatory traditions and patterns of governance, and these were also influential in shaping the nature and content of professional regulation. Despite these variations, by 1900 the medical profession in all four provinces had extensive regulatory powers and control over entry to practice, and possessed quasi-judicial powers to discipline practitioners.

Dentistry

Dentistry emerged as a distinct specialty in the Western world in the eighteenth century (Bremner 1964; Gullett 1971). Some activities now in dentistry's scope of practice – especially tooth-pulling – were done by barber-surgeons in earlier centuries. Most dental historians credit the emergence of dentistry as a separate art and science to Pierre Fauchard, an eighteenth-century Frenchman, who called himself a "dental surgeon" and whose practice, and book about dentistry, provided a foundation for the dental profession in the West for well over a century (Bremner 1964; Pierre Fauchard Academy 2015). The scope of practice outlined by Fauchard may sound familiar to readers today: dentists filled cavities, prevented cavities through education about diet and through providing regular check-ups and cleanings, straightened teeth (orthodontia), and constructed dentures. Fauchard also discredited prevailing theories of dental disease, paving the way for a more scientific approach (ibid.). Fauchard's ideas spread elsewhere in Europe through the eighteenth century, and found their way to America (probably with French assistance during the American Revolution), altering dental practice there beginning in the late eighteenth century (Bremner 1964; Gullett 1971).

Dentistry expanded in the United States in the opening decades of the twentieth century, but dental services were primarily used by the wealthy. Tooth-pulling continued to be a task performed by a wide variety of practitioners, from medical doctors to blacksmiths. The more elite services provided by dentists – full and partial dentures and filling teeth – tended to be expensive. Only the well-to-do could afford them. Nonetheless, in this era, dental disease was prevalent, and even young adults might suffer considerable tooth loss. The potential market for dental services was a large one. In the 1830s, American dentists began to form societies. Their stated goal was to distinguish educated and ethical dentists from their unscrupulous counterparts, some of whom made a public spectacle of pulling teeth for entertainment (Gullett 1971). The first dental college was established in Baltimore in 1840. Through education, dental leaders sought to establish dentistry as a "medical" profession. Elite dentists sometimes had training in medicine, and they wanted to raise the status of their occupation closer to that of medicine.

Modern dentistry came to Canada largely through the United States. It is true there were barber-surgeons in colonial Quebec, and some early practitioners were largely self-trained tradesmen (Gullett 1971); however, the first trained dental specialists in Ontario, Quebec, and Nova Scotia were American-born and/or American-trained men (Adams 2000). Dental training in this era was by apprenticeship, although those who could afford to do so might attend a US dental college, or lectures at a medical college. Apprenticeships could last as long as four years, but many were as short as a few months in duration (Gullett 1971; Adams 2000). Dentists trained in Michigan, New York State, Massachusetts, or Pennsylvania sought new markets in which to establish their practices, and the Canadian colonies provided an excellent setting as there were very few people providing dental services of any kind in the mid-nineteenth century. Practitioners in other fields (blacksmiths, gunsmiths, medical doctors) might occasionally pull teeth or make dentures as a sideline (Gullett 1971; Adams 2000). Others roamed the countryside selling their services. Although finding someone to pull a sore tooth was not particularly difficult, finding someone to make dentures, so that those without teeth could eat hard foods, was a challenge. Making dentures required considerable craft skill in this era (Adams 2000).

The expansion of the middle class in the mid-nineteenth century in Canada also raised the demand for dental services, which contributed to specialization and an increase in the number of practitioners. Members of the middle class could better afford dental services, and may have enjoyed a diet with more treats and sugars, leading to a higher need for dental services. Technological change also facilitated dental practice, and raised the demand for dentistry (Gullett 1971; Gidney and Millar 1994). First, the discovery of anaesthesia in the mid-nineteenth century was a boon, since for the first time dental operations could be done with little pain. Second, the invention of vulcanized rubber revolutionized the making of dentures; after mid-century dentures were easier to make, cheaper, and more comfortable for the wearer. It was probably this development that spurred professional activity in the 1860s (Gidney and Millar 1994). Trained and "ethical" dentists faced increased competition from lesser-trained itinerants, who attempted to take advantage of the new technology, producing an inferior product for an inferior price. Established, trained dentists felt threatened by the lesser trained.

In response, trained dentists in Ontario joined together and formed the Ontario Dental Association in 1867. Their primary aim in organizing was to seek legislation that would undermine the untrained itinerant dentists by showing "the public who [was] qualified" (ODA 1867). Untrained "quacks" were "hurting the public" and "qualified dentists who had to maintain established offices" (ibid.). The association had other aims as well, including the promotion of "professional and social intercourse among dental practitioners in the Province of Ontario" and the investigation of "the principles and practice of the profession and collateral sciences" (ibid.). Only dentists with established offices, who had been practising for five or more years, and who could provide proof of moral character were allowed to join the association (Adams 2000: 30). The driving force behind the association was Barnabus W. Day, a dentist with an MD degree, and several of his counterparts based in communities east of Toronto (O'Donnell 1898; Shosenberg 1992). All of these individuals were formally trained (one other had an MD degree, and a third had attended some lectures at a medical college). They sought to establish dentistry as an occupation that required training, both practical and scientific. They quickly gained the support of the majority of trained dentists in the province. Their first order of business was to prepare legislation in their favour.

In pursuing this goal, dental leaders were savvy, focused, well connected, and perhaps lucky as well. They quickly earned the support and endorsement of medical leaders. Not only did the provincial medical council formally endorse the bill, but they appear to have provided some guidance in its preparation, as did an MD MPP who helped write the bill and shepherded it through parliament. Dental leaders circulated a petition that was presented to the legislature early in 1868: this petition had the names of sixty-eight dentists (believed to represent a majority of trained dentists in the new province), as well as twenty-eight medical doctors, including members of the professional elite, a prominent druggist, and the mayor of Toronto (Gullett 1971: 279–82). As Gidney and Millar (1994: 217) have commented, the founding members of the Ontario Dental Association appear to have been "men of reputation and influence who knew how to work the levers of power." In early 1868, the newly formed Ontario provincial parliament was meeting for the first time. At this moment, legislators were quite receptive to their requests.

The speed with which all this transpired is notable. The initial meeting of nine dentists to explore the formation of an Ontario Dental Association occurred in January of 1867. The first official meeting of the association occurred in July 1867, when some thirty-one dentists convened to establish the society, formulate rules, and plan their direction (ODA 1867). It was the following January when the association convened again in Toronto (this time with over sixty members in attendance) to review the draft legislation and see its introduction in the Ontario legislature. A group of about 100 dentists and their supporters marched en masse to the parliament buildings to hear the introduction of the bill and to demonstrate their support for it (Shosenberg 1992; Adams 2000). Two short months later, dentists in Ontario had their act.

In 1868, as we have seen, medical leaders recognized that their own regulation had limitations, and they recommended a different structure for dentistry, which appears to have been a mix between the UK Royal College of Surgeons, and Ontario's Law Society. It is possible that regulatory patterns in Lower Canada influenced the dental bill, but professional histories, and evidence from the act itself, provide no evidence of such a connection. The act established an incorporated body – the

Royal College of Dental Surgeons of Ontario – and named twelve ODA members as a board of trustees and board of examiners (a mix of ODA founders and newer members from Toronto and Southern Ontario).[10] In the original bill, board members were entitled to choose their successors, but legislators objected to this provision, and an election system was established (MacNab 1970). Entry to practice was modelled after the ODA's own stringent membership provisions: all those in established practice for five years or more (who could provide proof of this fact from reputable citizens) were entitled to a licence without examination. All others would be examined; those who passed the exams, and provided evidence of "integrity and good moral character," would be granted a licence to practise dentistry. Practice without a licence became illegal (Ontario 1868). There was a great deal of support for the act. One legislator voiced hesitation over the clause requiring those not in established practice for five years to write the exam, but indicated he was willing to accede given that several dentists in this category expressed a willingness to undertake the exams (MacNab 1970). Given the limited opposition, and presented with such overwhelming support from practitioners and medical doctors, legislators agreed to the bill, and it became law in the spring of 1868. The potential for dissent was evident, however, and dentists appear to have mitigated it by offering exams that were less than stringent in the profession's early years (Elliot 1870). Dental leaders were forward-minded and sought to ensure that the next generation of dentists conformed to their image of a dental professional.

Thus, Ontario dentists achieved status as self-regulating professionals with little anguish, hardship, or struggle. They formed an organization, wrote an act, presented it, and successfully saw it through the house. It is evident, however, that some activity did go on behind the scenes. Dental leaders clearly mobilized social contacts and political resources effectively. Ties with medical leaders, and medical doctor MPPs were invaluable. Their well-to-do clientele may also have been helpful; certainly, it is likely that many legislators themselves (or their family members) patronized dentists. There is no evidence that a group organized to oppose their efforts; the few complaints received were from dentists negatively affected by the act. It is not clear how many itinerants would have even been aware of it. In 1867–8, trained dentists were numerous, and they successfully organized and focused their diverse membership on a shared goal. With this goal achieved, in subsequent years the ODA suffered from division, internal conflict, and a lack of direction (Gullett 1971; Shosenberg 1992). Nonetheless, the association soon found another goal – improving the profession and raising its status; achieving regulatory legislation did not bring them public status or respect. They had to win over the broader public, over the next fifty years, for that to be achieved (Adams 2000).

Regulatory initiatives in Quebec followed shortly after Ontario dentists achieved success. Dentistry had long been practised in Quebec, and many well-respected professional and public leaders emerged. Nevertheless, there were fewer dentists in Quebec than in Ontario in the late 1860s: perhaps forty to fifty trained men (Bernier 1989; Gullett 1971).[11] The earliest attempt to regulate dentistry in the region occurred in the 1840s, when medical legislation was being debated. Dentist Aldis Bernard, a future mayor of Montreal, sought to have some clauses respecting dentistry inserted into a bill then before the legislature, but his proposals were lost in a fire, and then abandoned (Gullett 1971: 35). In 1860, another Montreal dentist approached his colleagues to gauge support for a potential dental act. Although practitioners were favourable, they determined that the legislature was not, and once again abandoned the idea. The timing seemed right in 1868, and that fall a group of Quebec dentists, led by Aldis Bernard and others in Montreal, met to form a dental association, and review the Ontario dental act closely (Gullett 1971). Over the next several months, they developed their own act. In February of 1869, their petition was presented in the Quebec legislative assembly, and a month later Edward Brock Carter, a lawyer and MLA for Montreal Centre (and an MD's son) presented the bill in the legislature (Quebec 1869b). The bill was carefully reviewed in the legislative assembly, but few substantial revisions appear to have been made (*Montreal Herald* 1869). It was passed by the assembly in late March and approved by the legislative council shortly thereafter (Quebec 1869b). The Quebec act received royal assent in April of 1869, a mere seven months after dentists first met to form an association.

Some sections of the act were virtually identical to those passed in Ontario, but the act was longer, more detailed, and had slightly different provisions. The act established and incorporated a regulatory body, but this was not labelled a college; rather, the act named the Dental Association of the Province of Quebec (formed by the profession in 1868) as the profession's regulatory body. The first board of eleven dentists mostly based in Montreal and Quebec City was named, but subsequent boards would be elected. All dentists who had established practices for a period of two years (Ontario dentists required five) were eligible for a licence, but those who practised less than two were required to pass an examination, unless they possessed a recognized dental diploma (Quebec 1869a). Those seeking a licence also had to provide "satisfactory evidence of his apprenticeship, integrity and good morals" (ibid., s. 16). As in the Ontario act, the rights of physicians and surgeons were confirmed. Further, the Quebec act conferred broad regulatory powers on the regulatory board (as in Ontario). This legislation was tweaked over the next few years to adjust the grandfather clause (respecting the entry of those in practice when the act was passed) and entry requirements (Quebec 1870, 1874).

There are signs that in Quebec, as in Ontario, the dental profession had close ties with the medical profession. Quebec dental leaders wanted to establish a dental school like their Ontario counterparts did in the mid-1870s. However, the smaller size of the profession in Quebec, combined with the need to establish dental education in two languages, made doing so too difficult (Gullett 1971). Their solution was to require students to take courses at the medical school and augment them with training in dentistry either through apprenticeship or through other means. In the early 1890s, the profession established a dental school in the province with instruction in both English and French, but required students to take courses in medical subjects at McGill or Laval University (Gullett 1971: 85). Quebec dentists required medical school matriculation for entry-to-study dentistry. Thus, in Quebec, as in Ontario, there are signs of professional dentists collaborating with and receiving some support from the medical profession, in their professional projects.

Influenced by legislative activity in Ontario and Quebec, Nova Scotian dentists pursued dental legislation in 1869–70. There is no evidence of a provincial dental association active in this era. In fact, a decade prior, only five dentists were identified in the entire province, all of them based in Halifax (Gullett 1971: 33). The 1871 census of the province counted twenty dentists (seven in Halifax) (Canada 1873). Dental historians credit the drive to secure legislation for dentists in the 1870s to one man: Alfred Chipman Cogswell, "a member of one of Nova Scotia's most prominent families … [and] the province's leading dentist from the 1860s to the turn of the century" (Gullett 1971: 72). Cogswell trained in Maine and practised in New England before establishing a practice in Halifax in 1859. In the late 1860s he attended the Philadelphia Dental College (ibid.). Like his Ontarian counterparts, Cogswell mobilized the support of his fellow dentists and physicians. In 1870 the legislature received a petition from "physicians and surgeon dentists" in the province, asking for an act "to prevent incompetent persons from practising dentistry" (Nova Scotia 1870). The bill was introduced by MD MLA George Murray. It faced some opposition in the legislative assembly, but nonetheless, moved fairly quickly through the house, and once passed was forwarded to the legislative council for approval. The council did not approve the act, however, and the bill was dead. After a promising beginning the bill's promoters may have thought they would achieve regulation for dentistry in Nova Scotia as easily as it had been obtained in other provinces, but it would be twenty more years before dentistry would be regulated in Nova Scotia.

The debates surrounding the 1870 dental bill are illuminating, and worth looking at closely to understand the forces at work. As in Ontario, the bill proposed to grant a licence to practise to all those who had been in established practice for five years. All others would have to pass an examination (Nova Scotia 1870: 146). Unlike Ontario, however, the bill would simply establish a board of examiners, composed of three dentists and two physicians, to examine candidates in scientific and dental subjects (this was in keeping with other professional legislation in the province). During the legislative debate on the bill, its sponsor Dr Murray explained that the bill would exclude people who "came to this country pretending to be qualified to practice Dentistry, but who in reality robbed our people" (ibid.). Opposition to the bill centred around two key concerns. First, it was feared that if practice was restricted to those who passed an examination, "the country might be left without dentistry," or might have to pay too much for it (ibid.). Some held that the bill was sponsored by Halifax practitioners who sought (unfairly) to exclude competitors. Thus, legislators were worried about the impact of the legislation in rural areas. Second, and most important, there was uncertainty over the nature of dentists' skills, and whether training was truly necessary for practice. MLA Robert Chambers, a merchant from Colchester County, was one of the most vocal opponents of the bill. He argued that

> It was well known that some persons could acquire such a profession in half the time that it took others. If the bill passed, and a person not a dentist were to invent an improvement in dentistry, the public must wait for three years before he would be qualified to make use of it.

Further, Chambers argued that dentists did not need formal training:

> One of the best dentists in Boston was a mechanic from this province who had gone to Boston, learned dentistry, and practiced it very successfully. Another very successful dentist had been a cordwainer. These persons had no diploma, but they got a large practice because they gave satisfaction (ibid.: 146–7).

In his support of the bill, Dr Murray countered these arguments:

> Something more than mechanical skill was needed for the practice of dentistry. Dentists made use of very powerful poisons, and a great deal of mischief might be done in the application of these drugs by persons who did not understand their use, though they might have mechanical skill … A diploma with a medical man was a guarantee to the public that he had gone through some medical … training, and it would have the same benefit as regards dentists. (ibid.)

Barrister and cabinet minister Jared Troop spoke at length in favour of dentistry's regulation. He argued the legislation would have benefits for dentists and the people of Nova Scotia:

> The bill had been recommended by a large body of the medical and dental faculty and these persons should have some guarantee that they would be protected after spending time and money in the study of their profession. It should be placed beyond the power of pretenders and quacks to mutilate persons who were unfortunate enough to get into their clutches, and he thought that any member of the dental profession who had high attainments would prefer to have such a law so as to prove that he was complying with the test which it applied to his qualifications. The bill would give a superior class of medical dentists to the country and anyone who doubted the value of such an effect as that need only go to any gentleman in Halifax who had pursued the course of study pointed out in the measure and a few minutes conversation would dissipate his doubts. (ibid.: 147)

To summarize this debate, it appears that opponents feared regulating dentistry would restrict the supply of practitioners, benefit some at the expense of others, and leave the country without practitioners. Further, some believed that training was not necessary for successful practice, and hence such a measure was not only unnecessary, but potentially dangerous. Supporters (and the professionals in the legislature were among the most vocal of the bill's supporters) countered that training was necessary, that the trained were an honourable group of gentlemen deserving of some protection from the unscrupulous and untrained, and that the legislation would benefit the public by ensuring practitioners had the knowledge to practise skilfully and safely. The bill only narrowly passed by a vote of 15 to 13.

In the legislative council, some (including an MD) spoke in favour of the bill, but the council was concerned about the impact of the legislation in the countryside. In the end, council members rejected it, but asked for the bill to be published "for the information of the country." Their rejection resulted "not so much from hostility to the bill, as from the wish that its provisions should be generally known before it was passed" (*Halifax Chronicle* 1870: 2). The council intimated that the promoters should try again another year, and they would likely have a more favourable result at that time.

Despite the bill's defeat, there appeared to be considerable support for the regulation of dentistry in the Nova Scotian legislature and the bill's promoters were optimistic enough to try again the following year. In 1871, a petition and bill were introduced in the legislative assembly, again by MLA Dr Murray. When the bill was before the Committee of the Whole, however, an intense debate erupted (Nova Scotia 1871: 215–18). Opposition to the bill was along the same lines as the previous year. Critics (including the provincial secretary) claimed that dentistry was more trade than science, and hence the legislation was not necessary. Its impact would likely be higher fees. Further, "the country people were not fools – they knew who were qualified to pull teeth, and could take care of themselves without such a bill being passed" (Young, ibid.: 217). Moreover, it was argued that the act would benefit dentists, not the public. The bill's supporters reiterated their earlier arguments: dentistry was a science, and "it was dangerous to allow unskilful and ignorant persons to practice a science like that" (Dr Murray, ibid.: 216). Further, it was said that dentistry was "as important as any other branch of surgery" (Hill, ibid.: 218). In the end, however, a motion to defeat the bill passed by a margin of 13 to 8 (*Halifax Chronicle* 1871: 2).[12] It is worth remembering that in 1870 and 1871, medicine was not self-regulating in Nova Scotia. These acts would have granted dentists regulatory recognition that even their medical colleagues did not possess.

Dentists and their supporters did not immediately give up. Bills to regulate dentistry were promoted in 1877 (too late in the session to advance), 1878, and 1879. All three bills disappeared in, or were rejected by, the legislative committee on private and local bills, without explanation. After their defeat in 1879, dentists waited over a decade before trying again: it was not until 1891 that another bill to regulate dentistry was presented to the Nova Scotia legislature.

Gullett (1971: 72–3) credits A.C. Cogswell as being the prime mover behind this act as well, but by this time, he appears to have acquired some powerful allies. The 1891 bill "to incorporate the Dental Association of Nova Scotia," although a private bill, was introduced by the attorney general, and hence enjoyed government sponsorship. The bill was slightly amended in the assembly, but passed with little controversy (and no recorded debate). The amendments brought the proposed dental act in line with the earlier medical act, requiring that the board be partially appointed (instead of entirely elected as the original bill proposed), and requiring lieutenant governor approval for board regulations (Nova Scotia Archives 1891). The legislative council agreed to the bill without amendments. The act itself had some clauses that resembled the Ontario and Quebec acts, but was also similar to the Nova Scotia medical act. It incorporated "The Dental Association of the Province of Nova Scotia" (similarly to Quebec's legislation). It named thirty-one dentists as association trustees; they were based in towns and cities throughout the province. At the time, this must have reflected the majority of practitioners in the province: Gullett (1971) claimed there were forty dentists in the province in 1889. The act also established a provincial dental board to regulate the profession, the association, and especially entry to practice (Nova Scotia 1891). It appears that by 1891, the profession's standing and its claims that formal education was necessary for effective practice were on firmer ground. Similarly, the endorsement of dentists throughout the province countered earlier fears that dental regulation would be detrimental to the countryside.

In the few years that followed, dentists requested minor revisions to their acts (largely housekeeping considerations that would improve the functioning and expand the powers of the regulatory board), and these passed with little debate or controversy. By 1900, dentistry was one of only four self-regulating professions in Nova Scotia.

As in Nova Scotia, the regulation of dentistry in British Columbia may owe much to the efforts of a single dentist in the region, at least according to dental historians (Gullett 1971: 70). Thomas Joseph Jones was an Ontario-born dentist, who was trained in Ontario and practised in that province for twenty years. He even had served a term as president of the Ontario Dental Association. In 1884 he moved to British Columbia, settling in Victoria, and shortly thereafter pushed for regulatory legislation (Gullett 1971). However, requests for a dental act predated Jones's arrival in the province. The first bill was presented in 1883, and was rejected before it could even be read a second time.[13] Jones may have played a role behind the scenes in bringing about the next attempt in 1886. Nevertheless, the 1886 bill was preceded by a series of petitions requesting that "persons practising dentistry be required to pass examination" (*Victoria Daily Colonist* 1886f: 3). In total, eight different MLAs presented petitions supporting such legislation. The presence of petitions suggests that there was some organization within dentistry, or at least a group of people mobilizing support for the bill, but dentists were not formally organized in the province at the time.[14] The British Columbia Dental Association was not established until 1891 (with Jones as organizer and president).

The act was presented by merchant MLA John Grant. There were no MDs in the BC legislature at this time, and very few lawyers. The majority of MLAs were merchants and businessmen. In presenting the bill, Grant emphasized that it was "liberal" and "what it asked for was not unreasonable" (*Victoria Daily Colonist* 1886e: 3). Anyone with a diploma from any dental college in Canada or elsewhere in the world could obtain a licence. Grant assured his colleagues that dentistry was already regulated in many Canadian provinces, in the United States, and in several European countries. There was general support for the bill. MLAs argued that it guaranteed "to the public a certain measure of security that none but competent dentists would be allowed to practice" (ibid.). The Honourable John Robson claimed that "medicine and law and dentistry were the three professions that came first in necessity on behalf of the public" (ibid.). The little recorded opposition pertained to specific provisions only: for instance, one MLA feared that the government would have to bear the costs of paying the examiners, given the wording in the original bill. Minor amendments were made to the act when the house was in committee, and it passed easily in March 1886 (British Columbia 1886c). Thus, while their counterparts in Nova Scotia had debated the necessity of training for dentists fifteen years previously, BC MLAs in 1886 did not question dentists' expertise, or whether regulation would benefit the public.

The 1886 act, however, did not establish dentistry as a fully self-regulating profession. It simply established a board of examiners to review diplomas, credentials, and examine candidates for entry to practice, and made it a crime to practise dentistry without a licence (British Columbia 1886a). The author of the bill – it is not clear who this was – must have had a good understanding of the mood of the house, since this very limited bill passed without controversy, during the same session that such intense debate surrounded legislation pertaining to the profession of law (and to a lesser extent medicine) touched on in chapter 3.

BC dentists sought an expansion of their regulatory privileges in the mid-1890s, successfully expanding their self-regulatory powers around entry to study and entry to practice with legislation in 1895 – although the profession did not get everything it asked for at this time (British Columbia 1895; *Victoria Daily Colonist* 1895b: 6). A bill to alter the profession's entry requirements by allowing those trained outside the province to practice without fulfilling a residency requirement (counter to the profession's wishes) was introduced by an MLA in 1899, but it failed to pass as well (British Columbia 1899; *Victoria Daily Colonist* 1899: 5). It was not until 1908 that the profession requested and achieved status as a self-regulating profession. Debate about this latter bill focused not on self-regulation for dentistry, but on measures in the bill that appeared to be directed at a private dental company that was providing dental services. Many protested that companies could not provide dental services (only licensed individuals could), while critics protested that the government had no right to legislate against a private business. This debate is informative in its depiction of dentistry (as legislators saw it) at the time:

> The practice of the dental profession involved special qualifications and personal ability, and should never be permitted under the guise of a company with limited responsibility. The very idea of such a thing was offensive to the sense of propriety. It was absurd to speak of dentists as mere mechanics, for, as a matter of fact, dentists should be men of high professional ability. (*Victoria Daily Colonist* 1908: 2)

The majority opinion seemed to hold that the owner of the company could practise dentistry legally himself, but to employ non-dentists to do work under his general direction was against the law. The bill passed in short order. From 1908 on, dentists had a "College of Dental Surgeons of British Columbia" that was granted fairly extensive powers to regulate itself and the profession more broadly in the province (British Columbia 1908).

This look at the regulation of dentistry across the provinces highlights several considerations. First, it is clear that dentists' motivation for seeking regulation was to eliminate their less-trained competitors, but as with medicine, legislators were active participants in the regulatory process, and passed legislation when they felt there was some legitimate grounds for it. Second, support (or in the case of British Columbia a lack of opposition from) the medical profession was quite influential in dentists' efforts to win regulatory legislation and the privileges of self-regulation. In Nova Scotia, this support was not initially sufficient, however, to counter legislators' concerns. Third, it is evident that other social ties were also frequently important. Dentists' social and political connections were particularly important in Ontario, but also appear to have been relevant in Quebec, and were at least mentioned in Nova Scotia (where supporters in 1870 commented that they were impressive gentlemen). In several instances, their legislation was guided through the house by MD MLAs. Fourth, organization was clearly important. It was in those locales where dentistry was best organized – Ontario and Quebec – that the profession succeeded in winning sweeping legislation, in short order. At the same time, it is not clear that it was the sustained campaigns of these organizations that won them legislation, but rather their short-term mobilization of political resources. Organization may have been important to the extent that it demonstrated professional unity and shared goals. Notably, it was only once province-wide unity was demonstrated in Nova Scotia that the dental act was finally passed. Fifth, claims to competence, and successfully establishing the link between training and competence, was important in shaping legislators' opinions. Ontario, Quebec, and BC legislators appeared to need little convincing that trained dentists were safer practitioners than the untrained, but several Nova Scotian legislators disagreed – arguing that formal education and training had no connection to competence at all. Last, a look at interprovincial differences highlights the importance of the "mood" of the legislature when regulatory requests are made by professions. Some legislatures were more open, at certain points in time, to the claims made by dental leaders than were others.

Land Surveying

Often overlooked in studies of professions, even in Canada, land surveying is one of the oldest regulated professions in the country, dating back to Canada's early colonial days. It was particularly important in the settlement of New France (Quebec) and Upper Canada / Ontario. In New France surveyors helped to lay out property borders. In the late eighteenth century, once it acquired the colony, Britain commissioned land surveyors to survey and map the land, and to divide it into plots, which were sold, given away as rewards for loyalty or service, granted to the church, or kept in the hands of the state. In many regions, surveyors predated settlement, laying out entire regions and townships in grid-like patterns – establishing order and structure in the countryside. Writing of Ontario, surveyor historian John Ladell (1993: 9) explains:

> It was land surveyors acting for the Crown who laid out the first townships in the province, and it was crown surveyors who eventually carpeted virtually all of Ontario south of the French River, and much of northern Ontario, with a mosaic of roughly rectangular townships ... Dispatched into what was often wilderness unseen by any European, the surveyor was the first to examine the land in detail, noting its quality and its suitability or otherwise for settlement. Where the land seemed good, they laid out – on the instructions of their political masters – the first townships and then subdivided these into the lots that the early settlers took up. In many cases the surveyor selected the location for a future town.

Surveyors helped to establish roads, provincial and national boundaries, canals, and Aboriginal reserves. To a new and growing colony carved out of the wilderness by colonial powers, they were invaluable.

Land surveying in the seventeenth and eighteenth century required a rare mix of talents: land surveyors had to be literate, numerate, and ideally possess a talent for drawing, or at least a steady hand. Further, they had to be familiar with the tools of their trade. To do their work they had to travel to the region to be surveyed, and walk and learn the land, often working under extremely difficult conditions. In New France and early Quebec, there were few men with these talents who could afford to spend the (sometimes lengthy) time required to survey an area, away from their homes, farms, or businesses. Thus, many early land surveyors were also notaries and sometimes architects, as Vachon (1962) recounts for the mid-to-late seventeenth century. Given the low literacy levels in New France at the time, literate men were called on to fulfil many roles.

It was after the British took over that land surveying in the colonies expanded. In 1785, the legislative council passed "An Ordnance Concerning Land Surveyors and the Admeasurement of Lands," which provided instructions for the conduct of surveys, and required surveyors to keep field books, make plans, and register these with the surveyor general of the colony. The surveyor general was a high-ranking member of the government who supervised surveys and commissioned surveyors (called deputy land surveyors). Under the law, surveyors would be appointed by the government, and before taking up their duties they were required to undergo examination and provide an oath of allegiance before the surveyor general. A list of qualified surveyors was to be kept (Ladell 1993: 73–5).

Surveying was considered crucial in the new colony, as Britain sought to establish British settlers in Canada. After the American Revolution tens of thousands of Loyalists moved north to the British colonies. Families and officers who had demonstrated loyalty to the Crown were promised land (Ladell 1993: 78). At the time, the region that became Ontario was sparsely settled by Europeans. To prepare for the Loyalists, colonial authorities sent out deputy surveyors to survey the land, divide it into townships and plots, and then map them for the authorities and new settlers alike. When the Canadian colony was divided, and Upper Canada became a separate province in 1791, land surveying was deemed a priority by the new lieutenant governor John Graves Simcoe (ibid.: 88–9). Simcoe believed the post of surveyor required "great professional abilities and equal integrity" (ibid.: 89). It was crucial that land surveys be accurate, and that land surveyors be skilled and trustworthy.

Although plans had not initially been made to establish a post of surveyor general, Simcoe believed he could not proceed without one (Ladell 1993). To fulfil his goal of establishing Upper Canada as a British colony, and defending the land against potential American encroachment, it needed to be settled by loyal subjects, the sooner the better. Upper Canada's first (official) surveyor general was D.W. Smith, who in conjunction with the lieutenant governor established the pattern of settlement for the colony, and created plans and processes for the deputy land surveyors to follow. Some land was marked for sale, but other plots were reserved for the clergy and the Crown. For the latter groups land would be a source of revenue, and for the government, patronage (Gidney and Millar 1994). Land was granted "to leading officials and deserving citizens as a reward for services rendered" (Ladell 1993: 93). Indeed, Simcoe hoped, through such land grants, to establish a landed aristocracy for the colony. Government officials were able to become land-rich. Some surveyors benefited as well. Although land surveying did not pay much, and the pay was not regular, some land surveyors took their pay in land (a certain percentage of all they had surveyed), and thereby became well-to-do.

A new ordinance respecting land surveying was passed in 1798. In the earliest years in Upper Canada, then, surveys were conducted according to the 1785 ordinance, under which surveyors were examined by the surveyor general. At first these examinations appear to have been cursory and superficial, but under Simcoe they became more challenging field exams (Ladell 1993: 94). The 1798 ordinance pertained predominantly to the conduct of land surveys, regulating how land surveyors did their work. Entry to practice remained by commission or appointment, examination, and oath. The number of surveyors so employed was small: only fourteen were identified in 1805 (ibid.: 108). It would be 1818 before new legislation regulating land surveyors was established: at this time entry requirements were raised. Regulation remained in the hands of the government. Candidates would be examined by the surveyor general (or deputy surveyor general) concerning their "knowledge of the theory and practice of surveying" (ibid.: 118). To obtain a licence, they would further have to give an oath, and post "two sureties for £500" (ibid.). Their assistants would also have to pass an oath.[15]

A minor, but meaningful, act affecting surveyors was passed in 1841. This act made it illegal for anyone "to hinder or molest any land surveyor carrying out his lawful duties" (Canada 1841; Ladell 1993: 138). Further, the act enabled land surveyors to administer oaths to people providing information about boundaries or lost markers. This legislation extended the authority of the land surveyor – as an agent of the government and the Crown – to conduct his work. A few years following, a new land surveyors' act was passed in the united colony of Canada, which would pertain to surveyors working in both Lower and Upper Canada. The 1849 act established a clear penalty for illegal practice. No one was allowed to survey lands "for hire or profit within Upper Canada or Lower Canada, or act in any ways as a Land Surveyor within either portion of this Province, for hire or profit, unless he shall be duly authorized to practice as a Land Surveyor according to the provisions of this act" (Canada 1849b, s. ii). To practise as a land surveyor, one needed to be at least twenty-one years of age, and have a specified preliminary education which included geometry, knowledge of Euclid, trigonometry, map drawing, astronomy, and other subjects. Further, he had to have served for three years as an apprentice to a licensed land surveyor (ibid., s. iii). After the apprenticeship, prospective land surveyors had to be publicly examined by a board of examiners consisting of the commissioner of Crown lands (who had replaced the surveyor general), and "6 other competent persons to be appointed from time to time by the Governor, Lieutenant-Governor, or Person administering the Government of this Province" (s. iv). Finally, candidates had to provide a certificate attesting to their "character for probity and sobriety," and testify under oath regarding their practice and instruments (s. iv), as well as provide a bond with two sureties (£ 250), and swear an oath of office (s. ix). The act also affirmed the provision that no one could interfere with surveyors' work. Moreover, it empowered the board of examiners to suspend or remove a surveyor if they found him "guilty of gross negligence or corruption in the execution of the duties of his office" (s. x). In 1852, this act was revised to establish separate examining boards for each province (Ladell 1993: 156).

Thus, in the mid-nineteenth century, land surveying became one of the earliest regulated – but not self-regulating – professions in Canada. The year 1849 marked the year that law acquired status as a self-regulating profession in Quebec, and was merely two years after powers of self-regulation were granted to medical doctors and notaries. At this time, land surveyors had a board of examiners, but this was not elected; it was appointed by the government. In this manner the regulation of land surveying was similar to the regulation of medicine in Upper Canada at the time, with two notable exceptions. First, an important government official, the commissioner of Crown lands, played a key role. Second, land surveyors' regulatory legislation contained more stringent discipline provisions than most other professions, and more assurances of "good behaviour" – testimonies as to character, an oath, a bond, and questioning under oath. This profession would be more government controlled than its counterparts. The regulation of medical doctors, notaries, and lawyers was often justified as being in the public interest, and necessary to protect consumers. The main consumer of land surveyors' services was the state. It appears that state actors were unwilling to devolve powers of self-regulation upon them, but rather sought to regulate them more directly. At the same time, it is important to note that land surveyors were not numerous, they tended to work in isolation, and they do not appear to have been organized. While Quebec lawyers, notaries, and medical doctors demanded the right of self-regulation, it is not clear that similar requests were advanced by land surveyors.

In the 1850s, regulatory legislation was altered again to raise entry standards, to clarify that there was to be a preliminary exam prior to apprenticeship, and to increase the difficulty of this exam. The apprenticeship was reduced in length for those with Canadian university training in engineering and/or land surveying. Land surveyors, henceforth, would be required to be well educated (Gidney and Millar 1994).

At the time of Confederation, then, land surveying was regulated in Ontario and Quebec, but not in Nova Scotia. Under the British North America Act, property was the jurisdiction of the provinces, and hence land surveying continued to be regulated at the provincial level (Surveyor General 1936). Nonetheless, shortly after Confederation the government of Canada purchased the Northwest Territories from the Hudson's Bay Company, and desired to have these lands surveyed (ibid.). At first the government employed provincial land surveyors (from Ontario and Quebec) to survey the land "because no others were available"; however, in 1872, they determined they needed to have "better control over the Surveyors of Dominion lands" and so they created "Dominion Land Surveyors and a Board of Examiners for their admission" (ibid.). At this time, all provincial land surveyors were automatically appointed dominion land surveyors. This system of reciprocity continued for several years, but "as each one was acting independently, grave abuses arose, and the arrangement was discontinued" (ibid.). Thus, for a time, dominion land surveyors were the only profession regulated on a federal level. As separate provinces were formed in the West, they established and regulated their own provincial land surveyors, eventually rendering dominion land surveyors unnecessary (ibid.).

In the decades following Confederation, land surveying changed significantly. By the mid-1880s virtually all of southern Ontario – the most inhabited part of the province – had already been surveyed (Ladell 1993: 181). The same was true for much of Quebec. Many surveyors were in private practice, occasionally winning an assignment from the provincial Department of Crown Lands, or working as dominion land surveyors in the Northwest Territories. Others took municipal or other local contracts. Very few "of the perhaps two hundred land surveyors [in Ontario] ... were now carrying out crown surveys in the bush" (ibid.). The typical land surveyor in the 1880s was an urban-dweller. Rather than being strictly provincial government employees, they looked elsewhere (even if just to the federal and municipal government levels) for work, turning their focus to drainage, waterworks, and other related enterprises. Many had training in engineering, and did the work of civil engineers. It was in this new context that provincial land surveyors began to identify common interests, organize, and seek legislative change.

Dominion land surveyors working in Manitoba were the first to do so (Association of Canada Lands Surveyors 1999). They formed a society in the mid-1870s, and in 1881 successfully won incorporation and self-regulation from Manitoba's provincial government. Regulation in Quebec followed soon after. Thomson (1967) credits one surveyor, C.E. Gauvin, for being the driving force behind professional advance. Gauvin wrote to the province's commissioner of Crown lands, Edmund James Flynn, recommending incorporation and self-regulation of land surveying, to establish "desirable standards of ability, conduct, and knowledge," and to weed out "parish surveyors" who were unofficial and untrained (ibid.: 67). Flynn was favourable, so Gauvin and his colleagues hired a lawyer to prepare legislation and petitioned the legislature for an act "to incorporate The Land Surveyors of the Province of Quebec" in 1881 (Thomson 1967; Quebec 1881). The commissioner of Crown lands presented the bill, and it was referred to the Committee on Miscellaneous Private Bills; however, that committee reported that the bill should be treated as a public one, just like legislation regulating lawyers and medical doctors (Quebec 1881). After this, the bill simply disappears (ibid.). In 1882, the commissioner of Crown lands returned with a public bill to regulate Quebec land surveyors. The bill was amended by the assembly, but passed with little controversy in the month of May.

Under the act, the Incorporated Land Surveyors of the Province of Quebec were granted the right to regulate for the "government, discipline and honor of its members" (Quebec 1882, s. 2). The organization was granted the power to regulate itself, registration fees, association elections, property, entry-to-study, entry-to-practice, and even the right to establish a fee schedule for employers other than the government. From the beginning they were granted full disciplinary provisions allowing them to deny certificates, conduct investigations, hold hearings, summon witnesses, administer oaths, and so on (ibid., s. 14, 20–7). Practice was closed, but everyone currently in practice was entitled to registration without examination. Surveyors would not be employed by the government if they were not up-to-date on their dues (Casgrain in Ladell 1993: 198).

Although there had been some initial discussions about forming a similar organization in Ontario, nothing came to pass until 1886, when a surveyor named Willis Chipman rallied prominent surveyors to the cause, and brought them all together at a meeting in Toronto (held in the parliament building) to discuss the formation of a society (Ladell 1993; Thomson 1967). The initial meeting was fairly well attended, and most (but not all) present were in favour of such an association, which they promptly formed. Through association the members hoped to share knowledge, as well as raise their status to that of their contemporaries in other professions who had experienced advances in education and standing in recent years (Ladell 1993: 191; Gidney and Millar 1994). Some were keen to seek legislative advance and incorporation, but others were reluctant, so land surveyors decided to proceed slowly. Right from the first, however, it is clear that some surveyors saw the association as a medium through which they could influence government policy. A legislative committee was formed immediately, and the minutes of the initial meeting are replete with references to the positive impact such an association could have on government policy (Ladell 1993). Association leaders felt that self-regulation was a goal towards which they would strive, but that it was best not to request it too soon. In the words of the association co-founder and secretary Willis Chipman: "We must first become a united body, and be able to present our request to the Legislature so intelligently, so justly, and so forcibly, that they cannot do otherwise than comply" (in Ladell 1993: 187).

It would be several years before Ontario land surveyors would seek incorporation and self-regulatory status, but it does appear that they soon influenced government policy. In 1887 members of the Association of Provincial Land Surveyors of Ontario were consulted by, and worked closely with, the commissioner of Crown lands (then Timothy Blair Pardee) to redraw the Act respecting Land Surveyors and the Survey of Lands (Ladell 1993: 192).

In 1890 the association began to speak of incorporation in response to "growing dissatisfaction" with unqualified people doing work in the field. In 1891, association members discussed self-regulation in earnest, but some had reservations. A few members were uneasy with the idea that all land surveyors would be forced to join the organization, but many were in favour of incorporation. One prominent surveyor in the provincial Department of Crown Lands indicated that he thought the government would be supportive of self-regulation because it would relieve them of the annual expense ($400) of running the board of examiners (Ladell 1993: 198). The association resolved to seek incorporation, and shortly thereafter met with the commissioner of Crown lands – future premier A.S. Hardy – to discuss the matter (ibid.: 199). In preparing the draft bill, association members hired a lawyer, and worked with him and Hardy to produce a measure satisfactory to all. The commissioner himself introduced the bill in the 1892 parliamentary session.

The "Act to incorporate the Association of Ontario Land Surveyors and to amend the Act respecting Land Surveyors and the Survey of Land" incorporated the provincial association and established it as the regulatory body for the profession (Ontario 1892). A council of the association was formed, consisting of the commissioner of Crown lands, two men appointed by him, and six others elected by the profession. The council was empowered to regulate the association, entry to practice and entry to study, and was given disciplinary powers similar to the Quebec association's (ibid.). An earlier draft of the bill contained a clause concerning the regulation of fees, similar to Quebec's, but the association was advised that Ontario legislators would object to such a clause, so they removed it (Ladell 1993: 204). In other respects the Ontario and Quebec acts were quite similar.

Thus, while land surveying had been regulated in Quebec and Ontario since the eighteenth century, practitioners did not seek or achieve self-regulation until late in the nineteenth century. By 1900, however, they possessed regulatory powers that placed them alongside lawyers, medical doctors, and dentists. Regulation of land surveying in British Columbia developed around the same time.

As in Ontario, land surveyors were active in British Columbia from the colonies' earliest days. The position of "surveyor general" was first established on Vancouver Island in 1851 (Association of British Columbia Land Surveyors 2015). Additional surveyors were commissioned as necessary, as the colonies on the island and the mainland grew. It was first the surveyor general, and then the chief commissioner of lands and works, who appointed land surveyors in the province up to the early 1890s (ibid.). In 1886 the BC legislature passed legislation pertaining to the conduct of surveys in the province, but it did not formally regulate land surveyors. Here, as in colonial Canada, land surveyors were commissioned by the government. There were no formal criteria for entry to practice; the province hired those men already certified as dominion land surveyors (since 1872), and others deemed capable.

In 1890 a group of BC land surveyors met and formed the Association of Provincial Land Surveyors (Thomson 1967). They resolved to petition the legislature for legislation to establish qualifications for entry to practice and "prevent unqualified persons [from] acting as surveyors" (ibid.: 74). In 1891, the commissioner of lands and works, Forbes George

Vernon introduced a bill, and the "Act respecting Land Surveyors" passed a few months later. Like its predecessors in Upper and Lower Canada in the mid-nineteenth century, the act established a board of examiners consisting of the surveyor general and five land surveyors appointed by the lieutenant governor. The board could examine candidates, grant commissions, and administer oaths. This act, though, also contained disciplinary provisions: the board of examiners could suspend surveyors deemed guilty of "gross negligence or corruption," and it was empowered to hold hearings and gather evidence in the conduct of its duties (British Columbia 1891, s. x). Current dominion or provincial land surveyors with credentials from other provinces were eligible to practice. Here, as in early Ontario and Quebec, leading surveyors worked closely with the government (specifically the commissioner of lands) – the main employer of land surveyors – to bring about regulation.

Full self-regulation for BC land surveyors came in 1905 when legislation was passed to establish and incorporate the "Corporation of Land Surveyors of the Province of British Columbia." It is not entirely clear that the land surveyors' association was formally behind the bill, as it was not mentioned in reports on the legislation, and Thomson (1967) reports that the association had become dormant. This legislation may have been the result of discussion between members of the board of examiners and the commissioner of lands and works. The 1905 legislation established the regulatory body and a board of examiners (the first would be appointed by the government, but subsequent examiners would be chosen by the profession). The association was given powers similar to those granted in Ontario and Quebec. The act also raised standards for education and entry to practice, and restricted practice to British citizens. It is telling that newspaper reports on the bill stressed that it would "relieve the government of responsibility in connection with the examination of surveyors" (*Victoria Daily Colonist* 1905: 8). Thus, as in Ontario, self-regulation was lauded as a cost savings for the government. By 1905, the land surveying profession was on a similar footing to its counterparts in Ontario and Quebec.

It was not until the twentieth century that land surveying was regulated in Nova Scotia. Nova Scotia was an older colony with different settlement patterns (and less land), and land surveyors do not seem to have played as pivotal a role in the colony's early history. Certainly, the Nova Scotia government employed land surveyors, and in 1881 they affirmed that dominion land surveyors could work in the province. The province seemed to feel no need to establish criteria for provincial surveyors in the nineteenth century. In 1910 the government introduced a bill to regulate land surveyors. In presenting the bill, Attorney General Alexander MacLean explained that the "system of surveying which has obtained in Nova Scotia in past years has not been satisfactory, and the greatest uncertainty and confusion prevail[ed]," largely due to "incompetent surveyors" producing "inaccurate surveys" (Nova Scotia 1910: 147). Incompetence stemmed from the fact that Nova Scotia was the only Canadian province not regulating surveyors, he claimed. Although the bill appears to have been the attorney general's project, he read a letter supporting land surveying regulation from Hiram Donkin, the Deputy Commissioner of Works and Mines (ibid.: 148). The establishment of land surveying, then, was a government initiative aimed at establishing more accuracy in surveys, and raising the quality and trustworthiness of land surveyors in the province. If land surveyors themselves encouraged the legislative development, they were not mentioned in legislative debates. The act itself followed the pattern of initial regulation in British Columbia, Ontario, and Quebec, in establishing a board of examiners. Nova Scotia's board, though, had few regulatory powers. Instead, power to determine entry requirements resided with the governor, who appointed the board (presumably the governor would consult with practitioners on these issues). It was not until 1959 that the profession became self-regulating in Nova Scotia.

Reflecting on these histories, it is clear that land surveying is both similar to, and different from, other regulated professions. Historically, land surveying was state regulated and land surveyors were directly employed by the state – unlike their counterparts in most other professions (many of whom were self-employed). It was primarily once land surveyors were less crucial to state projects, and more often employed by others, that they developed a separate professional identity, formed organizations, and sought self-regulation. Nonetheless, not all land surveyors were organized when they won self-regulation. Like other professions, land surveyors' professional projects were aided by state contacts. Their close ties with the commissioner of Crown lands and his department provided a crucial ally when pursuing regulatory legislation. State actors supported their regulation. Further, they recognized land surveyors' claims to expertise and integrity, since surveyors had been regulated from colonial times. Some professional groups had to prove that trained practitioners were more competent than the untrained, but this was not the case in land surveying. Thus, the regulation of land surveying was clearly shaped by the profession's relationships with state actors, which varied across province and era.

Discussion

In chapter 1, I argued that to understand professionalization and professional regulation one needed to consider both professional leaders' activities (including social closure and collective mobility projects) and state actors' decision making. These case studies of medicine, dentistry, and land surveying in four Canadian provinces provide the opportunity to do this. While variations are evident across profession, province, and era, the case studies reveal several commonalities that provide considerable insight into processes of profession creation in late-nineteenth-century Canada.

Looking at occupational groups' activities to create professions highlights the significance of social closure, and reveals the strategies pursed by occupational leaders seeking regulatory change. In each of medicine, dentistry, and land surveying, there is evidence that occupational leaders professionalized to secure their position in their market, and to reduce the competition they faced from less-trained practitioners. Leaders in these groups also attempted to increase their status, their opportunities, and their rewards. Thus, the pursuit of regulatory legislation was part of social closure projects, as many have claimed (Murphy 1988; Witz 1992; Saks 2010). Further, there is some evidence that to achieve their goals, professional leaders used some collective mobility strategies. Many did organize, and endeavoured to win the support of state actors. Other research (not presented here) shows that medical doctors and dentists in particular carried out sustained campaigns, mobilizing a variety of resources to win over the public (Adams 2000; Gidney and Millar 1994; Bernier 1989; Larson 1977; Starr 1982).

However, the actual winning of professional self-regulation in the nineteenth century, in most cases, did not require a sustained campaign. Not all the professions were provincially organized when they sought regulatory legislation. Those that were sometimes organized only immediately before they pursued regulation (within a year). In fact, for most, the goal of organizing was primarily to obtain regulatory legislation. Organization seems to have been important less for resource mobilization than because it provided state actors with evidence of shared professional interests and unity. When practitioners from across a province stood behind a bill, then legislators were more likely to support it.

They were unwilling to indulge one group of practitioners at the expense of others. Further, except for dentistry in Nova Scotia, regulatory legislation was granted usually at the first request, and if not, then at the second. Professional leaders drew on political and social resources, and these alone seemed to be sufficient to win, and subsequently to defend, professional self-regulation for these groups. All the groups studied here had connections with state actors and/or MLAs, or they forged such connections to achieve their legislative goals.

The sociological literature on the state's role in profession creation alternatively casts state actors as passive recipients of and responders to aspiring professionals' requests, or purposive planners seeking to establish professions to achieve state or political goals. As the case studies show, in nineteenth-century Canada, the reality lay between these extremes. In most instances, state actors regulated professions only after they received a request to do so. Thus, state actors were often reactive, rather than proactive. This said, there were times when the impetus for regulation came from state actors, most often from professionals serving in the legislature, or from state leaders who felt they had something to gain (as in the regulation of land surveying in early Ontario). Further, legislators were far from passive in this process. Take, for example, the regulation of medicine in Ontario. The legislation medical doctors received in 1869 was significantly different from what they requested. State actors actively debated, critiqued, and altered professional legislation. It was frequently (but not always) contentious. State actors occasionally voiced an interest in self-regulation over the alternative of state regulation because it was cheaper, and did not require state resources. In passing legislation, state actors believed they were serving the public interest, and providing a benefit to society.

Nevertheless, it is not always clear that in regulating professions in the nineteenth century, state actors were trying to marshal expertise in service to the state (as Halliday 1987 suggests), or pursue political goals (following Abbott 2005). The exception is land surveying, where state leaders clearly saw land surveyors as possessing expertise that would benefit the state, enabling leaders to achieve their goals for the colonies (especially in Ontario). In line with Foucauldian explanations of governmentality, land surveyors may have served state actors by providing them information about the land, thereby enhancing their ability to govern (see Scott 1998: 44–51). This led to a highly state-directed mode of regulation and state employment. It was only once these principal aims had been achieved, and state actors needed them less, that land surveying was established as an independent self-regulating profession. There is no evidence that state actors sought to draw on dentists' knowledge at all. Nor is there strong evidence to support such an argument for medicine. Canadian legislators were committed to regulating a range of medical practitioners each with their own knowledge bases, and distinct claims to expertise. Legislators had little interest in using medical expertise when they first regulated the profession (except perhaps in times of epidemics and war). They simply sought to pass legislation that distinguished the trained from the untrained. It was not until the 1880s and 1890s that state actors began to draw on medical expertise, as they implemented several public health initiatives. At this point, in most provinces, medicine had been self-regulating for quite some time. Indeed, contrasting the experiences of medicine and land surveying suggest that it may have been precisely because state actors did not see medical expertise as being in service to the state that they were willing to grant it status as an autonomous, self-regulating profession.

Abbott (2005) has argued that we should see the state and professions as linked ecologies. Further, he has suggested that regulatory outcomes are shaped by the confluence of professional interests with state interests. These case studies suggest that in nineteenth-century Canada – at least in three of the four provinces considered here – the state and professions are best seen as not simply linked ecologies, but overlapping ecologies. Roughly 30 to 40 per cent of MLAs in Ontario and Nova Scotia were professionals; the percentage approached 60 per cent in Quebec. British Columbia was the only province with 20 per cent of MLAs (or less) trained in a regulated profession (law). At times, professionals were able to influence regulatory outcomes from inside the legislature. This is clearest in medicine, where MD MLAs advised their professional colleagues about legislation, introduced bills in the legislature, and worked within committees and on the house floor to advance legislation in their profession's favour, and undermine legislation against their interests. MD MLAs also supported dentists' legislation in several of the provinces (as did lawyers in many cases). While land surveyors do not appear to have benefited from having practitioner-MLAs, their close relationship with the office of the Commissioner of Crown Lands ensured that regulatory legislation was introduced by a leading member of government, with the full support of the government. These connections, and overlapping membership in both the professions and state ecologies, may help explain why so many of the requests advanced by professions in this era succeeded (with a few exceptions, like dentistry in Nova Scotia), and the few challenges to professional power failed. In this context of overlapping ecologies, the boundary between political goals and professional goals can become blurred.

As I argued in chapter 3, when they regulated professions, state actors were giving privileges to people like themselves – in terms of class background, educational background, gender, and race. Professional leaders and state actors shared similar world views, and similar political and social goals. Professional leaders were active not only in provincial legislatures, but at the community and municipal level as well. Through their professional activity, and their other various social and political roles, they were social leaders within their communities. Professional regulation both acknowledged these roles and reaffirmed them. In this manner, the regulation of professional groups may have contributed to social order and social support, as Streeck and Schmitter (1985) and others have claimed. Who aspiring professionals were, whom they knew, and how they were educated were often more important than (or at least as important as) their expertise in shaping regulatory outcomes. Legislators were willing to regulate for learned men, and even to protect learned men from untrained/unscrupulous men. Although professional legislation distinguished the trained from the untrained, except for land surveying, legislators demonstrated little interest in exactly what professionals did, or how they did it.

Before concluding this chapter, it is important to consider interprovincial differences in regulation. Political historians have revealed the presence of distinct political cultures across Canada, and these differences contributed to interprovincial variations in regulatory patterns. For instance, Ontario has been depicted as a province convinced of its "pre-eminence" in the country; this encourages it to be a trail blazer in some legislative areas (Wiseman 2007: 118). In its regulation of medicine and dentistry the province was certainly innovative, regulating dentistry before any other region in North America, and uniting all medical branches in one college. In contrast, Nova Scotia has tended to be more conservative and cautious; its regulation is shaped by local concerns and tradition (ibid.: 151). The legislature has been dominated by a conservative upper-class elite of businessmen and lawyers (Beck 1978: 179). This conservatism might be seen in the fact that Nova Scotia was the last of the provinces examined here to regulate dentistry and land surveying (at times by a significant margin), and its regulation of medicine at first followed the US pattern more than that common in other provinces. Further, the concern with locality comes through in legislative debates.

British Columbia has a raucous political culture characterized by polarities and heated debate (Wiseman 2007; Robin 1978). This political culture is evident in the content of debates, and may also capture the polarity in professional regulation, where the province was both willing to follow other provinces' lead in this era but still chart its own path. While in other provinces, professionals were well represented in parliament, in British Columbia, in addition to several lawyers, legislators were predominantly "acquisitive merchants … industrial and landed proprietors, whose wealth derived chiefly from investment in land, transportation, mines, lumbering, salmon canneries and flour mills" (Robin 1978: 41). Their participation brought a distinct, brash character to legislative debates, and ensured distinct traditions of regulation (Robin 1978).[16] In the late nineteenth century it also encouraged localism, where legislators promoted local and private interests over broader interests (ibid.: 42). Here, ambivalence surrounding professional regulation was strong.

In contrast, the Quebec legislature was more willing to establish self-regulating professions in a variety of fields and did so earlier than others. Quebec, historically, has combined "French culture" with British institutions (Massicotte 1989; Wiseman 2007), and this has profoundly shaped the emergence of professions, as well as the involvement of professionals in government, as we saw in chapter 2. The links between professionals and legislators may have been particularly strong here in the nineteenth century, given low literacy and education rates: MLAs were disproportionately professionals and merchants who were more highly educated than the vast majority of Québécois (Massicotte 1989; Wiseman 2007). These individuals appear to have a shared vision of Quebec society and social life that encouraged the formation of autonomous, self-regulating professions, and gave leaders the power to govern not only themselves but their fields of endeavour.

These differences, however, are of degree only. Wiseman (2007) argues that Canada as a whole has been characterized by a political culture that is more concerned with groups and group rights, than its American counterparts, who tend to focus on individuals and individual rights. This propensity to be concerned with groups – with classes of people – may be reflected in the extent to which Canadian provinces regulated professions in the nineteenth century, and how they regulated them.

Thus, Canada regulated more professions, earlier, than many other regions in the world. While some countries merely established criteria for entry to practice (a diploma) and encouraged individuals to meet a set standard, Canadian provinces tended to incorporate professional bodies, thereby uniting all practitioners together under an elected board of practitioners, who had at times extensive powers of governance, and the power to shape entry to study, entry to practice, and practice itself.

Chapter Five

The Expansion and Alteration of Professional Self-Regulation, 1900–1930s

In 1904, Canadian prime minister Wilfrid Laurier famously declared, "The twentieth century shall be the century of Canada and of Canadian development. For the next seventy-five years, nay for the next hundred years, Canada shall be the star towards which all men who love progress and freedom shall come" (Granatstein et al. 1990: 102; Morton 2001). With this statement, Laurier both captured the optimism and prosperity that pervaded Canada at the turn of the twentieth century and encapsulated his political agenda, geared towards business development, "freer" trade, immigration and settlement of Canada's west, and economic prosperity. Laurier would establish new provinces, carving Alberta and Saskatchewan out of the Northwest Territories, and encourage the immigration of Europeans to farm the land. The country would also witness considerable internal migration, as Canadians based in central and eastern Canada, especially Ontario, moved west. Further, rural Canadians moved to urban centres; accordingly, Canadian cities experienced significant growth, especially in the West, where Vancouver grew by 271 per cent between 1901 and 1911 alone.[1] In this era of progress, there was considerable investment in infrastructure – railroads, roads, public works, utilities (Granatstein et al. 1990; Barman 1991). There was also investment in schooling, seen as more important than ever in a thriving economy in which non-British immigrants would be encouraged to learn British customs (Granatstein et al. 1990). Statistics and "scientific facts" calculated by the government, aided by experts, were used to demonstrate Canada's "scientific progress" towards prosperity.

With rising demand for schooling, utilities, roads, and other infrastructure – all areas of provincial responsibility under the British North America Act – the size of the civil service increased: "New departments, bureaus, and branches of provincial administration multiplied as the provinces tried to cope with growing demands for public services" (Granatstein et al. 1990: 119). The expanding provincial state bureaucracy generated new jobs for clerks and a variety of other educated white-collar workers. The healthcare sector grew as well, creating new occupations and professions, and widening opportunities in established ones. Education expanded with the creation of new universities and new university programs (including professional programs); this was also an age of university reform (Barman 1991; Humphries 1985; Bell 2009).

Economic trends combined with changing gender roles to produce new opportunities for women in the opening decades of the twentieth century: nineteenth-century women workers found jobs in manufacturing and domestic service especially, but the twentieth century saw women employed in retail sales, teaching, and clerical work (Cohen 1988; Prentice et al. 1996). While prominent professions like medicine and law would remain male-dominated, women were slowly breaking down the barriers and entering these fields (Chunn and Brockman 2009; Hacker 1974; Kinnear 1995). Women also worked as nurses, and to a lesser extent in new health occupations. The opening decades of the twentieth century witnessed significant economic and social change that affected professions profoundly.

The landscape for professional regulation altered as well during this era. As provincial states expanded, governments' relationships with regulated professions began to change. All provinces regulated more professions in this era than in the nineteenth century, but how they did so, and how willing they were to delegate governance responsibilities to professions, varied. Nationally, there was rising public support for free trade, and many Canadians were opposed to market protections. For some, professions were "close corporations" that did not contribute to public well-being, but acted in professionals' own interests.[2] These sentiments put pressure on established professions to demonstrate their value to the public, and encouraged legislators to be cautious when granting professions regulatory powers. As new occupations pursued professional projects, they sometimes faced reluctant legislators, as well as opposition from established professions concerned that the upstarts were infringing on their rights and privileges. Provincial legislatures continued to spend a considerable amount of time debating and discussing professional regulation during this era, standardizing modes of professional regulation that were implemented on a more piecemeal basis during the nineteenth century.

This chapter explores these trends in professional self-regulation in Nova Scotia, Quebec, Ontario, and British Columbia from 1900 through the 1930s. As in chapter 3, I begin by outlining what was regulated, and how, across the four provinces during these four decades. Most of the growth in self-regulating professions occurred in the healthcare field, although professions in a cluster consisting of architecture, engineering, land surveying, and accounting increased as well. I explore how these professions were regulated, and what regulatory privileges they were granted. Next, I briefly consider the origins of professional regulatory legislation, arguing that, in this era, organized occupational groups instigated most regulatory activity, but that state actors and other groups also influenced regulatory outcomes. Subsequently, I look at the rationales provided, and debates surrounding, professional self-regulation. Here, I consider the regulation of high-status professions with more regulatory powers, and those which were granted fewer powers. Then, I provide evidence of emerging standardization in regulatory patterns, within each province, paying particular attention to Ontario, and that province's Hodgins commission. Last, I document broader participation in regulated professions by class and gender, and consider the implications for professional regulation. The overview provided in this chapter is complemented by a case study on the emergence of alternative health professions – and the role of state and professional actors in shaping regulatory outcomes – presented in chapter 6.

Overview of Regulation across Four Canadian Provinces

In 1900 the provinces of Nova Scotia, Quebec, Ontario, and British Columbia had between four and eight self-regulating professions each; law, medicine, dentistry, and pharmacy were regulated in all. Most of the provinces also regulated land surveying. Quebec and Ontario both regulated several additional professions. In the period between 1900 and 1940, the number of self-regulating professions established by statute more than doubled. By 1940, Quebec had sixteen self-regulating professions, while Ontario and British Columbia recognized fifteen and fourteen respectively. Nova Scotia continued to have fewer, but had experienced a substantial increase, counting twelve self-regulating professions in 1940. Table 5.1 provides a list of these self-regulating professions and the year in which they were granted powers of self-regulation by statute.[3] Those newly regulated during this era are highlighted (as are some of those regulated after 1940).

Table 5.1 Self-regulating professions in 1940, by date self-regulation achieved

Profession	Ontario	Quebec	Nova Scotia	British Columbia
Lawyers	1797	1849	1872	1874
Medical doctors	(1839)	1847	1872	1886
Notaries public	1869	1847		
Dentists	1868	1869	1891	1886
Pharmacists	1871	1870	1876	1891
Land surveyors	1892	1882	1910	1891
Architects	1890	1890	1932	1920
Chartered accountants	1882	1927	1913	1905
Engineers	1922	1898	1920	1918
Stenographic / shorthand reporters	1891			
Veterinary surgery	1920	1902	1913	1901
Optometrists (and opticians)	1919	1909	1921	1920
Nurses	1922	1920	1922	1918
Drugless practitioners	1925			(Naturopathy)
Osteopaths	(DP act)		(Med act 1921)	(Med act 1909)
Chiropractors	(DP act)			1934
Chiropodists	(DP act)			1929
Naturopaths	(DP act)			1936
Funeral directors and embalmers	1928		1938	
Certified public accountants	1926	1927		
Forest engineers		1921		
Dispensing opticians		1940		
Professional chemists		1926		

As table 5.1 shows, there is considerable consistency across the four provinces concerning which professions were self-regulating in 1940. Ten professions were regulated in all: law, medicine, pharmacy, dentistry, land surveying, engineering, accounting, veterinary medicine, optometry, and nursing. Quebec legislated four self-regulating professions that were not regulated in the other three provinces: notaries, professional chemists, forest engineers, and dispensing opticians. British Columbia and Ontario regulated alternative health practitioners – chiropodists, chiropractors, and naturopaths – but they did so differently. Ontario established one umbrella act to govern these three practices (as well as osteopathy, massage, and physiotherapy), while British Columbia established the three as independent self-regulating professions.[4] Across the provinces, the majority of the new self-regulating professions were in the healthcare field – nursing, optometry, veterinary medicine, and various alternative health practices. The rest fell into the fields of engineering, architecture, and accounting. The former cluster of occupations provided services directly to the public, while the latter frequently provided services to various levels of public administration and businesses. All regulated professions were said to have implications for the public interest. During this era, there were a few professions that sought and failed to achieve regulatory legislation in the alternative health field; all but one of these occupations (osteopathy) succeeded in winning regulatory self-regulation eventually, in at least some provinces.

Beyond these professions, there were several other occupational fields in which practitioners were required to take out a licence before practising, and in some instances may have had to pass an exam. For instance, private detectives in Ontario after 1909, and Quebec after 1915, were required to obtain a licence from the provincial treasurer. Real estate agents in British Columbia after 1920 were similarly required to obtain a licence from the government, although there appears to have been no test of competence required. In the early decades of the twentieth century, the lines between regulated occupations and self-regulating professions were typically clear: unlike self-regulating professions, regulated occupations had no established education requirements for entry to practice, and there was no body comprised of practitioners granted regulatory authority over entry to practice and practice itself (Adams 2010). Nevertheless, this demarcation began to blur: some groups – for instance, barbers in British Columbia and stationary engineers in Ontario – were regulated in a manner similar to self-regulating professions. The 1924 act to incorporate BC barbers established a board of examiners, and closed practice; however, there were no concrete training criteria for entry to practice, beyond a short apprenticeship and knowledge of sanitary regulations. Moreover, in 1906–7, people wishing to work as stationary engineers in Ontario had to pass an exam, but the occupation was regulated by the lieutenant governor, not an incorporated body. Thus, to summarize, in the years before the Second World War, provincial governments increasingly regulated entry to practise a variety of occupations, but only some were granted status as self-regulating professions.[5] The rest of this chapter focuses solely on self-regulating professions.

With so many professions established, it is perhaps not surprising that professional regulation remained an area of frequent activity within provincial legislatures: 556 bills respecting professional self-regulation were presented in the four provincial legislatures during this forty-year period. That represents roughly 139 bills per province during the period – and an average of 3.5 per province per year. Of these bills, a higher percentage passed in this era compared to the previous one. Fewer than one third of all bills presented across province failed (see table 5.2 and figure 5.1). Quebec was the province which debated the most bills respecting professions, although there was a noticeable drop in legislative activity respecting professions in the 1930s.[6] Failed bills were most common in established professions: law, medicine, pharmacy, and dentistry. Nevertheless, it was also the case that some new professions applied to the legislature more than once before achieving legislation. This was particularly true for alternative health professions like chiropractic, osteopathy, and optometry. Some of these aspiring professional groups did not achieve regulation before 1940 (in Quebec and Nova Scotia), while others had to petition for legislation numerous times before succeeding. Thus, in at least some cases, sustained campaigns by aspiring professional groups were necessary to achieve even limited powers of professional self-regulation.

Table 5.2 Bills 1900–1940

	Ontario	Quebec	BC	NS	Total
Failed	41	52	36	37	168
Passed	88	117	86	97	388
Total	129	169	122	134	556

Figure 5.1 Bills 1900–1940: Failed and passed

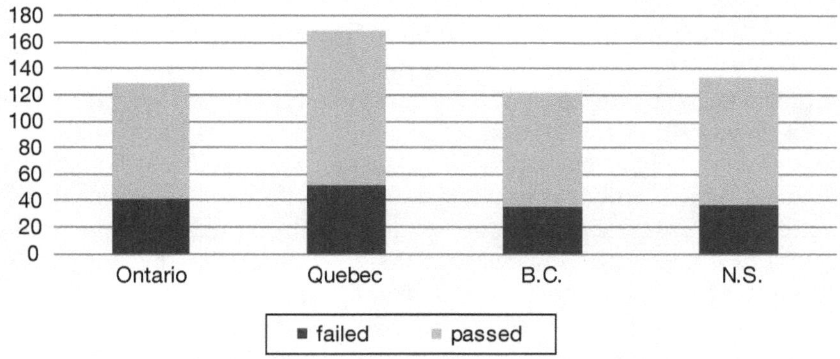

In all four provinces, the professions that experienced the most regulatory activity were the oldest, well-established professions of law, medicine, dentistry, and pharmacy. For example, across all four provinces, the profession of law was the subject of 103 bills. Medicine was the subject of 69 bills. There was hardly a year when medical or law profession legislation was not being considered, in at least one of the provinces. The regulation of these professions was constantly being tinkered with. Some of the bills dealt simply with administrative concerns – precise wording in the acts that needed clarification or alteration. However, many acts brought changes to the regulation and entry requirements of established professions. Professions sought to raise entry requirements, extend periods of formal schooling, and strengthen disciplinary provisions that would extend regulatory bodies' authority over professional practitioners' conduct. Established professions like law and medicine were particularly concerned with defending their turf against infringements by unlicensed practitioners (Moore 1997). Medicine sought legislative change to improve the profession's ability to prosecute "illegal practitioners," defined by professional leaders as virtually anyone providing health services without a medical licence or medical supervision. The courts did not agree with medicine's point of view, and thus, medical doctors appealed to the legislature for legislative change to strengthen their position and regulatory privileges (Adams 2012).

Regulatory Patterns and Powers

Between 1900 and 1940, professional regulatory patterns continued to resemble those witnessed in the late nineteenth century. Most regulated professions were closed, and a corporate body representing all practitioners was either established or acknowledged. This corporate body was governed by an elected board. Considering all self-regulating professions, across province, approximately two-thirds (65 per cent) were regulated in this fashion. Of the remaining self-regulating professions, 21 per cent possessed a restricted title, whereas only 14 per cent were governed by a regulatory board, usually appointed by the government. As table 5.3 shows, regulatory patterns varied by profession and province. Eight of the most common, well-established professions were closed, with an incorporated regulatory body: lawyers, medicine (board only in Nova Scotia), pharmacy, dentistry, land surveying (board only in Nova Scotia), engineering, architecture, and veterinary medicine. Veterinary surgery/medicine had fewer regulatory privileges than its counterparts, and at times was closely monitored. Two other professions – chartered accounting and registered nursing – were restricted title professions across all provinces. Provincially, British Columbia and Quebec had the most incorporated body professions, with twelve and eleven respectively. This represents a substantial change for British Columbia, which had only three such professions in 1900 (medicine, law, and pharmacy). Quebec maintained its tradition of regulating in this fashion, but created few new closed professions after 1910, instead creating more restricted title professions (see also Dussault 1978).

While Ontario continued to have several closed self-regulating professions, the province appeared to be more reluctant than the other three provinces to grant new professions substantial governance powers. In this era, engineering was the only new closed and incorporated self-regulating profession that was granted fairly significant governance powers across all provinces. Architects had been a restricted title profession before, but acquired more regulatory power and more closure in the 1930s. Veterinary surgery had been state-regulated (but not self-regulating) for part of the nineteenth century, but in the 1920s won some limited powers of self-regulation as well. During this era, Ontario also established several professions regulated by an appointed board (optometry, embalming, and drugless practice). These professions were, at best, only nominally self-regulating. As we will later see in chapter 6, this trend in health regulation appears to owe much both

Table 5.3 Regulatory structure by profession and province, 1940

Profession	Incorporated body, closed	Regulatory board only	Restricted title
Law	ON, QC, NS, BC		
Medicine	ON, QC, BC	NS	
Notaries		QC	
Dentistry	ON, QC, NS, BC		
Pharmacy	ON, QC, NS, BC		
Land surveying	ON, QC, BC	NS	
Architects	ON, QC, BC, NS		
Chartered accountants			ON, QC, NS, BC
Civil engineers	ON, QC, NS, BC		
Stenographic reporters			ON
Veterinary surgery	QC, NS, BC, ON		
Optometrists (and opticians)	QC, BC	ON, NS	
Nurses			QC, NS, BC, ON
Drugless practitioners		ON	
Chiropractors	BC		
Chiropodists	BC		
Naturopaths	BC		
Certified public accountants			QC, ON
Funeral directors		ON, NS	
Forest engineers	QC		
Dispensing opticians	QC		
Professional chemists			QC

to the power of the medical profession to curtail the privileges their competitors received, and to Ontario state actors' reluctance to delegate authority. In many ways, Nova Scotia's regulatory patterns resemble Ontario's, with a mixture of closed and incorporated, regulatory board, and restricted title professions; however, Nova Scotia did not regulate drugless practice during this era.

In the language of social movement theory, Quebec and British Columbia provided better opportunity contexts for professionalizing groups in the early twentieth century. Quebec, in particular, established several new professions, and seemed to do so with few controversies and rejected bills. The only Quebec groups to request some recognition and not succeed in these four decades were osteopaths, chiropractors, and funeral directors. British Columbia established eleven self-regulating professions in this period. Nevertheless, several professions (especially chiropractic and naturopathy) had a difficult time winning recognition until the 1930s. Nova Scotia also provided a somewhat favourable context for professionalizing groups, as several new self-regulating professions were established before 1940. Overall, during this period, distinct provincial (and regional) patterns of regulation persisted.

With respect to the powers delegated by provincial state actors to professionals, they too varied across profession and, to some extent, province. There were at least two classes of professions in this era. The first were established and prominent self-regulating professions created in the nineteenth century – law, medicine, dentistry, pharmacy, Quebec notaries, land surveyors – with the addition of engineers and, to a lesser extent, architects. These professions were the most privileged and enjoyed the most extensive regulatory powers and privileges. These professionals were typically incorporated into a body with an elected regulatory board, and granted the right to regulate entry to practice and discipline professional practitioners. In this era, disciplinary provisions were expanded, so that most of these professions in most provinces enjoyed the right to conduct hearings and mete out a variety of penalties – privileges enjoyed by only a few in 1900. This cluster of professions experienced other changes in their regulatory provisions in this era. For instance, as university education became more standard for professional training, regulatory bodies played less of a role in setting standards for entry to study; university standards were adopted. Moreover, scopes of practice were increasingly defined in legislation. Early legislation usually regulated a profession without specifying what exactly practitioners did. Without a definition, however, it was difficult for self-regulating professions to prosecute illegal practitioners (Adams 2012). This problem intensified as new occupations arose (especially in healthcare), providing competition for established professions. To defend their turf, many established professional groups requested that definitions of practice be added to their regulatory legislation.

Another legislative change in this period concerned entry to practice: the number of professions with character requirements increased. Law, land surveying, dentistry, pharmacy, and architecture had character provisions in most of the provinces, requiring new entrants to provide references or "proof" of character, sobriety, and probity. Professions like land surveying required oaths of office. As I have documented elsewhere (Adams 2016b), several professions also had citizenship requirements. These requirements prevented anyone who was not a "British subject" by birth or naturalization from obtaining a licence to practise. Here, the right to regulate (and practise) professions was restricted to those who met the criteria for serving in provincial legislatures (male citizens, of age, before women received the right to vote). Historically, citizenship restrictions were linked with "trustworthiness" (ibid.). Table 5.4 provides a list of professions restricting entry to practice by citizenship up to 1940. These restrictions became more popular in the mid-to-late twentieth century. Professions most likely to be governed by citizenship requirements in the early twentieth century included law, land surveying, pharmacy, optometry, and notarial practice.

The second "class" of professions consisted of the restricted title professions, and the "new" health professions, specifically optometry, nursing, and drugless healing (chiropractic, chiropody, and naturopathy in British Columbia). These professions were granted fewer regulatory privileges than their more established counterparts; in many provinces, drugless healing was not formally regulated at all. To some extent veterinary medicine falls into this group as well, since its regulatory privileges were not as extensive as other closed, self-regulating professions. These professions had less authority over entry to practice and few disciplinary powers, their scopes of practice were narrowly defined, and the privileges of established professions were typically reaffirmed in their legislation. For example, in Quebec, licensed physicians and sellers of eye glasses who did not practise optometry were exempt from the provisions of the optometry act (Quebec 1909a). The other provinces' optometry acts explicitly excluded medical doctors.

Thus, while there were many new self-regulating professions established in this era, they were arrayed hierarchically, with one group of

Table 5.4 Professions with citizenship requirements, 1940 (by year of implementation)

	British Columbia	Nova Scotia	Ontario	Quebec
Law	1877	1939	1912	1936
Land surveying	1905	1910		
Notarial practice	1893			1893
Architecture	1920		1935	(1953)
Pharmacy	1935	1930		(1953)
Optometry	1921	1921*	1919*	
Engineering				1933
Forest engineering				1921
Chiropractic	1934			

* Citizens were entitled to an exemption only.

established professions (nineteenth-century professions plus architecture and engineering) maintaining extensive regulatory powers, while others had fewer powers and privileges, and were sometimes subject to close government oversight.

Who Initiated Professional Regulatory Legislation?

It is not easy to determine the origins of every single one of the 550 bills respecting professional regulation introduced in the four provincial legislatures between 1900 and 1940. Nevertheless, it is clear that professions were the driving force behind the majority of legislative initiatives. Most of the new professions regulated (engineering, accountants, forest engineers, optometry, and other alternative health professions) were the product of requests advanced by professional organizations on behalf of their members. Some of these requests were granted very quickly – for instance, forest engineers in Quebec and chiropodists in British Columbia. Other aspiring professional groups, like optometry, undertook sustained campaigns to win legislation. Some professions had to mobilize a variety of resources, and lobby and compromise with government leaders and legislators to achieve their goals: for instance, engineering in Ontario (Millard 1988), and chiropractic in British Columbia and Ontario (Biggs 1986, 1989).

During this era, leaders in established professions endeavoured to influence the regulation of other groups. This was particularly the case in the medical profession, which played an active role in the regulation of nursing, optometry, and drugless practice. Other institutional actors and businesses affected by regulatory outcomes also weighed in. Thus, professional regulation was not simply the product of negotiation between professional leaders and state actors; consumer groups, and employers and companies, also voiced their opinions and shaped professional regulation.[7]

Nonetheless, it is still the case that state actors and professional leaders worked together to bring about regulatory outcomes. For instance, when medical doctors or lawyers wanted to make a change to their regulatory acts, they would approach a government leader, discuss the change, and if there was support, both parties might be involved in writing a bill, which would then be presented in the legislature by a government leader. State actors were often active behind the scenes in other instances as well. For example, engineering leaders met with government officials before pursuing regulatory legislation (Millard 1988). Further, nursing regulation in Ontario, British Columbia, and Nova Scotia did not begin with a petition. Rather, nurses approached provincial governments directly with their requests (Whittaker 1984), and frequently their legislation was introduced by members of the governing party. When nursing was regulated in Nova Scotia in 1922, it was cabinet minister Robert Emmett Finn who introduced the bill. In Ontario in 1922, it was provincial secretary Harry C. Nixon. While nurses provided the impetus for the bills, state actors were heavily involved in their creation.

At times, legislation was created by state actors themselves, after little or no consultation with the affected groups; however, this was rare, and usually negative for the profession involved. These instances are most apparent in Ontario. For instance, in 1919, the Ontario government introduced a new medical act in the legislature: the bill proposed to remove some of the powers of self-regulation from the College of Physicians and Surgeons of Ontario (Ontario 1919b). Medical leaders were appalled and protested the bill. In response, the government withdrew the bill, claiming that they had believed it had been approved by the medical profession.[8] Ontario optometrists were not as fortunate in the 1930s when faced with state actors' efforts to scale back their privileges. In 1933, a conservative party backbencher introduced a bill to repeal the optometry act (Ontario 1936). There was a growing feeling in the legislature that the optometry regulatory board was "using its influence and perhaps its disciplinary powers to ensure that a high price was paid for glasses" (MacNab 1970: 133). The 1933 bill lapsed, but when a few years later there was a change in government, the issue was raised again. New premier Mitchell Hepburn had campaigned against practices operating in restraint of trade, and the optometrists were among his first targets (ibid.). In 1936, Hepburn himself introduced a bill to repeal the optometry act. Attorney General Arthur Roebuck introduced another bill during the same session to establish a government-appointed board, which would regulate registration and education, subject to the approval and oversight of the lieutenant governor. It was not until the 1940s that optometrists would have some of their powers of self-regulation reinstated. As these examples show, legislation that came straight from state actors during this period tended to restrict professional privileges. Acts that established or extended privileges for professions tended to be spurred by requests from professional groups, even if many were the product of negotiations and discussions between government leaders and professional leaders. State actors also actively debated, amended, rejected, and approved legislation.

Regulatory Rationales

In the nineteenth century, when legislators debated if professions like medicine and law should be granted powers of self-regulation, they discussed the potential gains to the public and the profession. As we have seen, they tended to pass legislation to regulate professional groups whose leaders possessed a good formal education, and who, because of their social backgrounds and training, appeared trustworthy. To paraphrase Dan Malleck (2015: 61), regulatory legislation sought to ensure that only "the right type of person" was empowered to provide these potentially dangerous or significant services. Those in favour of professional regulation cast it as serving the public interest by raising the quality of services provided, and enabling the public to distinguish the trained from the untrained. By the twentieth century, these arguments had been largely accepted, and the tenor of legislative debates shifted. Rather than considering "if" professions should be regulated, legislators were more concerned with "how" they should be regulated, and who was deserving of self-regulation. Or, perhaps more accurately, "who else" was deserving. When making these decisions, they relied, at times heavily, on the knowledge and expertise of leaders in established self-regulating professions. Professionals who held elected office in legislative assemblies continued to be influential. However, state actors did not just listen to professional groups, in this era, but to various business, institutional, and sometimes consumer groups as well. Although established professions were influential, they were not all-powerful. Legislators were wary of established professions' efforts to extend their power, and were not reluctant to check them when they felt they were reaching too far.

Legislative and social debates surrounding professional legislation varied not only by province, but by profession. The distinction, highlighted earlier, between established, powerful, and closed professions, on the one hand, and restricted title and new professional groups, on the other, was significant. For aspiring (and less influential) professional groups, debates often centred on trustworthiness, education, and expertise. At the same time, professional interests and public interests were emphasized, as in the nineteenth century. For established groups whose claims to competence and authority had been previously accepted, regulatory debates centred more on the scope of a profession's authority, and its relationship to other occupations in related fields of practice. Legislators debated whether requests for new powers were "reasonable" and who might be harmed by them. Given these differences, I review debates for each grouping separately in the paragraphs that follow.

New and Restricted Title Professions

As noted in chapter 3, the first acts regulating a profession – especially if the act originated as a private bill – often included a preamble providing a rationale for the legislation. In the early twentieth century, such preambles were most common in Quebec, which passed more private bills in favour of aspiring professional groups than did other provinces. Professions established in Quebec during this period included optometry, public accounting, registered nursing, forest engineering, and professional chemistry. Some of these groups also obtained professional legislation in other provinces before 1940. As in the nineteenth century, preambles to professional legislation tended to highlight its advantages to both the professional group and the "public interest." For example, the 1920 "Act to incorporate the Association of Registered Nurses of the Province of Quebec" simply explained that nurses had petitioned for legislation on the grounds that it would "be both in the interest of the nursing profession and of the public" (Quebec 1920). Forest engineers' legislation in 1921 affirmed their commitment "to safeguard the public interests concerning the management of the forests of the province," and stated that incorporation would allow them to achieve their goals (Quebec 1921).

Not infrequently, no public interest claim was advanced at all; rather the focus was on what the aspiring profession might gain. For instance, the 1909 Quebec "Act to incorporate the Association of Opticians" explained that several petitioners had formed an

> Association of Opticians of the Province of Quebec, with a view of promoting the social and professional advancement of the science of optics by the establishment of laboratories, by scientific investigations and the diffusion of such science by the establishment of special courses of lectures, and the placing of the profession of optician upon a regular footing by the granting of diplomas and other certificates of capacity and efficiency, and that the said petitioners are of the opinion that if they and their successors were incorporated and vested with the powers above mentioned, they might more effectively attain the object of their association. (Quebec 1909a)

Similarly, a group of accountants in Ontario sought incorporation to increase "the knowledge, skill and proficiency of its members in all things relating to the business or profession of an accountant or auditor," to regulate and control "the conduct of its members," and to discipline members for misconduct (Ontario 1926). These examples support a neo-Weberian interpretation of profession creation. That is, workers organized, appealed to the legislature for privileges, and the legislature granted them, at times with little controversy.

Although these preambles are useful, they provide merely a surface justification for legislation. They cannot reveal the debates and concerns surrounding it. For these, it is helpful to turn to records of legislative debates.[9] Some legislation generated little discussion, but other pieces were very controversial. Debates surrounding new professions – especially in the healthcare field – were shaped by inter-professional conflict, competing claims, and questions about aspiring groups' expertise. The cases of optometry and nursing are illuminating.

The medical profession was particularly active in shaping regulatory outcomes for optometrists and nurses. In most provinces, medical doctors were vocally opposed to the optometrists' requests for professional self-regulation. They initially had some success in delaying optometry regulation, and subsequently in shaping its content. Medical doctors tended to regard nursing regulation more favourably, although they did voice opinions on how that regulation was best structured, and sought a role for themselves on regulatory bodies.

One of the earliest recorded debates on optometry regulation occurred in Nova Scotia in 1907, when members of the Nova Scotia Optical Society petitioned for an act to incorporate the organization and regulate the sale of lenses (Nova Scotia 1907a). At this time, the field was entirely unregulated. Optometrists had previously applied for a similar act in 1905, but their bill had been rejected by the province's legislative council. In 1907 there was some support for the bill, and a legislative subcommittee reported it favourably to the house. However, when the call for the bill's second reading arrived, MLA Dr Henry Arthur March spoke vociferously against the bill, arguing that it promised to grant "professional status to a class that only deserved public attention because of their incapacity to do what they professed to be able to do" (Nova Scotia 1907b: 495). Moreover, he charged them with the illegal practice of medicine. Dr March continued to say that his opposition was based solely on the public interest: "It was the duty of the legislature to protect the public against these men" (ibid.: 495). March's colleague, MLA Dr Arthur Samuel Kendall also spoke against the act as potentially "legalizing a fraud, and one which would cause serious injury to a palpable number of people of Nova Scotia" (ibid.: 498). A few other (non-MD) MLAs also spoke against the bill. These speeches seem to have swayed others, and the bill was defeated by a vote of 16 to 10 (Nova Scotia 1907a). Medical doctors argued that optometrists did not have sufficient education and training for the work they proposed to undertake, and further that the eye was such an important organ its treatment was best left to medical doctors (ibid.). Thus, optometry regulation was initially rejected on the basis of inferior training and expertise, as well as practitioner trustworthiness. The opposition of the medical profession was influential. Optometrists were cast as unscrupulous frauds who were a danger to the public. It was 1921 before optometry was regulated in Nova Scotia.

Legislators in Ontario also turned back several bills sponsored by optometrists. The first was presented in 1911, and, unusually, a debate broke out at the bill's first reading concerning optometrists' intentions. An MD MPP, Arthur Edward Ross, criticized a circular optometrists had sent throughout the province warning practitioners that they would be required to sit for examinations after March 1st. To legislators this appeared to signal an intention to create a close corporation, and raise money from registration fees (*Globe* 1911; MacNab 1970). Legislators were strongly opposed, and when the second reading of the bill was called a few weeks later, the bill was withdrawn (MacNab 1970; Ontario 1911). Optometrists tried again in 1912 and 1913. These bills also met with considerable opposition. Speaking of the 1912 bill, MPP and lawyer Isaac Benson Lucas argued that while the bill claimed to protect the public "too much power was sought by the association" (*Globe* 1912a: 9). A newspaper editorial on the 1913 bill warned against "onerous monopolies" (*Globe* 1913: 6). In the end, both bills were rejected on the grounds that they proposed to create a "close corporation" and were of little benefit to the public (MacNab 1970). Again, there seems to have been some question about optometrists' intentions (and trustworthiness).

It was not until 1919 that optometrists succeeded in getting an act in Ontario. A recently completed provincial assessment of optometry was disparaging, arguing that optometrists possessed "no education worthy of the name"; however, optometrist leaders appeared willing to improve (Hodgins 1918: 40).[10] Legislation offered an opportunity to increase practitioners' expertise, and thereby raise the quality of services provided. In this instance, then, legislation did not recognize a pre-existing claim to expertise. The resulting act provided very few privileges (Ontario 1919a). Entry to practise optometry would be governed by a government-appointed board, with medical doctor (and optometrist) representation. Those who passed the required exam would be registered, and could obtain a "certificate." Qualified optometrists then in practice who were British subjects could obtain a certificate and exempt themselves from registration. This particular clause is significant, suggesting that the legislation's intention was to control, rather than empower. While some professional legislation granted powers to the trained and trustworthy, Ontario's optometry act allowed the trained and trustworthy to avoid regulation. Thus, optometrists were only nominally self-regulating in 1919.[11] Questions about their skill and their trustworthiness had been raised by medical doctors and the provincial report. While legislators resolved to regulate the group, they were reluctant to delegate regulatory authority to them.

Medical opposition and controversy also surrounded the regulation of optometry in British Columbia. When a bill to regulate optometrists was presented in the BC legislature in 1921, a special committee was formed to investigate. The committee heard from medical eye specialists who argued against the measure, and optometrists arguing in its favour (Macdonald 1921). The legislative committee also considered optometry legislation in other provinces, and the report on optometry from Ontario's 1918 commission. Committee chair M.A. Macdonald claimed the following considerations guided the committee's decision:

> We addressed ourselves to the question as to whether or not optometrists can be safely entrusted with the power to perform this mechanical work without medical knowledge of the eye and the diseases affecting it or disclosed by it. And further, if conceded that they can safely be entrusted with this power will they be able to render a greater public service, ensuring greater competence and efficiency, if the proposed legislation is enacted? (ibid.: 120–1)

Thus, the focus of the legislative special committee was on practitioner "trustworthiness," knowledge, competence, and the public interest. The committee argued that optometry was a mechanical art, and that the public would be best served by seeing a medical doctor first. Nevertheless, it acknowledged that members of the public did not generally do this, and "they must have the right to be their own judges in this respect" (ibid.: 121). If optometrists were sufficiently knowledgeable, the risk of them providing treatment to the public would be minimal. Thus, the committee recommended legislation to regulate entry to practice, and further, that medical doctors hold a place on the optometrists' examining board to ensure that optometrists' knowledge was sufficient. To enhance optometrist "trustworthiness" the committee also amended the bill to restrict practice to British subjects.

The regulation of optometry does not appear to have been controversial in Quebec. There is no surviving record of debate on optometrists' legislation in 1906, but since that bill merely incorporated a society, opposition was unlikely to be strong. The reconstituted Quebec legislative debates record no discussion on the 1909 optometry bill which extended the profession's regulatory powers.

Debates surrounding the regulation of optometry in British Columbia, Nova Scotia, and Ontario reveal several legislative concerns in this era. First, expertise and knowledge were emphasized. Legislators questioned whether optometrists possessed (or should possess) a high degree of knowledge and skill to do their work. Legislators regarded optometrists' knowledge as inferior and largely "mechanical," and saw regulation as a way of raising practice standards. Second, the medical profession was often influential. Medical opposition was, at times, sufficient to defeat a bill. When optometrists were regulated, medical doctors were invited to be part of that regulation to ensure that optometrists demonstrated sufficient knowledge and expertise. Optometrists were not fully self-regulating; the medical profession had input. Third, trustworthiness and the public interest were important considerations. In 1907, Nova Scotian legislators questioned the motives and integrity of optometrist practitioners, as did their Ontario counterparts when rejecting optometry bills in 1911, 1912, and 1913 (and when deregulating optometrists in the 1930s). BC legislators voiced concern over the trustworthiness of BC optometrists as well, but in the end decided that they could be trusted (with medical oversight and a citizenship requirement to ensure this trust).

Some of these same themes emerge in debates over the regulation of nursing, especially in Ontario, where it was particularly controversial. Ontario did not establish a restricted title for nurses until 1920, but the Ontario legislature seriously debated nursing regulation as early as 1906. Legislation introduced in the provincial parliament in March of that year proposed to establish a graduate nurses association whose council would be composed of eleven nurses and four medical doctors who would have the power to set education standards for nurses and examine them (AO 1906). All council members would have to be British subjects (s. 9). Those who successfully passed the exams would be provided with a certificate; trained nurses with two years of experience in the field already would be eligible for a certificate without examination. Only the registered could be appointed to work as nurses "in any hospital, asylum or other [health] institution, maintained by the Province of Ontario" (AO 1906, s. 25; *Globe* 1906a: 8). If passed, then, the bill would have established a restricted title that conferred employment benefits, but not a "close corporation" (*Globe* 1906b: 13). Although the bill was not introduced by a member of cabinet, it seems to have enjoyed considerable support among government leaders. Graduate nursing groups and some hospitals also supported the legislation.

The 1906 bill was referred to a select committee of nineteen MPPs after second reading: six of these individuals (almost a third) were medical doctors by training (Ontario 1906). The committee heard from many interested parties, some of whom supported the bill, while others did not. In particular, representatives from some hospitals objected to certain aspects of the bill, including their lack of involvement on the proposed regulatory council. Other hospitals requested the act be delayed for a year, so that they could "study" it further (*Globe* 1906c).

Perhaps most concerning to many was the heavy involvement of nurses on the proposed regulatory council. A newspaper article on the bill expressed the following concern: "As now drawn there is nothing to prevent every one of the fifteen members of the council being women, a grave objection in the sight of those who are opposed to an organization of such a public nature being controlled absolutely by women" (*Globe* 1906c: 7).

The special committee revised the bill to reduce nursing representation on the council to five, and increase medical doctor and hospital board representation (MacNab 1970: 117). The revised bill required the four medical doctor members of the proposed council to be men (see AO 1906, revised bill s. 6). The clause requiring provincial institutions to employ only registered nurses was deleted. Although the bill as revised was recommended by the special committee, so many concerns were raised when the bill was discussed by the legislature as a whole that it was returned to the committee for additional consideration (*Globe* 1906c; Ontario 1922a). While the bill was before the special committee again, tempers flared. Some charged that members of the special committee had attempted to derail bill by not showing up to discuss it (*Globe* 1906d: 12).[12] Nevertheless, the bill was amended further by the committee and returned to the house. When the order came for its consideration, however, the bill was withdrawn. By this time it was late in the session, and there may not have been enough time to see the bill through. MacNab (1970: 118) argues that nurses requested the bill's withdrawal after the special committee removed the clause requiring that nurses working in provincial institutions be registered. In the end, it appears that difficulties accommodating all interested groups (especially nurses, medical doctors, and hospital representatives), and concerns over granting women regulatory authority, combined to defeat the bill. Since women did not possess the right to vote provincially in 1906, the bill may have been ahead of its time.

Nursing regulation was also initially controversial in British Columbia in 1916 when the first bill to regulate nurses was presented. Nurses had sought legislation in previous years, but the government refused their requests for bills (Whittaker 1984). In 1916, there was heated discussion over several days concerning the bill to establish an incorporated regulatory body and board of examiners for nurses (British Columbia 1918b). At the heart of the debates was MLA and MD Dr Henry E. Young, who insisted he approved of the principle of the bill, but had concerns about its execution, and hence sought to amend it substantially. Dr Young's key concern is encapsulated in the following excerpt from a speech he gave to the legislature on 11 May 1916:

> As drafted, it [the bill] gave unlimited power to the nurses, while there was not a single clause to provide for the proper regulation of nurses themselves, viewed from the standpoint of the public. The profession was not an independent one, but was interlocked with the medical profession ... It was, therefore, but just that the medical profession should be in a position to supervise the regulations affecting the conduct of nurses. (*Victoria Daily Colonist* 1916, p. 7)

Dr Young, thus, advocated for more medical doctor participation on the nursing council to ensure nurses' conduct was properly regulated. Like his counterparts in Nova Scotia when they discussed the regulation of optometry, Dr Young argued his concerns were solely for the public interest: "He wanted the bill to go through, but the legislature was not there for the purposes of creating special privileges" (ibid.). Young's comments were countered by Premier William John Bowser, who argued that placing just two medical men on the nurses' council should be sufficient, since contemporary women were more than capable of regulating themselves, as long as they had government oversight (ibid.). Another MLA, Mr Parker Williams, agreed with Dr. Young, stating that "two doctors on a board of twelve would have little effect against ten determined ladies" (ibid.). For him, more medical supervision was required, at least initially. In the end, debate on the bill was so heated, and so many amendments were proposed and discussed (many by Dr Young), that enthusiasm for it waned. The bill was defeated at third reading (British Columbia 1920b). As in Ontario, legislators were ambivalent about delegating regulatory authority to women, and it was difficult to please the various stakeholders involved (especially the medical profession).[13]

Legislation to regulate nursing in British Columbia was passed a few short years later in 1918, with much less controversy. This legislation incorporated the Graduate Nurses' Association and established a regulatory council consisting of twelve nurses. A restricted title was established. Although the first council would be appointed by the medical profession, subsequent council members would be elected by nurses. The council was given very limited regulatory powers: the right to regulate the register, examinations, and the right to revoke certificates. A board of examiners was established, and members were appointed by the lieutenant governor: two members would be members of the College of Physicians and Surgeons, and four would be members of the nursing association (British Columbia 1918a). Thus, nurses were granted self-regulation, with some medical profession oversight and input, in 1918, shortly after they received the right to vote in the province.

An act to establish a restricted title for nurses in Ontario did not come to pass until 1922, after nursing had been regulated in most other provinces, and women had been granted the right to vote.[14] This bill was introduced by Provincial Secretary Harry C. Nixon on behalf of the government (Ontario 1922a). Unlike in British Columbia, Ontario's 1922 nursing act gave next to no regulatory authority to nurses. The act simply established a register for trained nurses, and a restricted title, "registered nurse." It was the government, represented by the lieutenant governor, who was granted power to establish the register and training programs, and pass regulations under the act (Ontario 1922b). Under the regulations, a "Council on Nurse Education" with nursing, medical doctor, and hospital representation was instituted to advise the government (MacNab 1970: 120).

Other provinces gave more authority to nurses. Nova Scotia's 1922 nursing act fell in between BC's and Ontario's: it established an examining board with both appointed nurse and medical doctor members charged with examining candidates and maintaining a register (Nova Scotia 1922). Quebec's legislation was like British Columbia's to the extent that it incorporated a regulatory body for nurses and granted them limited regulatory privileges (Quebec 1920). In the latter province, nursing regulation appears less controversial. There is no surviving recorded debate on nursing regulation in 1920, although the bill was amended in subcommittee and by the legislative council. A 1922 amendment to the bill did raise some concerns by an unnamed group in Montreal, but these were addressed in subcommittee amendments (Quebec 1922). Nonetheless, there is evidence that the medical profession had reservations about nursing regulation: in 1927 the College of Physicians and Surgeons instigated a petition (ultimately abandoned) to bring nursing regulation into the hands of the medical profession (Kinnear 1994: 162–3).

A consideration of nurses' regulation reveals several forces shaping regulatory decisions, and highlights both what had changed since the nineteenth century, and what had not. In chapters 3 and 4, I argued that who professionals were had implications for regulatory outcomes. Successful professions were led by highly educated, high-status, white men. The granting of regulatory privileges to female nurses represents a significant change. For much of the nineteenth century, women were not even entitled to practise in male-dominated professions. Leading a profession was unthinkable. By the early 1920s, in British Columbia, Quebec, and Nova Scotia, nurses were granted some limited regulatory privileges – typically after they had obtained the right to vote (Whittaker 1984). Nevertheless, gender continued to be a concern (Kinnear 1994). In the years that followed, nurses advocated for an expansion of their regulatory privileges and powers, while some medical doctor leaders and state actors remained reticent (ibid.).

Linking the case of nursing with that of optometry reveals that there were more than gender issues at work here. Both nursing and optometry were regulated in order to control entry to practice and raise education standards; few governance responsibilities were conferred. In many provinces, the professions were granted powers of self-regulation, but medical doctors had a place on regulatory boards. The medical profession actively lobbied to restrict the autonomy and authority of these regulated health professions. Medical doctors held strong opinions on nursing and optometry regulation, and the profession was established enough to influence legislative outcomes (Coburn et al. 1983). Medical doctors were not the only group weighing in, however. Provincial legislators also expressed ambivalence about the regulation of these groups. Other interested parties also voiced concerns, especially representatives from hospitals (for nurses), and businesses selling eye glasses (optometry). In Ontario in 1906, opposition from hospitals may have been a decisive factor in defeating the nursing bill. At the time, hospitals ran nursing schools, and staffed their hospitals, at little expense, with nursing students (McPherson 1996). They may have felt that their existing practices were threatened by nursing regulation. An Ontario royal commission on health-profession regulation identified this training system as a barrier to regulation and good practice, since training was uneven from one institution to the next (Hodgins 1918). In the twentieth century, a variety of stakeholders voiced opinions on professional legislation. When legislators made regulatory decisions, they had to balance the concerns of several groups with their own beliefs about what was appropriate.

In making decisions about the regulation of new professional groups in the early twentieth century, provincial legislators appear to have focused on practitioners' knowledge and education, their competence, and their "trustworthiness" and responsibility. Many expressed reluctance to create "close corporations" with the kind of authority and privileges earlier professions had been granted. Regulation was frequently imposed to control, and enforce, higher standards. In these instances, legislators regulated to establish expertise, not to recognize a claim advanced by a professionalizing group. Nonetheless, there were differences across each province, with Ontario being the most reluctant to extend professional privileges in the 1910s and 1920s.

Established and Closed Professions

Although medicine and other established self-regulating professions were influential in this era, they were not all-powerful. In fact, the established professions of medicine, law, pharmacy, and dentistry had more bills turned back than did upstart and aspiring professions on average. Throughout this period, established professions attempted to extend and consolidate their authority, and to raise entrance standards. They were frequently challenged by legislators, but these challenges did little to undermine their professional power.

One telling example occurred in British Columbia in 1909. A new medical act was presented in the legislature in the spring of that year, which sought many changes, the most controversial of which were raising the length of medical education to five years, establishing a definition of medical practice, and prohibiting the practice of osteopathy in the province. The bill's presenter, MLA Dr James H. King, argued that the bill was in keeping with legislative developments elsewhere, passed to protect the public (*Victoria Daily Colonist* 1909a: 2). The bill angered some legislators, who interpreted it as a power grab. The following are excerpts from socialist party MLA James Hawthornthwaite's speech:

> [He] paid a tribute to the devotion and charity frequently shown by doctors. For this reason the profession should be doubly careful when asking for legislation not to do anything to injure this good impression. So this bill came rather as a shock, as it was generally believed that the profession was already well protected. There was no public demand for it ... [He] agreed that the public should be protected from quacks. His party did not stand for licensed ignorance, but too much power was demoralizing ... Principal practitioners here are allopaths who may think that they have all knowledge, but history shows that accepted practice half a century ago

> is often discarded today and it is admitted that but little is yet known of medical science. Nature and nursing do most of it. He quoted authorities to show that medicine is still largely empirical and for that reason too much power should not be given to one branch of the profession. (*Victoria Daily Colonist* 1909b: 17)

Hawthornthwaite and others were particularly bothered by clauses that would exclude osteopaths from practice. When the bill was in committee, this clause was changed such that the act did not prohibit osteopathy, but granted the College of Physicians and Surgeons the right to regulate entry to practise osteopathy. Thus, even as some critiqued medicine's efforts to extend their power, legislators extended that power by granting allopaths the right to regulate osteopaths. The definition of medical practice and the five-year course of study were also highly controversial (*Victoria Daily Colonist* 1909c: 5). The former clause passed once amended by Dr King to provide exemptions for dentists, pharmacists, opticians, as well as nurses and chiropodists engaged in "ordinary practice" (ibid.: 3). With all these exemptions, it appears that the definition was a weapon with which doctors sought to tackle practice by drugless healers like chiropractors. The five-years clause passed on division.

A similar debate erupted in Quebec in 1909 when the Quebec medical profession sought to expand medical education to five years. The 1909 "Act to amend and consolidate the law respecting physicians and surgeons in the Province of Quebec" (Quebec 1909b) was the subject of hours of discussion over several days; legislators considered each section very carefully. The bill's sponsor, MLA and medical doctor Charles-Eugène Côté, explained that the bill's main purpose was to extend medical education from four years to five in order to allow medical students time to acquire necessary practical experience. Although the act made additional amendments, it was this change that was most contentious. Opponents charged that this provision (and a few others) would raise the cost of medical education, rendering it less accessible, and committing "une injustice envers les étudiants pauvres" (M. Lavergne [Montmagny], in Quebec 1909c). Critics further charged that the extra year was entirely unnecessary. There were many legislators who were critical of medicine's requests, and were by no means willing to acquiesce without good reason. The bill's supporters countered these criticisms by claiming that medical doctors were themselves the best judges of what was needed:

> Tous les conseils médicaux de la province l'ont approuvé et ils sont bien les meilleurs juges. Devant cette unanimité, comment les députés qui ne connaissent pas les exigences de cette profession soutiendraient-ils l'opinion contraire? On n'a pas apporté une seule bonne raison contre le bill. (Tessier, in Quebec 1909c)
>
> [All the medical boards in the province have approved this, and they are the best judges. Given this consensus, how can members who do not know the requirements of the profession support the opposite view? There has not been one good reason brought against the bill.]

Another MLA, Henri Bourassa, declared himself in favour of the bill because the medical profession had requested it and because it would raise the level of the medical profession (Quebec 1909c). Thus, some legislators were willing to support the bill because they trusted the medical profession's judgment, and because the profession appeared to be united behind it. For some others, however, such reasons were not sufficient. Even those generally in favour of the bill debated the wording of specific clauses closely and endeavoured to ensure the bill was fair.

In both these examples, the medical profession received most of the privileges requested, but this was not always the case, as the number of failed bills in this era reveals. Significantly, legislators did not simply act as a "rubber stamp," as some sociologists imply is usually the case. Professional requests were actively debated and contested. Legislators voiced concerns over established professions' abuse of their power, and they raised concerns about how regulatory change would affect other workers, students, and the public more generally. At the same time, legislators expressed confidence in established professions. They trusted them to regulate in the public's interest, and many believed that established professions generally made decisions based on their superior knowledge of their own profession. Legislators were often willing to defer to their wisdom. Nonetheless, there were moments when legislators believed that a profession's request was out of line, and they rejected these bills outright.

Most professions in this category were established in the nineteenth century, except for engineering, which was regulated in most provinces between 1918 and 1922. Engineering is worth a closer look since it was one of only a few "new" self-regulating professions to be granted regulatory privileges similar to the established professions'. Engineering was not a new practice, or even a new profession, in the twentieth century.

It dates back to around the 1850s in Canada, and had been regulated in Quebec (and Manitoba) since the 1890s (Millard 1988). Like land surveyors, engineers were important to an expanding country, and played a key role in building railroads and other physical infrastructure in Canada. Engineers had organized nationally in 1887: the Canadian Society of Civil Engineers was committed to uniting all branches of non-military engineering, and fostering educational and professional advancement (ibid.). Although the society made some effort to achieve regulatory legislation in the 1890s – and succeeded in Manitoba and Quebec – the group's primary goals were educational and professional. High entry standards demarcated its members as high status and highly qualified (ibid.: 31–2).

By the opening decades of the twentieth century, engineers were not entirely happy with their lot. For educated and highly skilled individuals, working on important business and public contracts, they believed they were underpaid, underemployed, and too often treated with disrespect by the public and their employers. The latter often overlooked Canadian engineers in preference to their American counterparts. Engineers felt their employers often ignored their advice, but tried to blame them when something went wrong (Millard 1988). The First World War raised engineers' public profile and social status: "The war gave engineers an unprecedented opportunity to demonstrate their usefulness, not only at the front … but also at home" (ibid.: 101; see also *Globe* 1921a:13). However, the post-war prospects for Canadian engineers appeared bleak as a result of over-crowding. According to Millard (1988: 124), between 1881 and 1921 the numbers of engineers in Canada increased 778 per cent. Post-war immigration to Canada threatened to exacerbate the situation (Girard and Bauder 2007). The solution, engineering leaders believed, was professional regulation.

Engineers had established relations with political actors and were generally well respected. They also had experienced and respected men at the helm. In Ontario, Willis Chipman – the man behind the organization of land surveying in the province – led the way. The profession also had an engineer MPP willing to shepherd a bill through the house. Engineers' goal was self-regulation, which they explained was necessary to ensure public safety since government "officials … might not be conversant with engineering" (*Globe* 1921a: 13). Legislation was passed in Quebec and Nova Scotia with no controversy and little debate in 1920, but it faced strong opposition in Ontario from mining companies and mining engineers in the north for whom the bill represented a scheme by "incompetent" engineers "whose services at present are not in demand" (*Globe* 1921b: 3). Mining engineers and business leaders had formed an influential organization in the late nineteenth century; the former do not seem to have possessed a professional identity distinct from their employers' (Millard 1988). Despite the profession's efforts to achieve a compromise with the mining group, the latter vociferously opposed all attempts at legislation, and especially at closing the profession. These opponents charged that "the spectacled section of the profession whose ability lies chiefly in technical verbiage, have flocked to the support of the bill like sheep, while those who are actually doing things in the field and making good are generally opposed to the measure" (*Globe* 1921b: 3). Nevertheless, the bill had some support from legislators, and it was sent to a select committee that did not report until 1922 (Ontario 1921, 1922a). By this time the act had been revised to minimize its impact on mining engineers and mining companies (*Globe* 1922a: 2). It was amended further in the legislature to prevent professional closure – engineering would be a restricted title profession, with the designation "professional engineer" providing a "badge of distinction" (*Globe* 1922b: 15; Millard 1988). Engineers could continue to practise, without registration, as long as they did not claim to be "professional engineers" (Ontario 1922c; Girard and Bauder 2007; Millard 1988).

Engineering legislation also received some opposition from mining interests in British Columbia (*Victoria Daily Colonist* 1920a: 15). Indeed, provincial premier John Oliver himself objected to the bill, arguing that while he had "no desire to prevent engineers from having a recognized standing," he feared the bill would have a negative impact on non-professional men in the mining industry (*Victoria Daily Colonist* 1920b: 9). However, other legislators argued that the concerns of the mining industry were easily dealt with. Since practice would not be closed, mining engineers had no real reason to object. In his support for the bill, MLA John Walter Weart argued that "the promoters of the bill were seeking protection, not alone for themselves, but for the public, and were just as entitled to organize themselves in an association as were other bodies to whom that privilege had been extended by the legislature" (*Victoria Daily Colonist* 1920c: 5). The bill was passed with some amendments shortly thereafter (British Columbia 1920a).

Why were engineers granted fairly extensive regulatory privileges while many of their counterparts in other professionalizing occupations were not? The comments of Premier Oliver and MLA Weart are revealing. Both men agreed that engineers as a group of men were deserving of status. Unlike nurses and drugless healers (discussed in chapter 6), all engineers were men in the 1920s. Indeed, many were well-respected men who had undergone years of training: apprenticeships for engineers were lengthy, and some undertook university training. Engineers more readily resembled their counterparts in other closed, self-regulating professions. Moreover, their work was viewed as being of significant social importance, and they had rendered a valuable service during the war. For these reasons, legislators appear to have regarded their regulation more favourably than they did that of other petitioners in this era.[15]

To summarize this lengthy discussion of the rationales and debates surrounding professional regulation between 1900 and the 1930s, several important trends must be noted. Professional regulation continued to be cast in terms of the public interest. Although preambles (especially in Quebec) make reference to professional interests as well, legislators were reluctant to establish "close corporations" and give extensive privileges to new professional workers. That said, they did not undermine the closed self-regulating professions they had previously established. In fact, they tended to expand long-standing professions' powers (concerning discipline and entry requirements) during this era. When making regulatory decisions, legislators also discussed professionals' trustworthiness, their characteristics (for instance, gender and citizenship), and their knowledge. Higher-status applicants, like engineers, with a convincing claim to expertise were more likely to get privileges, and obtain more extensive privileges, than lower-status applicants such as nurses and optometrists. The former had regulatory powers conferred upon them, while some in the latter group were regulated to control them. Legislators also took into account the arguments of groups who might be affected by professional legislation, especially other professions (medicine) and employers, tempering regulatory privileges to accommodate opponents.

Signs of Standardization

Patterns of professional regulation differed slightly across provinces. As noted earlier in the chapter, Quebec regulated the most professions in this era, and created some new restricted title professions that were not regulated elsewhere. In British Columbia, many new self-regulating professions were established in the early 1900s, and most were closed with an incorporated regulatory body. Nova Scotia regulated fewer professions, but three of them were regulated by a board, not an incorporated body. Finally, Ontario seemed reluctant both to establish new professions and to grant those professions extensive regulatory powers. As we have seen, Ontario's legislation regulating optometry and nursing was more restrictive than that passed in the other three provinces. Although there are clearly commonalities across the provinces in terms of what was regulated and when, it is the emerging standardization within provinces that stands out. Provincial precedents for regulation had been established, and these precedents provided templates upon which legislation for new professions could be based.

This emerging homogenization is consistent with DiMaggio and Powell's (1983) work on isomorphism – coercive, mimetic, and normative processes, encouraging standardization. Both coercive and mimetic processes seem particularly relevant here: once a pattern of regulation had been established, state actors sought to create others that were similar in form (coercive isomorphism); and new organizations tend to model themselves after similar bodies "that they perceived to be more legitimate or successful" (ibid.: 152). Thus, new professions came to be structured in ways similar to previous professions.

At first glance, Ontario may appear to have been the major exception to this trend, since the regulation of professions, especially those established in the 1920s, does not closely resemble the legislation that preceded it. However, Ontario was probably the province that most strongly attempted to standardize and rationalize professional regulation in this period. There were two major events that signal this trend. First, in 1911 and 1912, the province redrew virtually every single piece of legislation regulating professions, with the exception of the medical act. In 1911 the acts regulating dentistry, pharmacy, land surveying, architects, chartered stenographic reporters, veterinary surgery, chartered accountants, and others were revised. All were standardized in their look and structure, and the wording of specific provisions was altered and clarified. Some professions were granted new powers, but for the most part, their regulation remained largely the same. In 1912, legislation regulating lawyers was also revised. Second, to guide its regulatory activity in the field of healthcare, the Ontario government appointed the Hodgins commission, which conducted an in-depth investigation into the education and regulation of a variety of healthcare practices, most of which were not regulated in the province. This commission was a landmark because it established rationales for professional regulation. Whereas previously regulation had been granted by legislators in response to requests, on a largely ad hoc basis, the Hodgins commission sought to determine who was worthy of regulation. Because it was so influential in Ontario (and indeed in other provinces), the Hodgins commission is worth looking at in some detail.

In the early 1910s, the Ontario legislature was inundated with requests for regulatory legislation from health groups. Medical doctors wanted to alter their legislation to enhance their ability to prosecute alternative healthcare practitioners for the illegal practice of medicine. In turn, alternative health groups like osteopathy, chiropractic, and optometry wanted their own legislation to increase their status, and protect them from medical prosecution. Nursing legislation had been debated since 1906. Other health occupations were on the rise. In response to these conflicting claims, Premier James P. Whitney vowed to establish a royal commission in 1912–13. He warned professional groups that no new legislation would be passed until the commission had provided its advice. However, Whitney's death, the onset of the First World War, and a provincial election delayed the commission (Adams 2012). It was not until 1915 that Whitney's successor, Premier William Hearst, appointed Justice Frank Egerton Hodgins as commissioner to investigate and advise the government on health professional education and regulation. Hodgins's task was to "inquire into all the different branches of the medical profession who are looking for legislation for the proper recognition of their profession" (*Globe* 1915b: 7). More specifically he was asked to explore the "establishment, creation, control and regulation of any new body intended to have relation to medicine," as well as the relationship of such bodies "to each other or to the Province" (*Globe* 1915a: 7). Hodgins began his work right away, holding multiple hearings with a variety of organizations representing the different occupational groups as well as educational leaders. Further, he explored health professional practice and regulation in other provinces, and throughout the United States, seeking out the advice of those south of the border. Hodgins met with several groups more than once.

Justice Hodgins took two years to conduct his investigation, and the commission was a costly one for the Ontario government, at a price of $8000 (Archives of Ontario [AO] 1919a). Hodgins's lengthy 177-page *Report on Medical Education in Ontario* was presented to parliament by Provincial Secretary William David McPherson in February 1918. For Hodgins (inspired by his instructions from the government), regulation was closely tied with education, and his report focused on the education and knowledge bases of each of the professions and practices he investigated. Furthermore, it was clear that, for Hodgins, medical education was the standard by which other groups would be judged; however, that did not stop him from criticizing medical education and practice. Hodgins (1918) reported on ten different practices: chiropractic, Christian Science, dentistry, homeopathy, medicine, midwifery, nursing, optometry, osteopathy, and physical therapy. In their meetings with Hodgins, various organizations representing each practitioner group took the opportunity to make their case for regulatory change.

In his report, Justice Hodgins made many influential recommendations. For instance, he recommended changes to the regulation of medicine, the structure of the medical council, and the role of medical schools. He reprimanded medical doctors for their reluctance to embrace manual therapies, which the experience of the First World War and the rise of alternative treatments like massage and osteopathy demonstrated were valuable. He recommended that medical doctors receive training in physical therapy, and that they take on a leadership role in developing treatment in this area.[16] Hodgins also recommended regulation for optometry, believing regulation could enforce higher standards for optometrists, whom he felt were poorly educated for their work. With provinces and American states near Ontario regulating optometry, Hodgins (1918: 40) feared the province was becoming a "dumping ground for those unable or unwilling to qualify" elsewhere. The Ontario government responded with legislation shortly thereafter. With respect to nursing, Hodgins (ibid.: 42–5) recommended that nurses be regulated and a restricted title be established to distinguish the trained from untrained; he also recommended that nurses have a voice in their own affairs. Hodgins was less supportive of drugless therapies. He found absolutely no merit in chiropractic, because of chiropractors' rejection of medical science and their low (and uneven) education standards (33). The rise of a medically oriented physical therapy occupation would provide similar services much more safely, he believed. Hodgins was more ambivalent about the regulation of osteopathy.

Hodgins's recommendations were taken seriously by the Ontario government, and shaped regulatory legislation for years to come. However, his report had a broader significance. It represented an attempt by the government to establish a rationale and a fair set of criteria to guide professional regulation. The main criterion emphasized by Hodgins, as noted, was scientific (medical) education. Those professions regarded most favourably (like medicine, dentistry, osteopathy) embraced scientific medicine. Those specialties disregarded by Hodgins (like chiropractic) rejected it. Hodgins's report was the single most important report shaping, and rationalizing, the regulation of health professions in Ontario until the 1960s, when the government established other commissions to take a fresh look at the issue.

Further, the Hodgins report demonstrates the extent of, and limitations to, medical dominance in the early twentieth century. Medicine was the most powerful health profession in the province and it had a strong impact on health regulation generally. Other health professions were judged on the basis of how similar they were to medicine (or at least how similar they appeared to be in the eyes of an educated professional lawyer and judge). Nevertheless, this status did not protect the medical profession from criticism, and it did not mean that they achieved all their professional goals. In the 1910s, medicine hoped to eliminate virtually all alternative health practices. However, upon Hodgins's advice, the Ontario government regulated many of these practices in the decade following.

Ontario's Hodgins commission was not the only one established during this period. British Columbia established a smaller commission to investigate the regulation of drugless practice in British Columbia in the 1930s, and Saskatchewan instituted a brief review on the same subject in the 1910s. However, Hodgins's report was more sweeping and influential. Other provinces (especially British Columbia) also drew on Hodgins's report when considering health profession legislation in the 1920s and 1930s. All these commissions represent initial attempts to standardize professional regulation. These processes merely intensified between the 1940s and 1970s.

Who Was Regulated?

In chapter 3, I showed that regulated professionals in Nova Scotia, Quebec, Ontario, and British Columbia were well-educated gentlemen. They tended to have a classical education. In Quebec, professional leaders were much more likely to be literate social leaders than their nonprofessional counterparts. In Ontario and Nova Scotia, professional leaders were disproportionately of British descent, either Ontario- or British-born, and predominantly Protestant. Their liberal education marked them as members of a societal elite and they disproportionately held leadership positions in their communities, government, and other social institutions (see also Gidney and Millar 1994; Miller 1991; Boily 1967; Brunet 2009; Moore 1997).

In the opening decades of the twentieth century, this profile changed fairly dramatically. Optometrists, nurses, and other newly regulated groups like chiropractors possessed a more modest socio-economic status (Biggs 1989). Nurses and some alternative health providers were women. Alternative health providers were disproportionately foreign-born and foreign-trained, and most were from Europe or the United States of America (Adams 2017b; Adams and Etherington 2015). As we have seen, nineteenth-century professionalism was bound up with socio-economic status, a liberal education, gender, and race; however, by the twentieth century, professionally relevant education was increasing in importance.[17] Further, as we have seen, legislation placed less focus on entry-to-study, especially in terms of requiring elitist components of a liberal education (knowledge of Latin or Greek, for example). Rather, it became common to require more general credentials: university matriculation or secondary school completion.

Nonetheless, it would obviously be naive to conclude that class, gender, and race were no longer relevant, and that by the late 1930s, it was solely expertise that determined regulatory outcomes. I have argued that in this period professions could be divided into two groups. The first group predominantly consisted of closed, incorporated self-regulating professions with considerable regulatory autonomy and authority. These professions were strongly white and male-dominated and, in some cases, exclusively so. Practitioners in these professions were highly educated, and tended to come from middle-class and elite social backgrounds.[18] The second group consisted of professions with limited powers of self-regulation: restricted title professions in which regulatory bodies had few powers, or were subject to considerable oversight. Some of the restricted title professions – notably chartered accountants, forest engineers, and professional chemists – were highly male-dominated, and required high levels of education for entry to practice. In contrast, optometrists did not possess extensive education and were largely regarded as tradesmen by legislators and others at the time. Nursing was becoming a career for middle-class women, but nurses were not uniformly of high status. Chiropractors tended to have limited education, and were predominantly from working-class backgrounds (Biggs 1989). Some alternative health practitioners were members of ethnic minorities (Adams 2017b). For these latter groups, professional regulation was controlling, as well as empowering. Thus, the full privileges of professional self-regulation were not extended to lower-status practitioners in this era. Status, class, gender, and ethnicity continued to matter.

The implementation of character and citizenship requirements for several professions in this period supports this argument. As the emphasis on education and training increased, so did requirements for proof of character, and in some cases citizenship (Adams 2009a, 2016b). In British Columbia, such restrictions prevented Asian men and women from participating in several regulated professions. The foreign-born could practise other professions only after they had been naturalized. Thus, ethnicity, race, and citizenship continued to be relevant to professions and their regulation in the opening decades of the twentieth century (see also Girard and Bauder 2007). Self-regulation remained tied to trustworthiness, which was in turn linked with status, citizenship, and social characteristics.

Discussion

During the opening decades of the twentieth century, professional regulation in the provinces of Nova Scotia, Quebec, Ontario, and British Columbia expanded. New groups were regulated. Some of them, like engineering and architecture, were granted privileges commensurate with those conferred upon several nineteenth-century professions. Others were granted fewer regulatory privileges. In these latter instances, regulation did little to empower, and more to control entry to practice and practitioner conduct. In all cases, regulation represented a contract between a professional group and state actors, through which the latter either delegated some of their authority to govern an area of social endeavour, or appointed representatives to regulate a field under their general oversight. The second regulatory form was more common in Ontario and Nova Scotia, and can be seen in the regulation of optometry, nursing, and drugless practice. The nature of these "contracts" and the structure of professional regulation varied across each province, but there are signs of standardization within the provinces, as well as concern with establishing rationales and justifications for professional regulation. There are also similarities across the provinces, as there was considerable overlap respecting which groups were regulated (and when). When a profession was regulated in one province, state actors in neighbouring provinces sometimes expressed concern that there could be an influx of untrained practitioners into their own province, unless they followed suit.

As the size of the provincial state infrastructures increased, and government reach extended, state actors may have been less inclined to delegate authority. Further, legislators and members of the public disdained "close corporations," and legislators were reluctant to pass legislation that closed practice entirely. Many members of the public were opposed to market restrictions believed to raise prices. Moreover, at least some legislators were concerned about potential abuses of professional authority. Medicine and law were powerful professions, and legislators expressed some concern that these professions would abuse their power. Nonetheless, they did little to curtail these professions' power, and passed legislation to extend their disciplinary authority. Medicine's powers of regulation were also extended to include allied and alternative healthcare workers as well.

As neo-Weberian theories of professions contend, professional regulation was usually instigated by requests and campaigns pursued by aspiring professional groups. However, social closure theory is unable to explain all regulatory outcomes which, as this chapter has shown, were quite variable. As we have seen, professionals made numerous requests between 1900 and the 1930s; many were not granted. The Weberian concept of status may help explain some variable outcomes, since higher-status, influential groups appear to have won more power and autonomy than others. Collective mobility models would suggest that outcomes might vary based on resource mobilization. Chapter 6 provides a closer examination of the applicability of these models to professionalization in this era. To understand regulatory outcomes we need to look beyond professional requests to consider legislators' decisions about what regulatory outcomes made sense for the people of their provinces. Their decisions were often influenced by their own backgrounds and interests, as the activity of professionals holding seats in provincial legislatures makes clear. Further, state actors' decision making was shaped by their assessments of professionals' claims to expertise and education, as well as their social backgrounds and trustworthiness. If legislators had doubts that professionals could handle the responsibility of self-regulation, they granted government officials supervisory authority over professional regulatory bodies. Legislators continued to justify regulation in terms of the public interest.

Although expertise was a consideration for legislators, its significance varied, and not in accordance with some sociologists' hypotheses.

Professional regulation was not simply a reward for experts, or recognition of a claim to expertise. Nor did it signal, necessarily, that a group of workers had skills state actors needed, as Halliday (1987) argues for lawyers in the United States. Rather, as the case of optometry shows, legislators sometimes regulated when they did not accept the knowledge claims advanced by a professionalizing group, and they sought, through regulation, to raise practitioners' education. Thus, while knowledge claims were important to regulation, competence continued to be intertwined with other considerations and characteristics, including social background, education, and trustworthiness.

Legislative outcomes were also shaped by inter-professional conflict and interactions in this period, especially in the healthcare field. Regulation for health professions was influenced by the medical profession, which sought initially to eliminate doctors' competition, and subsequently to control it. In Abbott's (2005) terms, tensions within the system of professions, or professions' ecology, interacted with political events and concerns to shape regulatory outcomes. The role of inter-professional conflict, and resource mobilization, in shaping the regulation of alternative health professions is the focus of chapter 6.

Chapter Six

Contests over the Regulation of "Drugless Healers," 1900–1930s

In the opening decades of the twentieth century, a variety of new health occupations emerged and expanded in Canada, from the nurses and optometrists discussed in chapter 5 to osteopaths, chiropractors, naturopaths, and other "drugless" healers. At the same time, the medical profession became a more dominant force in this era. The legislative challenges to medicine's status as a self-regulating profession that occurred in some provinces in the 1890s were behind them (Naylor, 1986; Gidney and Millar 1994). The effectiveness of medical science was increasingly recognized by public leaders and citizens alike (Clow 2001; Coburn et al. 1983). Nevertheless, the influx of osteopaths beginning in 1900 (Adams 2012), and other drugless healers shortly thereafter (Adams and Etherington 2015; Mills 1966), was perceived as a threat. Medical leaders cast alternative health practice as a public safety concern, and were quick to take action, both through the courts – charging alternative health practitioners with the illegal practice of medicine – and through legislative initiatives. Faced with prosecution, alternative health practitioners organized and fought back, in part by seeking legislative change to establish their occupations as legitimate self-regulating professions.

These contests played out in provincial legislatures, and behind-the-scenes lobbying of government officials, as well as in the judicial courts and in the court of public opinion during the first four decades of the twentieth century (and beyond). Although the main contests occurred in British Columbia and Ontario, neither Quebec nor Nova Scotia were immune. At the time, the outcome of these contests was by no means certain. Medicine enjoyed a dominant position in the market and had a good relationship with government leaders and legislators, but chiropractors, osteopaths, and other drugless healers had considerable public support. Policymakers were uncertain about what policy approach was the most politically prudent. Legislators' ambivalence is evident when one considers legislative activity during this period. In the British Columbia legislature, thirty bills were introduced between 1909 and 1939 respecting the regulation of medicine and other health practices (of which twenty actually passed). In Ontario eighteen bills were introduced over the same period, of which only six were successful. Both these provinces established a royal commission and several legislative committees to identify regulatory solutions. Bills respecting the regulation of osteopathy and chiropractic were also introduced in Quebec, with no success. In contrast, there was little activity in Nova Scotia, where an amendment to the medical act in 1921 incorporated osteopathy into medicine. Overall, this was a time of intense social debate, inter-professional conflict, and legislative activity surrounding the regulation of alternative health practices.

By the time the dust had settled in the late 1930s, none of the groups had achieved exactly what they wanted, but some were more content than others. Medical doctors had managed to maintain their dominant position in the healthcare field, but did not succeed in completely undermining their alternative health counterparts. Some new health practitioners, such as chiropractors in British Columbia, had achieved self-regulation and autonomy, while others had been severely restricted, in terms of both their scope of practice and their regulatory authority. In Quebec, alternative health practitioners continued to practise unregulated.

This chapter explores the professional projects of, and inter-professional conflict between, medical doctors and alternative health care providers, with a particular focus on osteopaths, chiropractors, and other drugless healers (including naturopaths). Further, it examines the impact of these projects and inter-professional conflict on legislators' decision-making and regulatory outcomes. Although I recount major events in each province, my focus is on Ontario, and to a lesser extent British Columbia, where the contests were most intense, and where surviving archival records document state-profession interactions more fully. Drawing on the theoretical concepts outlined in chapter 1, I identify the social closure and collective mobility projects pursued by established and aspiring health professions, and examine state actors' decision making, in the face of competing professional claims. In so doing, I demonstrate the utility of combining a focus on professional projects with a linked ecologies perspective to understand professional regulation.

Ontario

Various health services were available to Ontarians in the early twentieth century. Homeopathic medical doctors continued to provide a treatment alternative to regular medicine (Connor 1998). Moreover, several health practices that originated in the late nineteenth century in the United States, including Christian Science, osteopathy, chiropractic, and naturopathy spread into Ontario (and to a lesser extent British Columbia and other provinces) between the 1890s and 1910s. In addition to these health specialties, there were others that promoted health, or treated specific ailments, including chiropody, which treated foot problems (such as corns, bunions, and blisters) (Adams 2017b), physical culture (exercise and bodybuilding to achieve health benefits), massage, and Turkish baths.[1] Scattered practitioners providing treatment not linked with an alternative system of health or medicine could also be found, as Barbara Clow's (2001, 1997) research on Mahlon W. Locke, "toe-twister," and other practitioners has shown. These alternative providers were popular with the Ontario public: not only were their services cheaper than those provided by medical doctors, but they were often more effective for particular ailments.

The modern reader may be tempted to regard these various healers as "fringe" practitioners, but many appear to have been accepted service providers in early-twentieth-century cities and towns (and in some more rural settings as well). Among the most popular practices in the early twentieth century was Christian Science, which according to Jasen (1997/8) found its largest following in Ontario and the Western Canadian provinces, beginning in the 1880s. Christian Scientists regarded illness as an illusion of the mind; then, as today, they believe healing can be obtained through faith and prayer (ibid.). As a religious practice, Christian Science did not seek professional regulation. Rather, medical legislation was altered to provide an exemption for practitioners. More central to regulatory debates at the time were osteopaths, who appear to have entered Ontario in 1900, and chiropractors, who became quite numerous in the province in the two succeeding decades (Adams 2012; Biggs 1989; Mills 1966). Osteopaths advanced perhaps the most compelling case for regulation in the 1910s and 1920s, but never succeeded in becoming independent self-regulating professionals in the provinces examined here. In contrast, chiropractors' claims to expertise and education were not accepted by policymakers, but their popularity (and medicine's opposition to them) made them impossible to ignore.

Osteopathy was founded by Andrew Taylor Still, a largely self-trained medical doctor who had exposure to a variety of medical therapies. Beginning in the 1870s, Still provided health services mixing the practices of bone-setting with the tenets of magnetic healing (Gevitz 2004; Whorton 2002). Osteopaths believed in the body's power to heal itself. Illness occurred in bodies that were not structurally sound, and the task for the osteopath was to return the body to its proper state, through manipulation, so that the body could heal (Whorton 2002; Miller 1998). Hence, historically, osteopathic treatment entailed "the manual manipulation of bones and soft tissue with the goal of restoring the structural integrity so the circulatory, nervous and other body systems could function in a natural and healthy way" (Miller 1998: 1740). Still had immediate success with his treatment methods, and the practice spread quickly after Still established a school in Kirksville, Missouri, in 1892 (Gevitz 2004). Other osteopathy schools opened elsewhere in the United States in succeeding years. Osteopathy became a regulated health profession in the late 1890s and early 1900s in many American states, but to win regulation, osteopaths had to change their educational curriculum, expanding attention to medical science (Gevitz 2004). Although osteopathy had begun as a "drugless" therapy, osteopathy schools expanded the curriculum to include obstetrics, surgery, and even pharmacology in the early twentieth century (ibid.). By the early 1900s, then, osteopathy offered a real alternative to medicine – one that promised to incorporate the best medical advances with manual therapy to provide more complete, holistic, treatment, less reliant on drugs and surgery than regular medicine. In the opening decade of the twentieth century, osteopathy was the main alternative to regular medicine in the United States (Gevitz 1988b: 124); many North Americans rejected the medical profession's reliance on drugs, and eagerly sought such alternatives.

American-trained osteopaths set up practice in Ontario (and Quebec) in early 1900. Some of the early practitioners were Canadian-born, while others were Americans seeking a new market (Adams 2012). Although most of the earliest practitioners were men, several were women: Still was "a staunch supporter of women's rights" (Whorton 2002: 151). Medical doctors acted swiftly to this influx, and early practitioners were charged with the illegal practice of medicine and illegal use of the title "doctor," sometimes within weeks of establishing a practice (Adams 2012).[2] In the face of this prosecution, local and provincial osteopath organizations were formed; groups provided moral and financial support to practitioners facing criminal charges (Hodgins 1918). The success of these prosecutions was mixed. The medical profession did not always obtain convictions, and legal action did not stem the tide. Osteopaths continued to enter Canada. Estimates suggest that there were five osteopaths practising in Quebec in 1911 (Mills 1966), and in 1916, three in British Columbia and twenty-one spread across Alberta and Saskatchewan (Hodgins 1918). The largest number of practitioners entered Ontario where, by 1913, there were an estimated seventy-five practising osteopaths (ibid.).

In 1909, the Ontario medical profession charged Toronto osteopath Robert B. Henderson, a leader in the Ontario Association of Osteopathy, with the illegal practice of medicine. The case was tried before a local magistrate, who refused to provide a verdict, sending the case to a higher court (*Toronto Star* 1909). The final judgment given in the case was a boon to osteopaths and other drugless practitioners. Since Henderson did not prescribe medicine, County Judge Morson reasoned, he was not practising medicine. The judge provided advice to the medical council of the College of Physicians of Surgeons: "If the Ontario Medical Council desires the meaning of the word 'medicine' extended to cover the present case they must apply to the Legislature" (*Toronto Star* 1910: 1; CPSO 1938: 21). This verdict not only effectively legalized drugless practice in Ontario, but it spurred professional projects by both the medical profession and osteopaths. Medical doctors sought regulatory change to establish a definition of medicine that would eliminate drugless practice once and for all. Osteopaths sought status as a legitimate, regulated health profession, equivalent to medicine in terms of its powers of self-regulation.

Osteopaths began immediately, petitioning the legislature for a bill in 1910 (Ontario 1910a).[3] However, their petition was deemed inadmissible for procedural reasons, and hence, no legislation was forthcoming (Ontario 1910b). The osteopaths resolved to try again. To many social actors in the early 1910s, the regulation of osteopathy seemed likely and reasonable. State actors appear to have been open to the idea, and members of the Ontario Association for Osteopathy were committed to this path. Several medical leaders felt it was inevitable, and began discussing how osteopathy regulation might best be structured in order to maintain medicine's interests (Bruce 1912).

The medical council's own lawyer, Z.A. Lash, began working – on his own initiative – on a legislative solution. Lash was a prominent Ontario lawyer, considered to be "the great corporate counsel of his era," and a skilled legal drafter (Moore 1997: 153). Late in 1910, Lash was corresponding with provincial premier James P. Whitney on medical council business (which he did frequently), and offered to draft an amendment to the medical act to "take care of the Osteopaths" (Archives of Ontario [AO] 1910a). He asked Whitney to send him a copy of the draft bill that had been prepared but not presented, and a copy of the medical act. Lash was on friendly terms with Whitney, addressing his letters to "My dear Sir James," and his offer to draft a bill appears to have been a personal favour, not official business for either the government or the medical council. Indeed, when Lash sent Whitney his detailed memorandum on osteopath and medical regulation in mid-December 1910, he called it "a sort of Christmas gift, in the interest of the State!" (AO 1910b). Although Lash had originally intended to draft a bill, he explained to Whitney that since the issues were so complex, he was unable to do so. Instead, he provided Whitney with an extensive brief, containing a short history of osteopathy, an up-to-date overview of its regulatory status in the United States, and a reflective legal opinion on the regulatory issues at stake. Notably, Lash recommended that before the government proceed, it consider establishing an independent commission to investigate "their numbers and importance, with a view to judging whether the time has come for legislative recognition" of osteopaths (AO 1910c: 4). Assuming they were "entitled to regulation in some form," the question was whether it would be best to incorporate osteopathy under the medical act, or to regulate it separately (AO 1910c). Although he noted arguments for and against both paths, he seemed in the end to lean towards incorporating osteopaths under the medical act, recommending that the government sound out the osteopaths and members of the medical council to get their perspectives (ibid.).

Whitney took this advice into consideration. Shortly thereafter the government seems to have worked with the medical council and osteopathic leaders on a revision to the medical act that would incorporate osteopathy (Ontario 1912a). When that failed, the government established the Hodgins commission to investigate education and regulation in the healthcare field.

It was in 1912 that a revision to the medical act was proposed. Both osteopath and medical doctor leaders were ambivalent about this legislative solution. The 1912 bill would have brought osteopathy regulation under the control of the medical council, as the 1869 medical act did for eclectic and homeopathic medicine. Significantly, however, it made no provision for osteopathic representation on the medical council (Ontario 1912a). The bill proposed to establish high entry requirements: successful completion of a program at an approved American osteopathic college and (more challenging for osteopaths) equivalent matriculation requirements and exams for entry to practice, with the substitution of an exam in osteopathy for one in medicine (Ontario 1912a).[4] Osteopath leaders would have preferred a separate act. They were uneasy about joining the body that had dragged them through the courts over the last decade, and wary about such high matriculation and exam standards. Yet, many were won over by a generous grandfather clause allowing all osteopaths in the province who had graduated from an approved school, and practised for five years or more, to register without examination (Ontario 1912a: ss. 2, 3). Opposition from the medical profession could not be appeased, however.

The medical council supported the act. While medical leaders were disdainful of osteopaths and their claims, given state actor and public support for osteopaths, many believed that the best way to deal with the osteopaths was to absorb them. Once incoming osteopaths were required to have education equivalent to medical doctors, and pass the same exams, they would pose no threat to the public. Further, some felt, once they were exposed to medical science, practitioners would realize the error of their ways and abandon osteopathy (Bruce 1912; CMAJ 1912; *Toronto Star* 1912): "The faddists would soon disappear if they were required to spend five years in study and pass exams of a stringent kind" (McGillivray 1914: 655). Upon its introduction by an MD MPP, the "Act to amend the Medical Act" was referred to a select committee for consideration. The twelve-member legislative committee included four medical doctors, as well as two barristers, two accountants, and a few businessmen (Ontario 1912b).

When word of the bill spread through the medical profession there was outrage (CMAJ 1912; Bruce 1912). Medical leaders were highly divided. The medical council argued that the best way to undermine osteopathy was to ensure that there was only one route into medical practice – through the medical council (Bruce 1912; CMAJ 1912; McGillivray 1914). However, other doctors deplored the osteopaths as cultists (CMAJ 1912), and "ignorant, brazen-faced charlatans" (CMAJ 1915: 1092); they were unwilling to be associated with the osteopaths. A

1912 *Canadian Medical Association Journal* editorial criticized the medical council, claiming that those with the "true interests of the profession at heart" were "plainly disgusted with the attempt to drag the traditions of an honourable profession in the mire" (CMAJ 1912: 515). This element within the Ontario medical profession was so vocal that the MD MPP who introduced the bill, Dr Jamieson, apologized for the controversy and had all provisions relating to osteopathy deleted from the bill (*Globe* 1912b).[5]

While this action quelled the controversy, it did nothing to solve the overarching problem, and osteopaths and medical leaders continued to lobby the government for legislation. Although some medical leaders still argued incorporating osteopathy was the best solution (McGillivray 1914), others advocated for a revision to the medical act that would define the practice of medicine in a manner that would render osteopathy illegal, thereby enabling medical doctors to eradicate the practice in Ontario (CMAJ 1915). Osteopaths sought a regulatory body of their own. With optometrists, nurses, and others also asking for legislation around this time, Premier Whitney promised that he would establish a royal commission (AO 1919a).[6]

As discussed in chapter 5, the Hodgins commission was significant not only for its influence over the regulation of medicine and other health practices, but because it seemed to signal a change in the Ontario government's approach to professional regulation. The commission also profoundly shaped professional projects in the 1910s, as it opened up an opportunity for aspiring professional groups to organize, and state their case to a receptive audience, with the hope of winning professional legislation. After several delays, Justice Hodgins was appointed commissioner in 1915, and shortly thereafter began holding hearings with interested professional groups and individuals. Hodgins not only spoke to major provincial associations like the Ontario Medical Association and the Ontario Association of Osteopathy, but smaller groups such as the Academy of Medicine, and a variety of mainstream and alternative health providers. In his report he explained that he "heard the evidence or opinions of 207 persons, many of them more than once"; he also visited "14 cities, 5 of them more than once," and inspected 17 institutions (Hodgins 1918: 4).

When the commission was announced, the roughly 100 chiropractors in the province organized, forming at least four distinct associations: the Canadian Chiropractors Association, the Dominion Chiropractors Association, the Ontario Chiropractic Association, and the Drugless

Physicians Association (DPA)[7] (Biggs 1989: 138).[8] Each had a distinct membership. Chiropractic was split at the time. "Straight" chiropractors restricted their practice to chiropractic treatment through spinal manipulation; they were represented by the first two above-named organizations. In contrast, "mixers" combined chiropractic treatment with other therapies including electrotherapy, hydrotherapy, light therapy, and even osteopathy and naturopathy. They were represented by the latter two groups, with the most eclectic (and dually trained) joining the DPA (Biggs 1989). Chiropractic was another US transplant, having been established by (Toronto-born) D.D. Palmer in Iowa in the late 1890s (Whorton 2002; Biggs 1989). Chiropractors believed that illness was caused by "skeletal subluxations" (dislocations), and that once the "subluxation" was adjusted, the patient would be cured (Whorton 2002: 169). Chiropractic spread to Canada in the early 1900s, experiencing slow growth at first, followed by rapid growth in the late 1910s and early 1920s.

Each of the Ontario chiropractic groups met with Hodgins; some made a clear impression, but not a positive one. D.D. Palmer's son and then head of chiropractic in the United States B.J. Palmer met with Hodgins and declared that chiropractors had no use for chemistry or bacteriology, and no use for diagnosis (*Globe* 1915d: 7). Further, he reportedly declared that "bacteriology was the greatest of all gigantic farces ever invented for ignorance and incompetency" (Hodgins 1918: 125; Sutherland 1998: 164). Chiropractors, including Canadian Chiropractic College head Ernst Duval, rejected medical science, and saw advanced training as useless (Hodgins 1918). These extreme views were more commonly expressed by straight chiropractors. Mixer chiropractors were less opposed to medical science, and more moderate in their views.

Hodgins's report was eagerly awaited as established and aspiring professional groups hoped it would support their regulation and lead to positive regulatory change. Hodgins made definite recommendations concerning the regulation of medicine, osteopathy, and chiropractic, among other groups. As noted in chapter 5, he supported medicine's drive for a definition of the practice of medicine, and proposed a definition that was a variation on that suggested by the profession itself. Nonetheless, he criticized the medical profession for its failure to embrace "physical methods" of treatment that had been shown during the First World War to be so valuable (Hodgins 1918: 8–16). Medicine was urged to alter its educational curriculum to expand training in physical therapy for medical doctors, and to take the lead on further developments in this field. In addition, Hodgins recommended changes to the composition of the CPSO's medical council, with more government oversight of the council's activities, and affirmed that separate council exams should be required for entry to practise medicine (a medical degree from a provincial university was not sufficient).

Hodgins devoted more attention to osteopathy in his report than any other single specialty, documenting not only the state of osteopathy in the province, but also investigating osteopathy education and regulation in the United States. While osteopaths in the OAO tended to be highly trained, and committed to professional advance, there were others in the province who were only partially trained, either at fly-by-night colleges that sprung up in the province or at chiropractic mixer schools that provided some training in osteopathy on the side (at least some of these partially trained osteopaths were affiliated with the Drugless Physicians Association) (Hodgins 1918). Hodgins was ultimately ambivalent about the regulation of osteopathy. As osteopathy education in the United States increasingly resembled allopathic medical education, he felt the two professions might merge. Further, he was troubled by the lack of osteopathic schools in the province of Ontario, and unwilling to tie provincial licensing to American institutions. Thus, he felt that regulation was premature for all osteopaths, although he clearly saw osteopathy as a useful practice (in keeping with his opinion that manual therapies had been ignored for too long). Hodgins recommended that osteopaths in practice in Ontario as of "June 30th 1913" – symbolizing the date when Premier Whitney called for the commission – "be licensed to continue as osteopaths only" as long as their education met the standard set by the American Osteopathic Association (Hodgins 1918: 31). For Hodgins this was "a matter of equity more than of legal right," and indeed "somewhat of an indulgence" to these older practitioners, but one that "will not hurt the medical profession" (ibid.). The number of practitioners affected was small enough to "prevent any great harm being done to the public" (ibid.).

Osteopathic leaders took Hodgins's recommendations as an endorsement of their practice, and within a few years, this became accepted wisdom. Hodgins's report was almost 200 pages in length, and although some gave it a close reading, and prepared detailed responses to it (Ontario Medical Association [OMA] 1918; DuVal 1918), the nuance of Hodgins's argument respecting osteopathy was lost. In the 1920s, not only osteopath leaders, but medical leaders and state actors frequently refer to Hodgins as having endorsed osteopathy regulation, providing further impetus to osteopaths' professional projects (see, for instance, AO 1919a; CPSO 1938).

There was no possible confusion about Hodgins's assessment of chiropractic. For him, chiropractors' "repudiation of all modern scientific knowledge and methods is such that it would be impossible to recommend any way in which they could be allowed to practise by which the public could be safeguarded" (Hodgins 1918: 32–3). He continued to explain that those to whom he spoke "saw no necessity for preparatory qualifications, [and] ridiculed and repudiated diagnosis, bacteriology and chemistry" (ibid.: 33). Although Hodgins noted that chiropractic had many supporters, he could not bring himself "to the point of accepting, as part of our legalized medical provision for the sick, a system which denies the need of diagnosis, refers 95 per cent of disease to one and the same cause, and turns its back resolutely upon all modern medical scientific methods as being founded on nothing and unworthy even to be discussed" (ibid.). Chiropractors' rejection of medical science, and their flawed theory of illness, made it "dangerous" to sanction their practice in Ontario (ibid.).

As noted, Hodgins spoke to numerous chiropractic groups, and a careful reading of his report reveals some differences in his responses to them. It is Dr Duval and the straight chiropractors who are particularly marked for disdain and rejection. Hodgins actually includes the Drugless Physicians Association in his discussion of osteopathy, noting that virtually none of the groups' members are fully trained osteopaths. While the presence of lesser-trained drugless practitioners in the province fostered Hodgins's ambivalence towards osteopathy regulation, he nonetheless did not entirely reject their methods or practice, as he did for straight chiropractors.

Hodgins's report was sweeping, and its recommendations taken seriously by all groups involved. The Ontario government chose not to act immediately on Hodgins's recommendations, stating that it needed time to consider its many recommendations (*Globe* 1918a, 1918b). Late in 1918, government leaders did sit down with medical doctors, osteopaths, chiropractors, and drugless physicians to get their feedback on the report and decide how to move forward (*Globe* 1918b).[9] The medical profession was, on balance, supportive of the Hodgins report (OMA 1918; CMAJ 1918), as were, for the most part, the osteopaths. At least some chiropractic organizations protested the report, criticizing Hodgins for his medical bias (DuVal 1918), while others attempted to distance themselves from the controversial anti-science stance taken by the former (Drugless Physicians Association 1919).

In the fall and winter of 1918–19, the Conservative government drafted a new medical act in accordance with Hodgins's recommendations. This draft bill was circulated to government leaders and executive council for consideration (AO 1919a, 1919b). The bill proposed significant changes to medical regulation, altering the make-up of the medical council and reducing its powers of self-regulation, as recommended by Hodgins. Not only did the bill require the medical council to get approval from the government to pass regulations, but it also granted the government veto power over those regulations, and empowered the lieutenant governor to pass regulations governing medicine (without council approval). The draft bill also proposed to establish a licensing board to govern entry to practise osteopathy, chiropractic, and other forms of drugless practice like electrotherapy and hydrotherapy (AO 1919c). All trained osteopaths currently practising (with proof of moral character) would be given a licence to practice with no conditions; other healers faced some restrictions, but would be eligible to practise on satisfying a licensing board of their competence and moral character. The bill granted the lieutenant governor the right to appoint the licensing board, and pass regulations governing practice (ibid.). While the draft act proposed to license current practitioners, it made no explicit provisions for the registration of new practitioners. It, thus, appears to respond to Hodgins's recommendation that current osteopaths be allowed to practise, but that no provision be made for new entrants to practise in the province.[10]

The contents of the bill reflect Hodgins's (1918) recommendations, but may also have reflected state actors' views of the different alternative health practitioners. According to memos and assorted other records from the attorney general's office (AO 1919a), some state officials regarded the "position of the osteopaths" to be "a reasonable one" (ibid.: 3). Without regulation, "ignorant and unscrupulous people will avail themselves of the freedom thus created for the purpose of money-making and for other purposes even more objectionable" (ibid.). However, at least some of the chiropractors did not impress: they gave "the impression that neither their knowledge nor their qualities were such as those who practice healing should possess" (AO 1919a: 3–4). Further, the campaign of some segments of chiropractic "to destroy the confidence of the public in the medical profession," and their leadership in the anti-vaccination campaign, was regarded as a potential danger to the public (AO 1919a). Thus, the 1918–19 draft bill gave more recognition to osteopaths than others. Regardless, the draft bill was never officially introduced. It was rejected by caucus, largely because of its proposals concerning the regulation of drugless practice (AO 1919a): "Great objection was taken to putting chiropractors and others out of business on political grounds" (AO 1919b). Although state leaders saw little merit in chiropractic, they were well aware that many consumers used chiropractors' services; state actors were reluctant to legislate against them.

When Premier Hearst introduced a bill to amend the medical act late in April of 1919, only the clauses redrawing the powers and composition of the medical council remained (Ontario 1919b). Medical leaders were appalled and acted swiftly to oppose this legislation that, in their eyes, "would have rendered the authority of the medical council abortive and nullified its very existence" (Ferguson 1919: 1095). The government immediately withdrew the bill, claiming that it was "an eleventh hour measure hurriedly compiled under a misapprehension of the views and attitude of the medical profession" (ibid.). Evidently, the Hearst government was unclear about how to deal with the contests surrounding health professional regulation. The problem was taken out of their hands by the subsequent election that brought a terrible defeat to the Conservative party, and carried the United Farmers of Ontario – Labour party coalition into power.

The new government was elected on a popular mandate of government economy, support for rural issues, infrastructure development, and prohibition (Badgley 2000; Johnston 1986). Agrarian populism was high immediately following the First World War, partly in reaction to policies at multiple levels of government that were deemed anti-farmer (Badgley 2000; Eidlin 2015). After the 1919 election, the make-up of the legislature changed dramatically. Roughly half (47%) of all MPPs were farmers. Only 12% were members of regulated professions; most of these practitioners were lawyers (who represented 9% of all MPPs). Several MPPs were tradesmen. To secure an attorney general, the new premier, E.C. Drury, had to convince former Liberal William Edgar Raney to join the party and seek a seat through a by-election; none of the coalition's MPPs were lawyers. There were only two MD MPPs in the legislature at the time: Mimico practitioner and long-serving conservative Forbes Godfrey and Londoner Hugh Allen Stevenson, who represented the Labour party. Whereas in previous years, the medical profession could shape legislative change from within the legislature, with such low representation the medical profession was forced to alter its tactics.

The new premier and attorney general were soon briefed on the regulatory challenges facing them in the health profession field (AO 1919a). Like his predecessors, Premier Drury met with representatives from medicine and the various osteopath, chiropractic, and drugless practice groups to discuss legislation, but nothing was immediately brought forward. There appears to have been an expectation that legislation was imminent, however. Chiropractors attempted to prevent the introduction of legislation detrimental to them by mobilizing their patients. The premier's office was inundated with hundreds of letters attesting to the benefits of chiropractic, and begging the premier not to be swayed by efforts of the medical profession to legislate them out of existence (AO 1921). However, Drury refused to dictate a legislative solution; rather, he reputedly asserted "that there should be no Medical Legislation unless the Medical Doctors and the Osteopaths got together on a definite Bill" (Ontario Association of Osteopathy [OAO] 1923: 1; *Globe* 1921c). Further, he outright refused medicine's request for legislation that would make alternative health practice illegal (MacNab 1970: 47). In keeping with his populist political views, Premier Drury supported the principle of consumer choice: when in poor health people should be able to choose the practitioner they wanted (MacNab 1970: 47; Johnston 1986). Further, Drury's government was not particularly friendly to medicine. Drury believed medical doctors were using their prescribing privileges to circumvent prohibition – a cause he was passionate about. His government's clamp-down resulted in the removal of conservative MPP Dr Forbes Godfrey's prescription-writing privileges (Johnston 1986: 162). At the same time, there is no evidence that Drury was a particular supporter of osteopathy or chiropractic. Nevertheless, his government was reluctant to legislate against these practitioners because they enjoyed substantial public support. In the end, no new legislation affecting medicine, osteopathy, or chiropractic was brought forward until 1923.[11]

By 1923, the medical profession was frustrated about the lack of legislative progress, and decided to lobby the government heavily and take steps to win over the public (Routley 1922, 1965). The Ontario Medical Association and medical council established a joint committee to construct a medical bill and met regularly with the provincial premier on the legislation (Secord 1923; Routley 1965; Ferguson 1930: 85). Although the premier was initially reluctant (Routley 1965), after several months of negotiations, the government and medical leaders agreed on a bill. To ensure the bill's success, medical leaders were forced to accept a compromise, since legislators were unwilling to pass legislation highly detrimental to alternative healers. Through this medical act, medical doctors hoped to establish a definition of medical practice that could be used to prosecute alternative health practitioners like chiropractors and osteopaths, and ultimately rid the province of these alternative healers. The medical bill presented, though, exempted osteopaths, chiropractors, and other drugless therapists from prosecution for the illegal practice of medicine, as long as they registered with the provincial secretary (with proof of qualifications and good character) within sixty days. The act also empowered the government to draft regulations to govern alternative practitioners' entry to practice (Ontario 1923a).

Medical leaders believed that there was little support for their position in the legislative assembly, acknowledging that the chiropractors' lobby had been effective in winning over legislators, and that many state officials were sympathetic to the osteopaths' claims. Lacking an effective presence in the legislature, medical leaders lobbied legislators to persuade them to pass the act, going so far as to identify the personal physician of every MPP and mobilizing member support (Routley 1965: 41–2). Medical doctors "deluged" legislators "with approximately five thousand telegrams from every corner of the province asking for" legislation favourable to the profession (Secord 1923: 555). Many telegrams were sent directly to the premier as well (AO 1923).

There was considerable protest against the bill by the Ontario Association of Osteopathy, whose members were appalled by the medical council's tactics and with being "dumped out into the discard with chiropractors, divine healers, drugless healers, and other healers ad infinitum" (OAO 1923: 1). At the time, osteopaths' training was virtually equivalent to that of orthodox medicine, and they were horrified that the act not only failed to acknowledge their claimed status as a medical profession, but linked them with those who rejected medical science and education as "absolutely unnecessary" and a "danger to the people" (DuVal 1918: 3, 19). The chiropractic response to the legislation was divided. The Drugless Physicians Association – whose members were chiropractic mixers and lesser-trained osteopaths – supported the bill, as did members of the Ontario Board of Chiropractors (AO 1923). However, at least some chiropractors, predominantly straights and those associated with the chiropractic school in Toronto, were opposed, reportedly because they did not "wish to standardize their courses" (ibid.).[12] Chiropractors, then, appear to have been divided by training and treatment methods: those who were formally trained (in the United States) at mixer schools favoured the legislation, while many straight chiropractors and the lesser trained opposed it. In the end, the premier was able to obtain osteopaths' agreement to the bill, with the promise that he would provide them with more favourable legislation after the next election (*Globe* 1923b, 1924). Premier Drury himself introduced the bill in parliament on April 27 1923. To smooth its passage through the house, he first met with leaders from the other parties to discuss it (*Globe* 1923a: 12). After all the lobbying and negotiations, the bill moved through the house quickly, and was only modestly amended in the committee of the whole (Ontario 1923b).

The 1923 revision to the medical act appeared, at first, to have solved the contests around the regulation of medicine and drugless healing in the province. Medical practitioners had obtained legislation providing their long-awaited definition of the practice of medicine, and the act promised to curtail drugless practice in the future. At the time, there was growing concern about the increase in the number of drugless healers – and especially chiropractors – in the province. In 1915, there were approximately 100 chiropractors in Ontario, but by 1923 the number had grown to 550 – a 450 per cent increase in only eight years (Mills 1966). At least some of these new practitioners were not formally trained. The new legislation promised not only to legitimate and legalize the practice of osteopaths, chiropractors, and drugless healers in the province, but also to curtail the rapid growth of (especially untrained) practitioners in succeeding years. Legislators appear to have seen the act as a measure that would serve the people – and therefore match the populist platform of the dominant party – while simultaneously addressing the needs of the major professional groups who had been lobbying them. Ultimately, however, this legislative solution was not effective.

An election held in June 1923 brought the defeat of the United Farmers – Labour coalition government and the return of the Conservatives to power. This defeat ended discussions among state and professional leaders intended to establish regulations under the 1923 medical act (AO 1923).

The new Conservative government led by G. Howard Ferguson was more sympathetic to medicine than the previous one. There were six MD MPPs elected, along with two dentists and two pharmacists (members of these professions often supported medicine in disputes against drugless healers); all but one of these ten were members of the Conservative party. Long-serving Conservative MD MPP Forbes Godfrey was a member of cabinet, and soon became Ontario's first minister of health. Although Ferguson was a lawyer by training, his father was a medical doctor (as well as a politician) (Oliver 1977), and Ferguson appeared supportive of medicine's claims.

In 1924, Ferguson's government sat down with leaders from the various chiropractic and osteopath associations, and medical leaders, in an attempt to draft regulations under the 1923 medical act. The tone of these meetings appears to have been quite different than those under previous governments. Osteopath leaders affiliated with the OAO complained to the media that their concerns were not being heard. Rather, they claimed, "medical politicians" tried to dictate terms to the osteopaths, without compromise (*Globe* 1924: 13). Osteopaths sought legislative privileges that reflected their education and training, and the status of osteopathy in the United States (where its regulatory privileges were identical to medicine's in many states). Medical doctors and their government allies refused to accommodate osteopaths. While some state actors clearly remained sympathetic to osteopaths' case, with medicine unwilling to compromise, and a government leadership sympathetic to medicine's stance, osteopaths' prospects for positive regulatory change were poor.

Talks continued into 1925, but reaching a solution that satisfied all groups seemed impossible.[13] Some drugless healer groups were willing to compromise with the medical profession, and accept a circumscribed role, but the osteopaths were not (CPSO 1938). With negotiations at a standstill, the government began to consider other legislative options. An informal back-room meeting conducted after official talks broke down appears to have provided a solution. In March 1925, four practitioners, representing chiropractors, drugless healers, and "pseudo-osteopaths"[14] met with a lawyer in the attorney general's office and made it clear they were "content to have an Act drawn providing for a Board for the purpose of registering and licensing persons who treat the human body by physical manipulation without the use of drugs" (AO 1925). The official advised the Attorney General that it would be "a comparatively simple matter" to deal with "these people" (ibid.). It was suggested that additional measures could be put in place later to deal with the osteopaths (ibid.).

This backroom meeting in mid-March of 1925 (combined with several meetings with the CPSO-OMA joint legislation committee) led to the

1925 Drugless Practitioners Act, which was presented in the provincial parliament a mere three weeks later. State officials seem to have felt confident about moving forward, given that the four men who approached them appeared to have represented a variety of drugless practices. In reality, however, all four of the men who approached the state employee were affiliated with the Drugless Physicians' Association, although they held other association affiliations as well. Thus, the Drugless Practitioners Act was at least partly brought about through the savvy lobbying of the Drugless Physicians' Association, and their willingness to accommodate the medical professions' stance on drugless practitioners' regulation. At the same time, the medical profession was "very active" in securing the act (Ferguson 1930: 92). Their heavy lobbying, and their ability to ally themselves with the premier, minister of health, and attorney general, were important. Government leaders appeared committed to regulatory solutions that would satisfy medicine, without eliminating alternative health practice.

The other groups involved had little impact on the legislation. Trained osteopaths and members of other chiropractic groups were only informed about the act days before its presentation in the legislature. They protested, with no success (*Globe* 1925a, 1925b). Osteopaths later contended they were promised that subsequent legislation would be passed to provide them with due recognition (and government records suggest that this was certainly the intention of some within the AG's office) (*Globe* 1931; AO 1925). With this promise they muted their opposition. The attorney general, W.F. Nickle, introduced the act on 3 April 1925, and within a week it had passed. At the same time, an amendment to the medical act was passed that repealed the 1923 medical act, and made it illegal for anyone other than a licensed medical doctor to use the title "Dr"; hereafter, drugless practitioners could not call themselves "doctor" even if they held a doctorate degree (Ontario 1925a).

Compared to other acts regulating professions, Ontario's 1925 Drugless Practitioners Act is an oddity. Although the act provides a general definition of drugless practice, it specifies neither the occupations it seeks to regulate nor the criteria for entry to practice. The act principally establishes a board of regents, appointed by the lieutenant governor, and empowers it to pass regulations identifying the groups to be covered under the act, and to establish criteria for entry to practice. The act also protects the rights of medical doctors (Ontario 1925b). It was only under the regulations passed in 1926 that the groups affected by the legislation were identified: osteopaths, chiropractors, and drugless healers, as well as masseurs and chiropodists.[15] It is not entirely clear whether it was the original intention to bring the latter two groups under the act. Neither is it clear if they were included in any of the meetings with medicine and government leaders in the years prior to the act. The chiropodists, for one, do not appear to have been organized (at least provincially) before the passage of the act (Adams 2017b).

In the decade following the passage of the Drugless Practitioners Act, contests over the regulation of drugless healing continued to play out in the courts, the newspapers, and in the legislature; however, these contests were less intense, and in the end brought little change. In the spring of 1925, the government appointed five men to serve on the board of regents. Dr T.W.G. McKay, an MD and regulatory body veteran who had previously served as an examiner for the CPSO and on the optometry board, was appointed to the important role of secretary-treasurer, and hence main liaison with the government on regulatory matters.[16] Also named to the board of regents was chiropractic mixer (and drugless healer) A.W. (Archie) MacFie – a London, Ontario, practitioner and a driving force within the Drugless Physicians Association, who government records reveal was quietly influential in shaping regulatory outcomes. MacFie was the son of a Southwestern Ontario farmer; he had received formal training in chiropractic (earning his DC and a Master's degree) at Ross College in Indiana.[17]

Two prominent leaders in the OAO, Robert B. Henderson and Hubert Pocock, were also named to the board. Henderson, who held the title of chairman, was born in Oxford County around 1867, the son of a farmer. He was well educated, having attended high school in Ontario before attending the University of Minnesota, and later studied law in Ohio. He then studied osteopathy at the top (and founding) school, the American College of Osteopathy in Kirksville, Missouri. He served a term as professor at the school before setting up practice in Toronto in 1900 (*Toronto Star* 1941: 33); Henderson was one of the first osteopaths in the province. The thirty-nine-year-old Hubert Pocock grew up in London, Ontario, the son of a successful boot and shoe merchant. He also studied at the Kirksville school, and pursued additional training in Michigan before establishing a practice in Toronto around 1912. Less is known about the final member of the board, James Newburn, a Sudbury-based chiropractor who grew up in a farming household and was slightly younger than the other board members, being only thirty-two when appointed. When choosing board of regents members, it is evident that state actors chose practitioners who, on the whole, were better educated than the majority of drugless healers, men who could at least play the part of gentlemen. Further, at least three (MacFie, Henderson, and Pocock) had been meeting with state actors, representing their respective associations, for several years. The government sought trustworthy men to draft regulations and enforce them during what was bound to be a contentious process.

The first task of the board was to establish regulations under the act and determine criteria for entry to practise the different specialties. Government leaders worked closely with the board of regents to produce the regulations (*Toronto Star* 1926a). Almost immediately, there was controversy. Given the make-up of the board, it is perhaps not surprising that board members sought to establish high education requirements for entry to practice. Straight chiropractors and a small group of osteopaths who had no formal training (referred to as "pseudo-osteopaths") protested as soon as a draft of the regulations was circulated late in 1925 (*Toronto Star* 1925; *Globe* 1925c). A chiropractic school had been established in Toronto, and its course did not meet the minimum requirement – indeed, many straight chiropractors' schooling did not (Biggs 1989). Mixer schools tended to run longer courses, as they combined training in chiropractic with other treatment modalities like naturopathy (Gort and Coburn 1997; Biggs 1989). Compromises were made to grant the pseudo-osteopaths licences to practise (despite the protests of trained osteopaths), and to establish a special exam for students at the Toronto Chiropractic School (AO 1929). There would be no exceptions, however, for future practitioners, and so the regulations effectively reduced practitioner numbers and limited practice by the untrained.

According to numbers provided by the board early in 1928, there were 91 osteopaths, 16 pseudo-osteopaths, 158 chiropractors, 235 joint chiropractor and drugless therapists, and 35 (sole) drugless therapists licensed to practice in the province. The board had also licensed 45 chiropodists and 79 masseurs (AO 1928). Most of the registered had been practising before the act was passed. Only an additional three osteopaths, 25 chiropractors, and 22 drugless therapists had been added in the province between 1926 and 1928. In fact, the overall numbers of drugless practitioners in the province were in decline (Gort and Coburn 1997: 148). Further, the board reported increasingly "harmonious inter-relations" between "legally qualified Medical practitioners and the Drugless Practitioners" (AO 1928: 4).

Immediately after the board and its regulations were established, the medical profession began prosecuting illegal practitioners under the DP Act (*Toronto Star* 1926b, 1929). This activity led to a decline in practice by the untrained in the province. Early in 1926, several leading osteopaths sought to establish a college in the province, but when their requests for permission to establish a hospital (for treatment and training purposes) and to grant degrees were turned down, they abandoned the project (AO 1926–8). Not long after, the medical council sought to enforce its new monopoly over the use of the title "Dr" by prosecuting high-profile osteopaths and chiropractors. Board of regents member Hubert Pocock was the unfortunate target, along with chiropractor W.J. Ellison (*Globe* 1927a, 1927b). The issue was a controversial one, and many newspapers and members of the public were on the side of the osteopaths: surely, it was argued, someone who had earned a doctorate degree could use the title "Dr" (*Globe* 1928). While the lower courts sided with Pocock and the drugless healers, medical leaders appealed to a higher court, and in 1927 won the judgment they had sought (CMAJ 1927; *Globe* 1927b).[18] Drugless healers could not call themselves "doctor" any more.

This exclusion was one that a range of alternative healers felt keenly, and spurred some joint legislative activity in 1934 and 1938; cooperation among chiropractors was encouraged by the merging of their several associations in the 1930s (Biggs 1989; *Toronto Star* 1933). Chiropractors, osteopaths, and drugless healers jointly sponsored bills that would enable them to use the title "Dr" and expand their powers of self-regulation (Ontario 1934a, Ontario 1934b, Ontario 1938). None of these bills was successful. Osteopaths pursued legislation that would remove them from the confines of the Drugless Practitioners Act, and give them a level of professional status and recognition they felt was commensurate with their education and training in 1933 (Ontario 1933a). The legislative committee reviewing the bill noted medical opposition, but saw enough merit in the bill that they recommended a select committee be established (Ontario 1933b: 173). Medical leaders would not compromise and indeed stepped up their efforts to investigate osteopath education and practice, with the goal of showing it lacking.[19] Osteopaths' efforts were further opposed by other drugless healers who contended that such legislation would give osteopaths an unfair advantage (MacNab 1970). The Drugless Practitioners Act would remain on the books until the end of the century, although certain groups managed to escape its confines, beginning with chiropody in 1944.

By the late 1930s legislative activity had slowed. The medical profession had succeeded in maintaining its dominant position in the healthcare field, and while osteopaths, chiropractors, and drugless healers were accepted healthcare providers, the confines of the act discouraged the spread of drugless practice in years to come. Osteopaths continued to be trained in the United States, where their scope of practice was virtually equivalent to that of allopathic medical doctors. They were not interested in setting up practice in Ontario, where the scope of practice was so limited (Adams 2012; OAO 1966). High standards in the province, combined with educational trends in the United States, also limited growth in chiropractic and drugless healing (naturopathy) in the province (Adams and Etherington 2015).

Reflections on the Ontario Case

This look at contests over the regulation of drugless healing in Ontario between the 1910s and 1930s is both sociologically rich and theoretically important. It not only provides some evidence supporting neo-Weberian and collective mobility approaches to profession creation, but also demonstrates the value of ecological approaches. The regulation of osteopathy, chiropractic, and drugless healing was the product of resource mobilization, inter-professional conflict, and linked ecologies.

Considering events from the professions' points of view, it is clear that both established and aspiring professions were engaged in social closure projects. The medical profession pursued exclusionary social closure, through both the courts and legislative change, with the goal of eliminating alternative healers' opportunities to practise in the province. When they won new legislation, they again used the courts to prosecute illegal practitioners; remember that it was the CPSO that first prosecuted unregistered drugless healers under the Drugless Practitioners' Act (*Toronto Star* 1929). The OAO pursued what Witz (1992: 48) and other neo-Weberians call a "dual closure strategy": trained osteopaths attempted to battle the medical profession's exclusionary social closure, while at the same time trying to secure their own occupational boundaries by excluding lesser-trained osteopaths and chiropractors from their ranks. Chiropractors and drugless healers could be said to have pursued usurpationary closure strategies, in an attempt to change their excluded status (see Witz 1992: 49).

To achieve these closure goals, practitioners mobilized several resources. They formed organizations, they mobilized their patients (chiropractors especially), they courted the support of major newspapers (osteopaths especially), and they lobbied government leaders. The medical profession used their position inside the legislature when that opportunity was available to them, and when it was not, they lobbied individual legislators, and drew on common social connections to win over their state actor audience. Leaders in all groups took advantage of the opportunity provided by the Hodgins commission to advance their case. All this activity would have required financial resources as well. Professional groups hired lawyers to help argue their cases, and hence would have needed to pay lawyer fees. Further, face-to-face meetings with government leaders took place in Toronto, and several professional leaders had to cover the cost of travelling. These campaigns were carried out over a period of fifteen to twenty-five years (depending on the group), and thus were sustained campaigns requiring considerable organizational and personal resources.

It is also evident that inter-professional conflict between medical doctors and drugless practitioners shaped regulatory outcomes. In these battles, some groups had more success than did others. Medical doctors had an insider position, and good, well-established relations with government leaders. Osteopaths also made a favourable impression with state actors. While drugless physicians were fairly well regarded, many state actors appear to have agreed with Hodgins that chiropractors were "dangerous" and ignorant. They were not, however, willing to alienate the public by regulating against them.[20] In the end, government leaders embraced a compromise position that upheld medicine's dominant position, and legitimated but controlled chiropractic and others. There is evidence, though, that state actors had difficulty keeping track of all the different organizations representing the various groups and advancing competing claims. In the end, it seemed simplest to pass the Drugless Practitioners Act, lumping all such practitioners together, and allowing the regulatory body to sort out the differences. Although not an ideal solution from the point of view of many practitioners (especially the trained osteopaths), this solution reduced inter-professional conflict, and allowed members of all groups to continue practising, while curbing the growth of drugless practice by the untrained.

This case study also provides support for theories that cast state actors as active participants in regulating professions – even if their activity was a response to claims and requests advanced by professional actors. They provided far more than an "administrative rubber stamp" (Gilb 1966: 223). When state actors received competing claims, they were uncertain about what legislative solution would be best. The Hodgins commission, and repeated meetings with the practitioners involved, signal their efforts to find a solution and to resolve the inter-professional conflict. The various Ontario governments invested considerable time and both financial and personnel resources.[21] When they decided on a legislative solution, government leaders embraced it: either the premier or attorney general shepherded the bills through the legislature. Nonetheless, state actors' activity does not entirely conform to Foucauldian models. Certainly, although it could be said that regulatory solutions contributed to societal governance, there is little evidence that this was conscious or explicit. State actors did not demonstrate any clear regulatory agenda, even though the regulation of healthcare professions in this era shows signs of standardization and rationalization, as I argued in chapter 5.

At the same time, it is not clear that Ontario legislators were the strategizing politicians seeking short-term political gains that one finds in Abbott's (2005) account of medical regulation in New York State in the late nineteenth century. When they discuss the rationales for regulation, state actors usually comment on the public interest, and the need to distinguish the trained from the untrained and unscrupulous (AO 1910c, AO 1919b).[22] They attempted to strike compromises that would suit multiple claimants. This said, there is certainly evidence that state actors' regulation was shaped by their political goals. Legislators in the Hearst government reportedly opposed legislation that would restrict chiropractors purely "on political grounds" (AO 1919b). Similarly, the Drury government, elected in a surge of agrarian populism, was committed to allowing members of the public freedom to choose their health provider. For political and ideological reasons, they were unwilling to legislate drugless healing out of existence. Thus, politics and parties did shape regulatory outcomes. It is not entirely clear, however, that the solution established in 1925 – the Drugless Practitioners Act – served the political interests of state actors in any broader sense. It provided a solution to a legislative problem by appeasing most of the competing groups, and resolving an issue that was likely a drain on state resources. Further, it was a solution that the pro-medicine Ferguson government was satisfied with. It is not evident that it served state interests or the government's political interests beyond this. Additional interests are not mentioned in legislative debates or internal state memoranda.

The fact that no clear state agenda is evident may reflect that at this time, these two ecologies – the professions and the state (here represented by the provincial legislature) – continued to be overlapping, rather than linked, ecologies. Thus, professionals' concerns could also be state actor concerns; the two were not entirely separate. The legislature under the Ferguson government had twenty-seven MPPs who were members of regulated professions – almost one quarter of the total. These individuals held positions of power and influence. As noted, Ferguson, whose father was a licensed medical doctor, was a lawyer. The new minister of health was a medical doctor politician, while the attorney general was, of course, a lawyer. Professionals could use their institutional roles and influence in the legislature and in key government posts to shape regulatory outcomes – outcomes that favoured the established medical profession over the lesser-educated upstarts. Legislators were not impartial or uninterested observers who needed to be convinced; rather, many were professionals with a foot in the professions ecology.

Class also shaped regulatory outcomes.[23] State leaders demonstrated a preference for interacting with the more educated and refined professional leaders. Legislators seemed to deal best with the medical doctor leaders who shared their class position. Government leaders periodically appeared at organized medicine's social events, and may have run in the same social circles. In contrast, they disdained the chiropractors, whom they described as ignorant and unpleasant. It is not surprising that the first secretary-treasurer of the board of regents was a medical doctor: it would be McKay who was the principal liaison between the board and the government. The success enjoyed by alternative health leaders such as Henderson, Pocock, and MacFie seems similarly class based. MacFie was described by one official as a "thought-taking" friend to "the Government and the Legally Qualified Medical profession" as well as "mighty sane and proper in his attitudes towards all professional relationships" (AO 1929). He had some influence with the government, helped to shape regulatory outcomes, and played a key role on the board of regents – initially as a member, and in 1934 as its secretary-treasurer – seemingly because of his ability to act gentlemanly. In contrast, other drugless healers were clearly regarded as inferior. Consider the following description found in a government memo:

> It is too true of course that many of these people are hampered by ancestral heredity and deficient earlier education and the fact that they nearly all belong to that type of human spoken of by more restful people as faddists, or charlatans, or a class of a rather misled EGO and the unlimited

faith in their own personal ability which does not seem to real students as a scientific attitude of mind." (AO 1928)

Chiropractors and other healers were often referred to as "these people," implicitly distinguished from "our people," among whom MacFie, as well as Henderson and Pocock with their respectable class backgrounds and education, could be (frequently) counted. It is significant, then, that alternative healers were regulated despite the fact that most could not claim to be professional gentlemen. As noted in chapter 5, this both demonstrates the changing meanings attached to professional regulation in the early twentieth century, and is reflected in the type of regulation they received, which was more controlling and state directed.

British Columbia

The influx of alternative health practitioners into British Columbia was more gradual. Nonetheless, as in Ontario, osteopaths, chiropractors, Christian Scientists, and other health service providers entered the province in the opening decades of the twentieth century, settling especially in Vancouver and Victoria. The first known osteopaths arrived between 1904 and 1908, while the first chiropractor appears to have set up practice in British Columbia around 1910 (Biggs 1986). Medical doctors reacted quickly, as recounted in chapter 5, approaching the BC legislature in 1909 for a revision to the medical act that would declare osteopathy illegal. Dr James H. King, an MD member of the legislative assembly (MLA) introduced the bill. When legislators accused medical doctors of seeking too much power, and misusing their authority, they amended the medical act to bring osteopathy under medical authority; practitioners would be regulated and examined by regular medical doctors (*Victoria Daily Colonist* 1909b). This compromise was made by the several MD MLAs then sitting in the legislature, with the support of the medical council. For legislators this compromise allowed consumer choice, while protecting the public by ensuring practitioners were well trained. The solution was clearly to the advantage of the medical profession, who used their regulatory powers to limit the number of osteopaths practising in the province. In 1909, before the legislation passed, Victoria and Vancouver city directories listed seven osteopaths; the following year only one remained (British Columbia City Directories 1909, 1910). Hodgins reports only three osteopaths in British Columbia several years later (Hodgins 1918). Medicine successfully enacted social closure, preventing the rise of osteopathy in the province.

Although the medical profession won the battle against osteopaths – who do not appear to have been organized or prepared to mount a professional project in 1909 – they had not won the war against drugless practice. After 1909, some BC osteopaths appear to have left the province, but a few simply continued practising under a different job title, reappearing in city directories in subsequent years as chiropractors or "physical culture" specialists. Chiropractic expanded in the province during the 1910s, but not at the rapid rate witnessed in Ontario. Medical doctors first tried to eliminate chiropractic through the courts, charging chiropractors for the illegal practice of medicine (Biggs 1986). They had some initial success, and responded with an aggressive attack: in 1920 the medical council had twelve Vancouver and five Victoria chiropractors charged and tried. In response, chiropractors organized.

They formed two distinct organizations (Biggs 1986): one represented predominantly straight chiropractors, the BC Chiropractic Association, and one represented chiropractic mixers and other drugless practitioners (including physical culture specialists and sanipractors[24] as well). The second organization went by various names, but was originally known as the BC Association of United Drugless Therapists.[25] C. Lesley Biggs (1986) suggests that chiropractic mixers and straights had a falling out; the straight practitioners seemed especially keen on separating themselves from the mixers (see also Adams and Etherington 2015). Very shortly after, in 1921, both organizations sought legislation to establish themselves as self-regulating professionals.

Private bills respecting drugless physicians and chiropractors were introduced in the legislature in early March. The bills appear to have been modelled after medical legislation, and would have created a regulatory college and council "with wide powers of examination" (*Abbotsford Post* 1921: 4). These bills were accompanied by petitions with many signatures from practitioners and their patients (Dennis 2009; Biggs 1986). The BC legislature established a select committee with "instructions to hear and consider representations in favour of the Bill[s] or objections thereto, and to report their findings and recommendations to the House" (British Columbia 1921a: 63). The six-person committee included a physician and a druggist. In committee, medical leaders spoke strongly against granting drugless practitioners and chiropractors self-regulation, while practitioners and some members of the public spoke in favour. The select committee recommended against the bills on the grounds that these healers' educational background and training was American, and the quality of that education was unclear and variable (Macdonald 1921). The committee also cited the conclusions of Ontario's Hodgins commission that chiropractic was unscientific and of questionable merit (ibid.). The committee, however, did propose a compromise solution similar to that adopted in 1909 for osteopathy: entry to practise chiropractic and other branches of drugless healing could be governed by the medical council. Legislators agreed with this suggestion, and subsequently the medical act was amended (British Columbia 1921b).

This solution likely suited medical doctors, who seem to have followed the path they had traversed a decade previously with osteopaths, and established entry requirements so high that no one could meet them. The act required examinations in subjects most chiropractors would not have had training in, encompassing "anatomy, physiology, chemistry, pathology, histology, neurology, physical diagnosis, gynecology, hygiene, [and] medical jurisprudence" (British Columbia 1921b, s. 2). Chiropractors declared they could not pass the examinations, and they refused to sit for them (BC Archives 1923; Biggs 1986: 13, 18). Instead, both chiropractors and drugless healers continued to lobby for legislation granting them the right of self-regulation. Between, 1921 and the mid-1930s, twenty bills were introduced to regulate chiropractic and/or drugless healing in British Columbia. Legislators responded to a 1922 bill to regulate chiropractic by further revising the medical act to allow chiropractors and drugless physicians representation on the entry examining board (British Columbia 1922). This did not address the core problem, and both groups continued to avoid the exams (Biggs 1986; Dennis 2009).

Chiropractors' and drugless physicians' bills were continually rejected over the succeeding years. When legislators rejected another bill in 1924, a legislative subcommittee explained that alternative healers should not be granted powers equivalent to medicine's, because they did not have training equivalent to medicine's (Perry 1924). Legislators were content with their 1921 solution. Once they had passed the medical council's exams, it was argued, drugless healers were free to specialize in whatever branch of medicine they desired (ibid.: 128). These verdicts were no doubt influenced by medical doctors, but this was accepted opinion among legislators as well. Although it was the norm in Ontario to staff legislative subcommittees on health legislation with

MD MLAs, in British Columbia this was less common. Nonetheless, medical doctors did have a chance to attend committee meetings (as did chiropractors and others) and state their case.

The situation intensified in the early 1930s, when both drugless physicians and chiropractors pursued professional advance, and the medical profession increased their prosecutions of alternative healers for the illegal practice of medicine.[26] With the public behind them, and the press on their side, these healers continued to appeal to the legislature for regulatory legislation. For several more years, they were turned away. Chiropractors charged that their bills did not proceed because of the tactics of "political doctors" (Sturdy 1932a). MD MLAs were accused of vote trading to rally support from their fellow MLAs in order to defeat chiropractors' legislation (Sturdy 1931, 1932b). Chiropractic leader Walter Sturdy (1932b: 1) accused medical doctors of "brow-beating intimidated unwilling members to sacrifice their personal beliefs" to defeat the bills. Votes on chiropractic and drugless physician legislation were typically open; that is, legislators were not required to vote along party lines, but rather according to their conscience (*Vancouver Sun* 1932, 1936).[27] MLAs who were medical doctors and members of the allied professions of dentistry and pharmacy (numbering seven in 1932 and 1933) routinely voted against the legislation, regardless of party affiliation. Although most votes were not recorded, a look at the recorded votes shows no evidence that these seven MLAs voted as a block on any other issue; the vast majority of other votes broke down along party lines. Thus, while it is clear that medical MLAs voted as a block against chiropractic regulation, there is no clear evidence of vote trading or intimidation. Further, it seems unlikely that these seven individuals could effectively sway voting outcomes in a fifty-person legislative assembly.[28]

Observers also accused the medical doctor MLAs (and a few of their supporters) of using a variety of tactics to stall or derail alternative health professional legislation when it was under consideration. This is particularly evident in 1930, when it appeared that the Conservative Tolmie government, alternative healers, and the medical profession had reached an agreement on a legislative solution. Despite this agreement, the MD MLAs "continued to conduct the most strenuous kind of lobby ... against the drugless bill" according to the *Vancouver Sun* newspaper (1930a, 1930b: 1). When the bill was under consideration, MD MLAs raised a point of order that resulted in the Speaker of the House ruling the alternative healers' bills out of order, before a vote could be held (*Vancouver Sun* 1930c: 2). Hence, the government's compromise was lost on a technicality. In 1931, MD MLAs helped to halt debate on chiropractic and drugless healing bills by calling for a royal commission on the subject of chiropractic regulation (British Columbia 1931). Medical doctors were also accused of calling for a vote on the chiropractor bill in 1933, when some of its key supporters were absent from the House (*Vancouver Sun* 1933). In 1936, an MD MLA sought to stall the bill sponsored by drugless physicians (then calling themselves naturopaths) by raising a point of order about the bill's status (*Vancouver Sun* 1936). Thus, MD MLAs resorted to a variety of tactics to undermine drugless healer legislation under consideration in the BC legislature. Nevertheless, armed with public support and considerable financial backing for their professional projects, chiropractors and drugless physicians kept returning to the legislature with new bills.

Faced with these repeated requests, and in light of medical opposition, the BC government established a royal commission to look into the issue (like their Ontario counterparts in a similar situation in the 1910s). Supreme Court justice Denis Murphy was appointed as commissioner, and he conducted hearings in late 1931 and early 1932.[29] Murphy heard from lawyers representing the medical profession, the BC Chiropractic Association, and the drugless physicians' association, then called the Institute of Sanipractic and Naturopathic Practitioners, as well as individual practitioners.[30] In his report, Murphy (1932) supported self-regulation for chiropractic on the grounds that chiropractors and medical doctors had different philosophies about disease and treatment, and hence it was inappropriate for the latter to regulate the former. Murphy (1932: 9) claimed that the terms of the commission precluded him from determining if the standard for entry proposed by chiropractors provided adequate protection for the public. Murphy opposed regulation for drugless practice because drugless physicians in the province embraced no singular theory of disease and had no uniform method of treatment. Practitioners combined some mix of chiropractic, natural medicine, diet, and physical exercise, and the use of electricity, water, and heat, among other treatments. Practitioners shared neither common training nor education. This lack of standardization and uniformity prevented regulation, Murphy contended. Further, he was troubled by drugless practitioners' claim to diagnose, which Murphy believed they were unqualified to do because they lacked medical training.

Despite the commission's recommendations, BC legislators rejected bills to regulate chiropractic in 1932 and 1933, partly because of the MD

MLAs' tactics described above. Chiropractors finally found success in 1934, when "An Act respecting Chiropractors" was passed to establish straight chiropractic as a self-regulating profession (British Columbia 1934). Chiropractors received a boost when new Liberal premier T.D. Pattullo publicly supported the bill, even though he had voted against chiropractors' bills in 1932 and 1933. Pattullo's endorsement revealed some ambivalence: he reasoned that since "these men had been practising for 20 years with every evidence of success, there must be some merit in what they are doing" (*Vancouver Sun* 1934a: 8; *Victoria Daily Colonist* 1934: 3). Pattullo's change of opinion seemed to match the mood of the house, and the act passed with little controversy, and despite the opposition of two MD and two pharmacist MLAs (a dentist voted in favour of the bill). Pattullo had been elected on a pragmatic platform of "getting things done" (Sutherland 1960; Fisher 1991), and believed the state should take an active role in solving social problems (Barman 1991: 254; Fisher 1991). Further, he was not reluctant "to create precedent" (Pattullo, in Fisher 1991: 249). His government's decision to regulate chiropractic after fourteen years of debate and discussion was consistent with his party's platform.

Drugless physicians – who were increasingly calling themselves naturopaths – were not so fortunate in 1934. Their bill was defeated. Further, the content of the chiropractic act negatively affected them. The legislation prevented chiropractors from practising any other treatment modality (British Columbia 1934, s. 11), thereby rendering chiropractic mixing illegal.[31] At the time, roughly two-thirds of drugless physicians used chiropractic techniques when providing treatment (Murphy 1932; *Vancouver Sun* 1934b). Straight chiropractors were quick to enforce the act, targeting BC naturopaths who used chiropractic treatments, and charging them with illegal chiropractic practice in 1934 and 1935 (BCA 1936). In response, the drugless healers returned to the legislature in pursuit of legislation. In 1936, they were successful: "An Act respecting Naturopathic Physicians" was passed (British Columbia 1936a). Although opponents tried to derail the bill on a point of order, arguing that it required the "consent of the crown," the lieutenant governor endorsed the bill, and it was passed shortly thereafter (in early April) (British Columbia 1936b: 179).

Naturopaths' legislation granted them little autonomy, and few regulatory powers, but they had succeeded in obtaining a measure of self-regulation in 1936, despite medical opposition, and concerns about their expertise and education.

Reflections on the BC Case

As in the Ontario case study, this overview of the contests surrounding the regulation of drugless practice in British Columbia provides support for the theoretical models introduced in chapter 1. Medicine, chiropractic, and drugless healers were engaged in inter-professional conflict in which they pursued social closure projects, and mobilized a variety of resources to achieve their goals. At the same time, it is evident that state actors were not incidental to processes of professional development, and there is clear overlap between the professions and state ecologies.

The BC medical profession used a variety of social closure tactics to undermine alternative health practitioners. Although in 1909 they sought to make osteopathy illegal in the province, the legislative compromise that granted them the power to regulate entry to practise osteopathy enabled the profession to undermine osteopathy's growth. Only a few practitioners could meet the criteria set by the medical council, and they were easily absorbed into the medical profession. Medicine's success was facilitated by the low number of osteopaths in the province, and their lack of organization. Osteopaths were not in a position to counter-mobilize against the medical profession. In the 1910s, medical doctors attempted to eliminate chiropractic and drugless therapy through the courts. This tactic was not successful, and it prompted chiropractors and other drugless healers to organize. Subsequently, medical doctors attempted to use the legislature to undermine these alternative practices, first by encouraging the legislative compromise that granted medicine the right to control entry to practise chiropractic (which was ineffective), and subsequently by using political tactics and lobbying to undermine alternative healers' ability to obtain legislation. Medicine's tactics and lobbying were effective for a time, delaying chiropractors' and naturopaths' achievement of self-regulation for roughly fifteen years. Nonetheless, their presence in the legislature was never strong enough to dictate legislative outcomes: evidently most legislators agreed with medical doctors that alternative healers like chiropractors and naturopaths were not deserving of self-regulation.

Chiropractors and naturopaths also engaged in social closure strategies that were primarily usurpationary in nature – they tried to fight the exclusionary closure enacted against them. Chiropractors could be said to be engaged in a dual closure strategy, since they were concerned with distinguishing themselves from the drugless physicians, even as they battled medical closure tactics. In these social closure projects, chiropractors and drugless physicians mobilized a variety of resources. In 1931, chiropractic association head Walter Sturdy claimed that his group had already spent $15,000 trying to get a chiropractic bill through the legislature (Sturdy 1931); the drugless physicians claimed to have spent around $25,000 (Dennis 2009: 116). Clearly these legislative drives were expensive, but chiropractors and drugless therapists could mobilize the financial resources to see the bills through. Patients were also mobilized, to sign petitions, write letters, and meet with legislators. Newspaper accounts and political speeches frequently make mention of the extensive public support alternative healers possessed. At first, the support of "many estimable citizens" was dismissed by legislators, who suggested that these citizens had been influenced by "the power of suggestion" (Macdonald 1921: 133). However, the consistent support of the public began to sway legislators' opinions. In 1931, Conservative premier Tolmie spoke in favour of chiropractic regulation on the grounds that "reports of cures made by some of the best citizens indicated there must be some merit in chiropractic" (*Vancouver Sun* 1931: 12). Tolmie's sentiments were echoed by Premier Pattullo only a few years later (*Victoria Daily Colonist* 1934: 3). Chiropractors did not have strong legislative support, unlike their medical profession foes, but their mobilization of resources, like financial and public support, eventually won legislators over.

As both Tolmie's and Pattullo's comments reveal, many legislators were ambivalent about chiropractic and naturopathy regulation. Others were downright opposed. As we have seen, some saw little merit in either practice. Commissioner Murphy, appointed by the BC government, argued that drugless healing was unscientific, and that drugless healers did not have the education necessary to provide services safely to the public. These statements were not contested by state actors. They did not regulate naturopathy and chiropractic because they were impressed with their education, training, or claims to expertise. Why, then, did they regulate them? First, it is worth noting that the influence of the medical profession within the legislature appears to have lessened in British Columbia during the 1930s. While medical doctors in Ontario clearly benefited from the Ferguson administration's sympathy for the medical profession's point of view, it is not clear that either the Tolmie or the Pattullo government was particularly sympathetic to medicine's position. Although Tolmie was a veterinarian and farmer, his government was aligned with business interests (Barman

1991). His Conservative government did not oppose medicine, but it did not champion it either.

Under Tolmie, some legislators seem to have been frustrated by the MD MLAs' tactics aimed at undermining chiropractors' legislation. For instance, according to a news article in the *Vancouver Sun*, legislators expressed their displeasure at the MD MLAs' tactics that derailed the drugless practitioner and chiropractic bills in 1930 by supporting an amendment to the medical act to allow Christian Scientists the right to practise without prosecution, despite MD MLA opposition (*Vancouver Sun* 1930c: 2). MDs' influence over the House may have been waning. The changing make-up of the legislature was likely also influential. During Tolmie's term as premier between 1928 and 1933, roughly one sixth of MLAs were members of health professions, and professionals made up roughly 30 per cent of all MLAs. Under Pattullo, however, the involvement of both health and other professionals in the legislature appears to have dropped down to 20 per cent. Thus, during the Pattullo administration the power of professionals to influence legislative decisions declined.[32]

Abbott (2005) argues that professional regulation is enacted when it works in both the state and professions ecologies. Did the regulation of chiropractic and naturopathy meet political goals in 1930s British Columbia? Possibly. Pattullo won the 1933 election by casting himself as a man who could "solve the province's problems," through enacting social change to benefit the public during the Depression (Sutherland 1960). Respecting the regulation of chiropractic, Pattullo resolved in 1934 to "settle the issue at this session" (*Victoria Daily Colonist* 1934: 3). Thus, the regulation of chiropractic was generally commensurate with the Liberals' and Pattullo's political platform.[33] However, when the 1936 act to regulate naturopathy was being considered, Pattullo publicly declared that he did not find the bill to be in the public interest, but he was willing to support it anyway (*Vancouver Sun* 1936). The ambivalence expressed by Pattullo for both pieces of legislation suggests that they were not closely aligned with his political goals or personal beliefs. Pattullo provided his support seemingly despite his personal feelings about them. It is possible, of course, that after twenty bills across fifteen years, legislators were simply worn down. Perhaps the political goal the legislation achieved was – as in Ontario – resolving an inter-professional dispute that had already taken up a considerable amount of the legislature's time and resources. However, if a problem in the professions ecology (inter-professional conflict over healthcare) had become a problem in the state ecology, then once again these ecologies appear to be overlapping – not merely linked.

Overall, there is little evidence that state actors' regulation of chiropractic and naturopathy was intended to achieve overarching political goals, or meet state interests, even though the legislation was not inconsistent with Pattullo's political ideology. The legislation passed was popular, and may have served the political goal of pleasing voters. With the establishment of universal suffrage after the First World War, parties may have courted the "popular" vote by regulating occupations patronized by average citizens, such as chiropractic and drugless healing.[34] Legislative outcomes cannot be entirely explained by referring to political motives. Nonetheless, it seems true – using Abbott's (2005) language – that the passage of the chiropractors' and drugless physicians' acts in the mid-1930s was a legislative solution that worked in both ecologies. I have argued, though, that the reason it worked well was because these ecologies were overlapping, and resolving interprofessional conflict benefited both. Moreover, it is worth noting that in those periods when the two ecologies overlapped more – those moments when there were many professionals in the legislature – it was difficult for new contenders to win professional privileges in the face of opposition from established professions. It was when the ecologies were more separate that challengers to the dominant medical profession could achieve some gains.

A Brief Look at Quebec and Nova Scotia

There were fewer contests over the regulation of drugless practice in Quebec and Nova Scotia, likely because there were fewer drugless healers. Neither province established self-regulating professions in this field in the opening decades of the twentieth century. Nonetheless, both provinces briefly considered regulating alternative health practice, and it is worth touching on these moments before concluding this chapter. In Nova Scotia, as in British Columbia, the right to regulate entry to practise osteopathy was granted to the medical profession, before osteopaths were organized or actively pursuing self-regulation. Chiropractic was not regulated.[35] In Quebec, bills to regulate osteopathy and chiropractic were introduced into the legislature in this era, but they were all defeated.

In Nova Scotia, medical doctors went on the offensive against alternative health practice in 1921. That year, they sought legislative change that would both define medical practice in a manner that would enable the medical board to prosecute alternative practitioners, and grant the board regulatory authority over osteopaths and others. Their legislation would make it illegal for anyone without a medical licence to purport to "diagnose or treat any human disease, defect, deformity or injury" (Nova Scotia Archives 1921; Nova Scotia 1921a), and provide treatment by way of drugs, medicine, operation, or manipulation (s. 3b). Since regular medical doctors did not typically treat by manipulation, this scope of practice seems designed to ensure that osteopaths (and unnamed others) who did treat by manipulation were subject to medical discipline and control. Further, the bill specifically required osteopaths and homeopaths to undertake the medical profession's entry examinations to receive a licence to practise (Nova Scotia Archives 1921). In effect, a practitioner would need a medical degree (or equivalent) before being eligible to practise osteopathy in the province. According to the 1921 census, there were thirty-one osteopaths and chiropractors in Nova Scotia at the time, twenty-six men and five women. Halifax city directories for this year identify only three osteopath practitioners in the city, and about the same number of chiropractors (McAlpine's Halifax City Directories 1921). Legislative debate suggests that other osteopath practitioners were spread across the province. There is no mention in the surviving records of a provincial osteopathy organization existing at the time. Chiropractors were not explicitly mentioned in the act, or in recorded legislative debate, so it seems that medical doctors' primary targets at this juncture were osteopaths.

Within the Nova Scotia House of Assembly the bill appears to have generated little controversy. The act was slightly amended by the committee on law amendments to adjust the phrasing of some sections. It was in the legislative council that the bill met with opposition, in defence of the osteopaths.[36] The Honourable Mr Henry C.V. LeVatte, a notary and council member from Cape Breton, spoke at length against the bill, and introduced several amendments. LeVatte's position was bolstered by petitions the attorney general had passed on to him protesting the act, from hundreds of people in the counties of Colchester and Annapolis. While LeVatte's concerns were numerous, his opposition at times seemed reluctant. He tempered his concerns by praising the medical profession, especially in his introductory remarks: "I am aware that a very prominent delegation appeared before the Committee, a delegation of celebrated men from all over this Province, and no doubt reliable men, and good professional men in every sense of the word …

They are men in whom, in their profession, I would have the utmost confidence (Nova Scotia 1921b: 79).

Despite his respect for medical doctors, LeVatte expressed concern for both osteopaths and their patients.

> I have not the slightest objection to some authority in the Province disciplining people who are administering drugs or working on the human frame but when we come to realize that with one stroke with the sound of the gun at the closing of this Legislature, the people who are today, whether osteopaths or anything else, until they get their license from these medical men, are out of business, and that all over this Province – I am not particularly referring to the City of Halifax, but all over the Province – these men who have their patients, and patients who say themselves, and whose friends say they are receiving benefit from them, will have no longer to take any treatment from these men. I may say that so far as the medical profession is concerned, it is an honourable profession, but it has a great many privileges in this Province and while our medical men, as soon as they get licensed to practice in this Province, to a large extent migrate to the towns and cities, odd men once in a while will go to the country sections and practice medicine; but in the remoter districts it is practically impossible, unless at very large expense, to secure the services of a doctor. (Nova Scotia 1921b: 79–80)

LeVatte felt that the legislation would deny osteopathy patients of the benefits of these services, and this was particularly problematic because in remote districts people might not otherwise have access to a doctor, given regular MDs' tendency to settle in larger towns and cities. This pattern of settlement was typical in the United States as well: osteopaths were more likely to settle in the countryside than were regular doctors, and there they met health needs that would have otherwise gone unaddressed (Gevitz 2004). LeVatte ended his lengthy speech with some recommended amendments that substantially tempered the force of the act: osteopaths undergoing the medical board's exams should be examined by other osteopaths, and those who had practised in the province for five years or more should be allowed to register without examination (Nova Scotia 1921b). The legislative council also added provisions protecting sellers of patent medicine, and religious healers (like Christian Scientists). When these amendments were returned to the legislative assembly, there were objections; further discussion ensued, but in the end, the council succeeded in altering the bill.

Surviving legislative records make no reference to protests from osteopaths concerning this legislation; rather, the protests that resonated were those from patients and the general public. Once again, public support for alternative health practice encouraged legislators to force medical doctors to accommodate them. Legislators clearly accepted medical doctors' claims, and seemed reluctant to suggest they might have ulterior motives, but were nonetheless willing to force them into legislative compromises. As compromises went, however, this was a small one. Although the legislation had been tempered by the legislative council, its impact was substantial. The 1931 census records only seven osteopaths in the province, a decline of 77 per cent from 1921. Entry to practise osteopathy in Nova Scotia came to require a medical degree (not simply a degree in osteopathy) (Royal Commission on Health Services 1965: 80). Thus, Nova Scotia medical doctors were effectively able to enact social closure against osteopaths in the province, with the assistance of state actors. Legislators expressed trust for the medical profession, but they indicated they needed to amend the legislation to protect the public. It is not at all clear that this regulatory outcome met broader political or state goals – other than legislators' desire to be responsive to the various requests placed before them, and to serve the interests of the people of the province. At the time, it is worth noting, 49 per cent of the members of the House of Assembly were members of regulated professions (12 per cent of the total were medical doctors or dentists) (Beck 1957, appendix M).

The first known osteopath to set up practice in Quebec did so in 1900: American-born Arthur S. Burgess established not only an infirmary in Montreal that year, but also a school to train other osteopaths with his older sister Flora Stolz (The Canadian Osteopath 1900).[37] However, the growth of this occupation and other alternative health specialities was slower in Quebec than in Ontario or British Columbia. There were reportedly only five osteopaths in Quebec in 1911 (Mills 1966), and the 1921 census counted only forty-eight osteopaths, homeopaths, and chiropractors combined (Canada 1924). Thus, there were likely few osteopaths in the province when bills to regulate osteopathy were introduced in 1918 and 1919. Joseph-Napoléon Francoeur, a Quebec lawyer and long-standing Liberal politician, introduced a bill to amend the medical act to include provision for osteopaths. The provisions, however, read like an independent act, and proposed to establish a separate osteopath body with its own regulatory board to regulate entry to practice and maintain a register. The two bills make no reference to the medical profession or medical practice (Quebec 1918a, 1919a). In 1918, the bill was referred to a subcommittee, but was never reported (Quebec 1918b). In 1919, it was rejected by the legislative subcommittee, but its sponsor, Francoeur, tried to have it reconsidered (Quebec 1919b). In his speech on the bill, Francoeur claimed that the regulation of osteopathy was a serious matter because osteopaths provided valuable services, and they deserved justice (Quebec 1919c). Another MLA reported that he and his family had received excellent treatment from osteopathic doctors. However, the bill was opposed by many in the house, especially the MDs. They called osteopaths quacks and charlatans. In a telling comment, medical doctor MLA George-Stanislas Grégoire argued,

> Les médecins devraient jouir de la même protection que les avocats. Comment les avocats réagiraient si les médecins en Chambre adoptaient une loi permettant à des gens qui ne sont pas avocats de pratiquer le droit? (Quebec 1919c)
>
> [Medical doctors deserve the same protection as lawyers. How would lawyers react if the doctors in the Assembly adopted a law allowing men who were not lawyers to practise law?]

Again, the bill was defeated. Osteopaths continued to practise in Quebec, but remained unregulated and vulnerable.

In this era, as in previous ones, Quebec's legislative assembly was populated by many professionals (as well as business people and industrialists) (Massicotte 1989). Here, as in several other provinces, the presence of MDs (and lawyers) in the legislature shaped professional regulation; medical doctors used their position to undermine legislation favourable to their competitors. As Dr Grégoire's comments reveal, some professionals felt it perfectly reasonable to pursue their professional interests within the legislature. This again suggests that the state and professions' ecologies were inter-penetrated at this time, not simply linked; the legislature became a field within which inter-professional conflict was waged.

Bills to regulate chiropractic were introduced in the Quebec legislature in 1936 and 1939 (Quebec 1936, 1939). The bills proposed to close the practice of chiropractic. The Quebec Chiropractic Association, which had been incorporated by letters patent in 1933, was recognized, and the board of this association was to be empowered to regulate entry to practice, restricted to those with diplomas in chiropractic from specified schools. The bills granted the board control over entry to study, and proposed high matriculation requirements (Quebec 1936, 1939). The proposed regulatory powers of the association were fairly extensive. Both the 1936 and 1939 bills survived second reading and were referred to legislative subcommittees for consideration, but both were rejected in committee. There is no surviving record of debate on the bills.

It is not surprising that chiropractors did not meet with immediate legislative success, given the difficulties they faced obtaining legislation in Ontario and British Columbia. Further, the powers requested were extensive, and may have been viewed as unreasonable. Chiropractic was not regulated in Quebec until 1973. The Lacroix Commission established in 1963 considered the regulation of chiropractic and osteopathy, and spoke in favour of their regulation, despite chiropractic's limitations. Regulation, Lacroix (1965) believed, would protect the public by restricting chiropractors' scope, raising their education, and ensuring that the poorly trained could not practise. Lacroix's recommendations informed the 1973 chiropractic act.[38]

Discussion

In the opening decades of the twentieth century, aspiring professional groups such as chiropractors, osteopaths, and drugless healers (naturopaths) mobilized resources in their drive for status as self-regulating professions. Practitioners formed organizations, hired lawyers, drafted bills, lobbied and negotiated with government leaders, and mobilized their patients to appeal to state actors on their behalf. These activities were costly, but in some locales, such as British Columbia, practitioners could mobilize the financial resources to support their activity. These professional projects began defensively, as drugless practitioners were negatively impacted by medical leaders' pursuit of social closure. Organized medicine first attempted to eliminate their practice, and subsequently to control their practice, through both the courts and legislation. Medical doctors had a great deal of success in their professional projects because they were well established by the early twentieth century, and their claims to expertise and status were accepted by state actors. Further, their participation in legislatures allowed them to delay and sometimes defeat legislation unfavourable to their interests from the inside. When they had little voice in the legislature, such as in Ontario in the early 1920s, they were still able to mobilize resources, including social capital, to win over state actors, and ultimately achieve favourable legislative outcomes. Nonetheless, in British Columbia and to a lesser extent Ontario, chiropractors and other drugless healers succeeded in winning regulation through their resource mobilization. Notably, they do not appear to have won regulation by convincing legislators of their expertise, but rather by convincing them of their popularity, and the existence of a public safety risk when the untrained were allowed to practice. In Nova Scotia and Quebec, alternative healers were less numerous and less well-organized; the medical profession was able to defeat efforts to extend their status and authority.

Nevertheless, this chapter has demonstrated that legislative outcomes were not simply the product of social closure and resource mobilization. Rather, state actors actively debated, negotiated, rejected, and accepted the claims and requests of established and aspiring professional groups. Their activity is not entirely consistent with theories of professions and the state. It does not appear that legislators regulated alternative health practice to draw on, or recognize, their expertise. There is some evidence that they regulated in the public interest, but this was not their only concern. While Spencer (1896) argued that states regulate professions to enhance state legitimacy, alternative health professions lacked status and legitimacy, and hence their regulation was unlikely to benefit the state. Further, while the extension of professional regulation to include drugless practice might be seen to enhance societal governance in a general sense, it is not at all clear that this was state actors' intention. The most convincing explanation for state actor activity is found in Abbott's (2005) theory of linked ecologies, although even here the fit is not perfect. There is some evidence that the regulation (or rejection) of alternative health practice suited political goals, and state actors' concerns. However, the evidence is not strong. Rather, it seems that these health practitioners were regulated by state actors because the latter decided to meet the demands of consumers (and professional groups), and because they wanted to resolve inter-professional conflicts between medicine and alternative practitioners.

State actors were not disinterested individuals who only legislated for professionals when they themselves could achieve political or social gains. Rather, they were interested individuals, sometimes professionals themselves, who sought to resolve a contradiction in the system of professions that had produced tension and problems in the political sphere. The professions ecology and state ecology were overlapping for much of this era, such that problems in one sphere had implications for the other. The place of medical doctors in legislatures ensured that they had greater institutional power with which they could shape legislative outcomes. However, they could not determine them. They did not get everything they wanted in every context.

These case studies also highlight the importance of social context. The different political environments, the varying structures of the provincial legislatures, and differences in the occupational and socio-economic backgrounds of legislators combined to shape professional regulatory outcomes. Further, when new professions were regulated, their regulation aligned, at least generally, with the governing party's political views, and was shaped by other political concerns of the day. Regulatory outcomes were also shaped by the opinions of consumers and members of the public.

The importance of context, and the value of combining theories of professionalization with state-centred approaches will be explored more fully in the following, final chapter.

Conclusion

This book has explored the emergence of self-regulating professions in four Canadian provinces up to the 1930s. It not only provided a historical overview of professional regulation in British Columbia, Ontario, Quebec, and Nova Scotia, but sought to apply and critically evaluate sociological theories of profession–state relations and professionalization. Previous research on professions has tended to focus on single professions in single locales, with a few notable exceptions (e.g., Krause 1996; Saks 2015; Burrage 2006). These exceptions rarely include Canada among the countries studied. However, Canada is an excellent focal point for research on professional self-regulation: some professions have been self-regulating in this country, continuously, for 150 to 200 years, and while professional self-regulation has been undermined elsewhere in the world, here it persists (Adams 2017a). Canada has embraced self-regulating professions to a greater extent than perhaps any other nation in the world. This present study contributes, then, not only to our understanding of Canadian history, but also to the sociological literature on professions nationally and internationally.

For the most part, professions scholars have studied profession creation from the point of view of the professions, exploring in detail how practitioners organized and endeavoured to raise their status. As noted, this literature has typically focused on workers in a single region. This book has approached the topic from a different angle, while building on the valuable contributions of these professional histories. First, this study considered all professions regulated in a region. If we accept Abbott's (1988) argument that professions exist in an ecology, and that what happens to one may have implications for others, it is valuable to study trends affecting professions as a group – while still acknowledging the differences among them. Second, this study has focused on profession creation from the point of view of the state. I have examined legislation establishing professional self-regulation, and considered the rationales, debates, and concerns of state actors making regulatory decisions. State actors have long been under-examined in sociological accounts of profession creation. At the same time, I have considered professionals' points of view and explored how the interests of both sets of actors at times converged to encourage professional self-regulation. Third, this study has taken a comparative approach, exploring regulatory trends across the four provinces. This comparative focus has allowed an investigation of the role of context, population, and social and political culture on profession creation. Combined, these innovations provide opportunities to test and re-evaluate sociological theories concerning professions.

In this chapter, I summarize the main study findings and consider their implications for theoretical accounts of professions and professional self-regulation. I also identify interprovincial differences in professional regulation, and explore their implications for future sociological and historical research. The differences between Canada and its main comparator countries, the United Kingdom and the United States, are also touched on. I end the chapter with a short review of more recent trends in professional self-regulation in Canada.

Professions, States, and Theoretical Understandings of Professional Regulation

Professional self-regulation in these four Canadian provinces was the outcome of both professional projects and state actors' activity. In the nineteenth century, the impetus for professional self-regulation came from both state actors and professional bodies. Evidence suggests state actors took the lead in introducing original legislation to establish self-regulating professions in a slight majority of cases. By the early twentieth century, professional bodies and organizations were more often the drivers of regulatory change in this area. State actors demonstrated interest in regulating law, medicine, pharmacy, land surveying, and sometimes dentistry. The extension of regulation to other groups was often more contested. When professions took the lead in fighting for regulatory privileges, social closure processes are evident. Here, educated and trained practitioners were concerned with the practice of the untrained, who not only hurt their ability to make a living, but posed a danger to the public. In response, they approached the government to request a bill, or drew a bill up themselves (with a lawyer's or legislator's assistance) for presentation in their provincial legislative assembly. Aspiring professionals sought legislation that not only granted them a privileged market position, but conferred upon them the regulatory authority to govern their own affairs. Legislators actively debated and revised this legislation, not hesitating to reject bills outright or revise them substantially.

In some cases, state leaders appear to have created self-regulating professions to achieve state goals (e.g., the early regulation of law and land surveying in Ontario). But state actors' interests in professional self-regulation were much broader. Legislators spent a considerable amount of time, almost every single session, debating professional legislation. They wrote, revised, and debated it, and negotiated with professional groups and other interested parties in between sessions. In some cases, they spent years working with groups to get it right, only to revise professional legislation shortly thereafter. Many regulatory acts required ongoing supervision from government leaders – for instance, some professions required the approval of the lieutenant governor when they passed new by-laws. Some acts charged the government with appointing regulatory board members. State actors monitored professional board activity, and if they felt professionals were abusing their powers, they threatened to intervene, and sometimes revised professional legislation to limit abuses of power. Thus, professional self-regulation cannot be understood as simply the outcome of professional projects, but was evidently the result of state activity and state projects as well.

State actors saw professional self-regulation as an act of delegation. They were devolving some of their own regulatory authority onto a group of professionals. They were reluctant to delegate authority to some groups of people – those they deemed untrustworthy, and those with little education. High-status professions like lawyers and medical doctors, then, received many more privileges than lower-status groups like optometrists or nurses. Gender, class, and citizenship shaped regulatory outcomes. While legislation establishing self-regulating professions empowered, it also controlled. Professional groups with a weak claim to expertise (and who were deemed less trustworthy) were more likely to have legislation that granted few privileges, while mandating specific training and practice criteria. When granting professional privileges, state actors concerned themselves with public-interest claims, which in the nineteenth century especially were tied with training and education. Raising the standard of education was deemed to be in the public interest (see also Adams 2016a), since it created more knowledgeable practitioners. State actors also considered consumer choice and availability of services when making regulatory decisions. In the twentieth century, legislators often regulated to resolve inter-professional conflicts as well. In granting the privileges of self-regulation to professional groups, state actors received in return low-cost regulation of important areas of economic and social activity; professions' regulatory boards were (and are) self-funding.

These findings have several implications for sociological theories. In chapter 1, I focused on three: neo-Weberian approaches enhanced by social movement theory, and Foucauldian and ecological approaches. Some support for each of these theories is evident, but I have found a combination of neo-Weberian and ecological approaches most helpful in interpreting the history of self-regulating professions in Canada.

Neo-Weberian approaches emphasize professions' pursuit of social closure to dominate a market for professional services, and raise their status (for instance, Saks 2010, 2015). This study finds ample evidence that professional self-regulation was often sought by professional groups in their pursuit of social closure. To achieve their goals they sometimes organized, and mobilized a range of financial, cultural, social, and ideological resources, just like social-movement resource mobilization models contend. It is important to emphasize, however, that these theories do not capture all historical situations and events. Sometimes the impetus for professional regulation came from state actors, and sometimes prominent professionals pushed for regulation, not a professional organization. In the nineteenth century in particular, little resource mobilization was necessary. Rather, groups of practitioners drew on their social and political contacts to win self-regulation either without formally organizing, or very shortly after they organized. These theories also say very little about how social closure is enacted, and what types of resources might shape regulatory outcomes. It is important, then, when using neo-Weberian theories, to pay close attention to social context. Previous neo-Weberian accounts of profession creation, for instance, have not identified the potential significance of civil rights and democratization movements that were so important to the emergence of professional self-regulation in nineteenth-century Quebec. Further, interprovincial differences in the regulation of alternative health practices appear to owe much to the number of such practitioners in a region and their internal diversity. Thus, it is not simply organization and resource mobilization, but also professional unity, the number of organizations (if any) representing professional groups, and the alliances and counter-mobilization among professional groups that shape outcomes. Scholars using neo-Weberian accounts should recognize the theory's limitations and endeavour to surpass them.

Perhaps the most significant limitation of neo-Weberian social closure theory is its inability to address state actors' roles in processes of profession formation and regulation. Neo-Weberians see state actors as integral to processes of profession creation (Saks 2015; Witz 1992), but do not theorize their activity. Weber (1968) himself was quite concerned with the state, politics, and governance, and hence it may be possible to enhance neo-Weberian theories of profession creation by returning to Weber and his ideas about social action, rationality, and politics (Saks and Adams 2016; Adams and Saks forthcoming). This is a fruitful area for future theorizing.

Many scholars have turned to Foucault to highlight the important role played by state actors in professionalization (Johnson 1993, 1995; Chamberlain 2013). For Terence Johnson, the creation of professions has been linked with state building (Johnson 1982, 1993; Larkin 1995), and professions are said to be part of the state broadly defined (Johnson 1993, 1995). Furthermore, for Johnson (1993) experts facilitate state governance and the exercise of power. This approach helpfully draws our attention to state actors, arguing that professions contribute to social governance. The fact that the formation of self-regulating professions in Canada is closely correlated with major changes in the state – the arrival of responsible government in the late 1840s and Confederation – provides support for these Foucauldian arguments. Professions are governance institutions, and self-regulating professions are closely connected to the state. Nevertheless, this theory has limitations as well. First, provincial governments established many self-regulating professions, and it seems unlikely that they did so, in every instance, to draw on professional expertise. The regulation of law (especially in Ontario, where regulation was state-initiated) may support the argument. The regulation of land surveying less so, because the occupation achieved self-regulation only once provincial governments ceased to be surveyors' major employers. There is no evidence that self-regulating professions like optometry or dentistry contributed valued expertise to the state. Foucauldian explanations cannot account for this variability. Second, Foucauldian scholars reject "the notion of the state as a coherent calculating subject" (Johnson 1993: 140); hence policy changes which incorporate expertise into the state for governance purposes may or may not be consciously made (ibid.). For Foucauldian researchers, it is not state actors' intentions that are important, but rather the effect of their actions. As a result, the theory downplays state actors' agency, and ultimately prevents researchers from understanding the concerns and intentions that might shape state actors' regulatory decisions.

Abbott's (2005) linked ecologies approach is more useful for interpreting this study's findings. Abbott argues that regulatory outcomes are determined by the linkages between the professions and state ecologies, and by the actions and interactions of actors in each. The approach is sensitive to social-historical context: social and political events and internal conflicts influence state and professional actors' activity. When Abbott (2005) applied his own theory to the case of medical regulation in New York State, he emphasized state actors' political motivations, suggesting that legislators only legislated for or against a profession when they had something to gain. In the four Canadian provinces examined here, this was less evident. In many instances, it is not at all clear that legislators had anything to gain through the legislation they passed. Indeed, the sheer volume of legislative activity respecting professions suggests that professional regulation was an ongoing concern. I have suggested that the overlap between the professions and state ecologies was particularly important in shaping regulatory outcomes. In many provinces, professionals composed between one-third and one-half of all legislators. Professionals, then, had the opportunity to shape regulatory outcomes from inside the legislature, and concerns in the professions ecology became concerns in the state ecology. Professional projects and regulatory outcomes also varied according to the amount of overlap. In certain locales and times periods, when there were few professionals in the legislature, professionals had to use different tactics to achieve their goals. They could not rely on those within the legislature to represent them. Further, groups like alternative health professionals were at a disadvantage when their medical-profession opponents were numerous in the legislature. More favourable legislation was passed when medical-doctor politicians were scarce.

Overall, Abbott's linked ecologies approach is not entirely able to explain the regulatory outcomes observed, but it does provide a helpful lens as it points researchers' attention to state actors, professional actors, and the linkages and interactions among them. Deserving of more attention in professions research is the role of politician-professionals.

In Canada, at least, they played a significant role historically in shaping regulatory outcomes. Here it is important to emphasize that serving in the legislature in the late nineteenth and early twentieth centuries was a part-time job for most politicians. They participated in the legislative assembly during the two to three months that it was in session, and then returned to their regular jobs for the rest of year.[1] This structure provides more opportunities for the self-employed – like professionals historically – to serve in the legislature. Moreover, in this legislative environment, it is not surprising that legislators maintained their occupational identities, and that these identities shaped their legislative decisions. In recent decades, politics has become a full-time job; the impact of this change on regulatory outcomes and political debates is a topic worthy of future research.

Ultimately, future research on professions and professional self-regulation would benefit from using a combination of theories. In particular, combining Abbott's (2005) linked ecologies approach with neo-Weberian social closure theory is useful in drawing our attention to both state actors and professional actors' activities, and considering the social contexts in which they interact. Essentialist theories and definitions of professions should be abandoned. No single conception of profession can be applied to all times and places. Rather, as Freidson (1983) has argued, we should continue to explore how professions are made and how they are defined. Theories that provide a framework to help us do this, without necessarily telling us how this is accomplished, may be most useful.

Before concluding this section, it is worth considering two other theoretical contributions. The first is the suggestion advanced by some, and articulated most clearly by Halliday (1987: xvi), that professional regulation brings "expertise to the service of power." In this book, I have largely rejected this as an explanation for professional self-regulation. When professions were first regulated, there is little evidence that state actors sought to draw on their expertise. State actors were often sceptical about professions' claims to expertise at the moment of regulation, and regulation was frequently a mechanism more to increase practitioner education and training than to recognize an existing claim to knowledge. Historically, legislators were concerned with competence – with ensuring that practitioners knew enough to practise safely. They tended not to draw on the expertise of self-regulating professions until well after they had been established, with the possible exception of law.

Although professionals may provide expertise to the state (as Halliday suggests), professions are not typically granted self-regulation because state actors desire their expertise.

The second approach worth mentioning is Durkheim's view on professions' potential role in society. When Durkheim (1984, 1992) wrote on professional associations and similar bodies, he was not trying to explain social phenomena, but to advocate for an expansion of such organizations to the benefit of society. Durkheim (1992) believed that professions could serve an intermediary role between the state and the public. In doing so, they could reduce anomie, and encourage ethical behaviour by extending professional ethics to economic activity. Other scholars like Streeck and Schmitter (1985) have built on Durkheim's views to argue that professions, along with community, market, and the state, contribute to social order. These are valuable insights that enhance our understanding of professional and social regulation. Further, they encourage researchers to explore interactions between professions, the state, communities, and markets. This is a promising avenue for future research. Durkheim's work had a more direct influence on professional regulation in Canada later in the twentieth century, when his ideas appear to have informed the transformation of professional regulation in 1970s Quebec.

Expertise

One recurring theme in this book concerns the role of expertise in the emergence of professions and professional regulation. Sociologists increasingly equate professionals and experts, seeing the two terms as interchangeable or arguing that the latter term is more robust and useful (Eyal 2013). American sociologist Steven Brint (1994) has argued that while initially professionalism in the United States and United Kingdom emphasized gentlemanly character and values, this soon disappeared, to be replaced by an emphasis on technical expertise. Gil Eyal (2013: 898–9) has gone so far as to advocate that the sociology of professions be replaced by a "more comprehensive" sociology of expertise. These arguments may plausibly apply to current events in the United States, but they find little resonance with the history of professional self-regulation in Canada.

Some professions scholars have cogently argued that it is not expertise that distinguishes a profession from other occupations, but its organization, and the linking of knowledge to status (Collins 1990; Johnson

1972; Saks 2012). The history of self-regulating professions in Canada supports this view. Professional self-regulation was not a reward granted to experts who advanced a convincing claim. There were several instances (for instance, naturopathy regulation in British Columbia) when legislators established self-regulating professions even as they questioned practitioners' expertise. Even though professionals historically advanced claims to expertise, their regulatory status and institutional authority did not necessarily rest on these claims. Legislators considered a variety of factors when making regulatory decisions, and placed as much emphasis on character as expertise. Nineteenth-century Canadians did not speak of expertise; rather, their concern was for practitioner competence and effectiveness. As we have seen, competence was tied to a liberal education, gentlemanly status, and trustworthiness. By the early twentieth century, professional expertise was linked more closely with post-secondary education and practical training. Scientific knowledge was privileged over other forms. Professional regulation sought to increase practitioners' effectiveness by increasing their training. Nevertheless, trustworthiness and character remained important considerations.

More broadly, the findings of this study suggest that expertise is a social construction. What exactly it meant to be an "expert" or to possess competence shifted over time. Scholars, who emphasize expertise as a foundation for (or conceptual replacement for) "profession," are at risk of reifying the concept, treating expertise as if it were concrete and historically unchanging. What exactly constitutes expertise, and the extent to which expertise provides a foundation for professionalism, varies across social-historical context, and should be the subject of sociological and historical research. Certainly, expertise cannot be a substitute or synonym for profession, as this study has shown.

Those who equate professionalism and expertise, or argue that the latter is a more robust concept than the former, pay too much attention to professions' knowledge claims, and neglect their normative, institutional, and regulatory roles. This is particularly the case with definitions, such as Eyal's (2013: 869), that tie expertise to efficiency. Professions have long had a normative influence that scholars from early-twentieth-century social theorist Émile Durkheim (1984) to twenty-first-century scholars like Freidson (2001), Scott (2008), and Leicht (2015) argue can be a positive force in society. Professional codes of ethics, combined with professions' legal responsibility to protect the public (which admittedly they do not *always* meet), encourage professionals to be public-minded – in a way that experts, with their commitment to use their skills to the benefit of their employers, need not be. Scott (2008: 223) argues that professionals are institutional agents: the "most influential, contemporary crafters of institutions." They may have a normative influence on social institutions and practices (Scott 2008; DiMaggio and Powell 1983), and they may exert cultural authority (Starr 1982) to an extent that experts usually do not.

This is an area ripe with opportunities for additional research. American scholars have been the most vocal advocates for a switch towards a sociology of expertise (Eyal 2013; Gorman and Sandefur 2011; Brint 1994), while many scholars in other countries continue to work within a sociology-of-professions framework. These theoretical divergences may reflect differences in social experience (Adams 2015). More international and comparative research on professions is needed to determine the extent to which meanings attached to "profession" vary. Already comparative research has explored differing regulatory traditions in the United Kingdom and the United States (Burrage 2006; Saks 2015), suggesting that regulation is only "of secondary importance in the constitution of professions" in the United States (Brint 1994: 24); universities have been more important. Thus, expertise may have been more central to profession formation and regulation in the United States than elsewhere. More research on international differences in regulation is needed.

Professional Self-regulation across Province and Nation

One of the innovations of this study is its focus on regulatory outcomes across four Canadian provinces. It is useful to reflect on interprovincial differences and consider their relevance for our ability to understand and theorize professional self-regulation. It is also valuable to consider briefly international differences (and similarities) between Canada, the United Kingdom, and the United States.

Cross-provincial Comparisons

Several interprovincial differences in professional self-regulation were documented in previous chapters. For example, Nova Scotia regulated fewer professions than the others, and British Columbia and Quebec established more autonomous self-regulating professions than the other two provinces. Who was regulated and when also varied across province.

Although this book did not explore the sources of interprovincial variations in depth, several contributory factors were nonetheless revealed.

Cross-provincial comparisons reveal the importance of occupational size, distribution, and practitioner unity to shaping regulatory outcomes. For example, dentistry was regulated in Ontario when there were over 200 practitioners. They were fairly spread out across the province. In contrast, there were very few dentists in Nova Scotia in the early 1870s, and most trained dentists appear to have been located in larger towns. Low practitioner numbers contributed to Nova Scotia legislators' reluctance to regulate for dentists in the 1870s. A lack of professional unity was also important. Ontario dentists must have impressed legislators in 1868 when they marched one hundred strong towards the legislature in a show of unity. In contrast, the lack of unity in Nova Scotia – and a concern that the legislation would benefit city dentists over their country counterparts – led to the dental bill's defeat. When dentistry was regulated in 1891 in Nova Scotia, most dentists in the province were behind the bill. Overall, if practitioners were numerous, organized, and unified across the province, then they were more likely to win professional self-regulation. Contrasting legislative outcomes across locale reveals the significance of practitioner numbers and unity.

Was population important in other ways? In a 2009 article I postulated that population density had an impact on regulatory outcomes in Canada (Adams 2009b). Specifically, I argued that Nova Scotia's higher population density may have discouraged professional regulation in that province, compared to other provinces with a lower population density. This explanation was consistent with Durkheimian perspectives on professional regulation: in areas where the population was more spread out across a broad territory, provincial governments may have seen professions as important intermediaries, facilitating governance by providing a link between the public and the state. In areas where the population was concentrated in a relatively small geographical area, as in Nova Scotia, such intermediaries may have been unnecessary. As a result, state actors might be less likely to establish self-regulating professions. Other scholars have advanced the opposite view: Brint (1994: 42) contends that occupational specialization is positively correlated with population density. As a result, one might expect more professions in high-density provinces. This look at professional self-regulation across the four Canadian provinces provides no support for the argument that population density influences regulatory outcomes either way.

Nevertheless, it appears that population distribution is important. Legislators appear to have taken population distribution into account when making regulatory decisions. In Nova Scotia, where Halifax was the main urban centre and the rest of the population was spread throughout the province, legislators were reluctant to regulate professions. They argued that regulatory solutions that worked in Halifax did not suit the countryside; rural areas could be left without needed practitioners. Such core-periphery distinctions were also sometimes drawn in British Columbia. The concentration of professional practitioners in Vancouver and Victoria meant that BC legislators were reluctant to pass professional legislation that would impact the entire province, especially in the nineteenth century. When they did pass legislation, they sometimes allowed exceptions; in this manner, the Inferior Courts Practitioners Act enabled non-lawyers to practise in lower courts (British Columbia 1873), and other legislation empowered notaries to perform tasks left to lawyers in many other provinces (Brockman 1999). Population distribution in Quebec contributed to regional forms of regulation, with some professional boards originally based in the three major centres of Montreal, Quebec, and Trois-Rivières.

The population in Ontario was by no means evenly distributed, but there were several larger towns and cities spread from Southwestern through Central and into Eastern Ontario. If it could be demonstrated that practitioners in various regions of the province (even just the urban centres) were united in seeking a regulatory outcome, state actors were more willing to grant it. In this manner, legislators took distribution and organization into account. Nonetheless, there were many instances where a professionalizing drive was located in and around major centres (Toronto and Montreal), and these practitioners' social connections won them regulatory privileges (for instance, architects and accountants in Ontario, or homeopaths and accountants in Montreal). Overall, population distribution seems to have shaped regulatory outcomes, although it did not play a strong role in determining them.

Political structures and culture were also significant. In Nova Scotia, the bicameral legislative structure in place until the late 1920s encouraged legislative conservatism (Beck 1957), and discouraged professional regulation. There were several instances when the legislative assembly passed professional legislation (for instance, regulating dentistry, engineering, and optometry), only to have the legislative council reject that legislation.[2] Internal parliamentary practices may have also played a role. In Nova Scotia and Ontario, much of the work on bills was done in subcommittee (White 1989: 39; Beck 1957: 277–8). Debates on bills, therefore, occurred behind the scenes, with only those receiving initial approval and revision being returned to the legislative assembly for further consideration. Quebec referred some bills to committee, but most bills were discussed by the committee of the whole. In British Columbia legislation was not usually referred to subcommittees; bills were considered, debated, and revised by the entire legislative assembly. In a context without political parties – these only emerged in British Columbia in the early twentieth century – and in which early legislators were often merchants and businessmen focused on local and industrial concerns, it is perhaps not surprising that debate was often heated, divisive, and raucous (Robin 1978). In the nineteenth century, in particular, the BC legislature was not especially friendly to professions seeking privileges. It was not until the early twentieth century, once patterns of professional regulation were established, that professional self-regulation was extended.

Political scientists have also identified different political cultures across the provinces that shape legislative patterns. As noted, the political culture in British Columbia has been a contentious one, characterized by (twentieth century) parties at both ends of the political spectrum. Both business and labour groups have been well represented in the legislature, exacerbating an already contentious political environment (Robin 1978). Compared to other provinces, fewer professionals served in the legislature, which appears in the long run to have been a disadvantage for established professions attempting to eliminate their competition, but a potential advantage for new groups (like chiropractors) seeking professional recognition. In contrast, the Quebec legislature was dominated by professionals (Massicotte 1989, 2009).[3] The result appears to have been a willingness to extend professional self-regulation to a variety of groups, except for those (like osteopaths and chiropractors) who were perceived to challenge established professions. Politics in Quebec were also profoundly influenced by French-Canadian culture, and a long-standing tension between democratic principles and respect for institutionalized authority. As touched on in chapter 2, these trends created a favourable context for the establishment of professional self-regulation.

Political scientists argue that Nova Scotia has tended to have a conservative political culture that discouraged regulatory innovation and encouraged the province to follow the lead of other provinces (Beck 1978). Although Nova Scotia regulated some professions differently from other provinces – establishing regulatory boards rather than incorporated colleges in some instances – it has tended to regulate professional groups after they achieved regulatory legislation in other provinces, in several instances adapting the legislation passed elsewhere. Ontario's political culture has been somewhat staid and influenced by business interests (Penner 1978; Wiseman 2007). This alliance with business has encouraged political conservatism, but there is also a reform tradition in the province that contributes to innovation (Penner 1978; Wiseman 2007). When regulating professions (and other social institutions), however, Ontario has not hesitated to innovate, and frequently has regulated professional groups differently from other provinces (e.g., in its regulation of drugless practice and nursing). Overall, there is evidence that political structure and cultures shape regulatory outcomes.

Location and local culture also contribute to interprovincial differences. Just as political cultures shape regulatory outcomes, so do social cultures. These have not been explored in any detail in this book, but can be seen in the significance of political and social concerns to the emergence of self-regulation in Quebec historically, and in the reluctance of the Drury government elected in a wave of agrarian populism to legislate against alternative healers. In Quebec, the linking of professional regulation with democratization, social and civil rights discourses, and ethnic empowerment movements is significant and deserving of more attention. Nevertheless, all provinces studied here were influenced by Britain, British culture, and each other; hence, they have much in common. Culture was a factor that not only differentiated the provinces from each other, but also tied them together. There were many regulatory similarities across the provinces which were likely encouraged by shared cultures.

Regulatory patterns across the provinces were also influenced by locale. For example, professional regulation in British Columbia had some similarities with regulation in nearby provinces (Alberta and Saskatchewan, not analysed here) and American states. The popularity of alternative health practices on the United States west coast contributed to their popularity in British Columbia (Adams and Etherington 2015). In a similar vein, Nova Scotia was politically and socially influenced by the New England region in the United States (Wiseman 2007); many early Nova Scotian medical doctors trained in New England, and this may have shaped medical regulation in the province.

At the same time, it is evident that regulatory patterns established in one province shaped professional regulation in the others. Here it is helpful to reference the work of DiMaggio and Powell (1983) on institutional isomorphism in organizational fields. DiMaggio and Powell explore organizational change, and identify processes that "make organizations more similar without necessarily making them more efficient" (147). At their point of origin, organizations in the same or similar fields may be quite different; however, the authors contend, "once a field has been established… there is an inexorable push towards homogenization" (148). This certainly appears true for Canadian professions, which despite their original differences, came to resemble each other within and across provinces. New self-regulating professions were modelled after older established ones, legislative practices in other locales were reviewed, and a conscious effort was made to standardize regulation, both within and across provinces. Combined, these trends encourage homogenization (DiMaggio and Powell 1983). Although differences within and across provinces are evident, there are also striking similarities in terms of which professions were granted self-regulation, and how they were regulated across provinces.

To summarize, exploring trends in professional self-regulation across provinces has highlighted the importance of several factors shaping regulatory outcomes. These include professional organization size and unity, population density and distribution, political structures, local cultures, and locale. At the same time, there are processes and pressures encouraging commonalities across provinces, and the emergence of Canadian patterns of professional regulation. These characteristics and others are deserving of more attention in research on professions. Further, they serve as a reminder to sociologists that patterns of professional regulation are not simply determined by general social processes, but that social context, regional character, and local institutions are quite important as well.

International Differences

This book has focused on professional self-regulation in Canada, not international variations in regulatory trends, aside from a brief look at nineteenth-century medical regulation across three countries in chapter 2. Nonetheless, the history recounted here has provided evidence of some international differences that are worth highlighting. In chapter 2, I showed that legislation regulating medicine in Lower and Upper Canada was more likely than legislation in the United States and United Kingdom to close medical practice, to incorporate all practitioners into one regulatory body, and to establish a regulatory board composed of elected professional practitioners. Canadian legislation also granted more sweeping powers to professional groups – including the right to determine entry to practice and entry to study. I postulated that professional powers granted in the Canadian colonies were more extensive than elsewhere because there were fewer established competing or alternative institutions and organizations. In the United Kingdom, medical regulation had to accommodate and build around centuries-old professional colleges, established universities, and newer professional associations. In the United States, scholars contend, the decline of professional regulation in the mid-nineteenth century led universities and other institutions to step into the vacuum to shape training and define professional practice (Burrage 2006; Brint 1994; Starr 1982). Thus, professional regulation in the United States also had to accommodate pre-existing institutions.

These differences are especially evident in the cases of law and medicine. When self-regulation was first implemented in the mid-nineteenth century, the Canadian colonies had few universities, and training programs for professions were still being developed. Although professionals were beginning to organize, there were few competing professional associations.[4] The size of the state was also small, and in the 1840s it was decentralizing (Bernier 1989). This environment was conducive to the emergence of self-regulating professions in Upper and Lower Canada, and encouraged the delegation of authority. When new professions like dentistry and pharmacy subsequently emerged, the institutional environment was similar. These self-regulating professions were established post-Confederation, when provincial governments were still constructing their institutional and legislative frameworks, providing more leeway for professionals to define their own social roles and responsibilities. In contrast, self-regulating professions were legislated in the United States and United Kingdom at a time when those countries already had established regulatory traditions and institutional frameworks in place. Thus, there were greater opportunities for professions and professionals in Canada to obtain considerable autonomy and authority. Initial patterns of professional regulation established traditions for later professions to follow, as we have seen.

Cultural differences between the three countries were likely also relevant. American ambivalence to government intervention in the economy brought ambivalence towards self-regulating professions. While the United States has regulated many professions, occupations, and other institutions, the tendency has been to establish multiple layers of regulation, and implement checks and balances, to ensure that no single organization is too powerful (Terry et al. 2012; Rhode and Woolley 2012). As a result, the regulation of professions like law and medicine was, in effect, shared by multiple institutions – professional societies, appointed regulatory boards, universities and training schools, the courts, employers, and other institutions (Terry et al. 2012; Burrage 2006). Scholars have linked the emergence of self-regulating professions to political decentralization in the United Kingdom as well (Macdonald 1995). In this environment, regional and specialist groups could regulate themselves. The result was many internal divisions within professions. Engineering, accounting, law, and medicine were historically divided into subfields governed by distinct regulatory bodies and organizations (Parry and Parry 1976; Berman 2006; Jordan and Richardson 1984; Willmott 1986; Brazier et al. 1993). Professional unity has either been absent for extended periods, or has been loosely legislated through the establishment of overarching bodies such as the General Medical Council.

In contrast, and perhaps because professional regulation occurs at the provincial and not the national level as in the United Kingdom, Canadian professions have been more unified, with fewer layers of regulation or competing organizations. Professional power has, thus, been more concentrated. This occurred despite the efforts of Canadian professionals and state actors to recreate British institutions in the colonies. As they attempted to establish British professions on Canadian soil, state actors and professionals innovated – sometimes intentionally to make adaptations suitable for the colony, and sometimes unintentionally. As I argued in chapter 2, Canadian professionals and state actors sometimes lacked close knowledge of the institutions they sought to emulate. Further, by legislating institutions that developed informally in the mother country, early Canadian leaders inevitably created something different. Today, Canadian professions are subject to layers of regulation, like their counterparts elsewhere, but these layers have developed over time (Adams 2017a). They were less evident historically.

Research should continue to explore international differences in regulation, both within Anglo-American countries and more broadly. There is a growing body of research on international trends and divergences in professional regulation that is contributing to a better understanding of regulatory trends, historically and in the present day (Burrage 2006; Saks 2015; Suddaby et al. 2007; Adams 2015). Nevertheless, many questions remain.[5]

Twentieth-Century Transformations

This book has explored professional self-regulation in Canada up to 1940. The end date is somewhat arbitrary. There is little to distinguish trends immediately before and after the Second World War. Nonetheless, by the late 1930s, the foundation of professional self-regulation in Canada, in all its complexity, had been laid. Change was on the horizon. With the expansion of the welfare state in the Second World War era and beyond, state actors' approaches to professional regulation began to shift. The number and the types of groups regulated expanded: teachers, technicians, and workers in a variety of sectors obtained powers of self-regulation (Langlois 2011; Dussault 1978; Prud'homme 2011; Adams 2010). These new groups were sometimes regulated differently from those who preceded them. New health professions were established. Moreover, major transformations in professional self-regulation would occur beginning in the 1960s.

It was the implementation of medicare that appears to have had the most significant impact. With provincial governments sharing the expense of healthcare, concern over the provision of professional services, especially the efficiency, coordination, and costs of those services, increased (Adams 2016a). Around this time, social and consumer movements protested against professions, with critics contending professions misused their powers: professionals were accused of being more concerned with their own incomes and authority than with public well-being (Adams 2016a; Haug 1980). Combined, these trends resulted in a change in professional regulation. In Quebec, the change was dramatic: the 1973 Professional Code completely transformed professional regulation in the province, eliminating long-standing professional regulatory bodies, and creating new orders accountable to a state-appointed body which oversaw them. In Ontario, there was a substantial change in healthcare regulation. For example, the 1974 Health Disciplines Act affected most health professions, subjecting them to more oversight, and making them more publicly accountable. In these provinces and others, the involvement of lay people and state actors on professional regulatory bodies increased. The autonomy and power of self-regulating professions has been reduced. The focus of some regulatory legislation has also changed: for example, health legislation in Ontario and British Columbia now regulates by the task. Legislation grants health professionals the right to perform certain regulated acts

(O'Reilly 2000). Professional regulation has been significantly transformed since the 1940s, but self-regulation remains a lasting principle.

Nevertheless, professional self-regulation is currently under attack – from state actors interested in reducing professionals' power, as well as other workers jealous of their privileges (Abel 2003; Saks 2015). Scandals surrounding misbehaving professionals encourage members of the public to regard them cynically and question their value (Dixon-Woods et al. 2011). The globalization of professional work in some fields provides an additional challenge to professional self-regulation (Flood 2011; Suddaby et al. 2007). Whether self-regulation as a regulatory form can survive these pressures in the coming decades is by no means certain.

To document these dramatic changes fully requires extensive analysis. This is a topic worthy of a future book. There is reason to believe, however, that the theoretical framework developed here to explore professional regulation historically is still applicable. Our ability to understand recent changes, and future trends, in professional regulation will be enhanced by drawing on both neo-Weberian and ecological approaches, and exploring the actions and projects of professional leaders, state actors, as well as businesses, consumer groups, and other actors who increasingly shape professional regulation. The activity of global actors, and not just local actors, must be taken into account.

Conclusion

Some American scholars have declared the sociology of professions to be dead, replaced by a focus on expert workers in organizational settings (Eyal 2013; Gorman and Sandefur 2011). Scholars in the United Kingdom have announced the end of professional self-regulation as the regulation of law and medicine is now conducted by bodies on which laypersons form the majority (Dixon-Woods et al. 2011; Evetts 2002; Flood 2011). In contrast, in Canada professional self-regulation continues, albeit in modified form, and the sociology of professions appears very much alive. In the introduction to this book I asked, "Is Canada merely a laggard, or are current trends a reflection of different traditions respecting professions and professional regulation?" Canada may eventually adopt the regulatory mechanisms recently implemented in the United Kingdom and Australia, but historically Canada was not a laggard. Self-regulating professions in medicine and law were legislated in Canada before many other nations followed suit. Further, historical evidence suggests that Canada has had distinct traditions of professional regulation. Self-regulating professions contributed to social governance, not only through their regulatory authority, but by the participation of professionals in important social and political positions. Here, professional regulation was not simply an outcome of professional lobbying or social closure campaigns, inter-professional conflict, or even state projects. All these processes, and many others, combined to shape regulatory outcomes. In this latter respect, however, Canada may not be distinct. The same processes and social actors may shape professional development in other regions. I know of no similar studies exploring state decision making respecting professional self-regulation elsewhere. In light of recent changes in state-profession relations, and dramatic economic and social change affecting professions, now is not the time to abandon the sociology of professions. Rather, it is time to recognize professions as persistent and vital, if changing, social institutions, and devote more attention to their evolving relationships with state and society.

Notes

Introduction

1 Some scholars highlight monopoly over the provision of certain services or a restricted title as being a key defining feature of professions (see for instance Witz 1992; Brockman 1998; Freidson 2001). In contrast, I emphasize market control since very few professions have historically enjoyed a true market monopoly, although monopoly remains a goal towards which many professions strive.

1 Theorizing Professions

1 Some scholars continue to search for an invariant definition. For a recent and sophisticated example see David Sciulli's (2005, 2009) work.
2 Medicine has never successfully held a monopoly over the provision of healthcare services, for instance, except in a few cases, such as the treatment venereal disease in some provinces, at some points in time. Nevertheless, the medical profession has historically endeavoured to enhance its market control.
3 These theories have been criticized for their neglect of emotions and identity, and for focusing disproportionately on rational, organized movements seeking political change (for example, see Goodwin and Jasper 2004; Della Porta and Diani 1999). These flaws are not fatal in the study of professionalization as aspiring professions tend to approach professionalization rationally, and direct their campaigns at state actors, as well as the public.
4 This is not true of Durkheim (1992), who is nonetheless vague about state decision-making processes: "The State, like the individual is often

mistaken as to the motives underlying its decisions, but whether its decisions be ill-motivated or not, *the main thing is that they should be motivated to some extent. There is always or at least usually a semblance of deliberation,* an understanding of the circumstances as a whole that make the decision necessary" (50, italics added).

5 Abbott's (2005: 247) view of the state as a complex "structure filled with competing subgroups" is similar to the view of the state advocated by other historical sociologists.

6 Abbott (2005) argues that the professions' ecology is also linked with the higher-education ecology; however, Burrage (2006) suggests that schools played a larger role in profession formation in the United States than elsewhere (for instance, see p. 586).

7 Here, I have been influenced by Giddens's (1993: 88–112) and Weber's (1968) view that action encompasses both "doing" and "not doing," and agency entails the capacity to act (and is not reducible to intention or action itself). I also adopt Giddens's insight that the rationalization of action is distinct from motivation, and that the latter can be unconscious. Thus, we may not be able to determine exactly "why" state actors made certain decisions historically, but I believe there is something to gain from looking at when and under what circumstances they acted (or did not) and what rationales they provided for their actions.

2 The Emergence of Self-Regulating Professions

1 The seigneurial system was a form of land distribution implemented in New France in the 1600s that was similar to feudalism. The system promised to distribute land in a systematic way: under it the seigneur would grant land to farmer-tenants (les habitants). Tenants would owe rent, taxes, and often labour to the seigneurs, and in return would be part of a community and enjoy its resources and protections, including, often, local courts (Mathieu 2013). The seigneurs were influential and powerful in New France, but their authority (and economic base) was weakened after the British conquest (Ouellet 1980a: 11).

2 Combining these "two distinct 'national' legal traditions" provided particular challenges for lawyers (Garneau 2009: 131).

3 Early colonial leaders, including Samuel de Champlain, believed that lawyers would charge high rates, delay proceedings, and complicate the administration of justice in the colony (Veilleux 1997: 18). Nonetheless, "notaries and bailiffs were authorized to represent the population before the courts" (Garneau 2009: 131; also Vachon 1962: 43).

4 "Ils ont seuls le droit d'avocasser, signer les requêtes, faire toutes ventes et licitations ordonnées par justice, suivant les règlements et taxes qui en seront faites par la dite cour" (Court of Common Pleas) (La Gazette du Québec 1765, cited in Veilleux 1997: 24).
5 It is estimated that only one in ten francophones in the province could write his or her name as late as 1800 (Curtis 2012: 7).
6 Another 1785 ordinance pertained to land surveying, and it will be discussed in more detail in chapter 4.
7 This said, large numbers of francophones in the countryside remained illiterate and did not have access to quality education through much of this period (Curtis 2012).
8 Garneau (2009: 136) explains that lawyers in training often clerked in different offices, and that over a quarter of them spent time training with someone from another linguistic group.
9 Those elected to the Quebec board were a fairly homogeneous group: stable, urban, majority francophone (Bernier 1981). The majority also held important municipal or local posts. They were more moderate than their Montreal counterparts who were active in the rebellions (Bernier 1981, 1989).
10 In the early nineteenth century the vote was tied to property, but a fair number of Canadiens met the requirements (Ouellet 1980a; Curtis 2012: 7); there were a large number of francophone voters whom the Patriots were able to win over.
11 In contrast, in France, notaries were state-appointed and "their corporate bodies were first established by the state" (Burrage 2006: 10).
12 Nelson had a successful and long medical career, but was also active politically. He had been arrested for his role in the rebellions, and was deported to Bermuda. Shortly thereafter his deportation was overturned and he set up practice in New York. By the early 1840s he was effectively pardoned, and in 1844 returned to Canadian politics (Thompson 1976).
13 Female midwives in the cities of Montreal and Quebec, and the town of Trois-Rivières were asked to "prove their competency before any two members of the College" and obtain a certificate before entering practice (10 & 11 Vic c. 26, s. xv). In this manner, urban midwives were regulated (but not self-regulating). Also, those doctors licensed in Upper Canada were exempted under the act, and allowed to practice in Lower Canada.
14 When before the legislative assembly, the bill was referred to a special committee, which included several lawyers (Veilleux 1997).
15 For some, the Loyalists in Upper Canada represent "the conservative counter-revolution to America's revolutionary liberalism" (Wiseman 2007: 25).

16 Provinces differed in their use of these two terms. In the Western provinces, "solicitor" was the term used, while in Ontario and some other provinces, the term "attorney" was more common.

17 These reform-minded professionals were part of a broader wave of British immigrants in the first half of the nineteenth century that sought to reform Upper Canadian institutions established by their more conservative predecessors (Wiseman 2007: 192).

18 Immigration of Irish- and Scottish-trained medical doctors was likely encouraged by legislation in England that did not fully recognize their training for entry into general practice in that country (Parry and Parry 1976: 114).

19 Eclectic medical practitioners "borrowed therapeutic principles and practices from both regular medical groups and other sectarian ones [especially the use of botanical remedies] in an attempt to use all that they thought to be beneficial" (Connor 1991: 504).

20 By the 1830s most US states had some form of medical regulation, but laws were not terribly effective (Shryock 1967: 23–4). By the mid-1840s, many states had repealed their legislation regulating both the medical and legal professions (Shryock 1967: 30–1).

21 The wording in the act itself is subtle (Upper Canada 1839: s. xii): "It shall and may be lawful for the Fellows of the said College [CPSUC] to grant such applicant a license … to practice Physic, Surgery and Midwifery, *or either*, as the case may be, in this Province" (italics added).

22 Of the 40 or so men named in the act (whose backgrounds could be traced), 20 were Scottish- or Irish-trained, and 19 claimed membership in a college of surgeons (mostly London or Edinburgh). Thirty of them were born in England, Scotland, or Ireland; eight were born in Canada, and only two were American-born. British doctors were likely also influenced by the movement to reform medicine occurring around the same time in the United Kingdom.

23 In this section, I focus on this legislation, rather than early-nineteenth-century US medical regulation, since it was the later legislation that provided the foundation for subsequent professional regulation in the United States.

24 An 1886 legislative amendment allowed five GMC members to be elected by registered medical doctors (Chamberlain 2013: 51).

25 Miller (1991: 61) describes the legal profession in nineteenth-century Nova Scotia the same way: "The English example had been adapted to suit the conditions of the colony." Wiseman (2007) has argued this was true for politics and state activity in general in the nineteenth century.

26 The 1869 Medical Act will be discussed in more detail in chapters 3 and 4.

27 Burrage (2006: 586) identifies similar processes in law, arguing that professional institutions were undermined by the American Revolution, and lawyers turned away from collegial organization. By the time they renewed their professional projects in the late nineteenth century they "had to accept that two powerful actors, schools and legislatures, had come, in their absence to shape the profession, and they could hardly hope to dislodge or override them."

28 As we will see in chapter 3, the Ontario legislature forced regular and irregular medical doctors to join together under one regulatory college in 1869.

29 In his study of American lawyers, Terence Halliday (1987: 54) argues that influential professions find a way to "create expert authority and convert it into moral authority." While in nineteenth-century Canada, expertise and moral authority were intertwined, it was not the case that the latter was a development subsequent to, and somehow separate from, the former. Rather, professionals' claim to expertise to some extent rested on their moral authority.

3 Self-Regulating Professions Post-Confederation

1 Indeed, the Nova Scotia General Assembly (like its counterpart in New Brunswick) did not even alter its numbering. The year 1867 marked the beginning of the 24th General Assembly in the colony/province.

2 Recall from the introduction that I define professional self-regulation as a type of regulation in which the authority to govern a profession is granted (by the state) to a body composed (predominantly) of professionals. An occupation may be regulated without being self-regulating.

3 Examples of the latter include efforts by the Patrons of Industry in Ontario to curtail medicine's powers in the 1890s (MacNab 1970; Naylor 1986), and similar attempts in Nova Scotia in the 1880s. Both are discussed more later in this chapter.

4 In addition to these bills affecting the profession as a whole, there were a significant number of bills to facilitate the entry to practice of individuals seeking an exemption from professional regulatory boards' rules (not analysed here). Private bills for entry to practise professions were very common in Quebec (Massicotte 2009: 97), even more than in Ontario (Adams 2005).

5 Nova Scotia came close to establishing accounting as a self-regulating profession in this era. An Institute of Chartered Accountants was incorporated in Nova Scotia in 1900 (Nova Scotia 1900), but no restricted title was established.

6 The Chartered Stenographic Reporters' and Architects' Bills were almost identical.

7 Mr Pardee's main concern was the barriers the act placed on Quebec and English-trained doctors' entry to practice in Ontario (*Globe* 1869a: 4). Pardee himself was a lawyer, and hence may not have been opposed to self-regulating professions in principle.

8 This debate is reminiscent of that which occurred in Ontario in 1822, touched on in chapter 2.

9 It was common for the Attorney General to have a formal role in the Law Society, thereby providing a bridge between the society and the government (Watts 1984).

10 The debate over the second reading occurred on division, which was tied 9 for and 9 against. The Speaker resolved the tie in favour of the second reading. The pharmacy amendment act passed before the bill to repeal the pharmacy act reached the Committee of the Whole, and hence was withdrawn (see British Columbia 1895, pp 108, 119).

11 Dr Munroe continued to criticize the main principle behind the bill: "But about those discoveries and remedies; that is the laughable part of it. It is presumed that some bushwhacker or some other person in this country thinks he discovers a remedy for certain diseases ... They are no discoveries at all; they are not worthy of the name" (Nova Scotia 1888).

12 There were a few women involved in the Chartered Stenographers' association.

13 In 1891 Ontario undertakers and embalmers sought an act establishing them as professionals. Many of the leaders behind the petition for legislation were undertakers who listed themselves as cabinet makers in the census. Embalmers succeeded in obtaining regulatory legislation in several provinces early in the twentieth century, but at first they were more state-regulated than self-regulating. The push to regulate embalmers formed part of the early-twentieth-century public health movement, and early legislation established boards of examiners to examine and license practitioners.

14 The convention in most provinces is to refer to members of the legislative assembly as MLAs. In Ontario, these individuals are commonly referred to as MPPs or members of provincial parliament.

15 Dussault (1978: 446) notes that some dental leaders in Quebec were influential and well connected as well.

16 The circumstances surrounding medical doctors' and dentists' professional projects will be discussed in more detail in chapter 4.

17 Medical doctors are a notable exception here.

4 Case Studies in Self-Regulation

1 Although the movement of the act through the legislative assembly is mentioned in the *Globe*, *La Minerve*, the *Quebec Mercury*, and the *Montreal Witness*, no debate or discussion on the bill was recorded.

2 To control practitioners further, the CPSQ also established a code of ethics in 1878 (Bernier 1983).

3 The speaker ruled the 1881 bill out of order "inasmuch as it proposed to amend a Tariff which does not exist" (Quebec 1881: 288).

4 There was so much protest over this and other matriculation changes that the council approached the legislature for a revision to their act to affirm their proposed policies. Faced with opposition to these policies from within the profession, the legislature overturned several matriculation regulations, and delayed the implementation of Greek as a compulsory requirement until 1869 (Gidney and Millar 1984).

5 At the bill's second reading, Dr McGill defended the exclusion of homeopaths and eclectics by stating that the council would be "more than happy to allow them to enter the Council and be registered along with themselves after an examination," but that they did not propose such an accommodation in the act because they did not want to be accused of "persecution" (in MacNab 1970: 13). While some within medicine agreed with McGill, there were many vocal opponents.

6 Indeed, MacNab (1970: 12) claims the medical council had discussed the possibility of amalgamation of the three different branches previously.

7 Some bills were proposed in the late 1870s pertaining to reciprocity in medical licensing with Great Britain, but none of these bills even reached second reading (Ontario, *Journals of the Legislative Assembly*, 1877, 1878, 1879).

8 Support for the regulation of botanic doctors had been given by the legislature in 1850 (Howell 1992: 8).

9 Howell (1981) shows that 72 per cent of Nova Scotian MDs in 1890 were trained in the United States. It is reasonable to assume that the majority of MDs in 1870 were also American-trained. These US ties shaped regulatory strategies and goals in the province.

10 Originally the bill named eight Eastern Ontario dentists as the first trustees. This did not sit well with dentists in Toronto and Southern Ontario, so the names of four additional men were added to the bill (Shosenberg 1992).

11 The 1871 census records 46 dentists in the province of Quebec, compared to 230 in Ontario (Canada 1873).

12 A Quebec dental leader argued that the presence of a flamboyant dental quack in Halifax in 1871 who argued against the dental bill may have influenced legislators' opinion on the subject (Beers 1871: 156).
13 I could find no surviving record of the debate on this bill. The *Victoria Daily Colonist* reports the bill's first reading, but not the debate on the second reading.
14 Gullett (1971: 70) suggests that a more informal provincial society predated the British Columbia Dental Association, and it may have pushed for the legislation.
15 This law also changed the payment system. Formerly, land surveyors had been paid by the day, but after 1818, their pay would be a percentage of area surveyed. This encouraged surveyors to rush through their work, and led to less accurate surveys (Ladell 1993: 118). The daily-rate pay system was reinstituted in 1829.
16 Robin (1978: 37) argues that several of these pioneer business leaders "became rustic capitalists who wielded their new power with the brash abandon of the parvenue."

5 The Expansion and Alteration of Professional Self-Regulation

1 Vancouver's population increased from 27,010 in 1901 to 100,401 in 1911. In 1901, Vancouver was the ninth largest city in Canada (Montreal, Toronto, and Quebec City were 1, 2, and 3 respectively). In 1911 it was fourth (behind Montreal, Toronto, and Winnipeg). Cities in Saskatchewan and Alberta grew at an even faster rate (*Canada Year Book 1922–23*, 171, in Granatstein et al. 1990: 118).
2 In Millard's (1988: 68) words, "close corporation" was the "popular term for an incorporated professional society closed to non-professionals."
3 Some of these professional groups were regulated years earlier. For example, funeral directors in Nova Scotia had been regulated since 1908; however, their initial legislation established a licensing mechanism, with no clear entry requirements or regulatory authority. I have dated self-regulation of embalmers and funeral directors to 1938, when a new regulatory board with more extensive regulatory powers was established. Similarly, a nursing association was incorporated in Nova Scotia in 1910, but a provincially acknowledged restricted title (and associated regulatory privileges) were not implemented until 1922.
4 Osteopathy was also regulated in several other provinces in one way or another. In British Columbia and Nova Scotia, osteopathy practice was governed under the Medical Act.

5 The distinction between regulated occupations and self-regulating professions is described in more detail in Adams (2010). For the purposes of this analysis, I have included teaching in this category of "regulated occupations." Teachers were regulated under provincial education acts throughout this period, but they were not self-regulating.
6 These bill totals do not include the scores of private acts passed in Quebec (and similar acts passed in Ontario) to facilitate the entry of specific individuals into a profession by waiving an entry requirement (often matriculation) in the opening decades of the twentieth century. Most of these acts were passed with the agreement of the respective professions.
7 The interplay between these various groups is touched on later in the chapter, and will be explored in more detail in chapter 6.
8 The bill was created by staff members in the attorney general's office following the advice of the Hodgins commission discussed later in the chapter. It is possible that there was some communication mix-up between staff members, the medical profession, and the government.
9 Such records are incomplete in this era. None of the four provinces published "Hansard" through the entire period investigated here. Records of debates exist for Nova Scotia and Quebec (reconstituted) for much of this period, but for Ontario and British Columbia one must rely on newspaper accounts of legislative events.
10 The Hodgins commission report is discussed in greater detail later in the chapter.
11 The 1921 legislation to regulate optometrists in Nova Scotia was very similar in its limitations.
12 It is not clear whether medical doctors were among those who missed meetings so that quorum could not be obtained. The committee chair was a medical doctor, and was generally supportive of the bill (although he too expressed reservations at times).
13 The regulation of nursing in Nova Scotia in 1920 was also very controversial, for similar reasons.
14 Some provision for establishing a register for trained nurses (to be maintained by the provincial secretary) was made in the 1912 Hospitals and Charitable Institutions Act; however, the register was not established until 1920 (MacNab 1970: 118). The 1922 nurses' act replaced these provisions.
15 A related, and equally important, question is why was engineering established as a (partially) closed self-regulating profession in Canada, while in Canada's main counterparts, the United Kingdom and United States, it was not? In most Canadian provinces engineering is at least partially closed, and engineers doing certain types of engineering work must be

licensed. I believe the answer lies in the patterns of professional regulation evident in Canada at the time. As we have seen earlier in this chapter, roughly two-thirds of self-regulating professions in Canada were closed with an incorporated body, including engineering's allied professions of land surveying and architecture. Further, engineers' work has implications for government projects and the public interest. Self-regulation had become the standard form for professions of this nature by the 1920s.

16 In a few short years, training for physical therapists was instituted at the University of Toronto, and the specialization expanded (Heap 1995a).

17 Since regulation frequently entails a delegation of governance responsibilities, the extension of suffrage to all men (regardless of income) and women in the post–First World War era likely influenced the extension of professional powers to those outside the elite.

18 Millar, Heap, and Gidney's (2005) analysis of the socio-economic status of first-year students in the University of Toronto's medicine, engineering, and dentistry programs in the first half of the twentieth century shows that most students had fathers engaged in professional or business occupations. Fathers' occupations varied across program: for instance, in 1932, almost 60% of medical students had fathers working in professions or business, compared to 47% of engineers and 44% of dentists. Many dental students (17% in 1932) had parents engaged in farming, while engineering students had fathers in supervisory or white-collar jobs (24%). Students were also predominantly Protestant in the early twentieth century, but the participation of Catholic and Jewish students increased in the 1920s and 1930s.

6 Contests over Regulation of "Drugless Healers"

1 For a good discussion of physical culture see Churchill (2008). The popularity of Turkish baths and beliefs about their health benefits date back to the 1860s in the United Kingdom (Kandela 1999), but they were quite popular in urban centres like Toronto and Vancouver in the early twentieth century.

2 Medical doctors were more likely to target men for prosecution, but women were charged as well.

3 One-third of the eighteen petitioners were women osteopaths practising in the province. The petitioners were based in Toronto, Hamilton, Berlin, and Haileybury (Ontario 1910a).

4 These provisions were somewhat like those passed in British Columbia in 1909.

5 All that was left in the bill was a clause acknowledging that a federal medical act would have force in Ontario. It passed easily (Ontario 1912c).

6 During his term as premier, Whitney established many commissions to provide advice on a wide range of specific legislative concerns (Humphries 1985)

7 The Drugless Physicians Association also went by the name "Drugless Practitioners Association." The organizers preferred the former title: this was the name they sought to register, but the government would not approve it. Since this was their preferred name, and the name on their letterhead in the 1910s and early 1920s, this is the name I use.

8 In 1915, the Ontario legislature received a petition and a bill to establish and incorporate a College of Chiropractic for Ontario (AO 1915). The association mentioned in the act is the Ontario Chiropractors Legislators Association; it is possible this group was connected with one of the other groups, perhaps the Ontario Chiropractors Association. The bill was regarded as highly flawed (AO 1915; *Globe* 1915c), and the legislature was unwilling to legislate for any alternative health group while the Hodgins commission was in progress; hence the bill was withdrawn.

9 According to the *Globe* (1918b), the premier (Hearst), attorney general (Lucas), along with two cabinet ministers (future premier G. Howard Ferguson and H.J. Cody) met with representatives from Christian Science (from Boston), the OMA, the medical schools, the Ontario Academy of Medicine, the Ontario Association of Osteopathy, the Ontario Chiropractic Association (Duval), and the Drugless Physicians Association (the list may not have been exhaustive).

10 The bill also provided exemptions for nurses, chiropodists, those giving massage or Turkish baths, and Christian Scientists. See also AO 1919d for an earlier draft of the same legislation.

11 Osteopaths petitioned for an act to regulate osteopathy in 1921, and while their petition was read and received, no legislation was forthcoming (Ontario 1921). A bill to regulate chiropodists was also introduced in 1921, but it was withdrawn and the order for its second reading discharged (Ontario 1921; *Globe* 1921c).

12 The secretary of the Drugless Physicians' Association, A.W. MacFie, took it upon himself to keep Drury informed of the opposing chiropractors' mobilization against the act, warning him of imminent activity, while confirming the Drugless Physicians Association's support for the government and the bill (AO 1923).

13 Not all the groups were represented at these meetings. A letter from the attorney representing the Chiropractic Association of Ontario indicated

that they had "no knowledge of the discussions" leading up to the 1925 legislation (AO 1925).

14 Government officials came to refer to lesser-trained osteopaths as "pseudo-osteopaths" later in the 1920s. I have borrowed this terminology to distinguish these partially trained practitioners from the fully trained, aggressively professionalizing osteopaths associated with the OAO.

15 In the mid-1930s, physiotherapists were brought under the act (Ontario 1937).

16 McKay had also served as the medical officer of health for Oshawa.

17 MacFie had attended high school in Glencoe, Ontario, and several years later, in the early 1910s, pursued chiropractic training at the Ross College of Chiropractic in Indiana. He graduated with honours in March 1914, and set up practice in London, Ontario. He made a good first impression in the city, as he was the only chiropractor and one of only two drugless therapists to be included in a 1915 volume entitled *London and Its Men of Affairs* (London: Advertiser Job Printing Co. Ltd., 1915); the book provided "portraits and biographies of the men prominent in the city's official, professional, and business life" (p. 9). Osteopath Eldon Detwiler was the other drugless practitioner included. MacFie appears to have had the social and cultural capital to win over influential people and advance his organization's cause.

18 The *Globe* (1927b) was a particularly strong supporter of alternative health practices, and even in its articles discussing the conviction of Pocock and Ellison, referred to them as "Dr. Pocock" and "Dr. Ellison" throughout.

19 Although the training was modelled after medical education, the medical men made much of the fact that osteopathic schools had fewer resources, including less well-equipped labs, and smaller hospitals, which, they argued, resulted in an inferior educational experience (Etherington and Ryerson 1934; Etherington 1935).

20 The expansion of suffrage to include all men and women post–First World War is likely relevant here.

21 Recall from chapter 5 that the Ontario government reportedly spent $8000 on the Hodgins commission.

22 For example, in his letter to Whitney, Lash (AO 1910c: 5) argues that professional regulation is intended "to prevent the harm to the public which ensued by things requiring knowledge and skill being done by persons without the necessary knowledge and skill, and to prevent frauds and impositions upon the confiding and innocent public which could readily be practised by unscrupulous persons." Further in 1919, a government official asserts that without regulation there is "grave danger" because

"ignorant and unscrupulous people will avail themselves of the freedom … for the purpose of money making and for other purposes even more objectionable" (AO 1919b: 3).

23 Here it is also important to note that while many alternative health practitioners were women, they do not appear to have figured prominently in professional campaigns or state lobbying. Further, while there were members of ethnic minorities practising professions, few served as professional leaders.

24 Sanipractic was a drugless practice that emerged in Washington state in the early twentieth century, similar to naturopathy in its commitment to healing through natural means, including "the science and art of applied prophylactic and therapeutic sanitation," utilizing "nature-cure treatments (water, light, heat, exercise, food, herbs, and so on), as well as manipulation" (Adams and Etherington 2015; Baer and Sporn 2009). A few Vancouver practitioners appear to have been educated in sanipractic in Washington state, and brought the practice to Canada.

25 Lesley Biggs (1986) provides this title, but in 1922 some sources refer to the association as the British Columbia Association of Sanipractic Physicians and a few years later as the Association of Sanipractic and Naturopathic Physicians (British Columbia Archives [BCA] 1922; British Columbia 1923). In a brief memoir, early naturopath A.W. Dennis (2009: 116) calls it the Association of Naturopathic Physicians of British Columbia.

26 Members of the public resented these prosecutions of alternative healers, leading the medical profession to ease off during the 1920s (Biggs 1986); attacks on alternative healers resumed in 1930.

27 Party politics had only arrived in British Columbia in the early 1900s (Barman 1991). Professional regulation was not strongly shaped by party politics in this era.

28 For this analysis, the *Journals of the Legislative Assembly* were reviewed for recorded votes (only some votes were recorded) to determine how the seven MLA health professionals voted on various measures. If they had promised to give their votes on other bills, in return for votes against drugless healing bills, it was anticipated that they might vote in tandem, but they did not. Subsequent analysis aimed to determine if there was evidence of vote trading between health professionals and lawyers, when the latter were engaged in inter-professional conflict with notaries and sought to legislate against them in the 1920s (see Brockman 1999); however, again, there was no concrete evidence that this occurred.

29 Murphy was an Ontario-educated lawyer and BC judge, who had represented Yale in the legislature between 1900 and 1902 (Pue 1995).

30 The focus of the commission was initially controversial. Murphy (1932: 3–4) had been directed to investigate the regulation of chiropractic and drugless practice, but medicine sought (and failed to achieve) an investigation of their scientific validity. Again, medicine's protests about the nature of the commission resulted in a short delay.

31 Section 11 of the act reads in part: "no person registered as a chiropractor under this Act shall engage in the practice of the diagnosis or treatment of the human body for disease, or the causes of disease, otherwise than as a chiropractor, unless he first applies to have his name stricken from the register ... and discontinues the use of the name 'chiropractor' ..."

32 The presence of the CCF as the official opposition during the Pattullo government may have further reduced the influence of elites such as professionals within the legislature.

33 Members of the two dominant parties (the Liberals and the CCF) voted on either side of the issue, but 21 Liberals voted for chiropractic regulation, while only eight voted against, and two of the latter were medical doctors.

34 While chiropractic services were particularly popular amongst the working class (Biggs 1989), there is some indication that their appeal may have been broader in British Columbia. As noted, some legislators argued that many "estimable" citizens patronized them.

35 Inter-professional conflict and debates around the regulation of chiropractic erupted in Nova Scotia in the 1950s. See, for example, Nova Scotia Archives (1953-66). Chiropractic was not regulated in Nova Scotia until 1972 (Nova Scotia 1972).

36 J. Murray Beck (1957) argues that by the late nineteenth century, the council largely acquiesced to the decisions of the government, but it tended in instances like these to provide some sober second thought. In earlier years, the council would have likely rejected the bill, but although they considered doing so, council members instead revised it to temper its impact.

37 Burgess did not have a long tenure in the province; he was gone within a decade. He and a French-Canadian wife appear in the 1916 census in Manitoba, and by 1920 they were living in Los Angeles.

38 Quebec and Nova Scotia were among the last Canadian provinces to regulate chiropractic and naturopathy (drugless healing) (Royal Commission on Health Services 1965: 76, 79).

Conclusion

1 Beck (1957: 275) explains that sessions typically lasted only seven or eight weeks in Nova Scotia. Massicotte (1989: 79) reports for Quebec that "from

1867 to 1960 the average number of sitting days per year was forty-five, and a typical session lasted approximately three months." He further explains that the part-time nature of politics made it difficult for employees to participate in politics, leaving the field clear for professionals and businessmen who had more flexible schedules.

2 Quebec also had a bicameral system, but the upper house rarely countered decisions respecting professional regulation made by the lower house.

3 Administrators, industrialists, and small and medium-sized business owners were also well represented (Massicotte 1989: 78).

4 The emergence of divisions in medicine subsequently (in the 1850s and 1860s) delayed the re-emergence of self-regulation in the Ontario medical profession.

5 It should be noted that in all three nations, democracy was also a crucial element in the establishment of self-regulating professions. The formation and regulation of professions in non-democratic countries looks substantially different. Suffrage also appears to have been important. Professional regulation extended to non-traditional groups after the implementation of universal suffrage in the post–First World War era.

References

Abbreviations

AO	Archives of Ontario
BCA	British Columbia Archives
CMAJ	*Canadian Medical Association Journal*
CNC	Castonguay-Nepveu Commission
CHA	Committee on the Healing Arts
CPSO	College of Physicians and Surgeons of Ontario
HPLR	Health Professions Legislative Review
MASA	Medical Association of the State of Alabama
ODA	Ontario Dental Association
OMA	Ontario Medical Association

Primary Sources

Abbotsford Post. 1921. "Drugless Physicians Act Is Introduced in the House." *Abbotsford Post*, 11 March, p. 4.

Archives of Ontario (AO). 1906. Bill no. 106: An Act Respecting the Graduate Nurses' Association. RG 49-39, File: Bill no. 106 of 1906, R224934.

Archives of Ontario (AO). 1910a. Letter from Z.A. Lash to Premier Whitney, 6 December. RG F5-1, Sr. James Pliny Whitney correspondence, box B273276.

Archives of Ontario (AO). 1910b. Letter from Z.A. Lash to Premier Whitney, 16 December. RG F5-1, Sr. James Pliny Whitney correspondence, box B273276.

Archives of Ontario (AO). 1910c. Enclosures accompanying letter of Z.A. Lash sent to Premier Whitney, 16 December. RG F5-1, 16–31 Dec., box B273276.

Archives of Ontario (AO). 1915. Bill no. 29 – An Act to incorporate the College of Chiropractic for Ontario (and accompanying notes), RG 49-39, B227902.

Archives of Ontario (AO). 1919a. "Amendments to the Medical Act." RG 4-32, no. 3846, B420036.

Archives of Ontario (AO). 1919b. Ontario Medical Act: Memorandum for the Attorney General (Nov. 19, 1919). RG 4-32, # 960.

Archives of Ontario (AO). 1919c. Bill Respecting the practice of Medicine and Surgery (second revise). RG 4-32, # 960.

Archives of Ontario (AO). 1919d. The Ontario Medical Act, 1919 (draft). RG 8-5, B226516.

Archives of Ontario (AO). 1921. EC Drury Correspondence. RG 4-5-0–45, 46 and 47, MS 1658.

Archives of Ontario (AO). 1923. EC Drury Correspondence. RG 3-4-0–290 and 291, MS 1665 and 1668.

Archives of Ontario (AO). 1925. Attorney General's Office, internal memos. RG 4-32, # 659, B248107.

Archives of Ontario (AO). 1926–8. RG 55-27, B226899: Company hold-up files, 1926–8, Canadian College of Osteopathy, RG 8, I-2-F.

Archives of Ontario (AO). 1928. RG 4-32, B247991; File containing # 224, letter dated 17 February 1928.

Archives of Ontario (AO). 1929. Attorney General Correspondence. RG 4-32, B248010 and B248011.

Association of British Columbia Land Surveyors. 2015. "History." http://www.abcls.ca/?page_id=309.

Association of Canada Lands Surveyors. 1999. "History" https://www.acls-aatc.ca/files/english/history/History.pdf.

Beers, W.G. 1871. "Poor Nova Scotia." *Canada Journal of Dental Science* 3 (5): 156.

Biggs, C. Lesley. 1986. "No Bones about Chiropractic? The Early Struggle for Licensing of Chiropractors in British Columbia." BC Studies Conference, 7 November. (BC Archives, Chiropractors' Association of British Columbia, MS-2536, vol. 15, box 7).

Biggs, C. Lesley. 1989. "No Bones about Chiropractic: The Quest of Legitimacy by the Ontario Chiropractic Profession 1895–1985." PhD dissertation, University of Toronto, 1989.

British Columbia. 1873. "An Act Respecting Practitioners in the County Courts and Other Inferior Courts." *Statutes of British Columbia*, 36 Vic., c. 41.

British Columbia. 1877. "An Ordinance Respecting Practitioners of Medicine and Surgery" *Consolidated Statutes*, c. 120.

British Columbia. 1881. *Journals of the Legislative Assembly*. Victoria: Queen's Printer. Pp. 18, 25.

British Columbia. 1886a. "An Act to Regulate the Practice of Dentistry in the Province of British Columbia." *Statutes of British Columbia*, 49 Vic., c. 7.

British Columbia. 1886b. "An Act Respecting the Profession of Medicine and Surgery." *Statutes of British Columbia*, 49 Vic., c. 13.

British Columbia. 1886c. *Journals of the Legislative Assembly*. Victoria: Queen's Printer.

British Columbia. 1889. *Journals of the Legislative Assembly*. Victoria: Queen's Printer.

British Columbia. 1890. "An Act to Amend the 'Medical Act.'" *Statutes of British Columbia*, 53 Vic., c. 30.

British Columbia. 1891. "An Act Respecting Land Surveyors." *Statutes of British Columbia*, 54 Vic., c. 17.

British Columbia. 1895. *Journals of the Legislative Assembly*. Victoria: Queen's Printer. Pp 108, 119.

British Columbia. 1899. *Journals of the Legislative Assembly*. Victoria: Queen's Printer,

British Columbia. 1908. "An Act Respecting Dentistry." *Statutes of British Columbia*, 8 Edward VII, c. 2.

British Columbia. 1918a. "An Act Respecting the Profession of Nursing." *Statutes of British Columbia*, 8 Geo. V, c. 65.

British Columbia. 1918b. *Journals of the Legislative Assembly*. Victoria: King's Printer.

British Columbia. 1920a. "An Act to Incorporate the Association of Professional Engineers of the Province of British Columbia." *Statutes of British Columbia*, 10 Geo. V, c. 108.

British Columbia. 1920b. *Journals of the Legislative Assembly*. Victoria: King's Printer.

British Columbia. 1921a. *Journals of the Legislative Assembly*. Victoria: King's Printer.

British Columbia. 1921b. "An Act to Amend the 'Medical Act.'" *Statutes of British Columbia*, 11 Geo. V, c. 38.

British Columbia. 1922. "An Act to Amend the 'Medical Act.'" *Statutes of British Columbia*, 13 Geo. V, c. 48.

British Columbia. 1923. "Bill no. 17: An Act Respecting Sanipractic Physicians." Victoria: King's Printer.

British Columbia. 1931. *Journals of the Legislative Assembly*. Victoria: King's Printer.

British Columbia. 1934. "An Act Respecting Chiropractors." *Statutes of British Columbia*, 24 Geo. V, c. 12.

British Columbia. 1936a. "An Act Respecting Naturopathic Physicians." *Statutes of British Columbia*, 1 Edward VIII, c. 42.

British Columbia. 1936b. *Journals of the Legislative Assembly*. Victoria: King's Printer.

British Columbia Archives (BCA). 1922. Minute book, volume 1, Chiropractors' Association of British Columbia, MS-2536.

British Columbia Archives (BCA). 1923. Minute book, volume 1, Chiropractors' Association of British Columbia, MS-2536.

British Columbia Archives (BCA). 1936. Minute book, volume 2. Chiropractors' Association of British Columbia, MS-2536.

British Columbia City Directories. 1909. Vancouver Public Library: www.vpl .ca/bccd.

British Columbia City Directories. 1910. Vancouver Public Library: www.vpl .ca/bccd.

Bruce, Herbert A. 1912. "Ontario Medical Association Presidential Address." *Canadian Medical Association Journal* 2 (7): 580–92.

Canada. 1785. "Ordonnance qui concerne les avocats, procureurs, soliciteurs et les notaires et qui rend plus aisé le recouvrement des revenus de sa majesté." *Statutes*, 25 Geo. III, c. 4.

Canada. 1788. "Ordonnance qui concerne les médecins …' *Statutes*, 28 Geo. III, c. 8.

Canada. 1841. "An Act to grant authority to Licensed Surveyors in that part of this Province called Upper Canada, to administer an oath in certain cases, and to protect them while in the discharge of their duty in Surveying Lands." *Statutes of Canada* 4&5 Vic., c. 9.

Canada. 1847a. "An Act to incorporate the Members of the Medical Profession in Lower Canada, and to regulate the Study and Practice of Physic and Surgery therein." *Statutes of Canada*, 10 and 11 Vic., c. 26.

Canada. 1847b. "An Act for the organization of the Notarial Profession in that part of this Province called Lower Canada." *Statutes of Canada*, 10 and 11 Vic., c. 21.

Canada. 1849a. "An Act to Incorporate the Bar of Lower Canada." *Statutes of Canada*, 12 Vic., c. 46.

Canada. 1849b. "An Act to repeal certain Acts therein mentioned, and to make better provision respecting the admission of Land Surveyors and the Survey of Lands in this Province" *Statutes of Canada*, 12 Vic., c. 35.

Canada. 1859. "An Act Respecting Homeopathy." *Statutes of Canada*, 22 Vic., c. 47.

Canada. 1861. "An Act Respecting the Eclectic System of Medicine." *Statutes of Canada*, 24 Vic., c. 110.

Canada. 1865a. "An Act to Regulate the Qualifications of Practitioners in Medicine and Surgery in Upper Canada." *Statutes of Canada*, 28 and 29 Vic., c. 34.

Canada. 1865b. "An Act to Incorporate the Montreal Homeopathic Association." *Statutes of Canada*, 28 Vic., c. 59.

Canada. 1867. "An Act for the Union of Canada, Nova Scotia, and New Brunswick, and the Government thereof, and for the purposes connected therewith" [short title: British North America Act]. *Statutes of Canada*, 30–31 Vic., c. 3.

Canada (Department of Agriculture). 1873, Census of Canada, 1870–71. Volume 2. Ottawa: I.B. Taylor.

Canada (Department of Agriculture). 1882. Census of Canada. 1880–1. *Volume 1: Population*. Ottawa: Queen's Printer.

Canada (Dominion Bureau of Statistics). 1924. Sixth Census of Canada, 1921, Volume 4. Ottawa: F.C. Acland, King's Printer.

The Canadian Osteopath: Devoted to the Interest of the Science of Osteopathy. 1900. Pamphlet. Volume 1, no. 1.

Chartered Stenographic Reporters Association. 1892. *Proceedings of the First Annual General Meeting of the Chartered Stenographic Reporters Association of Ontario, including the Act of Incorporation.* Toronto: Press of the Budget.

CHA (Committee on the Healing Arts). 1970. *Report, Volume 1*. Toronto: Queen's Printer.

CMAJ. 1912. "The Ontario Medical Council and Osteopathy." *Canadian Medical Association Journal* 2 (6): 514–15.

CMAJ. 1915. "The Ontario Commission." *Canadian Medical Association Journal* 5 (12): 1091–2.

CMAJ. 1918. "Editorial: The Report of the Commission upon Medical Education in Ontario." *CMA Journal* 8 (6): 556–8.

CMAJ. 1927. "Medico-Legal: The Use of the Term Doctor or Physician as an Occupational Designation." *CMA Journal* 17 (7): 849–50.

CNC (Castonguay-Nepveu Commission). 1970. *Report of the Commission of Inquiry on Health and Social Welfare: The Professions and Society*. Quebec: Queen's Printer.

CPSO (College of Physicians and Surgeons of Ontario). 1938. Untitled pamphlet on medical registration. Toronto: CPSO, 1938. P. 21.

Dennis, A.W. 2009. "Brief History of Naturopathy in British Columbia." In Iva Lloyd, *The History of Naturopathic Medicine: A Canadian Perspective*, 115–18, 301–3. Toronto: McArthur & Co.

Drugless Physicians Association. 1919. Letter addressed to Premier Hearst, dated 4 February 1919. Archives of Ontario, RG 4-32, no. 3846, B420036.

Dun and Bradstreet Reference Book. Toronto: Dun and Bradstreet Canada, 1867–81.

DuVal, E. 1918. The Chiropractic Criticism of Mr. Justice Hodgins' Report on Medical Education in Ontario. Archives of Ontario, 8-5, Medical bill, B226482.

Elliot, George Lewis. 1870. *An Account of my Stewardship*. Toronto: Bell, Barker and Co., City Stream Press.

Etherington, Frederick. 1935. "Osteopathy and Licensure." Read before the Annual Congress on Medical Education, Hospitals and Licensure, Chicago, 19 February 1935. Reprinted and published in CPSO, untitled pamphlet on medical registration and examination (Toronto: CPSO, 1938).

Etherington, Frederick, and E. Stanley Ryerson. 1934. Report on Osteopathic Colleges and Teaching in Kirksville, Philadelphia, Des Moines and Chicago. Joint Advisory Committee representing the CPSO, the OMA, and the Universities of Ontario engaged in the teaching of medicine.

Ferguson, R. 1919. "Retiring [Medical council] President's Address" *Canadian Medical Association Journal* 9 (12): 1095–100.

Foulkes, Richard G. 1973. *Health Security for British Columbians*. Victoria: Minister of Health.

Globe. 1869a. "The Medical Bill." 15 January, p. 4.

Globe. 1869b. "An Allopathic View of the New Medical Bill." 22 January, p. 4.

Globe. 1871. "Sale of Poisons." 27 January, p. 4.

Globe. 1876. "Quebec Legislature: The Medical Profession." 30 November, p. 4.

Globe. 1906a. "Perquisites Have Been Abolished: Graduate Nurses." 2 March, p. 8.

Globe. 1906b. "Nurses Support Their Bill: Deputation Waited on the Provincial Secretary." 10 March, p. 13.

Globe. 1906c. "Nurses Bill Has Been Held Over; Some Suggestions to Be Embodied as Amendments." 20 April, p. 7.

Globe. 1906d. "Fight on Nurses' Bill: Warm Time at Meeting of the Special Committee." 27 April, p. 12.

Globe. 1911. "Storm Brewing over Optometrists' Bill: Association Does Not Take Kindly to Snub Received in Legislature Yesterday." 2 March, p. 9.

Globe. 1912a. "Oppose Close Corporations." 19 March, p. 9.

Globe. 1912b. "Leave Osteopaths Out." 12 April, p. 9.

Globe. 1913. "Is This a Close Corporation?" 15 April, p. 6.

Globe. 1915a. "Government Appoints Medical Commission: Judge Hodgins Will Investigate All Forms of Practice." 30 September, p. 7.

Globe. 1915b. "Drugless Physicians Inquiry Commences: Chiropractors, Christian Scientists and Various Medical Folk of Ontario Affected." 18 October, p. 7.

Globe. 1915c. "Chiropractors Must Do Without College." 17 March, p. 6.

Globe. 1915d. "Empty Garbage Cans Harbor No Rats." 5 November, p. 7.

Globe. 1918a. "Profession to Peruse Report." 12 February, p. 9.

Globe. 1918b. "Healers Meet Ontario Government: State Their Attitudes on Proposed Definition of Medical Practice." 5 December, p. 7.
Globe. 1921a. "Engineers Seek Bill to Register Members." 7 January, p. 13.
Globe. 1921b. "General Opposition to Engineers' Bill." 21 December, p. 3.
Globe. 1921c. "Practise of Chiropody." 5 March, p. 14.
Globe. 1922a. "Bill 'Exempts' Mining Work: Professional Engineers Provided with Means of Registering." 1 March, p. 2.
Globe. 1922b. "Miners' Opposition Strong against Act: Proposals in Engineers' Bill Believed to Impugn Private Rights." 10 February, p. 15.
Globe. 1923a. "He Says Legislation Is Not Now in Order." 26 April, p. 12.
Globe. 1923b. "Medical Amendment Given First Reading." 28 April, p. 19.
Globe. 1924. "Osteopaths' Head Corrects Minister." 21 April, p. 13.
Globe. 1925a. "Proposed Bill Full of Import for Osteopaths." 2 April, p. 11.
Globe. 1925b. "Letters to the Editor: The Osteopathic Position." 6 April, p. 4.
Globe. 1925c. "Drugless Practice and Regulations Fully Considered." 11 December, p. 11.
Globe. 1927a. "Argument Is Heard of Osteopaths' Use of Title 'Doctor.'" 31 January, p. 14.
Globe. 1927b. "Dr. Hubert Pocock Issues Statement in Osteopathy Case." 11 June, p. 36.
Globe. 1928. "Letter to the Editor: Title or Occupation." 2 March, p. 4.
Globe. 1931. "Osteopath Charges Medical Physicians with 'Duplicity.'" 14 May, pp. 13–14.
Halifax Chronicle. 1870. "Dentistry Bill Deferred." 31 March, p. 2.
Halifax Chronicle. 1871. "The Dentistry Bill." 16 March, p. 2.
Health Professions Legislative Review (HPLR). c. 1989. *Striking a New Balance: A Blueprint for the Regulation of Ontario's Health Professions*. Toronto: Queen's Printer.
Hodgins, Justice F. 1918. *Report and Supporting Statements on Medical Education in Ontario, 1917*. Toronto: King's Printer.
Lacroix, Justice Gerard. 1965. Report of the Royal Commission on Chiropraxy and Osteopathy. Quebec.
Macdonald, M.A. 1921. "Interim Report of the Select Committee Appointed Pursuant to Resolution on 9th March." *Journals of the Legislative Assembly*. Victoria: King's Printer. Pp. 120–1.
Manitoba Law Reform Commission. 1994. *Regulating Professions and Occupations*. Report no. 84. Manitoba: Queen's Printer.
MASA (Medical Association of the State of Alabama). 1877. *Comments, Transactions of the Medical Association of the State of Alabama* 30: 39.

McAlpine's Halifax City Directories. 1921. Nova Scotia Archives, Microfilm no. 9726.

McGillivray, Dr C.F. 1914. "OMA President's Address." *CMA Journal* 4 (7): 654–7.

Mills, Donald L. 1966. *Royal Commission on Health Services: Study of Chiropractors, Osteopaths and Naturopaths in Canada*. Ottawa: Queen's Printer.

Montreal Herald. 1869. "Local Parliament," 25 March, p. 1 and 31 March, p. 1.

Murphy, Denis. 1932. *Report of the Royal Commission on Chiropractic and Drugless Healing*. Victoria, BC: King's Printer.

Nova Scotia. 1811. "An Act for the Better Regulation of Attornies, Solicitors and Proctors Practising in the Courts of Law and Equity in This Province." *Statutes of Nova Scotia*, 41 Geo. III, c. 3.

Nova Scotia. 1828. "An Act to Exclude Ignorant and Unskilful Persons from the Practice of Physic and Surgery." *Statutes of Nova Scotia*, 9 Geo. IV, c. 5.

Nova Scotia. 1870. *Debates and Proceedings of the House of Assembly*. Halifax: Queen's Printer. Pp. 146–7.

Nova Scotia. 1871. *Debates and Proceedings of the House of Assembly*. Halifax: Queen's Printer. Pp. 215–18.

Nova Scotia. 1872a. "An Act to Regulate the Qualifications of Practitioners in Medicine and Surgery." *Nova Scotia Statutes*, 35 Vic., c. 31.

Nova Scotia. 1872b. "An Act to Amend Chapter 130 of the Revised Statutes "Of Barristers and Attorneys." *Nova Scotia Statutes*, 35 Vic., c. 19.

Nova Scotia. 1872c. *Debates and Proceedings of the Legislative Assembly of the Province of Nova Scotia*. Halifax.

Nova Scotia. 1876. "An Act to Incorporate the Nova Scotia Pharmaceutical Society, and to Regulate the Sale of Drugs and Medicine Pharmacy." *Nova Scotia Statutes*, 39 Vic., c. 11.

Nova Scotia. 1883. *Debates and Proceedings of the House of Assembly*. Halifax: Queen's Printer.

Nova Scotia. 1885. *Debates and Proceedings of the House of Assembly*. Halifax: Queen's Printer. P. 300.

Nova Scotia. 1886. *Debates and Proceedings of the House of Assembly*. Halifax: Queen's Printer.

Nova Scotia. 1888. *Debates and Proceedings of the House of Assembly*. Halifax: Queen's Printer. Pp. 79–87, 91–110.

Nova Scotia. 1891. "An Act to Incorporate the Dental Association of the Province of Nova Scotia." *Nova Scotia Statutes* 54 Vic., c. 147.

Nova Scotia. 1898. *Debates and Proceedings of the House of Assembly*. Halifax: Queen's Printer. Pp. 127–8.

Nova Scotia. 1900. "An Act to Incorporate the Institute of Chartered Accountants of Nova Scotia." *Statutes of Nova Scotia*, 63 Vic., c. 154.

Nova Scotia. 1907a. *Journals of the Legislative Assembly*. Halifax: King's Printer.

Nova Scotia. 1907b. *Debates and Proceedings of the House of Assembly*. Halifax: King's Printer. Pp. 495–8.
Nova Scotia. 1910. Debates and Proceedings of the House of Assembly. Halifax: King's Printer. Pp. 147–8.
Nova Scotia. 1921a. "An Act to Amend the Medical Act." *Statutes of Nova Scotia*, 11–12 Geo. V, c. 29.
Nova Scotia. 1921b. *Debates and Proceedings of the Legislative Council*. Halifax: King's Printer. Pp 79–80.
Nova Scotia. 1922. "An Act to Amend the Act to Incorporate the Graduate Nurses' Association of Nova Scotia." *Statutes of Nova Scotia*, 12 Geo. V, c. 21.
Nova Scotia. 1972. "Chiropractic Act." *Statutes of Nova Scotia*, chap. 5.
Nova Scotia Archives. 1891. Original Bill: An Act to Incorporate the Dental Association of the Province of Nova Scotia, RG 5, series B: Original bills.
Nova Scotia Archives. 1921. Original bill (no. 192): A Bill Entitled "An Act to Amend Chapter 103 Revised Statutes 1900, the Medical Act." RG5, series B, vol. 132, no. 157.
Nova Scotia Archives. 1953–66. Records of the Nova Scotia Medical Association, respecting chiropractic, 2013–017, file 364.
O'Donnell, J. 1898. Excerpt from "Letters from Old Practitioners." *Dominion Dental Journal* 10 (10): 351–2.
Ontario. 1868. "An Act Respecting Dentistry." *Ontario Statutes*, 31 Vic., c. 37.
Ontario. 1869a. "An Act to Amend and Consolidate the Acts Relating to the Profession of Medicine and Surgery." *Ontario Statutes*, 32 Vic., c. 45.
Ontario. 1869b. *Journals of the Legislative Assembly*. Toronto: Queen's Printer.
Ontario. 1874. "An Act to Amend and Consolidate the Acts Relating to the Profession of Medicine and Surgery in Ontario." *Ontario Statutes*, 37 Vic., c. 30.
Ontario. 1883. "Act to Incorporate the Institute of Accountants of Ontario." *Ontario Statutes*, 46 Vic., c. 62.
Ontario. 1887. "An Act to Amend the Ontario Medical Act." *Ontario Statutes*, 50 Vic., c. 24.
Ontario. 1890a. "An Act Respecting the Profession of Architects." *Ontario Statutes*, 53 Vic., c. 41.
Ontario. 1890b. *Journals of the Legislative Assembly*. Toronto: Queens Printer.
Ontario. 1892. "An Act to Incorporate the Association of Ontario Land Surveyors and to Amend the Act Respecting Land Surveyors and the Survey of Land." *Ontario Statutes*, 55 Vic., c. 34.
Ontario. 1895. *Journals of the Legislative Assembly*. Toronto: Queen's Printer.
Ontario. 1906. *Journals of the Legislative Assembly*. Toronto: King's Printer.
Ontario. 1910a. Petition number 54 of 1910, Archives of Ontario, RG 49-38-2, B224804.

Ontario. 1910b. *Journals of the Legislative Assembly*. Toronto: King's Printer.
Ontario. 1911. *Journals of the Legislative Assembly*. Toronto: King's Printer.
Ontario. 1912a. "Bill 192: An Act to Amend the Ontario Medical Act." Archives of Ontario, RG 49-39, B227887.
Ontario. 1912b. *Journals of the Legislative Assembly*. Toronto: King's Printer.
Ontario. 1912c. "An Act to Amend the Medical Act." *Ontario Statutes*, 2 Geo. V, c. 29.
Ontario. 1919a. "An Act to Regulate the Practice of Optometry." *Ontario Statutes*, 9 Geo. V, c. 39.
Ontario. 1919b. "Bill 160: An Act Respecting the Practice of Medicine and Surgery." Archives of Ontario, RG 49-39, B227922.
Ontario. 1921. *Journals of the Legislative Assembly*. Toronto: King's Printer.
Ontario. 1922a. *Journals of Legislative Assembly*. Toronto: King's Printer.
Ontario. 1922b. "An Act Respecting the Registration of Nurses." *Ontario Statutes*, 12 Geo. V, c. 60.
Ontario. 1922c. "An Act Respecting Professional Engineers." *Ontario Statutes*, 12 Geo. V, c. 59.
Ontario. 1923a. "The Medical Act." 13 Geo. V, c. 35. Toronto: King's Printer.
Ontario. 1923b. *Journals of Legislative Assembly*. Toronto: King's Printer.
Ontario. 1925a. "Act to Amend the Medical Act." *Ontario Statutes*, 15 Geo. V, c. 48.
Ontario. 1925b. "The Drugless Practitioners Act." *Ontario Statutes*, 15 Geo. V, c. 49.
Ontario. 1926. "An Act to Incorporate the Association of Accountants and Auditors in Ontario." *Ontario Statutes*, 16 Geo. V, c. 124.
Ontario. 1933a. "Bill no. 108: An Act to Amend the Medical Act." Toronto: King's Printer.
Ontario. 1933b. *Journals of Legislative Assembly*. Toronto: King's Printer.
Ontario. 1934a. "Bill no. 86: An Act to Amend the Drugless Practitioners Act." Archives of Ontario, RG 49-39, B228037.
Ontario. 1934b. "Bill no. 87: An Act to Amend the Medical Act." Archives of Ontario, RG 49-39, B228037.
Ontario. 1936. *Journals of Legislative Assembly*. Toronto: King's Printer.
Ontario. 1937. "Regulations under the Drugless Practitioners Act, Province of Ontario." Archives of Ontario, RG 4-2, Drugless Practitioners 1938 (Correspondence re Legislation and Regulations), box 8, file 8.9, B435007.
Ontario. 1938. "Bill no. 27: An Act Respecting the Ontario Academy of Osteopathy and the Associated Chiropractors and Drugless Therapists of Ontario." Toronto: King's Printer. Archives of Ontario, RG 49-39, B228063.

Ontario Association of Osteopathy (OAO). 1923. Letter to E.C. Drury, dated 23 April 1923. Archives of Ontario, EC Drury Correspondence, MS 1665 – RG 2-4-0-290.

Ontario Association of Osteopathy. 1966. "Brief for Presentation to the Committee on the Healing Arts of Ontario." November 1966. 40pp.

Ontario Dental Association (ODA). 1867. Proceedings of the 1st session of the Ontario Dental Society, Cobourg, Ontario, July 1867.

Ontario Medical Association (OMA). 1918. *Report of the OMA on Judge Hodgins' Report on Medical Education*. Toronto: T.H. Best Printing Co., Ltd.

Perry, H.G. 1924. "Twelfth Report of the Select Standing Committee on Private Bills and Standing Orders" B.C. Journals of the Legislative Assembly. Victoria: King's Printer. Pp. 128–9.

Quebec. 1869a. "An Act to Incorporate the Dental Association of the Province of Quebec." Quebec Statutes, 32 Vic c. 69.

Quebec. 1869b. *Journals of the Legislative Assembly for the Province of Quebec.* Volume 3. Quebec: Augustin Coté's Printing Office.

Quebec. 1870. "An Act to Amend the Act of the Legislature of This Province, thirty-second Victoria, chapter sixty-nine, relating to the Dental Association of this Province." *Quebec Statutes*, 34 Vic c. 45.

Quebec. 1874. "An Act to Incorporate the Dental Association of the Province of Quebec." *Quebec Statutes*, 37 Vic c. 14.

Quebec. 1875. "An Act to Amend the Act of Incorporation of the Pharmaceutical Association of the Province of Quebec, and to Regulate the Sale of Poisons." *Quebec Statutes*, 38 Vic c. 37.

Quebec. 1876a. Journals of the Legislative Assembly for the Province of Quebec. Quebec: Queen's Printer.

Quebec. 1876b. "An Act to amend and consolidate the acts relating to the profession of medicine and surgery in the province of Quebec." *Quebec Statutes*, 40 Vic c. 26.

Quebec. 1879. "An Act to further amend and consolidate the acts relating to the Profession of Medicine and Surgery in the Province of Quebec." *Quebec Statutes*, 42–43 Vic c. 37.

Quebec. 1880. "An Act to Incorporate the Association of Accountants in Montreal." *Quebec Statutes*, 43–44 Vic c. 88.

Quebec. 1881. *Journals of the Legislative Assembly for the Province of Quebec.* Quebec: Augustin Coté's Printing Office.

Quebec. 1882. 'An Act respecting the land surveyors of the Province of Quebec and the survey of lands." *Quebec Statutes*, 45 Vic c. 16.

Quebec. 1898. "An Act to amend the law respecting Physicians and Surgeons." *Quebec Statutes*, 61 Vic c. 30.

Quebec. 1909a. "An Act to amend the act incorporating the Association of Opticians of the Province of Quebec." *Quebec Statutes*, 9 Ed VII c. 130.

Quebec. 1909b. "An Act to amend and consolidate the law respecting physicians and surgeons in the Province of Quebec." *Quebec Statutes*, 9 Ed VII c. 55.

Quebec. 1909c. Débats de l'Assemblée législative (débats reconstitués). 15 April. http://www.assnat.qc.ca/fr/travaux-parlementaires/assemblee-nationale/12-1/journal-debats/19090415/86613.html.

Quebec. 1918a. "Bill no. 151: An Act to amend the Revised Statutes, 1909, relating to osteopaths." Quebec: The Telegraph Printing Co. Obtained from the Bibliothèque de l'Assemblée nationale, Quebec.

Quebec. 1918b. *Journals of the Legislative Assembly of the Province of Quebec*. Quebec: The Telegraph Printing Co.

Quebec. 1919a. "Bill no. 160: An Act to amend the Revised Statutes, 1909, relating to Osteopaths." Quebec: The Telegraph Printing Co. Obtained from the Bibliothèque de l'Assemblée nationale, Quebec.

Quebec. 1919b. *Journals of the Legislative Assembly of the Province of Quebec*. Quebec: The Telegraph Printing Co.

Quebec. 1919c. *Débats de l'Assemblée législative (débats reconstitués)*. 14 March. http://www.assnat.qc.ca/fr/travaux-parlementaires/assemblee-nationale/14-3/journal-debats/19190314/91527.html.

Quebec. 1920. "An Act to incorporate the Association of Registered Nurses of the Province of Quebec." *Quebec Statutes*, 10 Geo V c. 141.

Quebec. 1921. "An Act to incorporate the Association of Forest Engineers of the Province of Quebec." *Quebec Statutes*, 11 Geo V c. 143.

Quebec. 1922. *Débats de l'Assemblée législative (débats reconstitués)*. 27 February. http://www.assnat.qc.ca/fr/travaux-parlementaires/journaux-debats/index-jd/recherche.html?cat=ex&Session=rd15l3se&Section=bills&Requete=363&Hier=80+-+Bill+amendant+la+loi+10+George+V%2c+chapitre+141%2c+concernant+l%27Association+des+gardes-malades+enregistr%c3%a9es+de+la+province+de+Qu%c3%a9bec+(Monet)_Comit%c3%a9+g%c3%a9n%c3%a9ral_363.

Quebec. 1936. Private Bill no. 94: An Act to incorporate the Chiropractic Association of the Province of Quebec. Quebec: The Chronicle-Telegraph Publishing Co. Ltd. Obtained from the Bibliothèque de l'Assemblée nationale, Quebec.

Quebec. 1939. Private Bill No. 109: An Act to incorporate the Chiropractic Association of the Province of Quebec. Quebec: King's Printer. Obtained from the Bibliothèque de l'Assemblée nationale, Quebec.

Routley, T.C. 1922. "Medical Organization." *CMA Journal* 12 (10, October): 711–14.

Routley, T.C. 1965. "Routley's History of the O.M.A." *Ontario Medical Review* 32: 38–43.

Royal Commission on Health Services. 1965. *Report*. Volume 2. Ottawa: Queen's Printer.

Secord, E.R. 1923. "President's Address." *Canadian Medical Association Journal* 13, no. 8 (August): 555.

Sheppard, Claude-Armand. 1970. L'Organisation et la Reglementation des Professions de La Santé et du Bien-Être au Québec. Tome 1, annexe 12. Commission d'Enquête sur la Santé et le Bien-Être Social. Gouvernement du Québec.

State of Alabama. 1877. "An Act to Regulate the Practice of Medicine in the State of Alabama." *Transactions of the Medical Association of the State of Alabama* 30: 37–39.

State of Illinois. 1877. "An Act to Regulate the Practice of Medicine in the State of Illinois." Approved 29 May. In force 1 July 1877.

State of New Mexico. 1882. "CHAPTER LV: An Act to protect the public health and regulate the practice of medicine in the Territory of New Mexico." *The General Laws of New Mexico: Including All the Unrepealed General Laws*. New Mexico.

State of New York. 1874. "Chapter 436: An Act to regulate the practice of medicine and surgery in the state of New York. *Statutes at Large of the State of New York*. (97th session, 1874).

State of Virginia. 1884. "Chapter 65: An Act to regulate the practice of Medicine and Surgery." Acts passed at a General Assembly of the Commonwealth of Virginia.

Sturdy, Walter. 1931. Clipping from *Vancouver Sun*, Sturdy Scrapbook, British Columbia Chiropractors Association Fonds, British Columbia Archives, MS-2536, vols. 10 and 11.

Sturdy, Walter. 1932a. "Citizens to Fight Medical Domination." *Vancouver Sun*, Clipping from Sturdy Scrapbooks, British Columbia Chiropractors Association Fonds, British Columbia Archives, MS-2536, vols. 10 and 11.

Sturdy, Walter. 1932b. Quoted in "Capone Rule by Doctors Says Sturdy." *Vancouver Sun*, 13 April, p. 1.

Surveyor General of Canada. 1936. Letter from F.H. Peters Surveyor General to H.B. Mathews Esq, Surveyor General, Department of Lands, Sydney, New South Wales, Australia, re Suggested Reciprocity in regard to the Surveying Profession, dated 28 January 1936. See especially Appendix 4. Library and Archives Canada, RG 88 337 – Correspondence re surveys – Surveyor General.

Toronto Star. 1909. "Doctors Prosecute the Osteopaths." 7 October, p. 1.

Toronto Star. 1910. "Osteopaths Won Appeal, Can Legally Practice." 23 March, p. 1.

Toronto Star. 1912. "Medical Council Recognizes Osteopathy as a Science." 5 July, p. 10.

Toronto Star. 1925. "Declares Osteopaths Are Dominating Board." 11 December, p. 11.

Toronto Star. 1926a. "Drugless Healers Have to Register, Act Now in Force." 22 January, p. 19.

Toronto Star. 1926b. "Women's Police Court: Charge Mrs. Elliott Is without License." 15 May, p. 2.

Toronto Star. 1929. "Girl Is Investigator." 5 October, p. 3.

Toronto Star. 1933. "Merger Is Proposed of Drugless Healers." 26 October, p. 25.

Toronto Star. 1941. "R.B. Henderson Dies, Noted as Osteopath." 22 October, p. 33.

Trebilcock, Michael J., Carolyn J. Tuohy, and Alan D. Wolfson. 1979. *Professional Regulation: A staff study of Accountancy, Architecture, Engineering, Law in Ontario prepared for the Professional Organizations Committee*. Ontario: Attorney General.

Upper Canada. 1839. "An Act to Incorporate certain persons under the style and title of the College of Physicians and Surgeons of Upper Canada." *Statutes*, 2 Vic c. 38.

Vancouver Sun. 1930a. "Drugless Healers and Chiropractors to be Authorized to Practice Their Callings." 3 March, p. 1.

Vancouver Sun. 1930b. "Breaking Faith Laid to Doctors: Healers and Medical Men Rally for Battle." 18 March, p. 1.

Vancouver Sun. 1930c. "Drugless Healer's Bill Killed." 20 March, p. 2.

Vancouver Sun. 1931. "Chiropractors' and Healers' Bills Dropped." 27 March, p. 12.

Vancouver Sun. 1932. "Government to Have Free Vote on Healers' Bill." 1 April, p. 4.

Vancouver Sun. 1933. "Chiropractors Bill Rejected." 17 March.

Vancouver Sun. 1934a. "Chiros Triumph after 17 Years." *Vancouver Sun*, 27 March, p. 8.

Vancouver Sun. 1934b. "Healing Licenses: Many chiropractors seek provincial permits June 2nd." Sturdy Scrapbooks, British Columbia Chiropractors Association Fonds, British Columbia Archives, MS-2536, vols. 10 and 11.

Vancouver Sun. 1936. "Naturopath's Bill." 30 March, p. 14.

Victoria Daily Colonist. 1873. "Legal Practitioners' Bill." 20 February, p. 3.

Victoria Daily Colonist. 1879a. "Medical Registration Bill." 21 April, p. 3.

Victoria Daily Colonist. 1879b. "Medical Registration Bill." 23 April, p. 3.

Victoria Daily Colonist. 1881a. "Legal Professions Bill."19 February, p. 3.

Victoria Daily Colonist. 1881b. "Legal Professions." 25 February, p. 3.

Victoria Daily Colonist. 1886a. "Medical." 24 February, p. 1.

Victoria Daily Colonist. 1886b. "Medical Bill." 26 February, p. 1.

Victoria Daily Colonist. 1886c. "Legal Profession." 25 February, p. 1.
Victoria Daily Colonist. 1886d. "Medical Bill." 17 March, p. 3.
Victoria Daily Colonist. 1886e. "Dentistry Bill." 25 February, p. 3.
Victoria Daily Colonist. 1886f. "Dentistry." 16 February, p. 3.
Victoria Daily Colonist. 1888. "Legal Professions Act." 1 March, p. 4.
Victoria Daily Colonist. 1889a. "A Protest." 7 March, p. 4.
Victoria Daily Colonist. 1889b. "The Medical Act." 27 February, p. 4.
Victoria Daily Colonist. 1891. "The Pharmacy Bill." 24 February, p. 2.
Victoria Daily Colonist. 1893. "Legal Professions Act." 29 March, p. 6.
Victoria Daily Colonist. 1894. "Legal Professions." 30 November, p. 6.
Victoria Daily Colonist. 1895a. "The Pharmacy Bill." 23 January, p. 6.
Victoria Daily Colonist. 1895b. "Dentistry Act." 8 February, p. 6.
Victoria Daily Colonist. 1899. "Dentistry Bill." 4 February, p. 5.
Victoria Daily Colonist. 1905. "Land Surveyors." 8 April, p. 8.
Victoria Daily Colonist. 1908. "Dentistry Act." 7 March, p. 2.
Victoria Daily Colonist. 1909a. "Medical Bill." 24 February, p. 2.
Victoria Daily Colonist. 1909b. "Medical Bill." 25 February, p. 17.
Victoria Daily Colonist. 1909c. "The Medical Bill." 7 March, p. 5.
Victoria Daily Colonist. 1916. "Nurses' Measure Is a Cause of Contention." 11 May, p. 7.
Victoria Daily Colonist. 1920a. "Opposition Shown to Engineers' Measure." 26 February, p. 15.
Victoria Daily Colonist. 1920b. "Sharp Criticism for Engineers' Measure." 18 March, p. 9.
Victoria Daily Colonist. 1920c. "Speak Good Word for Engineers' Bill." 20 March, p. 5.
Victoria Daily Colonist. 1934. "Chiropractic Bill Favored." 27 March, p. 3.

Secondary Sources

Abbott, Andrew. 2005. "Linked Ecologies: States and Universities as Environments for Professions." *Sociological Theory* 23 (3): 245–74. https://doi.org/10.1111/j.0735-2751.2005.00253.x.
Abbott, Andrew. 1991. "The Order of Professionalization: An Empirical Analysis." *Work and Occupations* 18 (4): 355–84. https://doi.org/10.1177/0730888491018004001.
Abbott, Andrew. 1988. *The System of Professions: An Essay on the Division of Expert Labor*. Chicago: University of Chicago Press.
Abel, Richard L. 2003. *English Lawyers between Market and State: The Politics of Professionalism*. Oxford: Oxford University Press.

Abrams, Philip. 1988. "Notes on the Difficulty of Studying the State." *Journal of Historical Sociology* 1 (1): 58–84. https://doi.org/10.1111/j.1467-6443.1988.tb00004.x.

Adams, Tracey L. 2017a. "Self-Regulating Professions: Past, Present, Future." *Journal of Professions and Organization* (Early online October 2016).

Adams, Tracey L. 2017b. "Chiropody/Podiatry: Interprovincial Differences in Profession Formation." *Canadian Bulletin of Medical History* 34 (2) 364-392. https://doi.org/10.3138/cbmh.177-20042016.

Adams, Tracey L. 2016a. "Professional Self-Regulation and the Public Interest in Canada." *Professions and Professionalism* 6 (3): 1–15. http://dx.doi.org/10.7577/pp.1587 (Published December; early online July 2016).

Adams, Tracey L. 2016b. "'When Citizenship Is Indispensable to the Practice of a Profession": Citizenship Requirements for Entry to Practise Professions in Canada." *Journal of Historical Sociology* 29 (4): 550–77. https://doi.org/10.1111/johs.12112.

Adams, Tracey L. 2015. "Sociology of Professions: International Divergences and Research Directions." *Work, Employment and Society* 29 (1): 154–65. https://doi.org/10.1177/0950017014523467.

Adams, Tracey L. 2012. "The Rise and Fall of Osteopathic Medicine in Ontario." *Histoire Sociale* 45 (89): 49–77.

Adams, Tracey L. 2010. "Profession: A Useful Concept for Sociological Analysis?" *Canadian Review of Sociology* 47 (1): 49–70. https://doi.org/10.1111/j.1755-618X.2010.01222.x.

Adams, Tracey L. 2009a. "The Changing Nature of Professional Regulation in Canada, 1867–1961." *Social Science History* 33 (2): 217–43.

Adams, Tracey L. 2009b. "Regulating Professions in Canada: Interprovincial Differences across Five provinces." *Journal of Canadian Studies/ Revue d'Études Canadiennes* 43 (3): 194–221. https://doi.org/10.3138/jcs.43.3.194.

Adams, Tracey L. 2006. "Sneaking in the Back Door? Social Closure and Private Bills for Entry into Ontario Professions, 1868–1914." *Histoire sociale / Social History* 39 (November): 405–23.

Adams, Tracey L. 2005. "Legislating Professionals: Private Bills for Entry to Practise Professions in Ontario, 1868–1914." *Journal of Historical Sociology* 18 (3): 172–200.

Adams, Tracey L. 2000. *A Dentist and a Gentleman: Gender and the Rise of Dentistry in Ontario*. Toronto: University of Toronto Press.

Adams, Tracey L., and Nicole Etherington. 2015. "The Emergence of Naturopathy in Two Canadian Provinces: British Columbia and Ontario, 1920–1970." *Histoire Sociale* 48 (96): 215–44. https://doi.org/10.1353/his.2015.0010.

Adams, Tracey L., and Mike Saks. forthcoming. "Neo-Weberianism and Changing State-Profession Relations: The Case of Canadian Healthcare." *Sociologia Problemas e Práticas* 86 (3).

Badgley, K. (and United Farmers of Ontario). 2000. *Ringing in the Common Love of Good: The United Farmers of Ontario, 1914–1926*. Montreal, Kingston: McGill-Queen's University Press.

Baehre, R. 1995. "The Medical Profession in Upper Canada Reconsidered: Politics, Medical Reform, and Law in a Colonial Society." *Canadian Bulletin of Medical History* 12 (1): 101–24. https://doi.org/10.3138/cbmh.12.1.101. Medline:11609091

Baer, Hans, and Stephen Sporn. 2009. "Naturopathy in Canada." In *Naturopathy around the World*, 359–60. New York: Nova Science Publishers.

Baker, Samuel L. 1984. "Physician Licensure Laws in the United States, 1865–1915." *Journal of the History of Medicine and Allied Sciences* 39 (2): 173–97. https://doi.org/10.1093/jhmas/39.2.173. Medline:6371126

Barman, Joan. 1991. *The West beyond the West: A History of British Columbia*. Toronto: University of Toronto Press.

Beck, J. Murray. 1978. "Nova Scotia: Tradition and Conservatism." In *Canadian Provincial Politics: The Party Systems of the Ten Provinces*, 2nd ed., ed. M. Robin, 171–204. Scarborough, ON: Prentice Hall.

Beck, J. Murray. 1957. *The Government of Nova Scotia*. Toronto: University of Toronto Press. https://doi.org/10.3138/9781442656741.

Bell, David G. 2009. "Slamming the Door on Brains: Two Early Twentieth-Century Law Schools and the Narrowing of Educational Opportunity." In *The Promise and Perils of Law: Lawyers in Canadian History*, ed. C. Backhouse and W.W. Pue, 31–48. Toronto: Irwin Law.

Berman, Elizabeth Popp. 2006. "Before the Professional Project: SUCCESS and Failure at Creating an Organizational Representative for English Doctors." *Theory and Society* 35 (2): 157–91. https://doi.org/10.1007/s11186-006-9000-2.

Bernier, Jacques. 1989. *La médicine au Québec: Naissance et évolution d'une profession*. Quebec: Les Presses de l'Université Laval.

Bernier, Jacques. 1983. "L'intégration du corps médical Québécois à la fin du XIXe siècle." *Historical Reflections / Réflexions Historiques* 10 (1): 91–113. Medline:11632132

Bernier, Jacques. 1981. "Vers un nouvel ordre médical: Les origines de la Corporation des Médecins et Chirurgiens du Québec." *Recherches Sociographiques* 22 (3): 307–30. https://doi.org/10.7202/055947ar.

Biggs, C. Lesley. 1989. "No Bones about Chiropractic: The Quest of Legitimacy by the Ontario Chiropractic Profession 1895–1985." PhD dissertation, University of Toronto.

Biggs, C. Lesley. 1986. "No Bones about Chiropractic? The Early Struggle for Licensing of Chiropractors in British Columbia." BC Studies conference, 7 November 1986. See British Columbia Archives, Chiropractors' Association of British Columbia, MS-2536, vol. 15, box 7.

Biggs, C.L. 1983. "The Case of the Missing Midwives: A History of Midwifery in Ontario from 1795–1900." *Ontario History* 75 (1): 21–35. Medline:11615035

Boily, Robert. 1967. "Les hommes politiques du Québec, 1867–1967." *Revue d'Histoire de l'Amérique Française* 21 (3): 599–634.

Bouchard, Gérard. 1996. "Naissance d'une élite: Les médecins dans la société Saguenayenne (1850–1940)." *Revue d'Histoire de l'Amérique Française* 49 (4): 521–49. https://doi.org/10.7202/305463ar.

Bourgeault, Ivy Lynn. 2006. *Push! The Struggle for Midwifery in Ontario*. Montreal, Kingston: McGill-Queen's University Press.

Brazier, Margaret, Jill Lovecy, Michael Moran, and Margaret Potton. 1993. "Falling from a Tightrope: Doctors and Lawyers between the Market and the State." *Political Studies* 41 (2): 197–213. https://doi.org/10.1111/j.1467-9248.1993.tb01402.x.

Bremner, M.D.K. 1964. *The Story of Dentistry*. 3rd ed. Brooklyn, NY: Dental Items of Interest Publishing.

Brint, Steven. 1994. *In an Age of Experts: The Changing Role of Professionals in Politics and Public Life*. Princeton, NJ: Princeton University Press.

Brockman, Joan. 1999. ""A Cold-Blooded Effort to Bolster up the Legal Profession": The Battle between Lawyers and Notaries in British Columbia, 1871–1930." *Histoire Sociale* 32 (64): 209–35.

Brockman, Joan. 1998. "'Fortunate Enough to Obtain and Keep the Title of Profession': Self-Regulating Organizations and the Enforcement of Professional Monopolies." *Canadian Public Administration* 41 (4): 587–621. https://doi.org/10.1111/j.1754-7121.1998.tb00222.x.

Brockman, Joan. 1995. "Exclusionary Tactics: The History of Women and Visible Minorities in the Legal Profession in British Columbia." In *Essays in the History of Canadian Law, Volume VI: British Columbia and the Yukon*, ed. Hamar Foster and John P.S. McLaren, 508–61. Toronto: Osgoode Society. https://doi.org/10.3138/9781442657021-017.

Brunet, Melanie. 2009. "'Good Government, without Him, Is Well-Nigh Impossible": Training Future (Male) Lawyers for Politics in Ontario, Quebec, and Nova Scotia, 1920–1960." In *The Promise and Perils of Law: Lawyers in Canadian History*, ed. C. Backhouse and W.W. Pue, 49–71. Toronto: Irwin Law.

Burns, Robert J. 1983. "Gray, Robert Isaac Dey." In *Dictionary of Canadian Biography*, vol. 5. University of Toronto / Université Laval. Online. http://www.biographi.ca/en/bio/gray_robert_isaac_dey_5E.html.

Burrage, Michael. 2006. *Revolution and the Making of the Contemporary Legal Profession: England, France, and the United States*. Oxford: Oxford University Press.

Canniff, William. 1894. *The Medical Profession in Upper Canada 1783–1850*. Toronto: William Briggs.

Caplow, Theodore. 1966. "The Sequence of Professionalization." In *Professionalization*, ed. H.M. Vollmer and D.L. Mills, 19–21. Englewood Cliffs, NJ: Prentice-Hall.

Casey, James. 1994. *Regulation of Professions in Canada*. Scarborough, ON: Carswell.

Chamberlain, John Martyn. 2013. *The Sociology of Medical Regulation*. Springer.

Chunn, Dorothy E., and Joan Brockman. 2009. "'Into the Rough of Things': Women Lawyers in British Columbia, 1912–1930." In *The Promise and Perils of Law: Lawyers in Canadian History*, ed. C. Backhouse and W.W. Pue, 245–63. Toronto: Irwin Law.

Churchill, David S. 2008. "Making Broad Shoulders: Body-Building and Physical Culture in Chicago: 1890–1920." *History of Education Quarterly* 48 (3): 341–70. https://doi.org/10.1111/j.1748-5959.2008.00155.x.

Clark, A. Kim. 1998. "Race, 'Culture,' and Mestizaje: The Statistical Construction of the Ecuadorian Nation, 1930–1950." *Journal of Historical Sociology* 11 (2): 185–211. https://doi.org/10.1111/1467-6443.00060.

Clow, Barbara. 2001. *Negotiating Disease: Power and Cancer Cure, 1900–1950*. Montreal: McGill-Queen's University Press.

Clow, Barbara. 1997. "Mahlon William Locke: 'Toe Twister.'" In *Alternative Health Care in Canada: Nineteenth and Twentieth Century Perspectives*, ed. J.K. Crellin, R.R. Andersen, and J.T.H. Connor, 114–38. Toronto: Canadian Scholars Press.

Coburn, David. 1999. "Professional Autonomy and the Problematic Nature of Self-regulation: Medicine, Nursing and the State." *Health and Canadian Society* (Winnipeg, MB) 5: 25–53.

Coburn, David, G.M. Torrance, and J.M. Kaufert. 1983. "Medical Dominance in Canada in Historical Perspective: The Rise and Fall of Medicine?" *International Journal of Health Services* 13 (3): 407–32. https://doi.org/10.2190/D94Q-0F9Y-VYQH-PX2V. Medline:6350198

Cohen, Marjorie Griffin. 1988. *Women's Work, Markets and Economic Development in Nineteenth Century Ontario*. Toronto: University of Toronto Press. https://doi.org/10.3138/9781442657526.

Collin, J. 1997. "Genèse d'une profession: Les pharmaciens au Québec au XIX siècle." *Canadian Bulletin of Medical History* 14 (2): 241–62. https://doi.org/10.3138/cbmh.14.2.241. Medline:11620461

Collins, Randall. 1990. "Changing Conceptions in the Sociology of Professions." In *The Formation of Professions: Knowledge, State and Strategy*, ed. R. Torstendahl and M. Burrage, 11–24. London: Sage Publications.

Connor, J.T.H. 1998. "Homeopathy in Victorian Canada and Its Twentieth-Century Resurgence: Professional, Cultural and Therapeutic Perspectives." In *Culture, Knowledge and Healing: Historical perspectives of homeopathic medicine in Europe and North America*, ed. R. Jutte, G.B. Risse, and J. Woodward, 111–38. Sheffield: European Association for the History of Medicine and Health Publications.

Connor, J.T.H. 1991. "'A sort of felo-de-se': Eclecticism, Related Medical Sects, and Their Decline in Victorian Ontario." *Bulletin of the History of Medicine* 65 (4): 503–27. Medline:1802316

Corfield, Penelope J. 1995. *Power and the Professions in Britain 1700–1850*. London: Routledge. https://doi.org/10.4324/9780203171226.

Creighton, Donald. 2012. *The Road to Confederation, 1863–1867*. Rev. ed. Don Mills, ON: Oxford University Press.

Creighton, Donald. 1994. "Mason, John James." In *Dictionary of Canadian Biography*, vol. 13. University of Toronto / Université Laval. Online. http://www.biographi.ca/en/bio/mason_john_james_13E.html

Creighton, Philip. 1990. "Harman, Samuel Bickerton." In *Dictionary of Canadian Biography*, vol. 12. University of Toronto / Université Laval. Online. http://www.biographi.ca/en/bio/harman_samuel_bickerton_12E.html

Creighton, Philip. 1984. *A Sum of Yesterdays: Being a history of the first one hundred years of the Institute of Chartered Accountants of Ontario*. Toronto: Institute of Chartered Accountants of Ontario.

Curtis, Bruce. 2012. *Ruling by Schooling Quebec: Conquest to Liberal Governmentality*. Toronto: University of Toronto Press.

Curtis, Bruce. 1997. "Working Past the Mythical Abstraction: Abrams and Foucault on State and Government." *Les cahiers d'histoire* 17 (2): 9–20.

Curtis, Bruce. 2001. *The Politics of Population: State Formation, Statistics, and the Census of Canada, 1840–1875*. Toronto: University of Toronto Press.

Davies, Celia. 2004. "Regulating the Health Care Workforce: Next Steps for Research." *Journal of Health Services Research & Policy* 9 (1, suppl.): 55–61. https://doi.org/10.1258/135581904322724149. Medline:15006229

Davies, Megan Barker. 1994. "MacNeill, Mary." In *Dictionary of Canadian Biography*, vol. 13. University of Toronto / Université Laval. Online. http://www.biographi.ca/en/bio/macneill_mary_13E.html.

Della Porta, Donnatella, and Mario Diani. 1999. *Social Movements: An Introduction*. Oxford: Blackwell Publishers.

DiMaggio, Paul J., and Walter W. Powell. 1983. "The Iron Cage Revisted: Institutional Isomorphism and Collective Rationality in Organizational Fields." *American Sociological Review* 48 (2): 147–60. https://doi.org/10.2307/2095101.

Dixon-Woods, Mary, Karen Yeung, and Charles L Bosk. 2011. "Why Is U.K. Medicine No Longer a self-Regulating Profession? The Role of Scandals

Involving "Bad Apple" Doctors." *Social Science & Medicine* 73 (10): 1452–9. https://doi.org/10.1016/j.socscimed.2011.08.031. Medline:21975027

Dunglison, Richard J., and Henry O. Marcy. 1883. "Report on Laws Regulating the Practice of Medicine in the United States and Canada." *Boston Medical and Surgical Journal* 109 (17): 390–3. https://doi.org/10.1056/NEJM188310251091703.

Durkheim, Émile. 1984. *The Division of Labour in Society* (1933). 2nd ed. New York: The Free Press. https://doi.org/10.1007/978-1-349-17729-5.

Durkheim, Émile. 1992. *Professional Ethics and Civic Morals.* (1957). London, New York: Routledge.

Dussault, Gilles. 1978. "L'évolution du professionalism au Québec." *Relations industrielles / Industrial Relations* 33 (3): 428–69. https://doi.org/10.7202/028889ar.

Eidlin, Barr. 2015. "Continuity or Change? Rethiking Left Party Formation in Canada." In *Building Blocs: How Parties Organize Society*, ed. C. de Leon, M. Desai, and C. Tugal, 61–86. Stanford, CA: Stanford University Press.

Evans, A. Margaret. 1992. *Sir Oliver Mowat*. Toronto: University of Toronto Press.

Evetts, Julia. 2002. "New Directions in State and International Professional Occupations: Discretionary Decision-Making and Acquired Regulation." *Work, Employment and Society* 16 (2): 341–53. https://doi.org/10.1177/095001702400426875.

Evetts, Julia, and Robert Dingwall. 2002. "Professional Occupations in the UK and Europe: Legitimation and Governmentality." *International Review of Sociology* 12 (2): 159–71. https://doi.org/10.1080/0390670022000012413.

Eyal, Gil. 2013. "For a Sociology of Expertise: The Social Origins of the Autism Epidemic." *American Journal of Sociology* 118 (4): 863–907. https://doi.org/10.1086/668448.

Fahmy-Eid, Nadia. 1997. *Femmes, santé et professions: Histoire des diététistes et des physiothérapeutes au Québec et en Ontario, 1930–1980*. Saint-Laurent, QC: Fides.

Farrell, D.R. 1983. "Roe, Walter." In *Dictionary of Canadian Biography*, vol. 5. University of Toronto / Université Laval. http://www.biographi.ca/en/bio/roe_walter_5E.html.

Ferguson, John. 1930. *History of the Ontario Medical Association, 1880–1930.* Toronto: Murray Printing Company, Ltd.

Fingard, Judith. 2003. "Johnston, James Robinson." In *Dictionary of Canadian Biography*, vol. 14. University of Toronto / Université Laval. http://www.biographi.ca/en/bio/johnston_james_robinson_14E.html.

Firth, Edith G. 1979. "White, John (d. 1800)." In *Dictionary of Canadian Biography*, vol. 4. University of Toronto / Université Laval. http://www.biographi.ca/en/bio/white_john_1800_4E.html.

Fisher, Robin. 1991. *Duff Pattullo of British Columbia*. Toronto: University of Toronto Press.

Flood, John. 2011. "The Re-landscaping of the Legal Profession: Large Law Firms and Professional Re-regulation." *Current Sociology* 59 (4): 507–29. https://doi.org/10.1177/0011392111402725.

Foucault, Michel. 1991. "Governmentality." In *The Foucault Effect: Studies in Governmentality*, ed. G. Burchell, C. Gordon, and P. Miller, 87–104. London: Harvester Wheatsheaf.

Foucault, Michel. 1979. *Discipline and Punish: The Birth of the Prison*. Trans. A. Sheridan. New York: Vintage Books.

Freidson, Eliot. 2001. *Professionalism: The Third Logic*. Chicago: University of Chicago Press.

Freidson, Eliot. 1983. "The Theory of Professions: State of the Art." In *The Sociology of the Professions*, ed. R. Dingwall and P. Lewis, 19–37 . London: Macmillan. https://doi.org/10.1007/978-1-349-16979-5_2.

Freidson, Eliot. 1970. *Profession of Medicine*. Harper and Row.

Garneau, Jean-Philippe. 2009. "Civil Law, Legal Practitioners, and Everyday Justice in the Decades Following the Quebec Act of 1774." Trans. Steven Watt. In *The Promise and Perils of Law: Lawyers in Canadian History*, ed. C. Backhouse and W.W. Pue, 129–39. Toronto: Irwin Law.

Garneau, Jean-Philippe. 2007. "Une culture de l'amalgame au prétoire: Les avocats de Québec et l'élaboration d'une langage juridique commun au tournant des XVIIIe et XIXe siècles." *Canadian Historical Review* 88 (1): 113–48.

Gevitz, Norman. 2004. *The DO's: Osteopathic Medicine in America*. 2nd ed. Baltimore: Johns Hopkins University Press.

Gevitz, Norman. 1988a. "'A coarse sieve': Basic Science Boards and Medical Licensure in the United States." *Journal of the History of Medicine and Allied Sciences* 43 (1): 36–63. https://doi.org/10.1093/jhmas/43.1.36. Medline:3276773

Gevitz, Norman. 1988b. "Osteopathic Medicine: From Deviance to Difference." In *Other Healers: Unorthodox Medicine in America*, ed. Norman Gevitz. Baltimore: Johns Hopkins University Press.

Giddens, Anthony. 1993. *The Giddens Reader*. Ed. Philip Cassel. Stanford, CA: Stanford University Press.

Gidney, R.D., and W.P.J. Millar. 1994. *Professional Gentlemen: The Professions in Nineteenth-Century Ontario*. Toronto: University of Toronto Press.

Gidney, R.D., and W.P.J. Millar. 1984. "The Origins of Organized Medicine in Ontario, 1850–1869." In *Health, Disease and Medicine: Essays in Canadian History*, ed. C. Roland, 65–95. Toronto: Hannah Institute for the History of Medicine.

Gidney, R.D. 2005. "'Madame How' and 'Lady Why': Learning to Practise in Historical Perspective" In *Learning to Practise*, R. Heap, W. Millar, and E. Smyth, eds. Ottawa: University of Ottawa Press, pp 13–42.

Gilb, Corinne Lathrop. 1966. *Hidden Hierarchies: The Professions and Government*. New York: Harper & Row.

Girard, Erik, and Harald Bauder. 2007. "The Making of an 'Arcane' Infrastructure: Immigrant Practitioners and the Origins of Professional Engineering Regulation in Ontario." *Canadian Geographer* 51 (2): 233–46. https://doi.org/10.1111/j.1541-0064.2007.00176.x.

Goebel, Thomas. 1994. "Professionalization and State Building." *Social Science History* 18 (2): 309–37.

Goode, William. 1966. "'Professions' and 'Non-Professions'." In *Professionalization*, ed. H. Vollmer and D. Mills, 34–45. Prentice-Hall.

Goodwin, Jeff, and James M. Jasper. 2004. "Caught in a Winding, Snarling Vine: The Structural Bias of Political Process Theory." In *Rethinking Social Movements*, ed. J. Goodwin and J.M. Jasper, 3–30. Lanham: Rowman & Littlefield.

Gordon, Colin. 1991. "Governmental Rationality: An Introduction." In *The Foucault Effect: Studies in Governmentality*, ed. G. Burchell, C. Gordon, and P. Miller, 1–51. London: Harvester Wheatsheaf.

Gorman, Elizabeth H. 2014. "Professional Self-regulation in North America: The Cases of Law and Accounting." *Sociology Compass* 8 (5): 491–508. https://doi.org/10.1111/soc4.12152.

Gorman, Elizabeth H., and Rebecca L. Sandefur. 2011. "'Golden Age,' Quiescence, and Revival: How the Sociology of Professions Became the Study of Knowledge-Based Work." *Work and Occupations* 38 (3): 275–302. https://doi.org/10.1177/0730888411417565.

Gort, E.H., and D. Coburn. 1997. "Naturopathy in Canada: Changing Relationships to Medicine, Chiropractic and the State." In *Alternate Health Care in Canada*, ed. J.K. Crellin, R.R. Anderson, and J.T.H. Connor, 143–83. Toronto: Canadian Scholars Press.

Granatstein, J.L., M. Irving Abella, T.W. Acheson, David J. Bercuson, R. Craig Brown, H. Blair Neatby. 1990. *Nation: Canada since Confederation*. 3rd ed. Toronto: McGraw-Hill Ryerson Ltd.

Greenwood, E. 1957. "Attributes of a Profession." *Social Work* 2: 45–55.

Gullett, D.W. 1971. *A History of Dentistry in Canada*. Toronto: University of Toronto Press.

Hacker, Carlotta. 1974. *The Indomitable Lady Doctors*. Toronto: Clarke, Irwin.

Halliday, Terence C. 1987. *Beyond Monopoly: Lawyers, State Crises, and Professional Empowerment*. Chicago: University of Chicago Press.

Hamowy, R. 1979. "The Early Development of Medical Licensing Laws in the United States, 1875–1900." *Journal of Libertarian Studies* 3 (1): 73–119. Medline:11614768

Haug, Marie. 1980. "The Sociological Approach to Self-Regulation." In *Regulating the Professions*, ed. R.D. Blair and S. Rubin, 61–80. Lexington, MA: Lexington Books.

Heap, Ruby. 1995a. "Training Women for a New 'Women's Profession': Physiotherapy Education at the University of Toronto, 1917–40." *History of Education Quarterly* 35 (2): 135–58. https://doi.org/10.2307/369630.

Heap, R. 1995b. "Physiotherapy's Quest for Professional Status in Ontario, 1950–80." *Canadian Bulletin of Medical History* 12 (1): 69–99. https://doi.org/10.3138/cbmh.12.1.69. Medline:11609100

Heap, Ruby, Wyn Millar, and Elizabeth M. Smyth, editors. 2005. *Learning to Practise: Professional Education in Historical and Contemporary Perspective.* Ottawa: University of Ottawa Press.

Holman, Andrew C. 2000. *A Sense of Their Duty: Middle-class Formation in Victorian Ontario Towns.* Montreal, Kingston: McGill-Queen's University Press.

Howell, C.D. 1981. "Reform and the Monopolistic Impulse: the Professionalization of Medicine in the Maritimes." *Acadiensis* (Fredericton, NB) 11 (1): 3–22. Medline:11620109

Howell, Colin. 1992. "Medical Professionalization and the Social Transformation of the Maritimes, 1850–1950." *Journal of Canadian Studies / Revue d'Études Canadiennes* 27 (1): 5–20. https://doi.org/10.3138/jcs.27.1.5.

Humphries, Charles W. 1985. *'Honest Enough to Be Bold': The Life and Times of Sir James Pliny Whitney*. Toronto: University of Toronto Press.

Jarrell, Richard A. 2005. "Klotz, Otto Julius." In *Dictionary of Canadian Biography*, vol. 15. University of Toronto / Université Laval. Online. http://www.biographi.ca/en/bio/klotz_otto_julius_15E.html

Jasen, Patricia. 1997/8. "Mind, Medicine, and the Christian Science Controversy in Canada, 1888–1910." *Journal of Canadian Studies / Revue d'Études Canadiennes* 32 (4): 5–22. https://doi.org/10.3138/jcs.32.4.5.

Johnson, Terence. 1972. *Professions and Power*. London: Macmillan.

Johnson, Terry. 1995. "Governmentality and the Institutionalization of Expertise." In *Health Professions and the State in Europe*, ed. T. Johnson, G. Larkin, and M. Saks, 4–13. London: Routledge.

Johnson, Terry. 1993. "Expertise and the State." In *Foucault's New Domains*, ed. M. Gane and T. Johnson, 139–52. London, New York: Routledge.

Johnson, Terry. 1982. "The State and Professions: Peculiarities of the British." In *Social Class and the Division of Labour*, ed. Anthony Giddens and Gavin MacKenzie, 186–208. Cambridge: Cambridge University Press.

Johnston, Charles M. 1986. *E.C. Drury: Agrarian Idealist*. Toronto: University of Toronto Press.

Jordan, A.G., and J.J. Richardson. 1984. "Engineering a Consensus: From the Finniston Report to the Engineering Council." *Public Administration* 62 (4): 383–400. https://doi.org/10.1111/j.1467-9299.1984.tb00571.x.

Kandela, Peter. 1999. "Turkish Baths." *Lancet* 353 (9152): 601. https://doi.org/10.1016/S0140-6736(05)75668-3. Medline:10029022

Kett, Joseph F. 1967. "American and Canadian Medical Institutions, 1800–1870." *Journal of the History of Medicine and Allied Sciences* 22 (4): 343–56. https://doi.org/10.1093/jhmas/XXII.4.343.

Kinnear, Julia L. 1994. "The Professionalization of Canadian Nursing, 1924–32: Views in the CN and the CMAJ." *Canadian Bulletin of Medical History* 11 (1): 153–74. https://doi.org/10.3138/cbmh.11.1.153. Medline:11639367

Kinnear, Mary. 1995. *Subordination: Professional Women 1870–1970*. Montreal, Kingston: McGill-Queen's University Press.

Kleiner, Morris M. 2006. *Licensing Occupations: Ensuring Quality or Restricting Competition?* Kalamazoo, MI: Upjohn Institute. https://doi.org/10.17848/9781429454865.

Krause, E. 1996. *Death of the Guilds*. New Haven, CT: Yale University Press.

Kuhlmann, Ellen, and Mike Saks. 2008. "Changing Patterns of Health Professional Governance." In *Rethinking Professional Governance*, ed. E. Kulhmann and M. Saks, 1–11. Bristol: The Policy Press. https://doi.org/10.1332/policypress/9781861349569.003.0001.

Ladell, John L. 1993. *They Left Their Mark: Surveyors and Their Role in the Settlement of Ontario*. Toronto: Dundurn Press.

Langlois, Simon. 2011. "La grande mutation des professions au Québec, 1971–2006." *Les Cahiers des Dix* 65 (65): 283–303. https://doi.org/10.7202/1007779ar.

Larkin, Gerry. 1995. "State Control and the Health Professions in the United Kingdom: Historical Perspectives." In *Health Professions and the State in Europe*, ed. T. Johnson, G. Larkin, and M. Saks, 25–30. London: Routedge.

Larson, Magali Sarfatti. 2013. *The Rise of Professionalism: Monopolies of Competence and Sheltered Markets*. Rev. ed. New Brunswick, NJ: Transaction Publishers.

Larson, Magali Sarfatti. 1977. *The Rise of Professionalism: A Sociologic Analysis*. Berkeley: University of California Press.

Leicht, Kevin T. 2015. "Market Fundamentalism, Cultural Fragmentation, Post-modern Skepticism, and the Future of Professional Work." *Journal of Professions and Organization*. Early online, November.

MacDermot, H.E. 1967. *One Hundred Years of Medicine in Canada*. Toronto, Montreal: McClelland and Steward Ltd.

MacDermot, H.E. 1935. *History of the Canadian Medical Association, 1867–1921*. Toronto: Murray Printing Co., Ltd.

Macdonald, Keith M. 1995. *The Sociology of Professions*. London: SAGE.
MacNab, Elizabeth. 1970. *A Legal History of Health Professions in Ontario*. Toronto: Queen's Printer.
Malleck, Dan. 2015. *When Good Drugs Go Bad: Opium, Medicine, and the Origins of Canada's Drug Laws*. Vancouver: UBC Press.
Martineau, Armand. 1967. "Programme des études au Canada durant la période 1760–1790." *University of Ottawa Quarterly* 37 (1): 206–30.
Massicotte, Louis. 2009. *Le Parlement du Québec de 1867 à aujourd'hui*. Quebec City: Laval.
Massicotte, Louis. 1989. "Quebec: The Successful Combination of French Culture and British Institutions." In *Provincial and Territorial Legislatures in Canada*, ed. G. Levy and G. White, 68–89. Toronto: University of Toronto Press. https://doi.org/10.3138/9781442678873-006.
Mathieu, Jacques. 2013. "Seigneurial System." In Canadian Encyclopedia. Online. http://www.thecanadianencyclopedia.ca/en/article/seigneurial-system/
McAdam, Doug. 1999. *Political Process and the Development of Black Insurgency, 1930–70*. 2nd ed. Chicago: University of Chicago Press. https://doi.org/10.7208/chicago/9780226555553.001.0001.
McAdam, Doug, and David Snow. 2010. *Readings on Social Movements: Origins, Dynamics, Outcomes*. New York: Oxford University Press.
McCarthy, John D., and Mayar N. Zald. 1977. "Resource Mobilization and Social Movements: A Partial Theory." *American Journal of Sociology* 82 (6): 1212–41. https://doi.org/10.1086/226464.
McPherson, Kathryn M. 1996. *Bedside Matters: The Transformation of Canadian Nursing, 1900–1990*. Toronto: Oxford University Press.
Millar, Wyn, Ruby Heap, and Bob Gidney. 2005. "Degrees of Difference: The Students in Three Professional Schools at the University of Toronto, 1910 to the 1950s." In *Learning to Practise*, ed. R. Heap, W. Millar, and E. Smyth, 155–87. Ottawa: University of Ottawa Press.
Millard, J. Rodney. 1988. *The Master Spirit of the Age: Canadian Engineers and the Politics and Professionalism*. Toronto: University of Toronto Press.
Miller, Bernard F. 1991. "The Legal Profession in Late Victorian Nova Scotia." *Nova Scotia Historical Review* 11 (1): 57–90.
Miller, Katherine. 1998. "The Evolution of Professional Identity: The Case of Osteopathic Medicine." *Social Science & Medicine* 47 (11): 1739–48. https://doi.org/10.1016/S0277-9536(98)00247-0. Medline:9877344
Millerson, Geoffrey. 1964. *The Qualifying Associations: A Study in Professionalization*. London: Routledge and Kegan Paul.
Monet, Jacques. 2006. "Act of Union." In *The Canadian Encyclopedia*. Online. http://www.thecanadianencyclopedia.ca/en/article/act-of-union/

Moore, Christopher. 1997. *The Law Society of Upper Canada and Ontario's Lawyers, 1797–1997*. Toronto: University of Toronto Press. https://doi.org/10.3138/9781442623378.

Morton, Desmond. 2001. "Text of remarks to a parliamentary committee considering a law to proclaim Macdonald-Laurier Day, at the Parliament Buildings, April 25, 2001." Proceedings of the Standing Senate Committee on Social Affairs, Science and Technology, Issue 8, Appendix A. https://sencanada.ca/en/Content/Sen/committee/371/soci/08ap-e

Murphy, Raymond. 1988. *Social Closure: The Theory of Monopolization and Exclusion*. Toronto: Oxford University Press.

Nancarrow, Susan A. 2015. "Six Principles to Enhance Health Workforce Flexibility." *Human Resources for Health* 13 (9): 1–12. http://human-resources-health.biomedcentral.com/articles/10.1186/1478-4491-13-9

Naylor, C.D. 1986. "Rural Protest and Medical Professionalism in Turn-of-the-Century Ontario." *Journal of Canadian Studies / Revue d'Études Canadiennes* 21 (1): 5–20. https://doi.org/10.3138/jcs.21.1.5. Medline:11617278

Neal, Mark, and John Morgan. 2000. "The Professionalization of Everyone? A Comparative Study of the Development of the Professions in the United Kingdom and Germany." *European Sociological Review* 16 (1): 9–26. https://doi.org/10.1093/esr/16.1.9.

Oliver, Peter. 1977. *G. Howard Ferguson: Ontario Tory*. Toronto: University of Toronto Press.

O'Reilly, Patricia. 2000. *Health Care Practitioners: An Ontario Case Study in Policy Making*. Toronto: University of Toronto Press. https://doi.org/10.3138/9781442675650.

Ouellet, Fernand. 1980a. *Lower Canada 1791–1840: Social Change and Nationalism*. Trans. Patricia Claxton. Toronto: McClelland and Stewart.

Ouellet, Fernand. 1980b. *Economic and Social History of Quebec, 1760–1850: Structures and Conjonctures*. Toronto, Ottawa: Gage Publishing Ltd.

Parkin, Frank. 1979. *Marxism and Class Theory: A Bourgeois Critique*. London: Tavistock Publications.

Parry, Noel, and José Parry. 1976. *The Rise of the Medical Profession: A Study of Collective Social Mobility*. London: Croom Helm.

Paton, Paul. 2008. "Between a Rock and a Hard Place: The Future of Self-regulation – Canada between the United States and the English/Australian Experience." *Journal of the Professional Lawyer*, 2008: 87–120.

Penner, Norman. 1978. "Ontario: The Dominant Province." In *Canadian Provincial Politics: The Party Systems of the Ten Provinces*, 2nd ed., ed. M. Robin, 205–21. Scarborough, ON: Prentice Hall.

Pentland, H.C. 1959. "The Development of a Capitalistic Labour Market in Canada." *Canadian Journal of Economics and Political Science* 25 (4): 450–61. https://doi.org/10.2307/138984.

Phillips, Jim. 2009. "The Court and the Legal Profession: Loyalist Lawyers and the Nova Scotia Supreme Court in the 1780s." In *The Promise and Perils of Law: Lawyers in Canadian History*, ed. C. Backhouse and W.W. Pue, 161–72. Toronto: Irwin Law.

Pierre Fauchard Academy. 2015. "About Pierre Fauchard." https://www.fauchard.org/publications/47-who-is-pierre-fauchard

Prentice, Alison, Paula Bourne, Gail Cuthbert Brandt, Beth Light, Wendy Mitchinson, and Naomi Black. 1996. *Canadian Women: A History*. 2nd ed. Toronto: Harcourt Brace Canada.

Price, David. 2002. "Legal Aspects of the Regulation of the Health Professions." In *Regulating the Health Professions*, ed. J. Allsop and M. Saks, 47–61. London: Sage. https://doi.org/10.4135/9781446220047.n4.

Prud'homme, Julien. 2011. *Professions à part entière: Histoire des ergothérapeutes, orthophonistes, physiothérapeutes, psychologues et travailleuses sociales au Québec.* Montreal: Presses de l'Université de Montréal.

Pue, W. Wesley. 1995. *Law School: The Story of Legal Education in British Columbia.* Vancouver: UBC Faculty of Law.

RCP (Royal College of Physicians). 2015. "History of the RCP." https://www.rcplondon.ac.uk/about-rcp/our-history.

Reader, W.J. 1966. *Professional Men: The Rise of the Professional Classes in Nineteenth-Century England*. London: Weidenfeld and Nicolson.

Rees, Victoria. 2013. "Transforming Regulation and Governance in the Public Interest." Report Prepared for the Nova Scotia Barristers' Society.

Rhode, Deborah L., and Alice Woolley. 2012. "Comparative Perspectives on Lawyer Regulation: An Agenda for Reform in the United States and Canada." *Fordham Law Review* 80: 2761–90.

Richardson, Alan J. 1989. "Canada's Accounting Elite: 1880–1930." *Accounting Historians Journal* 16 (1): 1–21.

Riddell, William Renwick. 1916. *The Legal Profession in Upper Canada: Its Early Periods*. Toronto: Law Society of Upper Canada.

Rinehart, James W. 2006. *The Tyranny of Work: Alienation and the Labour Process*. 5th ed. Toronto: Thomson Nelson.

Robin, Martin. 1978. "British Columbia: The Company Province." In *Canadian Provincial Politics: The Party Systems of the Ten Provinces*, 2nd ed., ed. M. Robin, 28–60. Scarborough, ON: Prentice Hall.

Romano, Terrie M. 1995. "Professional Identity and the Nineteenth-Century Ontario Medical Profession." *Histoire Sociale* 28 (55): 55–98.

Rose, T.F. 1972. *From Shaman to Modern Medicine: A Century of the Healing Arts in British Columbia*. Vancouver: Mitchel Press Ltd.
Roth, Julius A. 1974. "Professionalism: The Sociologists' Decoy." *Work and Occupations* 1 (1): 6–23. https://doi.org/10.1177/073088847400100102.
Rubin, Stephen. 1980. "The Legal Web of Professional Regulation." In *Regulating the Professions*, ed. R.D. Blair and S. Rubin, 29–60. Lexington, MA: Lexington Books.
Rueschemeyer, Dietrich. 1986. "Comparing Legal Professions Cross-Nationally: From a Professions-Centred to a State-Centred Approach." *American Bar Foundation Research Journal*. 11 (3): 415–46.
Saks, Mike. 2015. *Professions, State and the Market: Medicine in Britain, the United States and Russia*. London: Routledge.
Saks, Mike. 2012. "Defining a Profession: The Role of Knowledge and Expertise." *Professions and Professionalism* 2 (1): 1–10.
Saks, Mike. 2010. "Analyzing the Professions: The Case for the Neo-Weberian Approach." *Comparative Sociology* 9 (6): 887–915. https://doi.org/10.1163/156913310X522624.
Saks, Mike. 2016. "A Review of Theories of Professions, Organizations, and Society: The Case for Neo-Weberianism, Neo-institutionalism and Eclecticism." *Journal of Professions and Organization* 3 (2): 170–87.
Saks, Mike, and Tracey L. Adams. 2016. "Neo-Weberianism, Professional Formation and the State: Inside the Black Box." European Sociological Association, Research Group on Professions, Aveiro, Portugal, September 2016.
Sandvick, Clinton. 2009. "Enforcing Medical Licensing in Illinois: 1877–1890." *Yale Journal of Biology and Medicine* 82 (2): 67–74. Medline:19562006
Sciulli, David. 2009. *Professions in Civil Society and the State*. Brill.
Sciulli, David. 2005. "Continental Sociology of Professions Today: Conceptual Contributions." *Current Sociology* 53 (6): 915–42. https://doi.org/10.1177/0011392105057155.
Scott, James C. 1998. *Seeing Like a State: How Certain Schemes to Improve the Human Condition Have Failed*. New Haven: Yale University Press.
Scott, W. Richard. 2008. "Lords of the Dance: Professionals as Institutional Agents." *Organization Studies* 29 (2): 219–38. https://doi.org/10.1177/0170840607088151.
Senior, Hereward. 2006. "Fenians." In *The Canadian Encyclopedia*. Online. http://www.thecanadianencyclopedia.ca/en/article/fenians/
Shortt, S.E.D. 1983."Physicians, Science, and Status: Issues in the Professionalization of Anglo-American Medicine in the Nineteenth Century." *Medical History* 27 (1): 51–68.
Shosenberg, James W. 1992. *The Rise of the Ontario Dental Association: 125 Years of Organized Dentistry*. Toronto: Ontario Dental Association.

Shryock, Richard Harrison. 1967. *Medical Licensing in America, 1650–1965*. Baltimore: Johns Hopkins University Press.

Simmins, Geoffrey. 1989. *Ontario Association of Architects: A Centennial History, 1889–1989*. Toronto: Ontario Association of Architects / University of Toronto Press.

Snow, David, Sarah H. Soule, and Hanspeter Kriesi. 2008. *The Blackwell Companion to Social Movements*. Chichester, UK: Wiley-Blackwell.

Spencer, Herbert. 1896. *Principles of Sociology*. New York: D. Appleton & Co.

Stacey, Meg. 1995. "The British General Medical Council: From Empire to Europe." In *Health Professions and the State in Europe*, ed. Terry Johnson, Gerald Larkin, and Mike Saks, 116–39. London: Routledge.

Starr, Paul. 1982. *The Social Transformation of American Medicine*. New York: Basic Books.

Streeck, Wolfgang, and Philippe C. Schmitter. 1985. "Community, Market, State – and Associations? The Prospective Contribution of Interest Governance to Social Order." In *Private Interest Government: Beyond Market and State*, ed. Wolfgang Streeck and Philippe C. Schmitter, 1–29. London: Sage.

Suddaby, Roy, David J. Cooper, and Royston Greenwood. 2007. "Transnational Regulation of Professional Services: Governance Dynamics of Field Level Organizational Change." *Accounting, Organizations and Society* 32 (4–5): 333–62. https://doi.org/10.1016/j.aos.2006.08.002.

Suddaby, Roy, and Thierry Viale. 2011. "Professionals and Field-Level Change: Institutional Work and the Professional Project." *Current Sociology* 59 (4): 423–42. https://doi.org/10.1177/0011392111402586.

Sutherland, Donald C. 1998. "Chiropractic: From Rejection to Acceptance 1900–1980." *Journal of the Canadian Chiropractic Association* 42 (3): 163–70.

Sutherland, Neil. 1960. "T.D. Pattullo as a Party Leader." MA thesis, Department of Political Science, University of British Columbia.

Terry, Laurel S., Steve Mark, and Tahlia Gordon. 2012. "Trends and Challenges in Lawyer Regulation: The Impact of Globalization and Technology." *Fordham Law Review* 80: 2661–84.

Thompson, John Beswarick. 1976. "Nelson, Wolfred." In *Dictionary of Canadian Biography*, vol. 9. University of Toronto / Université Laval. Online. http://www.biographi.ca/en/bio/nelson_wolfred_9E.html

Thomson, Don W. 1967. *Men and Meridians: The History of Surveying and Mapping in Canada*, vol. 2, *1867–1917*. Ottawa: Queen's Printer.

Tilly, Charles. 2004. *Social Movements, 1768–2004*. Boulder, CO: Paradigm Publishers.

Tilly, Charles. 1998. *Durable Inequality*. Berkeley: University of California Press.

Tilly, Charles. 1978. *From Mobilization to Revolution*. Addison-Wesley Publishing.

Tipliski, Veryl Margaret. 2004. "Parting at the Crossroads: The Emergence of Education for Psychiatric Nursing in Three Canadian Provinces, 1909–1955." *Canadian Bulletin of Medical History* 21 (2): 253–79. https://doi.org/10.3138/cbmh.21.2.253. Medline:15568262

Torstendahl, Rolf. 2005. "The Need for a Definition of 'Profession.'" *Current Sociology* 53 (6): 947–51. https://doi.org/10.1177/0011392105058029.

Tunis, Barbara. 1981. "Medical Education and Medical Licensing in Lower Canada: Demographic Factors, Conflict and Social Change." *Histoire Sociale* 14 (27): 67–91. Medline:11633190

Twohig, Peter L. 2006. "Education, Expertise, Experience and the Making of Hospital Workers in Canada, 1920–1960." *Scientia Canadensis* 29 (2): 131–53. https://doi.org/10.7202/800522ar. Medline:18548900

Twohig, Peter L. 2005. *Labour in the Laboratory: Medical Laboratory Workers in the Maritimes, 1900–1950*. Montreal: McGill-Queen's University Press.

Vachon, André. 1962. *Histoire du notariat canadien 1621–1960*. Quebec: Les Presses de l'Université Laval.

Veilleux, Christine. 1997. *Aux Origines du Barreau Québécois 1779–1849*. Quebec: Septentrion.

Vollmer, Howard, and Donald L. Mills. 1965. "Some Comments on 'The Professionalization of Everyone?'" *American Journal of Sociology* 70 (4): 480–1. https://doi.org/10.1086/223885.

Waite, Peter B. 1963. *The Life and Times of Confederation, 1864–1867*. Toronto: University of Toronto Press.

Wallace, Elisabeth. 1950. "The Origin of the Social Welfare State in Canada, 1867–1900." *Canadian Journal of Economics and Political Science* 16 (3): 383–93. https://doi.org/10.2307/137811.

Watts, Alfred. 1984. *A History of the Legal Profession in British Columbia 1869–1984*. Vancouver: Law Society of B.C.

Weber, Max. 1978. "Classes, Status Groups and Parties." In *Weber: Selections in Translation*, ed. W.G. Runciman, trans. Eric Matthews. Cambridge: Cambridge University Press. [Excerpt taken from Weber's *Economy and Society*] https://doi.org/10.1017/CBO9780511810831.007.

Weber, Max. 1968. *Economy and Society*. Ed. G. Roth and C. Wittich. New York: Bedminster Press.

White, Graham. 1989. "Ontario: A Legislature in Adolescence." In *Provincial and Territorial Legislatures in Canada*, ed. G. Levy and G. White, 29–46. Toronto: University of Toronto Press. https://doi.org/10.3138/9781442678873-004.

Whittaker, Jo Ann. 1984. "The Search for Legitimacy: Nurses' Registration in British Columbia 1913–1935." In *Not Just Pin Money: Selected Essays on the History of Women's Work in British Columbia*, ed. B. Latham and R.J. Pazdro, 315–26. Victoria, BC: Camosun College.

Whorton, James C. 2002. *Nature Cures: The History of Alternative Medicine in America*. New York: Oxford University Press.

Wilensky, Harold L. 1964. "The Professionalization of Everyone?" *American Journal of Sociology* 70 (2): 137–58. https://doi.org/10.1086/223790.

Willmott, Hugh. 1986. "Organising the Profession: A Theoretical and Historical Examination of the Development of the Major Accountancy Bodies in the U.K." *Accounting, Organizations and Society* 11 (6): 555–80. https://doi.org/10.1016/0361-3682(86)90036-X.

Wiseman, Nelson. 2007. *In Search of Canadian Political Culture*. Vancouver: UBC Press.

Witz, Anne. 1992. *Professions and Patriarchy*. New York: Routledge. https://doi.org/10.4324/9780203167786.

Index

Kolibri 360 GmbH
Ferdinand-Jühlke-Straße 7
99095 Erfurt, Deutschland
produktsicherheit@kolibri360.de